MW01711391

NO RIGHT TO STRIKE

NO RIGHT TO STRIKE

The History of the New Zealand Police Service Organisations

David McGill

Published by Silver Owl Press
And sponsored by NZI Life

For the New Zealand Police Service Organisations

© New Zealand Police Service Organisations, 1992

All rights reserved. No part of this publication may be reproduced by any means, electronic, mechanical, electrostatic photocopying or otherwise, or stored in a retrieval system without the prior permission of the New Zealand Police Service Organisations, c/- Secretary, NZ Police Association, Box 12–344, Wellington.

Design: Bill Wieben
Editor: Anna Rogers
Major cover photograph: Peter Hunter
Inset cover photograph: Michael Hall
Typesetting: GP Print Limited
Printed through GP Publications Limited, Archives House,
10 Mulgrave Street, Thorndon, Wellington.

ISBN 0-9597979-2-0

CONTENTS

Dedicated to those police who helped me tell this story, including one who did so against his superior's wishes, which is another reason why this story needs to be told.

‘It is essential that the Police should not suffer in pay because they are deprived of the right to strike, and that it should be put beyond doubt that they *are* being paid fairly.’

Edmund-Davies Committee, England, July 1978.

Introduction

The New Zealand Police Association was registered on 28 October 1936 and is open to all members of the police up to and including the rank of senior sergeant. Membership is voluntary but virtually all who are eligible belong; at the end of 1990 only six of the 5200 frontline officers were not members.

The association is divided into regional and district representation on the national council, the policy-making body of the association. At its annual conference the national councillors elect the board of directors, consisting of the president, a vice-president and five members. The board meets monthly, chaired by the president, a serving member of the police on fulltime secondment to the association. The association employs a national secretary and a research and clerical staff, sharing resources with the Credit Union and the Welfare Fund on the 11th floor joint offices at 57 Willis Street, Wellington.

The objectives of the association include:

1. To maintain discipline, increase the efficiency, improve working conditions and promote the general welfare and contentment of the police of New Zealand.
2. To constitute the official channel of communication between its members as a body and:
   (i) The Minister of Police;
   (ii) The Commissioner of Police.
3. To foster good relations throughout the police.
4. To assist members and dependants and where necessary bring their claims before the department.
5. To publish *New Zealand Police Association Newsletter* and other literature that promotes the objects of the association.

The New Zealand Police Officers' Guild was incorporated on 1 June 1955 to promote similar objectives for the ranks of inspector up to deputy commissioner, to which all 240 eligible officers belong. A management committee directs an executive director to carry out the wishes of the national council.

Members of the association and guild contribute to the New Zealand Police Staff Benevolent and Welfare Fund and to the Police and Families Credit Union. The former provides insurance, welfare and holiday benefits; the latter provides modest loans and administers the movement of the government superannuation funds into the welfare fund, for first mortgage loans. The welfare fund and the credit union are run by boards of members; both have fulltime managers and staff.

The evolution of these service organisations is a story peppered with strong personalities who generated surges in individual service development. Often it was only the push from a powerful personality that could breach the steely habits and traditions of this most disciplined service.

In the New Zealand context these service organisations were late developers. That they have leapfrogged to the front ranks of what is in many ways a waning union movement is a tribute to the drive and vision of leaders and members. Yet part of the reason for such singular recent decades of success must lie in the long and harsh struggle against an oppressive system maintained by administrators, who chose to forget or ignore their origins in this hidebound system, and politicians who cynically and indifferently exploited this poorly provided-for long arm of their own vigorous Victorian laws.

Those police who stood up for a better deal for their fellows were as quickly cut down by the authorities within and above them. They are the martyrs who forged the will to win a better deal. Present-day success was built on their backs, at their expense. This story thus begins with the long and demanding struggle through the wilderness years. If that struggle is remembered, there will be no return to those bitter, exploited days.

Part I

The Wilderness Years

The well-being of the police service radiates from this recent *Newsletter* centrespread. It has taken the four police service organisations a long time to achieve this primary objective. This book tells the story of that struggle. *Yanse Martin*, New Zealand Herald *photograph*, Newsletter, *December 1991*

Chapter One

Our Victorian Policemen's Unhappy Lot

The Police Force differs from other branches of the public service. Policemen for many years have had to do dreary night duty, and it appears from the evidence that, although they are generally men of superior physical development, there is a tendency to break down at an age at which other government employees are still vigorous. Their occupation exposes them to great risks of injury and disablement. The duty of a Policeman appears to unfit him for any other kind of work, and he must retire at a comparatively early age if the Force is to be an efficient one. For these reasons we strongly recommend the establishment of a Police pension scheme.

There is a robust, undated ring about this report by the 1898 Royal Commission on the Police Force in New Zealand. The word 'Force' has gone as surely as New Zealand's colonial status, but its message remains as valid as it ever was. Most commissions fulfil the political wish to draw and dampen down immediate dissatisfactions. This commission proved a watershed in defining what police conditions of employment and service should be.

It was only by eventually banding together into an association that the police rank and file won the status envisioned by the commission. If they had recognised the commission point that they differed from other branches of the public service, the police might not have made the false move of joining the Public Service Association (PSA), and then been obliged to leave a body that could not meet their different needs or cope with their different status. The commission's extensive question and answer sessions revealed how different the police were always expected to be. It was when they surrendered to such common public pastimes as drinking and gambling that Joe Public found the police most wanting. The power of arrest carried with it an expectation of unimpeachable conduct.

Last century there was also the grim Victorian expectation that the police should do the job from duty rather than for money, and do it all hours of the day and night in uniforms they paid for, without taking holiday breaks or enjoying the normal social relaxations taken for granted by the rest of society. The colonial policeman's lot was not a happy one.

In proving this to be the case, the commission recorded over 1100 pages of evidence. Its members, barrister Albert Pitt and stipendiary magistrates Joseph William Poynton and Herbert Samuel Wardell, spent five months travelling

POLICE COMMISSION OF 1898.
Left to Right: Commissioner A. Hume, J. W. Poynton, Esq., S.M., — Wardell, Esq., S.M., Colonel Albert Pitt (Attorney General), New Commissioner John Bennett Tunbridge, E. W. Kane, Secretary to Police Commissioner.

(Photo from Det.-Sgt. D. McKenzie.)

The 1898 Royal Commission on the Police Force in New Zealand was the watershed in defining what police conditions of employment and service should be. The last century has been spent seeking those conditions. *Detective Sergeant D. McKenzie photograph from* Police Journal, *October 1939*

New Zealand interviewing policemen, politicians and the public. They chronicled six decades of poor police pay and conditions; they proposed far-sighted patterns the police have spent this century struggling to achieve.

The commission observed 'a great deal of discontent, dissatisfaction, and apathy in the Force', but was sure that 'life and energy' would be infused into the police by 'the granting of the rates of pay and the pension scheme now recommended'. The commission was convinced that the country must accept the additional expenditure if it 'desires to have a Police service characterised by vitality and earnestness, as opposed to one in which the duties are performed in a perfunctory manner, without heart or enthusiasm'.

Policing could not have begun here in more perfunctory or pallid fashion. As the lowest paid occupation, it attracted the personnel its rates could command. Captain William Hobson had arrived in January 1840 to annex the country with a force of one sergeant and four troopers of the New South Wales mounted police. Their role was really that of Hobson's bodyguard. Chief Police Magistrate Willoughby Shortland, effectively Hobson's second in command, was authorised to hire constables at 3s 3d per day, sub-constables at 2s 9d per day, less than the lowest labouring wage. Those drawn to policing were tradesmen either out of work or unable to get any, usually because they drank too much.

One month after Shortland employed a police boat crew at Kororareka (later Russell), they deserted over low pay. This goes on record as the first strike in New Zealand's history. The strikers were imprisoned for a month, but the Colonial Secretary's report to Hobson dated 29 May 1840 observed that the crew were paid too little to live in a creditable manner.

So the first police hired in New Zealand were among the country's first gaolbirds. Those who followed were no better, since Hobson did not have the money to pay better wages. The first Police Clerk in New Zealand, W.C. Hayes at Kororareka, was one of several who did not see out the first year, dismissed because of booze. The local newspaper condemned the 'disorderly police', notably a Kororareka policeman seen having a barney with his wife outside their tent.

The same men were required to suppress sly grog shanties. Little wonder that the first year of settlement generated violent clashes between the police and their fellow working class folk, and won them abuse as traitors to their class. Resignations were frequent, often coinciding with the inability to pay the extra £5 for a police uniform.

A similar situation developed in other early settlements such as Wellington and Akaroa. The two constables at Akaroa complained of 'almost actually starving from want of means to purchase stores'. Hobson changed quarterly pay to monthly and added an extra 3d per diem for those who undertook to buy their own uniforms, but these were no improvements when pay was months late.

At the beginning of 1842 Hobson appointed Henry Thompson Police Magistrate at the new settlement of Nelson. Here a population of 500 labourers made rowdy by the grog shop and inclined to petty theft provided the pool from which Thompson hired his six policemen. He could not pay them for most of the first year because all payments had to be approved from Wellington. His police began in debt.

Pay was nil, conditions appalling. Constable Figgis had for his home, office and gaol a raupo whare at the port. He was able to arrange that three seamen he had in charge would share the domestic chores. The fourth felon was foul

Commissioner Arthur Hume. *B. G. Thomson*

Policing began here as the lowest paid occupation, and attracted the personnel its rates commanded. The public were not impressed, as exemplified in this 1860s caricature of a Christchurch policeman. *Canterbury Museum*

in mouth and body and relief came only when a second whare was built for him. In June 1842 Figgis, attacked while attempting to arrest a drunkard, called for help in the Queen's name. John Clark refused the constable's call. When brought before Thompson, Clark said he refused to do the Queen a kindness until she paid him the money owed him.

The struggling administration introduced pay cuts in 1844. More police resigned, only the poorest in purse and performance remaining. Wellington citizens in particular complained loudly of random, unwarranted and aggressive arrests, including the locking up of a 'gentleman' who had gone to the station to bail out a friend. The station was no place for a gentleman, being without windows or sanitary facilities for prisoners. The Wanganui station was no better, being a damp, run-down shed, and the barracks at Onehunga were so flimsy that they were abandoned in favour of a tent. In this context the public understandably had little respect for the police.

Governor George Grey had no time for submissions from his enforcers. He resolved a police complaint about compulsory attendance at Church of England services by dismissing these 'police unionists'.

In 1852 regulations governing the police in New Zealand were issued, based on those of the London Metropolitan Police Force. There was no provision for any redress for members. Any man could be dismissed without the police chief having to give a reason. This arbitrary clause, written as Section 9 into the Police Force Act of 1913, was incessantly appealed against by the association before finally being removed by the Police Act 1958.

The year 1852 was also notable for the first widespread strike of sworn police. Eleven of the 13 police in Wellington struck for a rise from 3s 6d a day to 5s, to match the rising labouring wage. They claimed their wage could not meet the necessities of life. Grey assured them their grievances would be given due consideration, provided they returned to work. Later that year police in Canterbury petitioned for a pay rise on the grounds that a pound of butter cost more than half a day's pay, boots more than a week's pay.

Grey's delay provoked a June 1853 petition drawn up by John Adlum and circulated by police in Wellington, requesting 'any thing near the wages of a labouring man'. Police contracts ran out at the end of the month and police could leave without being penalised. Grey reluctantly awarded police an extra 6d a week, but declined to renew the contracts of the leaders of the police 'union' and had Adlum dismissed.

The introduction of provincial government that year did nothing to improve the policeman's lot. On the morning of 30 May 1872 three sergeants and 17 constables in Dunedin struck over a reduction of 1s a day. They compared their 12-hour beat duty, including the continuous night beat from 9 pm to 5 am and earning them less than 3s a day, with gaol warder duties. Warders did not, they argued, have a more demanding job.

There was some public support for them, but no official appreciation. Wellington's *Evening Post* newspaper expressed the superior establishment view with its sarcastic comment that the epidemic strike habit had spread to those 'who toil not, neither do they spin'. The paper saw the city of Dunedin under the guard of but two duty sergeants, 'who seem to have souls above filthy lucre', but the city was at the mercy of 'the light-fingered gentry'. Although there is no evidence that the city establishment succumbed to the light-fingered gentry, the light-pocketed police were sacked. When a public meeting passed a resolution asking the Superintendent of the Province to reinstate the men, he did not. Such an act, he said, would be subversive to discipline.

Earlier that year, Christchurch police had been successful with a petition to abolish pay cuts, but the two police 'union' leaders were dismissed.

The Otago Superintendent had been able to afford to sack his turbulent police because he could apply to Wellington for temporary use of Armed Constabulary. This first central government-controlled police force had been raised in 1867 to fight in the Land Wars. They did not necessarily make good beat constables; one was quickly dismissed for being drunk on duty. When the provinces were abolished in 1877, the provincial police forces were amalgamated with the Armed Constabulary, with a military officer in charge.

After a decade of this unsatisfactory situation, the Police Force Act of 1886 disarmed the police and established a national civil police force controlled by a commissioner. Although it was the start of an unarmed police dedicated to keeping the peace as opposed to conducting war, recruits came into it principally from the New Zealand military, the Indian Army and the Royal Irish Constabulary. Men of war did not quickly become men of peace. The military message was maintained by applying military standards. The commissioner was from the military, and with him came military standards of discipline and staffing.

The 1886 act specifically prohibited combinations—in other words, unions. Members had little right of redress, there was no pension scheme, transfers were used to discipline members and promotion was irregular. Demotion was a common punishment for trivial offences.

Demotion was also a kind of solution to the log jam of promotions that took place as the provinces dissolved. It was not enough, however, to allow men to progress through the ranks. Pay was not being reviewed, buildings were not being maintained. Police had one bonus over other workers, in that they were provided with houses, but they had almost no means of expressing dissatisfaction with wages and conditions and it was constantly alleged that the only means of advancement was through political influence. Police in Westland did petition successfully for minor wage and travel improvements between 1878 and 1880, but it was noted that such combining and petitioning was contrary to discipline and prohibited by regulations.

Many police must have found it ironic that the newspapers should be full of accusations that they were corrupt and inefficient because they were politically controlled. The argument for better pay was and is to remove any susceptibility to temptation and corruption, but then the minority who had succumbed to temptation, corruption and political favour tarred the entire force by their actions.

Alcohol was at the centre of the scandal. Christchurch prohibitionist and MP Thomas Taylor claimed that the police had been corrupted by ministerial influence, and that Premier Dick Seddon's sympathy for liquor interests was behind it. Accusations that the police were turning a blind eye to liquor offences forced on Seddon the 1898 Commission of Inquiry.

Incredibly, Taylor was allowed to travel with the commission as unofficial witness for the public prosecution of the police. He produced much evidence that liquor was sold during prohibited hours, and always alleged that this was due to police corruption. He quoted the *Lyttelton Times* that 'the Police in Christchurch were little better than the confirmed drunkards they were supposed to control'.

Taylor brought his case home to roost with the celebrated case of Constable Patrick McGill (no relation to the author). McGill confessed to being under the influence of alcohol while on duty at Riccarton racecourse on 5 November 1890. He was allowed to resign, but was then reinstated after Seddon took an interest in the case.

During Taylor's cross-examination of Police Commissioner Colonel Hume, it emerged that McGill had put in a quarter of a century of good service, had educated a large family and, at the time he left the force, was in poor circumstances. That consideration had led to his reinstatement. Taylor alleged ministerial influence that affected the efficiency, morale and discipline of the force. The commission, however, took the long view that those who knew McGill over the period of his service did not consider him of intemperate habits; the charge was 'quite disproved'. Taylor continued for a time to accuse the force of drunkenness, but he was always strongly challenged and eventually withdrew from the proceedings.

Boozers were the policeman's principal clients last century. Christchurch prohibitionist MP Thomas Taylor provoked the 1898 commission with his allegations of boozing and corrupt police. *B. G. Thomson*

What kept coming before the commission was the evidence of police disadvantages. Charles Slight told how, when he was in the police, he had supervised removal of cargo from a ship wrecked at Waikanae. He lost two uniforms 'through the salt water, tar, and dirt'. When he sought compensation from the Customs Department, Customs referred him to the underwriters, who in turn referred him to the contractors. He received no compensation. When he arrested a horse thief, his fellow constable got a rise, but he did not. When men junior to him were given rewards and promotion, he resigned.

Royal Commission member Poynton asked Slight for his remedy:

> This infernal system of political influence done away with. An honest, straightforward man has not a ghost of a show against political influence. The Commissioner should not be tied by the nose to a Minister at all. It is a disgrace to the service. I can speak from personal experience. I know if I had used political influence I could have got promotion over the heads of all these men, but I would not use it. I spurned the thought of it, because I thought if I was not worthy of promotion by my officer on my merits I was not worthy of the service.

Slight continued to deliver damning evidence of police conditions, such as having to pay for his own fuel and light and those of any prisoner at Pauatahanui. This went for all country stations.

While he still dogged the commission's hearings, it was often Taylor who drew out such evidence. Third-class Constable John Timothy Foley revealed in answer to a Taylor question not only that it was difficult for the police to detect breaches of the licensing law, but also that police were dissatisfied with having to pay for their uniforms, and with constables paying house rent while sergeants did not. Foley claimed that his promotion was blocked by the personal animosity of an inspector and the late commissioner. He produced lengthy evidence of complaints he had made that were not heard.

The Royal Commission provided a most thorough surgical operation, lancing the accumulated resentments of the past six decades. The poor pay, harsh discipline and rapid transfers were summed up in the example of the married policeman who was declared 'insolent' when he objected to nine transfers in 14 years. Police had had to watch the general public become enfranchised but had been denied the vote on the grounds that they numbered soldiers among their ranks and soldiers could not be permitted to vote. They were so understaffed that by 1896 they had sunk to the lowest ever ratio of police to popula-

Former Scotland Yard Chief Inspector J.B. Tunbridge was brought here as Commissioner of Police by the Seddon Liberal Government to clean up the police, alongside Colonel Pitt. *W.A. Bowring sketches, Canterbury Museum*

tion, one to 1530, and copped the blame for not controlling the colony's unbridled drinking habits.

Seddon's Liberal Government had imported retired New Scotland Yard Chief Inspector John Bennett Tunbridge to oversee new policing methods and then work with the Royal Commission to ensure that the London bobby image could be put in place.

The commission found that police numbers had not kept pace with the growth of the colony. Discipline was poor because there were not enough sergeants to enforce it. The Armed Constabulary ethos did not blend well with that of the police; constabulary men were untrained for police street duty and the requirement of drill duty interfered with police arrangements.

New Zealand police, the commission found, had a lower rate of pay than any Australian colony. After paying for uniforms and life insurance, married policemen in particular were at poverty level. Whereas lack of superannuation and promotion discouraged younger men, older men stayed in the force until they died because they had no retirement pension. The commission noted the strong feelings among police that political backing was needed to secure appointments or promotions, and that promotion was often barred by trivial offences committed years before. As a result policemen suffered discontent and discouragement, which had reduced 'to a minimum the esprit of the Force'.

So it was that a commission set up by those alleging police corruption should come to reflect, in the evidence it took from 500 witnesses, the grievances of present and former policemen.

The obvious recommended reform was to recruit from the general public, not the military. And the recruits should be trained first rather than being put straight on the street. There should be a pension scheme and a compulsory retiring age of 60 (65 for inspectors) to weed out those no longer up to the job and to prevent blocking of promotion, which caused so much loss of morale and so many resignations. Uniforms should be free. Promotion should not be just by seniority, but should also take account of fitness and efficiency. Policemen should stay no longer than five years in charge of a station, to avoid envy by other police and the danger of favouritism in the community. Police numbers must rise; the commission noted the New South Wales ratio of one to 702, less than half the New Zealand ratio.

The commission recommended extensive improvements in pay, leave, accommodation, compensation and retirement conditions. Despite some discipline problems and lack of numbers, the commission found the conduct of the force satisfactory.

But recommendations are one thing, their implementation another. Almost a century later, this is still being worked on. Indeed, there was some suggestion that mid-1980s Minister Ann Hercus had overstepped the boundary defined by the 1898 commission and implemented immediately, that the Commissioner of Police control all internal police administration such as promotions, transfers and dismissals. The commission proposal that the commissioner be a man of police experience had already been implemented.

Commissioner Tunbridge instigated many improvements. By 1903 staff had been increased by almost 100, more sergeants were appointed, policemen received 6d a day increase for every five years of service. Uniforms were free, a Police Provident Fund was underway, with deductions from pay, and married men without accommodation received a lodging allowance after a certain time.

All these improvements were, however, doled out from above. There was no machinery for men to air grievances; membership of any union was prohibited. The police were regarded by governments as there to break, not make, industrial action. Police were used against freezing workers in 1907, the Blackball coalminers in 1908 and, most bitterly, against the Waihi miners in 1912. Victorian authority was not yet ready to allow an organised voice advocating improvement of the policeman's lot.

The powers that be were not even ready to honour their promise to give the top policeman a free hand. After agitation from prominent local citizens, Tunbridge investigated the acquittal of a sergeant in Nelson on a charge of drunkenness. Having let the offender off with a caution, and reprimanded and fined two constables involved, Tunbridge soon discovered that he was not the sole authority in matters concerning his staff. Seddon's Cabinet responded to the local pressure by derating the sergeant and requiring the constables to resign. Tunbridge was left with little choice but to follow his constables' lead, resigning 'because of ill health'.

His successor, Walter Dinnie, was another English policeman. His six disastrous years as commissioner were

Commissioner Tunbridge being welcomed by Premier Seddon in 1897. Six years later he had made many improvements, only to fall foul of Seddon's interfering habits. *B.G. Thomson*

dominated by a scandal over the admittance to the Dunedin police of a man with a prior conviction. Thomas Taylor was once more prominent in parliamentary attacks on Dinnie's administration. A Royal Commission in 1909 found other examples of poor screening of candidates for the police, and that Dinnie had been 'absurdly lenient' with policemen guilty of heavy drinking. The old charges of political influence in the force and unfair and inconsistent promotions resurfaced. Dinnie's resignation was accepted by Prime Minister Ward in late 1909 and Undersecretary for Justice F.G.B. Waldegrave became commissioner.

Taylor kept unearthing more boozy scandals, such as a fellow Christchurch MP persuading an inspector of police to protect a prominent local citizen arrested for drunkenness by having him appear in court under a false name, having had the station sergeant falsify the charge book.

Any possible police reforms took a back seat to such scandals. On 1 April 1912 Inspector John Cullen was appointed commissioner. He got on well with his Minister Alexander Herdman and the new Prime Minister Bill Massey, who sent in special constables to settle the 1913 waterfront dispute. From the Opposition front bench Sir Joseph Ward charged that Massey had used the extreme measures of sending in farmers' sons to crack wharfies' heads while the regular police had been ignored.

Cullen did push through some reforms with the long-awaited Police Force Act of 1 March 1913. These included the introduction of qualifying examinations for promotion, tighter disciplinary provisions, a new pay scale, new appeal and inquiry provisions. His new regulations also, however, required policemen to drill in their time off, a return to the

Christchurch police in 1907 with another improvement, the new Swift bicycles. The catch was that they had to pay for them. Constable James Cleary, holding the third cycle from the right, paid £19 for the privilege, and the machine lasted him until his retirement. *B.G. Thomson*

previous century's military tack.

The gap between officers and men widened once more. The qualifying examinations were making the police a more professional group, but they were still working-class recruits, and some of the men were uneasy about being used to break strikes and protect strike-breakers or scabs, particularly when they knew their criminal records. They were being asked to crush their own social group, and to invite their scorn, while receiving none of the emerging rights of their own rapidly unionising class.

The police had enjoyed a headstart on the union movement with the establishment of the Provident Fund in 1899, but there had been little continuation of the initial improvements in staff, training and buildings. The police were part of an urban drift that concentrated them in larger groups, instead of, as before, scattered around country stations. They had to sit back and watch other urban groupings band together for better pay and conditions, and move ahead of them. They were forced to accept abuse from trade unionists who perceived them as the heavy arm of the establishment. Yet in 1913 there was encouragement from the newly reformed Public Service Association, which advocated that police should be permitted to join government service organisations.

The police now had, in Commissioner John Cullen, the first boss to come through their own ranks. Bringing with him the paramilitary thinking from the last century, he was noted more for promoting the pitched battles at Waihi than for listening to complaints from his own 'troops'. Whether he listened or not, he was receiving demands for better conditions, particularly in hours worked and days off. The era of the Victorian policeman's subservient lot was over. The resistance, however, was not, as the authorities moved swiftly to crush this rebellion in the ranks.

Chapter Two

The Silencing of the First Organised Police Voice

The public, the politicians and perhaps even the commissioned officers got a shock when they read the *Auckland Star* of Saturday 12 April 1913. The headline read 'Constables Want a Union to Better Their Life' and the item reported Auckland constables springing a surprise on their officers the previous night by deciding to form a Police Association 'of a nature approximating that of a trade union'.

The men met at Trades Hall. Arthur Rosser, as the organiser, pointed out that regulations forbade them to be members of the association, and discussed the question of forming 'an industrial union'. It was known that members

Prime Minister Massey and Police Minister Alexander Herdman were the final and quintessential examples of politicians suppressing any police grievances. The newspapers of the day were beginning to see the beat policeman's viewpoint. *B.G. Thomson*

of the New South Wales constabulary had formed an association, but it was not clear to the meeting whether police had the power to form a registered union under the Arbitration Act of New Zealand. It was therefore decided to form an association meantime, 'with a view to taking all the steps outside the Department, for the amelioration of working conditions'.

The meeting was of single members of the force living in barracks, and 40 to 50 were said to be prepared to subscribe their names to the association. A similar meeting was afoot in Wellington. Christchurch and Dunedin constables were said to be prepared to follow suit.

The Auckland meeting made it clear that what rankled the rank and file was their inability to get redress for their grievances through departmental channels. One specific complaint was having to drill on their day off, a military duty in which the 1898 commission had seen no value.

The *Auckland Star* approached Superintendent Mitchell, who was in charge of the Auckland Police District. He said the meeting was a total surprise and he was not aware of such grievances. The men had to put in one hour of drill a month and, if they took a real interest in their work and efficiency, this could hardly prove a hardship. The superintendent told the newspaper that the formation of an association was against police regulations, which were framed to preserve discipline, a necessity if the force were to be efficient. It was an offence to form a combination for the purpose of discussing police business. Other officers approached by the *Star* had no idea of such action and saw no necessity for it.

The paper, on questioning the men themselves further, discovered that a series of petty grievances had 'combined to make a constable's life unhappy'. Those on the beat objected to the 'constant encroachment made by the Department on the private life and time of the men'. A constable nominally did eight hours a day, actually a great many more. There was no recognition of this in pay or time off. A man might be on duty from 5 am to 9 am and 1 pm to 5 pm. If he had made an arrest on the first shift, he had to attend the Police Court to give evidence, which left him little or no time for a break or to eat properly. Having to drill on his one day off in four or five weeks, usually a Sunday, proved the last straw.

Minister of Justice and Police Herdman had but one response to organised complaints: 'This sort of thing will not be tolerated.' He and Commissioner Cullen travelled to Auckland where Cullen paraded the 70 constables, demanding to know their grievances. He was presented with chapter and verse by about half the men. Menial labourers could earn twice as much, up to 16s a day with night work; police pay was 'quite inadequate to the cost of living'. Furthermore, they had to pay out of it the mess bill of 3 guineas a month, £2 10s per annum for uniform and laundry, increasing amounts for boot upkeep. Married men paid abnormally high rentals to live near the station, or otherwise must rise at 3.30 am to arrive in time for the morning shift. No food was to be consumed from 7 pm until noon the next day, and regulations could not be breached by eating on the beat. Superior officers were prosecutors and judges of complaints. The men asked Cullen for an extra shilling a day and better allowances and conditions.

The *New Zealand Truth* reporter was seen off the premises by Senior Sergeant Dart, but he was informed that 'Cullen lost his temper and became a very angry party. He informed any man who did not like the job that his resignation would look well on the Commissioner's table.' The *Auckland Star* mildly concluded that every attempt had been made to break up the association.

Back in Wellington Cullen, in an *Evening Post* report of 18 April, assured the Auckland men that they had no better friend than their Minister Herdman and that their complaints would be passed on to him. Alas, the whole problem was 'a matter of money'. Such hand-wringing would not wash with anybody aware of the recently announced government surplus of £709,000. The truth was that New Zealand had one of the cheapest police forces in the world.

The newspapers were picking up on the discontent. The *Evening Post* reported from Christchurch on 21 April that one constable had told a reporter the locals would stand by the Auckland men because they were 'sick and tired of this humbugging, domineering way that is fast creeping into the New Zealand Police Force'. But a Sub-Inspector Mackinnon presented the party line—he knew of no grievances in Christchurch and they were 'a happy family'.

Cullen continued his damage control, on 1 May meeting 47 Dunedin constables and then telling the press there were no serious grievances. The same day the press published the news that Cullen had telegraphed instructions to Auckland that the identified Police Association secretary Charles Gordon Smyth be transferred to Greymouth 'in view of the part which Constable Smyth had taken in the attempt to form the association, and having regard to the fact that, because of his action, he was now regarded by his sergeant and officers with distrust, it was thought better (in his own interests) to remove him from their supervision'.

Within a few days Smyth was off to Greymouth, but not before his colleagues had presented him with a silver-mounted umbrella and a case of pipes. The *Auckland Star* announced that his successor as secretary had been appointed and that, reportedly, a Police Association had been formed in Dunedin. *Truth* on 10 May put a bolder cast on proceedings, saying Caesar Cullen's 'mailed fist' had descended on Constable Smyth, who 'struck out for his pals and received the glassy stare and the outraged authority glance'.

A month later Smyth was dismissed for a minor breach of regulations, namely leaving his post and making a false entry in the time book. Smyth explained he had mistaken the time and, when he realised his mistake, returned to his post but did not cross out the incorrect entry, a matter of one hour. Usually such a trivial offence was handled by the local inspector, probably with a 10s fine. In just such a case

Commissioner John Cullen travelled to Auckland in 1913 to hear what this talk of a police union was all about, before promptly crushing it. *Truth* took the policemen's side, constantly referring to 'Caesar' Cullen. *New Zealand Police Centennial Museum*

Constable Charles Gordon Smyth, No. 1770, was identified by Cullen as the first would-be Police Association secretary and became the first victim of such audacity. Smyth was transferred to Greymouth, and then drummed out of the force on a minor charge. This photograph was taken just in time, in about 1913 in Auckland a few months before, Superintendent Mitchell had fined a constable absent an hour from his beat 5s.

There was no doubt, in *Truth*'s view, that Cullen had acted at 'the behest of Minister Herdman'. The minister had been reported in the *Evening Post* of 12 April as having been confronted at Auckland railway station by 50 or 60 constables asking if their association could continue. Herdman had said no. They were permitted to meet in the station billiard room and their spokesmen were heard. Consideration would be given to their representations—a line Governor Grey had used last century, a line favoured by procrastinating politicians ever since; Herdman was famous for it.

The minister had gone public on 7 May, reported that day in the *Evening Post* as saying 'this sort of thing will not be tolerated'. In the event of any 'Labour trouble' the police 'must be under the direct control of the Commissioner and the Government'. He would not permit Rosser or any other Labour leader 'to interfere with the discipline of the force or to sow the seeds of discontent amongst its members'. He smugly told the paper that he had asked policemen in the four centres to speak out, but few were prepared to. The Auckland police behaviour was, he claimed, 'quite incomprehensible'; since the Waihi trouble 'a steady effort has been made to sow discontent in the ranks of the police'. Those 'fomenting disloyalty and strife' in the ranks were recent recruits and Arthur Rosser 'has been getting in touch with the junior men with a view of forming an association'.

Rosser denied this, telling the *Auckland Star* of 7 May that he had not been an agitator among the police. Discontent was there and had been for some time, but it was not sown by him. And the dissatisfaction was not restricted to junior men, but was felt by older and married men, all those rankers who had not enjoyed the recent benefits that had been restricted to the higher officers.

On 12 July *Truth* claimed that Herdman and the Reform Government had 'totally alienated the police by the dismissal of Smyth, and the recent rustication of Constables Baker and Bruton only accentuated the bitterness'. In Auckland Constable Baker had asked Herdman if there would be victimisation if he answered questions. He was told there would not be. Baker was transferred to Gisborne. The Reform Party, *Truth* suggested, 'do not believe in keeping their word with commoners'. Constable Bruton had clashed with the unpopular Constable Adam Murray, who was not welcome in the association. The next Bruton knew he was sent to Greymouth, the Siberia of New Zealand. Constable Mills of Auckland was also recorded by *Truth* as having been forced into resignation after a clash with a constable and an investigation by 'Tsar Cullen'. And a Constable Baylis had had to resign after failing to get police approval for his marriage. *Truth* gauged that, under existing conditions, the chances of making a decent profession out of the New Zealand Police were as much 'as a Dartmoor convict has of exercising his fancy in an aeroplane'.

The Police Force Act 1913 offered the only kind of compromise paternalistic rulers understood, promising that 'every reasonable consideration shall be given to complaints or representations from members of the Force and meetings would be permitted with the authority of the Commissioner or officer in charge'. However, the regulations introduced by the act also promised that 'combinations shall be severely dealt with as subversive to discipline' and 'no man is permitted to complain on behalf of another'. This dishonest regulation gave as justification that every man was 'held to be the best judge of his own grievances'. What it really did was ensure there would be no union. Police could, however, become members of the PSA.

The big difference for the put-upon police was that, by now, the newspapers had reported enough industrial unrest to begin appreciating why it was happening. The *Evening Post*, which had been so contemptuous of the police the previous century, now saw justification for police grievances. In February 1913 it had questioned the treatment of constables 'when the pay of the higher branches of the Force increased'. The constable, it wrote, 'is to be a picked man, strong in mind and body, courageous, adamant against all temptations of graft, a Sir Galahad against the evil-doer', and therefore worth more than the 8s a day 'pick and shovel rate'.

Herdman replied on behalf of the constables. They had a free roof in barracks for single men, 1s 6d a day for married men, which compared favourably with the Australian forces. What Herdman did not say was that single men were required to live in these barracks and could not leave at any time without telling the duty policeman where they were going. They were not permitted to go more than quarter of a mile from barracks. They must be in bed by 10.30, lights out at 11.

The *Evening Post* was not impressed that Herdman told the constables at Lambton Police Station 'to step out like men' rather than go behind his back with their complaints. The paper suggested they might fear doing this lest they suffer 'victimisation'.

It was no surprise that Auckland was the flashpoint. The *New Zealand Truth* was the most vocal of the new wave of press sympathy for the policeman's lot. Its issue of 19 April 1913 declared that 'Auckland has been known amongst constables throughout New Zealand as the worst station in the Dominion in which to work—particularly for single men'. Auckland had been cursed for years with bumptious, overbearing, would-be military martinet officers whose ideas of discipline were reminiscent of the good old days when a British soldier was flogged for having a loose button. Matters became considerably worse with the elevation of Cullen and the arrival at Auckland of Superintendent Mitchell. The reason was that Cullen was a proud member of the Royal Irish Constabulary and Mitchell had served in the Life Guards, who were just as strict. *Truth* claimed that Cullen's advertisements for recruits in Ireland proved his preferences. The result was that Auckland policemen with unblemished records and years of experience were resigning in double the numbers of any other centre over the last 12 months.

Cullen's new regulations made it an offence punishable by dismissal to sit down when on duty or to gossip or loiter without lawful excuse. Meal and tea breaks were almost unheard of, and any meal had to be consumed standing up. This meant a few sandwiches eaten at the roadside or in a shop doorway, often as a nightsoil cart passed by. To leave the beat for a cup of tea could attract a 10s fine, 2s more than a constable earned in a day. Married men living some distance from the station had no time between duty stints to get home, and were forced to go eight hours without food. The constable at the end of his Queen Street beat, standing with his hands behind his back in the military stand-easy position, would often be confronted by Mitchell, who would knock his hands asunder and lecture him on discipline and the proper way of standing.

The Auckland barracks had been inspected by *Truth*. A man was not permitted to hang his towel up on the wall to dry, but must store it in the soap box, where it stayed damp until it was used again. A man might not have any decoration on his wall, such as a photograph of a girlfriend, nor anything on the floor. He had to scrub, polish, window clean, mat shake, clean the office. Then there was the inspection. A night duty man might come off at 5 am, have a few hours' sleep before having to attend court, then be back to have his bed in perfect order. Any further rest would attract a fine and a black mark, which would count against promotion. The *Truth* reporter also learned of favouritism, with some juniors getting cushy clerical jobs in the watch-house or prisoner escort and country station relief, while men with 15 years in the job were passed over.

The rule from the top was harsh. Two Auckland constables had provided medical certificates attesting to their wives' poor health and the need to move. Cullen had dismissed their applications, saying a constable 'cannot pick and choose what stations he will do duty in'. Unlike the ordinary daily newspapers, *Truth* happily took the men's side to colourful degree, always referring to 'Caesar Cullen' and sneering at the way men were separated from their sick wives lest 'the heavens would fall and a host of Waihi miners would invade Auckland and steal the Grey statue and the Bank of New Zealand'.

The reporter was with the young unmarried constables, who included John Bruce Young, later to be commissioner, when they met Rosser at Trades Hall on 11 April. The dissidents had already made contact with those of like mind in the other main centres and had printed a rule book. They had the indication from married men and those in suburban stations that they would join the planned association. One constable said that if one of their number made an unsuccessful stand against a grievance, all members would send in their resignations. The response was the joining of the association by all but three men, who were not welcome because they were 'pimps and crawlers'.

Truth was most interested in Superintendent Mitchell's reaction. He asked his men to write down if they were at the Trades Hall meeting, include their names, state their grievances, state the sergeants objected to, and then forswear the association. He carpeted one constable, demanding details of the meeting, but was refused. 'If we are policemen,' one member declared under the pseudonym 'Stand Firm', 'we are also citizens and free men.'

The newspapers reflected public appreciation of policemen's rights. *Truth* claimed Cullen had his hands full trying to reform the police on obsolete lines, while Herdman, the 'jelly fortress' of Reform, felt threatened by policemen trying to better their conditions and remedy a few long-standing ills.

The government had taken a press pounding, and now it had to go under the democratic microscope of parliamentary debate on the Police Force Bill 1913. Rarely have police matters occupied so much space in Hansard before or since. On 8 July 1913 Oamaru MP E. P. Lee asked Herdman the grounds for Smyth's dismissal. Herdman said he was transferred because he 'persisted in taking an active part in the formation of a police association, which in the opinion of the Police Commissioner and myself was likely to subvert the discipline of the Force'. Herdman explained his dismissal by quoting the Greymouth senior sergeant who was suspicious of Smyth and visited him at 3 am, to find Smyth sitting before a big fire with his washing drying. Presumably the silver-mounted brolly had not kept off the worst of the Coast weather.

Herdman also told Parliament that Smyth had been 'insolent' to him at Auckland and that, in any case, he had already been suspicious of Smyth's fitness for the force. Smyth had claimed a refund for a suit of clothes alleged to have been damaged while he was procuring evidence against Wellington bookmakers.

There was more damning evidence against Smyth. He had not paid debts to the mess caterer for one month's board until, Herdman said, 'I forced him to pay.' Given that Smyth had only joined the force the previous year, aged 29, this seemed rather close attention for the minister to be paying him. Herdman went on to say that Smyth had admitted to Sergeant Fraser at Auckland asking for a transfer from Dunedin 'in order to take active steps to bring about the formation of this union'.

Herdman said Baker had been sent to Gisborne for telling an Auckland newspaper that his minister had said 'upon my honour' that what the police there told him would not be held against them. Herdman said he had not made that commitment. The police association would not, Herdman continued, be permitted because it was not in the interests of the police or the public that such a group should be formed, 'guided by men connected with the labour movement—that no association formed on union principles would be tolerated'. After the papers printed this statement, Baker continued to take an active part in the business of the association. In so doing he was guilty of insubordination and sent to Gisborne.

Riccarton MP George Witty asked Herdman about the 1893 regulation allowing police to join an association. That, Herdman replied, existed before the new regulations. His government had no objections, however, to the police joining the PSA, an association 'controlled and managed by responsible public servants'. The regulation dealing severely with combinations in the police was derived from the Royal Irish Constabulary, which he regarded as one of the best police forces in the world. The RIC was the source for the minister authorising a committee of inquiry into any claim for pay, leave, clothing or whatever.

'Why not allow constables to be represented?' asked Russell.

'That would be ridiculous,' said Herdman.

He went on to say that his bill would retain the commissioner's right to dismiss a constable. When L.M. Isitt asked if the accused could have legal advice, Herdman said no. 'If we were to import lawyers into cases, there would be no end to them. My experience of the Police Force is that they are fairly good lawyers themselves.' Herdman must rate as a prime example of the paternalistic, patronising, pompous and perfidious political powermonger.

Sir Joseph Ward, who believed in an association free of politics and an appeal board for the police, told Herdman he had made a mistake in not allowing the police to form an association. In government Ward had allowed associations of Railways and Post and Telegraph workers, and he pointed out that, if a contented police service was wanted, then they should not be put in a paddock by themselves and denied the means of protection, representation and defence admitted by legislation as essential to the rest of the public service.

Thomas Wilford, who was to succeed Herdman, asked him why he refused for the police what he approved for railway servants. Herdman replied that, should any industrial troubles such as a lockout or strike occur, the police were required to preserve law and 'enforce obedience to the law'. They could not perform these duties if they were

Sir Thomas Wilford

The first promotion examinations were supervised by Superintendent John Dwyer in the Christchurch Supreme Court on Friday 24 September 1913. Introduced into police regulations that year, they were the first move to make the force more professional and were perhaps seen by the politicians as a means of raising educational standards and thus muting working-class propensities for union agitation. Part of the same political thinking was to offer the police the right to join the professional bureaucrats of the PSA. *Christchurch Police Museum*

associated with or likely to be influenced by leaders 'on either side'. And the Railways and Post and Telegraph associations differed from the proposed police association in being controlled by 'responsible and well-known public servants'.

Opposition amendments such as right of appeal against a promotion decision and appeals heard by officers of a recognised association were unsuccessful. In the Upper House of the Legislative Council John Rigg also lost an amendment allowing a police association on the grounds that an organised body of men were easier to deal with, especially where there was discontent.

Despite such failures, many MPs clearly understood that change must come. Wanganui's W. A. Veitch said the time was not too far distant when there would be an appeal board and a police association. We had to trust the police every hour of the day and night, so why not trust them further and give them the means to organise and bring their opinions for the improvement of the service and their conditions before the head of the department and the minister? This would prove that those in control were in sympathy with their aspirations and anxious to improve their conditions.

Nelson Independent Harry Atmore blamed Herdman for the police trouble because he was born 'absolutely without any bowels of compassion' and was 'devoid of sympathy'. Atmore quoted the association rule book to show that it had no political purpose or connection with any political or industrial organisation. Its object was 'to improve the conditions of its members' and it sought to control the conduct and diligent execution of members' duties and 'promote concord ... between officers and men'. The rules also intended assistance to members and their families in need. Atmore characterised Herdman as Mrs Partington with her broom sweeping back the Atlantic, and repeated the charge of Cullen's predecessor that Cullen was a vindictive man.

Herdman may have felt that the educated public servants would muffle the working-class propensities of the police. His offer of marriage with the PSA or nothing carried with it the likelihood of divorce, as is generally the case with shotgun marriages. He must have had some inkling. Certainly he remained nervous through 1913. The deployment of specials during the Maritime Strike might have partly reflected uncertainty about the loyalties of some elements in his police force, although their nickname, 'Massey's Cossacks', suggests the heavy hand of his Ulsterman boss.

The police proved slow to join the PSA. Herdman's successor Wilford deferred permission to join, but the outbreak of war in 1914 deflected pressure to improve pay and conditions, or submerged any such moves under emergency regulations. Police organisation went underground. The most union-minded continued to operate the clandestine association. The victimisation of Charlie Smyth and others provoked more police to join the association, particularly in Wellington and Dunedin.

Smyth returned to his family bakery business in the Oamaru area. He died of cancer 13 years later, leaving behind a wife and five daughters and a burning desire among many policemen to establish their own association. When they finally did, the Auckland model rule book quoted in Parliament became the basis of the New Zealand Police Association rule book. Smyth has featured extensively in both oral and written records, taking on the status of patron saint of the New Zealand Police Association, a situation that must surely have Herdman, Cullen and Massey grinding their grave teeth.

NEW ZEALAND

Truth

THE PEOPLE'S PAPER

Largest Circulation throughout the Dominion

WELLINGTON: SATURDAY, FEBRUARY 11, 1922

333

TROUBLE IN THE CIVIL CIRCUS

The "Noo Zee" Police have withdrawn from the Civil Service Association on the ground that members of the Association are "too extreme." Some people allege that the real reason for the police pulling out is that they do not want to participate in the salary cut.

BILL: "HOOP-LA!"

THE HIND LEGS: "HOOP-LA! I DON'T THINK! THAT LITTLE HOOP'S NO GOOD TO ME. THIS IS WHERE I GET OUT."

PERSONS, PLEBS & PLUTES

Godfrey Turner, a well-known Press scribe, a native of Christchurch, passed out in London, whither he had gone to make a name for himself. He served his apprenticeship to the craft on the "Times" as a reader, and joined the "Sun" on its first appearance in 1914. He did some bright, original work for

Quite recently, in London the well known Irish Journalist and Commoner, T. P. O'Connor ("Tay Pay"), was entertained at dinner by a distinguished company, amongst whom was Hon J. G. Jenkins, ex-Premier of South Australia. In responding to the toast of his health, "T.P." delighted the assemblage greatly by delivering some Parliamentary

Prime Minister Massey provoked this cartoon and the police departure from the PSA when he exempted the police from civil service pay cuts

Chapter Three

The Short, Unhappy Marriage of the Police and the PSA

The police patriotically put aside their grievances when World War One erupted. Their wartime duties changed dramatically as offences dropped because almost half the eligible males were overseas. Emergency regulations required them to work longer hours in worse conditions maintaining surveillance on those left behind. Patriotism was worn thin by new grievances. Constables had to answer examination questions on special wartime statutes, but they had no time to study. By the end of 1915 considerable numbers began joining the PSA, the only permitted outlet for their grievances.

During this period Herdman told Parliament that 'throughout the ranks of the Force, contentment prevails. The men are satisfied with their lot.' When asked about employing women in the force, he said the government would communicate with other governments where women constables were employed, including the United States and Australia, and then decide. Herdman was the classic deferrer of decisions until they had been 'looked into'.

At the end of 1916 the police got a new commissioner, John O'Donovan, famous ever since for saying that every constable potentially carried the commissioner's baton. He was not pleased that his police could be unionised when they had the job of enforcing unpopular wartime regulations. Furthermore the PSA representing the police ran contrary to Regulation 172 of the 1913 Police Force Act, which stated that 'no man is permitted to complain on behalf of another, every man being held to be the best judge of his own grievances; nor shall any member of the Force write for or dictate to another any complaint to which he is not himself a party.'

This limbo status of the police in the PSA remained during Herdman's time. In February 1918 Herdman was promoted to the Supreme Court bench and replaced as minister by Liberal Thomas Wilford. O'Donovan immediately informed his new boss that, because the police had not been given the opportunity to form their own association, it was not known what proportion favoured belonging to their own group or joining the PSA. Wilford directed that there should be a ballot of the entire force to find out. This revealed that 34 wanted no police association, 87 wanted a police association and 697 voted for PSA membership.

The government respected the vote by adding, that December, to the rule against police forming combinations: 'Nothing in this regulation shall be held to prohibit members of the Force from becoming members of the Public Service Association.' Like any cagey politician Wilford added the proviso to 'reserve to the Minister the full right to limit hereafter and define the matters which may be discussed and dealt with by virtue of association, and to safeguard the preservation of discipline in such a manner as he may think necessary'.

Policemen had the legal right to confer, albeit under the beady eye of the minister. There was also the constraint of having to secure the permission of superior officers to meet as PSA branches. However, four policemen joined the PSA executive and negotiations began with the government over long-standing police grievances.

The Wilford-O'Donovan team were dedicated to giving the police a better deal, but they did not perceive the PSA as the appropriate presenter of police grievances. Wilford said he would prefer to deal directly with a separate police association than with a force influenced by an association that was part of the labour movement. This was a reversal of Herdman's thinking. It is quite possible that the big majority favouring PSA representation reflected fears in the ranks that Wilford and O'Donovan preferred a pussycat police association they could readily control.

John O'Donovan, new Commissioner of Police in 1916 and concerned that the police could be unionised while carrying out unpopular wartime regulations. In the last year of the war he proposed that the police be permitted to voice their union preference. He is celebrated for saying that every constable potentially carried the commissioner's baton. *B.G. Thomson*

The first stirrings of negotiation between police and administration began with the four policemen who were on the PSA executive from February 1919 presenting remits. Wilford and O'Donovan anticipated PSA pressure by setting up a commission of inquiry into police pay and conditions, particularly the old grievance that the detectives enjoyed privileges over the uniformed branch. The four hours on/four hours off/four hours on day shift had been unpopular for years. O'Donovan tested an eight-hour shift in Wellington, which was eventually extended to the whole country. Following the commission's report in June 1919, its recommendation of equal pay for equal rank was adopted.

Wilford and O'Donovan were principally concerned with bringing the force back up to strength. This included legislation extending the wartime appointment of temporary police. In Parliament Robert Semple said he had been assured the police did not object to temporary constables, but his own enquiries revealed that a large number did object. They feared it would be used as a lever against them in any desire to improve conditions.

Semple was one of the new Labour voices in the House speaking up for the police who, so recently, had been arresting them as pacifist agitators. Peter Fraser was most prominent, speaking to a Police Amendment Bill that all over the world police made claims for better pay and conditions and New Zealand might follow their example. 'I think if the government paid good wages and improved the conditions of the present Force, they would have no difficulty in getting the right class of men without creating a Second Force.' The real remedy, Fraser believed, was to make the force more attractive, by giving the men the pay and conditions they deserved. James McCombs of Lyttelton added that there was no police participation in superannuation, an area where the government saved money.

Prime Minister Massey blithely apologised for not involving the PSA in discussions on the desirability of temporary police. Wanganui's MP W.A. Veitch was provoked to criticise the PSA for not pressing reform of police appeal procedures. He thought police discipline too severe; the police should be lined up with other departments in matters of appeal.

The PSA executive that year angered the commissioner by asking for an audience with the Minister of Police. Wilford and O'Donovan listened to 18 remits, one for the establishment of an appeal board that included a union nominee, as enjoyed by other public servants. There were also pleas for optional retirement at 55 and cold weather clothing for southern police. Perhaps the biggest breakthrough was that police representatives on the PSA could now negotiate directly with the commissioner without having their careers threatened. Police and PSA enjoyed a honeymoon that climaxed with the PSA securing a general cost-of-living increase in 1920.

There were frictions as the PSA developed links with the Railway unions, which were tied in to the militant Alliance of Labour. Older members of the police objected to these connections. Some trade unionists were wary of being associated with the police, who so often had been strikebreakers. Both sides saw a conflict of duties.

The police were seen as being favoured by their pension scheme, more so when the government did not meet its share of superannuation and did not adjust rates of pay. In 1922 Massey ensured that the police would be perceived as the politicians' pet when he announced salary cuts for the public service but exempted the police, his reason being that they were in short supply.

The *Public Service Journal* editorial of 20 March 1922 said the PSA would under no circumstances 'have stirred a foot towards securing exemption for Police Officers from the salary cut, for the simple reason that when we secured cost-of-living salary increases in 1920, it was definitely understood that the Police were to participate, and the conditions then made in regard to decreases must needs apply also'. At the time, the *Journal* continued, it was well known that some of the police did not appreciate the PSA attitude. Since then, with a new commissioner, Arthur Wright, opposed to the police being linked with any other organisation, the force had been divided on membership of the PSA.

Massey then proceeded to include the police in the salary cuts. It was not clear what his game was, but one result was to split the police, with the entire Auckland branch deciding to stay in the increasingly militant PSA while, in July 1922, 50 police in Wellington, including three representatives on the PSA executive, resigned. The reason given was that the PSA was too militant, but the *Public Service*

William Fergusson Massey, the Prime Minister who pitted police against the PSA

Journal for that month said the action was 'not altogether unconnected with the fact that the Police Force were included in the salary cuts'. The implication was that those who resigned thought they could do better outside the PSA.

The 50 resignees resolved to form a police association, and saw Commissioner Wright about it. He wanted proof that they represented the general police view. Police branches in the PSA were asked to comment. Some left the PSA. Others such as Auckland, where future Commissioner John Bruce Young had been secretary, voted to stay on the grounds that leaving meant they surrendered collective bargaining power. For its part, the PSA announced that, if it could be shown the police wanted their own organisation, it would help. Two-thirds of the police indicated that they wanted to leave the PSA.

At the mid-year third national PSA conference the PSA executive stated that 'no good purpose could be gained by proceeding with Police matters'. The PSA would not represent the police until their numbers in the PSA totalled 350.

Police membership was going in the other direction, with 500 resignations by August. The intention may have been to join a new police association, but the commissioner was not responding to any such representations, and the news of police strikes in Australia and the United States did not incline him to indulge any requests for police unionism here.

The police drifted out of the PSA, and stayed adrift. Again they were without a mouthpiece, again there was trouble for any who dared complain, again district bosses would not pass on grievances. The result was depressingly clear in static police pay and conditions throughout the 1920s. The force had enjoyed only a temporary reprieve from the wilderness years.

P.G.1918/577.

Office of Minister of Justice.
Wellington. 30th. September.1918

To the members of the Police Force.

On oocount of the question having been raised since I have had charge of the Police Department as to whether members of the Police Force are entitled to join the Public Service Association notwith--standing the provisions of the Police Force Act and regulations,I have decided to endeavour to ascertain the wishes of the members of the Force by taking a ballot uppn the issue contained in the ballot-paper.

I may state that I have no objection to the members of the Force joining the Public Service Association nor have I any objection to the members of the Police Force forming an association of their own independent of the Public Service Association with an "executive" representative of the various branches, such executive to have the right to approcah me and make their representations personally on behalf of the association, if formed. Such executive would, of course,have to apply through the Commissioner for any appointment for an interview to be made with me.

The ballot-paper forwarded to members of the Police Force are to be returned to Mr. W.G.Riddell,Stipendiary Magistrate,Wellington, who will examine the papers and communicate the results to me. He will be the only person who will see such ballot-papers,and he will have no means of identifying the voter. After he has communicated the result to me he will be required to seal up such ballot-papers in envelopes and retain same for twelve months,after which time the same will be destroyed.

It will be noticed on the ballot-paper that instructions are given that members of the Force will not have to sign the paper or put any other mark upon it that is required by the striking out of the word "Yes" or "No" as the voter desires.

Thomas.M.Wilford.
Minister of Justice.

Memorandum.

The following are the issues which will be submitted in the ballot-paper referred to in the Hon.Minister's memorandum above;-

1. Are you in favour of having any Police Association?.
2. Are you in favour of having a police association separate from any other association? or
3. Are you in favour of admission to the Public Service Association?...

A ballot-paper and a copy of the Hon.Minister's menorandum will be forwarded to every member of the Force.

J.O'Donovan.
Commissioner of Police.

P.G.1918/707.

POLICE BALLOT.

Office of the Minister of Jistice.
Wellington, 18th. December.1918.

To the members of the Police Force.

Referring to my memorandum of the 30th. September.1918,published in the Police Gazette 1918, page 577, the result of the ballot as communicated to me by Mr. Riddell,S.M. the scrutineer, is as follows;-

Votes in favour of a separate Police Association..............87
Votes in favour of joining the Public Service Association.....697
Votes against forming any association 34
Informal votes...38

Chapter Four

An Outcast in the Wilderness Years

William Dunlop Thom demonstrated how easily a dedicated policeman could be made an example of in the new wilderness years from 1922 to 1935.

After resigning to serve with the armed forces in the Great War, Thom rejoined the police in 1919 and, like most policemen, joined the PSA. He was elected secretary of the Wellington Police Branch, a position not much sought after. For three successive years he was delegate for Wellington city at the annual PSA conference. The other police delegate was John Bruce Young, now representing West Coast Police on the PSA after his transfer to Greymouth in 1920.

Thom knew of no contact or co-operation between the police branches of the PSA. When he attended conference, remits would come forward from other branches that had never been discussed by his branch, and he could only speak on matters as an individual. The Commissioner of Police would not recognise the PSA as the mouthpiece of police members and refused to meet any deputation from the conference.

'You can imagine,' wrote Thom, 'the position I was in when I had to report these facts back to my committee and at the same time remind members that their subs for the following year were due.'

When it appeared that the PSA had overseen a cut in police salaries, Wellington members resigned. Thom later took the view that this was overhasty. They were back where they were before 1918. Being in the PSA may, he believed, have assisted them in forming an association.

Thom's mistake was to accept the good wishes and backing of Wellington members of the force to set about forming a police association. He organised a letter to every police station in New Zealand asking for their views on this proposal. Three-quarters of members stated they were in favour of forming a police association. There was no reply from Auckland. Thom believed he was outmanoeuvred there. The General Secretary of the PSA, hearing of his letters, travelled to Auckland and called a meeting of the police branch of the PSA. Few members were present, but the following morning the local newspaper said the Auckland police were not in favour of resigning from the PSA.

When Thom appeared, with his former chairman and vice-chairman of the PSA branch, at an interview with the commissioner to discuss forming a police association, Wright produced the Auckland newspaper cutting to show that members of the force were not unanimous in their wish for an association. They might never have been unanimous, but the commissioner had a reason for saying that nothing could be gained by discussing the matter. The

Constable William Dunlop Thom represented the police in the PSA and attempted to form a police association. He was transferred out of Wellington. Later he lost his sergeant's stripes for presenting a shiftwork grievance, and was transferred to Ross, about as far as he could be from any colleagues. A war veteran himself, he is seen here speaking at the unveiling of the Ross War Memorial

interview lasted two minutes. The commissioner was polite and formal. The repercussions of that meeting continued throughout Thom's long police career, beginning the following morning with notification of his urgent transfer. Given a choice, he took Feilding and was sent immediately, having to leave behind his wife recovering from surgery in Wellington Hospital.

His career picked up for a time, as he served at Palmerston North, Te Araroa and Ormondville, before gaining promotion to sergeant at Dunedin. There he led a delegation of sergeants to the officer in charge of the district concerning a shiftwork hardship. His sergeant's chevrons were removed. Soon after he was judged to have written an anonymous note and was transferred to Ross in Westland; there were no members to organise there.

Like most frontline police in those days, Thom worked alone much of the time. He did not meet other policemen. If he had a complaint, it had to be written to the commissioner and submitted through his superior, who might be the cause of the problem. Many complaints ended there. A rare successful stand against a superior was an off-duty policeman who called in to the station to see his mates and was charged with drunkenness by Inspector Donald Scott.

Superintendent Mackinnon inspects his Christchurch staff in 1926, during the wilderness years when the police had no voice in their own affairs. *Truth* had written of the glassy authority stare of military martinet officers. *Canterbury Public Library*

His case was only dismissed in court after his fellow constables testified in his defence.

Senior sergeants at city stations were known for the phrase, 'If you don't like the job, get out.' A third of those who joined in 1922 did just that, not inspired by the prospect of 15 years of dreary shiftwork under the petty tyranny of a senior sergeant before any chance of promotion. The rank and file had no more representation than they had had last century.

Once again, in the early 1920s, *Truth* took on the role of their unofficial mouthpiece, leading the press in the printing of police complaints under noms de plume. Gripes included uncompensated overtime, police boxers being debarred from public contests, free afternoons forfeit to general inspection parades, 12-hour days still being worked despite the introduction of the eight-hour day, beat men still getting only one Sunday off each month. The commissioner set the rules but he might not know of his district officers ignoring them; there was no way for a policeman to get his complaint past his superior.

The question of introducing a six-day week and leave provisions was raised in Parliament. The new Minister of Police, C.J. Parr, echoed his commissioner's position that leave would be given when men could be spared. They airily dismissed unsourced complaints as unsound, but no policeman was prepared to publish his own professional suicide notice in a newspaper.

On 8 September 1923 *Truth* asked 'Can men who are required to work broken time for a period of 15 hours a day be expected to be alert?' And what about the effect on their families, who did not see them until 10 every night? This 'sweated police force is a distinct menace to society and an encouragement to crime'. The simple solution was good pay and reasonable hours of work.

Former London bobby W.J. Jordan, now MP for Manukau, led the parliamentary questions about poor police morale. That month the government ordered a small increase in pay, mindful perhaps of threatened strikes and the need for police control.

The rising Labour Party beat the police drum loudly.

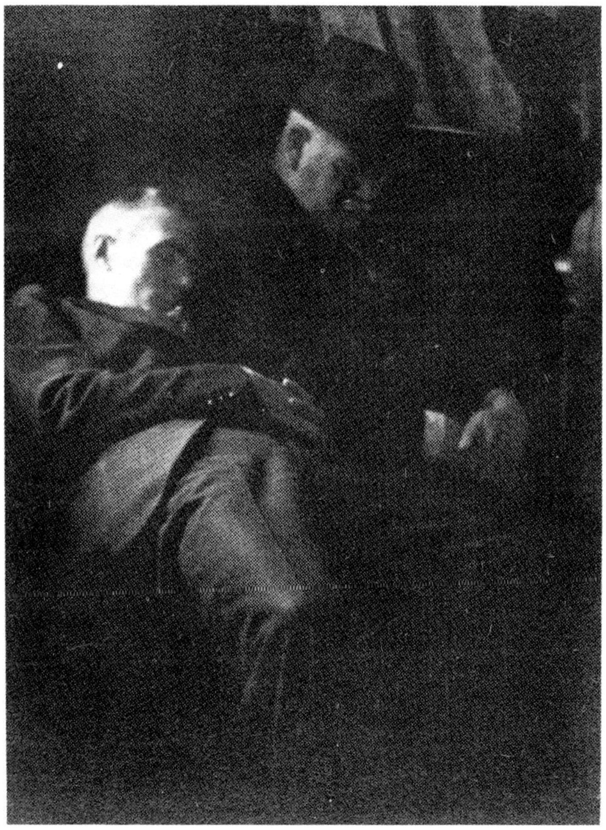

Detective Sub-Inspector Dunlop and Senior Sergeant Nelson effectively answer the *Truth* question of 8 September 1923: 'Can men who are required to work broken time for a period of 15 hours a day be expected to be alert?' *B.G. Thomson*

Constable Jack Cossill awaits his cuppa from Constable Ted Hotham in this photograph taken in 1934, when police ate on the beat. *New Zealand Police Centennial Museum*

Speaking to the 1928 report on the police, John A. Lee said 'there should be a channel through which police officers ... can make representation to the Government of the day for necessary increases in pay and for the rectification of grievances'. He noted no loss of efficiency when Queensland allowed a police organisation. New Zealand was paying less for police protection than any other country and was not paying 'our police that reward to which they are entitled'. Frequent areas of complaint were promotion, travel, superannuation and retirement age, the many dismissals without any right of appeal.

Napier's Labour MP W.E. Barnard spoke to the 1929 report, comparing New Zealand's ratio of one policeman to 1273 citizens at a cost of 6s 1¼d per capita with New South Wales' one to 715 at 10s 10¾d. New Zealand had 939 constables and a total of 1146 police. Barnard called on their behalf for the repeal of Section 9 allowing the commissioner to dismiss without appeal and forfeiture of superannuation.

Other Labour MPs joined in. D.G. Sullivan referred to the inadequate pursuit of offenders by train and taxi because the police did not have their own cars. He spoke of poor pay scales that saw a constable under three years of service on 15s a day compared with the lowest labouring wage of 15s 8d a day.

R.A. Wright called for the appointment of women police. Minister of Police Wilford fobbed him off with a challenge to define the age and type of woman he would want. Michael Joseph Savage asked why there were so many police transfers. 'One wonders,' he said, 'whether a policeman can call his soul his own.' In 1930 the Reverend Clyde Carr, MP for Timaru, wanted an inquiry into police dismissals. The new Police Minister, J.G. Cobbe, said there was no good purpose in discussing it.

On 7 August 1930 *Truth* trumpeted 'Give Them a Voice—Rank and File of the Police Anxious to Co-operate—Why not a Police Federation?' Of all the reforms required in the police, the most important was facilities for the force 'to co-operate in its own improvement'. The government took no action. The police administration was concerned only to identify the author of an anonymous typed memorandum dated 13 August 1930 advocating the formation of a police union.

Charles Belton, a detective before he resigned and founded the well-known real estate firm, wrote that when an eight-hour shift was proposed, there was strong opposition from many of the officers. They regarded men on call 12 hours a day seven days a week as 'only proper'. Belton noted that the men in one-man stations still had to pay for their own light. Another petty injustice was policemen having to pay for telephone calls made in the line of duty. This led to beat men forever scouring gratings and drains for coins, which were retrieved on a lump of gum stuck to a stick.

On 21 June 1931 Riccarton MP H.S.S. Kyle specified eight charges against a local sergeant that were proved wrong on appeal as an example of serious injustices in the police. The appeal had cost the sergeant £40. The sergeant was told to get out of Christchurch. 'There is something radically wrong with the superior officers in Christchurch,' he said in Parliament. He knew of intimidation 'going on for a long time'.

In 1932 there was discussion in Parliament of a speech by Superintendent Denis Cummings in which he said he had smashed a strike at Christchurch. When, Peter Fraser asked, were the police informed that it was part of their function to take sides against the workers in industrial trouble? The answer lay perhaps in the government action of employing, in the main centres, special constables or auxiliaries to help control the protesting unemployed. Speaking in Parliament in 1934, Auckland lawyer and MP F.W. Schramm said the rank and file police were strongly against these specials. He advocated spending money on more regular police. Savage spoke against any move that damaged police morale; Semple said he would regard specials as a vote of no confidence in the police. Jordan pointed out that auxiliary police in London had resulted in the undermining of the force there.

Police Minister Cobbe maintained the government line on auxiliary police and rejected the call for policewomen, despite the citing of their success in Britain and the United States. On the contrary, he said the reports were not favourable.

In 1935 Eden MP A.J. Stallworthy asked Cobbe to allow members of the force to make representations for its improvement. If there was reliable evidence that matters were not right in the police and such information was supplied, it would, Cobbe said, receive earnest consideration.

Schramm called for more constables and more leisure time for overworked policemen. He condemned the auxiliary police as 'tantamount to creating a detachment of strikebreakers who could also be used against existing police officers in the event of their having legitimate

The mounted police unit raised to control the 1932 tramway strike, when the politicians still saw the police as there to keep the workers in their place. *Christchurch Police Museum*

grievances they sought to bring before Ministers of the Crown'. Semi-private forces should be eliminated because there was no place for them in a democratic society. Furthermore, there were allegations of young men forced into enlisting with the auxiliaries to retain their civilian employment. In fact, these auxiliaries were never deployed, and in 1936 the Labour Government disbanded them.

The 27 November 1935 general election gave the long-time Labour champions of police reform the chance to practise their preaching. The unco-ordinated shadow police association that had lobbied the press and Parliament was about to become an organised reality. Labour would live up to its rhetoric.

The first Constable Thom at Ross heard of it all was when the new Labour Minister of Police, Peter Fraser, visited his station. Thom told him he had not heard of the Police Department circular inviting members to give their views on a police association. Eventually receiving a copy after writing to Greymouth district office, Thom read it and filed it in the station memorandum book. He was rebuked for this by his district commander. He had done so because he wanted to record the date of the circular's issue and the date

Michael Joseph Savage, one of the Labour Party leaders constantly asking parliamentary questions about police conditions. He asked why there were so many police transfers and wondered if a policeman 'can call his soul his own'

that he received it months after it was drawn up.

Thom was truly in the wilderness, but the wilderness years of no representation for policemen were about to end, too late to be of any assistance to Thom. On 25 April 1953 he wrote to the journal of the then well-established New Zealand Police Association. His 40 years would be up in 1954, and he suggested that his experiences might assist the association and 'let some of the laggards and half-hearted members see just what we had to put up with prior to 1936'. He believed that had Jack Meltzer been there as General Secretary of the Police Association when he struck his bother in Dunedin, he would, in 1953, be sitting in a superintendent's chair.

The irony of Thom's career was that the change to a Labour Government happened while he was still in Dunedin, but matters had not moved fast enough to save him. He was convicted there in 1935 of writing an anonymous letter on a subject in which he was not even interested and about an incident in which he was not involved. He was convicted on the evidence of a Christchurch handwriting expert named Collins, who was subsequently discredited in court. The case was heard by Inspector Allan Cameron at Christchurch, and Superintendent Denis Cummings was a member of the appeal board. Thom blamed himself and his distinguished counsel Alfred Hanlon for not countering the evidence of Collins with their own handwriting expert; he did this later with two experts and was vindicated by their opinions that he was not the writer of the letter.

Thom did submit his case to the fledgling Police Association, which advised him to have the case reopened and offered financial assistance. His wife was not well and she was very distressed at the thought of going through another trial. This, coupled with the fact that Thom was now broke, decided him to drop the matter.

Thom had no regrets, he said, about his unsuccessful attempt to form an association. He had the satisfaction of knowing that he had made an attempt to assist his fellow members. 'I finish my service,' he wrote, 'still retaining my ideas and ideals: support your Association in will and in deed. It may not be required to assist you, but it may assist your friend on the next beat.'

Constable Thom had transferred to Islington in Christchurch just before World War Two began. He worked up a group into the first parade of Home Guard in Canterbury and he wrote to the association journal trying to stir up interest in a police hostel. After the war he moved to Lower Riccarton where, although over 60, he carried on so that he could obtain his full superannuation benefits at 65. He recognised that the association had not by then obtained all its major planks, but that much had been achieved. He particularly appreciated the fact that a member charged with an offence against regulations could object to the charge being heard by an officer who had handled the file.

Thom ended his career as he began, a constable. Denis Cummings, on the other hand, moved up in 1936 to become Commissioner of Police. One of his unprecedented tasks was coping with the new Police Association.

Part II

The Formative Years

Chapter Five

The Political Go-Ahead for the Police Association

The New Zealand Police Association was officially given the go-ahead on Thursday 8 August 1936. At 9.30 that morning a deputation from the police met their minister, Peter Fraser, with a proposal to form an association. Fraser took the wind out of their sails by saying that there was no need for such a proposal, since it was already approved. The government was right behind them—why didn't they get on with it?

Three days later in Parliament seven MPs—A. L. Campbell of Chalmers, W. J. Jordan, Hawke's Bay's E.L. Cullen, Auckland West's M. J. Savage, A.H. Nordmeyer from Oamaru, Dunedin West's Dr D.V. McMillan and W.M.C. Denham of Invercargill—asked Fraser whether the government was prepared to consider favourably the formation of a police association. Fraser answered yes, adding that the government welcomed it and would do everything possible to help.

The Opposition, too, were by now in agreement. During the 28 August debate on the supply vote of £498,019, Cobbe showed his political mettle by telling Fraser that salaries for the police were inadequate; he apologised that, when he was minister, he had not had the money. He noted that men on public works were receiving more than constables. Christchurch North MP Sid Holland had nothing to apologise for. He said police trainees got the princely sum of 15s a day, about the same as relief workers. He called for an all-round pay increase for the police. It was refreshing, Fraser observed, to hear such words from the Opposition.

The police had never heard such words of encouragement before, so it was understandable that they had been slow to apply for an association. According to Auckland District Secretary of the association A.T. Gillum, 1 May 1936 was the date on which Detective Sergeant Arnold Bell Meiklejohn wrote out the application to form an association. As far as Gillum could learn, this was the earliest date 'that any man dared to attempt such a thing in the interests of all the men'.

Soon afterwards Meiklejohn was transferred, not to any Siberia of the service, but to Palmerston North, to take charge of the detective branch there. What is more, he got the job over the heads of other senior men who might have thought they had the right to that station. It seemed, under the Labour Government, that promotion would not be determined by favouritism and seniority.

Over 100 Auckland members farewelled Meiklejohn, who was praised as an inspiration for having the courage to put in the first report aimed at setting up an association. Meiklejohn replied that the idea had been successful in Australia and it must be in New Zealand. He spoke of a police union with access to the Arbitration Court as a long felt need. He reminded members that the association was their voice—be sure to send in remits in plenty of time for the conference. He also told them not to be afraid of their superiors. Meiklejohn represented the new mood; as an 'agitator', he was moving up, not down and out, as had Thom, who had passed his exams up to senior sergeant and felt he could have gone on if allowed.

Police Minister Peter Fraser not only told the police they could form an association, but told them to get on with it

The rise in confidence was rapid and widespread. Charles Belton at Hamilton also typed an application to form an association on 7 May, unaware that Meiklejohn had just done the same. However, those same officers Meiklejohn had warned Auckland members not to be afraid of were still there. Belton's application was returned with the question: 'Is Detective Belton free to state in what way an association would benefit, (1) the Force, and (2) the public?'

Belton said that the majority of the men favoured an

Some of the mid-1936 documentary response to Fraser's advice to the police to set up an association

[Police—100A.

NEW ZEALAND POLICE.

Police-station: WELLINGTON.

Date: 12th May 1936.

REPORT of CONSTABLE T.F.SMITH, *No.* 1793

relative to APPLICATION FOR PERMISSION FOR A DEPUTATION OF ABOUT SIX MEN TO WAIT ON THE HON. THE MINISTER OF POLICE WITH A VIEW to OBTAINING THE NECESSARY PERMISSION TO FORM A POLICE ASSOCIATION.

I respectfully apply for permission for a deputation of about six men to wait on the Hon. the Minister of Police with a view to placing before him the wishes of the members of the Force in the matter of a Police Association.

In this connection it is to be understood that should the Hon. the Minister, after having heard the views expressed by the deputation, feels satisfied that a Police Association is justified and accedes to our request, the Police Association is to be and must of necessity be distinct from any other organization and will not be affiliated with any other body.

Also, the Police recognise that loyalty to the Government is the first essential, whatever Government may be in office, and therefore cannot countenance for a moment an affiliation with any other organization.

Associations of a similar nature are now functioning throughout the Australian States with satisfaction to all branches of the service and it is felt generally throughout this service that an organization founded on similar lines would prove beneficial to all.

The Hon. the Minister of Police has stated his willingness to meet a deputation from the Police at such time and date as can be suitably arranged.

It is proposed to approach the Minister at an early date.

Const.No.1793.

THE SUPERINTENDENT OF POLICE,
W E L L I N G T O N.

300,000/8/35—7007]

Wellington,
4th. June, 1936.

To Members of the Police Force in the Wellington District.

Re Deputy Commissioner's Memorandum P. 36/544
(copy of which is attached).

In accordance with the above memorandum, we, the undersigned members of the Police Force in the Wellington District, hereby convene a meeting to be held in accordance with the Deputy Commissioner's instructions.

The meeting will be held in the Billiard Room at the Central Police Station, Wellington, on Tuesday next the 9th. June, 1936, at 7 p.m.

All members of the Force who can possibly do so, are earnestly urged to attend this meeting, as the subject is of paramount importance to all members of the Force.

If any member of the Force through duty, sickness or any other unavoidable cause, is unable to be present at the meeting, he is urged to forward to the meeting in an envelope addressed to "The Meeting Chairman, C/o Central Police Station, Wellington C.1.," a statement of one or other of the following:-

"I am in favour of the formation of a Police Association."
"I am not in favour of the formation of a Police Association."

with, if the member so desires, an expression of any views the member may wish to bring forward.

Sgd .... J. M. Pointon, H. E. Campin, J. W. Ellis,
E. F. Barry, Leo. Revell, N. W. Baylis,
S. C. Browne, N. J. McPhee, W. R. Murray,
G. Hogan, V. P. Cosgrave, F. N. Robinson,
P. Munro, F. Hayhurst.

All members of the Service who can be spared from duty may attend the meeting if they desire.
Those who cannot attend, may send in their views on the matter to the meeting.

(Sgd) D. J. Cummings,
Superintendent of Police
4/6/36.

[Police—100A

NEW ZEALAND POLICE.

Police-station: Christchurch

Date: 16th June 1936

REPORT of Senior Sergeant L. L. Calwell, No. 1394

relative to Meeting held re "Proposed Police Association"

Vide Commissioner's Memo. P. 36/544, of 29th May 1936.

I respectfully report that, in accordance with the permission granted by the Deputy-Commissioner, and arrangements previously made as shown by file attached, a meeting of the members of the Police Force in the Christchurch Police District was held at the Central Police Station (Library) at 3.30 p.m. on 15th June 1936, for the purpose of ascertaining the wishes of the members regarding the proposed formation of a "Police Association".

I forward herewith a copy of the minutes of that meeting showing the result thereof in accordance with the instructions contained in the last paragraph of the Commissioner's Memorandum.

The minutes taken will be handed on to the Committee which has been appointed for such further action as is necessary when the instruction regarding the ultimate outcome of the meetings held at other centres are received.

The meeting was conducted with the utmost dignity and orderliness and was marked by a very keen desire of all members of loyalty to the Department and an apparent genuine desire to approach the matter in a proper manner..

The original file is forwarded herewith.

The Inspector
of Police
Christchurch.

Senr. Sergt. No. 1394

The Secretary
Committee of Christchurch
Branch (Police Association)
Minutes of general
Meeting of 15/6/36 herewith
L. L. Calwell
16-6-36 Senior Sergeant

[?],000/8/35—7007]

Police Station, Nelson.
P. O. Box 43.
29th. July, 1936.

The District Secretary,
Proposed Police Association,
Christchurch

Dear Sir,

On the 24th. June, 1936, a meeting of members of the Force in the Nelson District was held in the watch-house at Nelson Station, to discuss the formation of a Police Association, in accordance with the memorandum of the Deputy Commissioner of Police, dated the 29th. May, 1936.

All members of the Force from out-stations who were unable to attend in person submitted their views to the meeting in writing.

On a vote being taken, it was carried with one exception that a Police Association be formed.

A report that the meeting had been held and the result of the meeting was submitted through the official channel for transmission to the Commissioner of Police, for the information of the Hon. Minister in Charge of the Police Department.

Yours faithfully,
James Jackson
Dist. Secy. (pro tem)

[Police—100A.

NEW ZEALAND POLICE.

Police-station WELLINGTON,

Date: 5th August 1963

REPORT of CONSTABLE T.F.SMITH, *No* 1793

relative to PROPOSED POLICE ASSOCIATION - NAMES OF DELEGATES TO WAIT ON THE HON. THE MINISTER IN CHARGE OF POLICE.

I respectfully report that all delegates have arrived in Wellington and will assemble in the Wellington Police Library at II a.m. today the 5th instant.

We had a brief discussion early this morning and it is the wish of the delegates that the Commissioner of Police meet the delegates at the appointed hour should he ofcourse desire to do so.

The names of the delegates are as follow:-

INVERCARGILL.	CHIEF DET J.B.YOUNG.
DUNEDIN	DO
TIMARU	SEN SGT D.HEWITT
CHRISTCHURCH	CONST.W.A.CALWELL
NELSON	CONST.F.H.HEALY
GREYMOUTH	SGT J.ISBISTER
WHANGAREI	SGT.O.TOCHER
AUCKLAND	DO
HAMILTON	SGT T.KELLY
GISBORNE	CONST.McCURRACH
NAPIER	CONST.BOWICK
NEWPLYMOUTH	DET.JENVEY
WANGANUI	CONST.F.W.EDWARDS
PALMERSTON NORTH	CONST.H.SHIELDS
WELLINGTON.	CONST.T.F.SMITH.

THE INSPECTOR OF POLICE,
WELLINGTON.

Const.No.1793.

300,000/8/35—7007]

Police Station,
Wellington,
7th August, 1936.

The Commissioner of Police,
WELLINGTON.

Sir,

As instructed by the Hon. Minister in Charge of Police yesterday, the Delegates present at the deputation returned to the library and went into Conference for the purpose of drawing up a set of proposed Rules and Constitution of the Association.

As a result of our deliberations, which continued to a late hour last night, and which we re-commenced this morning, we have drawn up a set of Rules which we forward herewith for the information of yourself and the Hon. Minister.

We wish it to be clearly understood that we were dealing with a very difficult matter, and that it is quite possible that some of the rules may not meet with the unanimous approval of all members. However we think we can say most definitely that the whole of the matters have been given very serious consideration and notwithstanding any complaints there may be, the Conference should be given credit for having acted in perfectly good faith.

This is the initial step in the formation of our Association and we do not think that any reasonable person could possibly expect the rules to be perfect. We also wish it to be clearly understood that they are laid down more or less as a temporary measure to get the association into working order at once and as the weaknesses of the rules are discovered, steps can be immediately taken by the members objecting, to have the rules altered in a constitutional manner.

The rule which is causing the most concern is the one in regard to the appointment of the General Secretary. This matter was the subject of a very lengthy discussion and the view of the majority of the Delegates are as laid out in the rules of the Association. It must be clearly understood by everyone that the appointment, duties and honorarium of the General Secretary are in the nature of an arrangement until we get some more definite information as to what the Association may require of him.

We omitted at our deputation to the Minister yeaterday to draw attention to Regulation 300 which relates to the use of influence by members of the Force. We feel that some amendment may be necessary to such Regulation so that it will not conflict in any way with the work of our Association.

We would also respectfully ask you to grant permission to all Districts for the holding of a general meeting so that the Delegates from the Conference may make a full report to their members, and that Officers in Charge of Districts be informed of that permission. These meetings will be necessary to have the rules confirmed.

We would like, Sir, for the information of members of the Police Force as a whole, some early notification from you by way of memorandum published in the Police Gazette, regarding the Association.

In conclusion, we desire to thank you and the Minister for the assistance and opportunities that have been afforded us to bring our Association into being.

We remain Sir,
Yours obediently
Police association Confc

per/ J.B. Young,
Chairman of Conference.

[Police—100A.

NEW ZEALAND POLICE.

Police-station: Coalgate.

Date: 9th August, 1936.

REPORT of Constable W. A. Calwell, *No.* 2227.

relative to Police Association; formation permitted by Commissioner and Minister in Charge of Police.

I beg to report having attended in Wellin[gton] a Conference of Delegates for the formation of a Police Association.

The assembled delegates waited upon the Minister in Charge of Police and the Commissioner who both consented to the formation of the Association, and, indeed, offered every facility for its formation.

I respectfully apply, therefore, for permission to take the necessary steps to invite all non-commissioned officers and men to join the Association and to pay their entrance fees of 2/6 each on next pay-day, the 14th insta[nt].

Also to call a general meeting after the parade at the end of the month for the purpose of presenting an out line of the proceedings of the Conference, to elect a Committee for the ensuing year, and for such other discus ion as may be necessary for the forming of a branch of th Association in the Christchurch District.

It may be worthy of note that the Hon. Minister inti ated that he was favourable to the suggestion that member ship of the Association be compulsory, and that the Commi -ioner is not adverse to the suggestion.

The Superintendent of Police,
CHRISTCHURCH.

W A Calwell
Const. No.2227.

The Inspector
Have no objection to the application. I have informed Constable Calwell
Alexander Cameron
Superintendent
10.8.36

The Senior Sergeant
for your information please. For Const Calwell to note Superintendent's memo of 10/8/36
Wallace
for Inspector
10/8/36

200.000/7/34—5382]

[Police—100A.

NEW ZEALAND POLICE.

Police-station: WELLINGTON.

Date: 23rd September 1936.

REPORT of CONSTABLE THOMAS FREDERICK SMITH, No. 1793

relative to THE FORMATION OF THE PROPOSED NEW ZEALAND POLICE ASSOCIATION.

I respectfully report that the Management Committee of the proposed N.Z.Police Association held a meeting on the 16th instant at Wellington.

It was resolved " That in view of the unanimous desire expressed by the members of the Police Force of New Zealand that an association be formed, the Hon. the Minister in Charge of Police be requested to introduce legislation in the form of an Amendment to the Police Force Act and Regulations, legalising the formation of such association and providing for compulsory membership for all non-commissioned officers and men". also " That as the association cannot be formed and registered until legislative authority has been given and the fact that there has been considerable discussion with regard to and apparent dissatisfaction with the progress in the formation of the association, it is respectfully requested that the matter be given urgent and favourable consideration ".

I may point out that all Police Districts have approved of the proposed rules (some with suggested amendments) excepting one distrivt from which we have had no reply yet. Although all districts unanimously favour the formation of an association, the approval of the proposed rules has retarded its progress somewhat. However, as pointed out by letter dated 7th August, 1936 to the Commissioner of Police and signed J.Bruce Young, Chairman of Conference, the rules are laid down more or less as a temporary measure to get the association into working order at once and as the weaknesses of the rules are discovered steps can immediately be taken by the members objecting to have the rules altered in a constitutional manner.

A copy of the rules is attached herewith for transmission through the Commissioner to the Hon. the Minister in Charge of Police for his approval.

THE SUPERINTENDENT OF POLICE,
W E L L I N G T O N.

Constable.No.1793.

300/00/8/35—7007]

[Police—100A.

NEW ZEALAND POLICE.

Police-station: WELLINGTON,

Date: 13th October 1936.

REPORT of Constable Thomas Frederick Smith, *No.* 1793.

relative to a request by the Management Committee of the N.Z.Police Association for an interview with the Hon. the Minister in Charge of Police.

I respectfully report that as Secretary of the Management Committee of the N.Z.Police Association, I was instructed to submit a report to the Commissioner of Police requesting that the Management Committee be granted an interview with the Hon. the Minister in Charge of Police at the earliest possible convenience in connection with matters concerning the Association.

As already intimated by the Hon. the Minister, that he is willing at any time to receive a deputation, it is now earnestly desired that he accede to this request.

THE SUPERINTENDENT OF POLICE,
W E L L I N G T O N.

Const.No.1793.

300,000/8/35—7007]

[Police—100A.

NEW ZEALAND POLICE.

Police-station: WELLINGTON.

Date: 30th October, 1936.

REPORT of Constable Thomas Frederick Smith, No. 1793.

relative to Amended Regulations as published in current Police Gazette, page 660.

I respectfully report that at a meeting of the Management Committee of the N.Z.Police Association (inc held on the 29th inst., I was instructed, as Temp.Gen.Secy, to submit a report to the Commissioner asking the following question :- " Does clause I of the Amended Regulations as published in the current Gazette page 660, mean that any meeting held by the Management Committee, District Committees, or any other meeting convened by a responsible body of the N.Z.Police Association (inc) is in breach of the Regulations unless the authority of the Commissioner or the Officer in Charge of the District is first obtained."?.

The Superintendent of Police,
WELLINGTON.

Const.No.1793.

The Commission of Police
D.C. Fraser
Supt of Police
30.10.36

8370/36

A circular as per copy attached will appear in tomorrow's issue of the Police Gazette.

D.J. Cummings
Commissioner.

24/11/36

300,000/8/35—7007]

Circular No. 9/36

Police Ass'n & Reg No 172 as amended

The Police Ass'n has any authority to hold meetings when such meetings are considered necessary.

In each District the Sec of the Ass'n shall notify the O in Ch. of the Dist in good time of the date whereon a meeting is to be held, so that the O/C of the Dist may make arrangements to relieve from duty as many men as is possible in the circs to enable them to attend the meeting.

D.J.C

C/r.

W.G.H

24/11/36

association, but few wanted to lead it. He charged ahead, getting permission to post notices declaring a meeting. He then circularised every district in the country with the proposed administration of the association, feeling himself to be 'more or less an unofficial general secretary'. He got agreement to his proposed rules from the 15 districts, but a temporary secretary was appointed from the Wellington members, Constable Thomas Frederick Smith.

Smith had been busy organising the application on his own patch, as Belton had on his, and Meiklejohn had in Auckland. The service then was lacking the communication facilities to organise readily on a national scale. Belton was a man in a hurry. He felt he could have risen to be commissioner, but when promotion did not eventuate, he resigned.

Tom Smith, No. 1793, was more a dyed-in-the-blue-serge copper. Sworn in in December 1912, he had served in Auckland and been lucky. During a downpour in 1914 he had objected to doing traffic duty in ankle-deep water and left his point. Unlike Smyth, he was not dismissed. The next year he applied for leave without pay to join the armed forces. Commissioner Cullen visited Auckland to tell men that they would not be allowed to join the army, and Smith was charged with 'accepting a position outside the police without prior consent'. Again he was lucky. The charge was dismissed and he caught the ship to Egypt, then on to France, where he lost the lower part of a leg.

Constable Tom Smith disobeyed police regulations to enlist in World War One. He lost a leg and was disbarred from returning to the force. Parliament overturned that. He limped back to Parliament to ask another favour, whether he could form a police association. The answer was yes. Smith was first acting secretary of the Police Association

Upon repatriation, he was disbarred from re-enlistment in the police, but a parliamentary enactment overturned this and he was posted to Wellington. Twice juniors were promoted above him. Ignoring the regulation against contact with MPs, he visited Parliament to seek political support for a police association. He was received with open arms, not only getting an interview with the new Police Minister Peter Fraser, but being encouraged to start an association.

He went through the usual channels of submitting a report to his superintendent for transmission to the commissioner asking permission to form a police association and take a deputation to the minister. When he showed the copy to some of his fellow coppers they were horrified and said he would be shot at dawn. He had, he told them, faced shellfire before, and would gladly do so again to improve working conditions. As it was, Smith was invalided into hospital when permission came back to hold a meeting to set up formation plans. The next Smith heard was that Auckland had put forward a similar request about the same time.

Smith, Belton and Meiklejohn were acting independently of each other in the same cause, hampered by lack of communication. Smith's application was dated 12 May. Finally it was a national memorandum P. 36/544 dated 29 May 1936 from Deputy Commissioner R.F. Madden to district superintendents which informed that the Minister of Police 'advises that the Government has no objection to the formation of such an Association'. Meetings could be held at district headquarters to find out the wishes of members.

The Wellington district meeting was in the billiard room of the Central Police Station at 7 pm on 9 June. One of those

Detective Sergeant Arnold Bell Meiklejohn of Auckland on 1 May 1936 made the first application to form a police association

Detective Charles Belton of Hamilton applied on 7 May 1936 to form a police association, unaware that Meiklejohn had already done so. Tom Smith followed with an application on 12 May. This lack of communication was one of the problems the Police Association would address. *Belton Family*

present was Bill Murray, who wrote to Meiklejohn on 15 June that the meeting had voted 152 to one in favour of forming an association.

The 15 June meeting at 3.30 pm of 164 Christchurch police in their central station was singular for including the acting superintendent, the sub-inspector and the senior sergeant on down, but constables were chosen to be chair and be secretary, possibly the first recorded occasion on which constables controlled their superiors. The vote was 104 to nil in favour of forming an association. It was agreed that Constable W.A. Calwell of Coalgate should write to his brother, Senior Constable A.G. Calwell of Melbourne, seeking details on their association. A month later the reply came back that his brother's association was dominated by the Chief Commissioner, who chose its office holders and made it of little use to its members.

On 14 June Timaru voted unanimously to form a police association. Dunedin met on 8 July and voted in secret ballot—55 were in favour of an association, one of a union, one opposed to both.

On 23 June Constable Tom Smith was back at work and circularising the news that the large majority of police wanted an association. The need now was for development of aims and objectives. He proposed using the 1000 strong Post and Telegraph Officers' Guild as a model for the 1219 strong police, with the same 2s 6d monthly levy to pay a secretary's honorarium, administrative costs, travel expenses and counsel before the Appeal Board.

At 11 am on 5 August Smith had delegates gathered in the Wellington Police Library. Dunedin and Invercargill delegate Chief Detective Young was elected to the chair. In attendance were Timaru Senior Sergeant D. Hewitt, Christchurch Constable Calwell, Nelson Constable F.H. Healey, Greymouth Sergeant J. Isbister, Auckland and Whangarei Sergeant O. Tocher, Hamilton Sergeant T. Kelly, Gisborne Constable McCurrach, Napier Constable Bowick, New Plymouth Detective Jenvey, Wanganui Constable F.W. Edwards, Palmerston North Constable H. Shields and Wellington Constable Tom Smith.

In a letter written that day Young assured the minister that the association they sought was going ahead without any antagonism to the department and would have no political purpose or connection with any political or industrial organisation. Its objectives were to promote the general welfare of the service and the conditions of its members, particularly in regard to housing, wages, hours of duty and other working conditions. Among the other now familiar objectives to foster fellowship and provide assistance, perhaps the most interesting was Young saying that the association would be the official channel of communication between non-commissioned officers and men as a body, and the commissioner and minister. Already it was accepted this group was not for the commissioned ranks to which Young would soon be promoted.

It was a very polite letter. These 13 delegates bent over backwards to make it clear they were not the 'crank' or 'agitator' type that Commissioner O'Donovan had vowed in 1918 would be 'weeded out when their propensities are discovered'. The delegates had no need to be concerned. Fraser welcomed them with open arms on 8 August. All they had to do was get their association act together.

Chapter Six

The Calm Man From Cumbria

Detective William Robert Murray was principal spokesman for the police delegates who met Peter Fraser at Parliament on 21 October 1936. Because of restlessness in the ranks, Bill Murray asked the minister to speed up the legislation permitting formation of the association. Fraser said the police had themselves to blame by not holding all their meetings and submitting the results. There was nothing to prevent the organisation going ahead, because he had already given them permission and approval. Fraser and Murray were the key players in forming the association. Fraser, Murray acknowledges, was in favour of a successful association, but the politicians did not realise the full extent of what the fledgling association wanted.

The delegates told Fraser it was the unanimous view that membership should be compulsory; Tom Smith and J.H. McComb told him it could not function successfully otherwise. Fraser did not agree—there might be a schism between association and non-association police. Every effort must be made to make the association successful on a voluntary basis, and he 'entirely disapproved of the backslider' who would not join. Later he was to say that if two men were eligible for promotion and one was not in the association, even though he was more efficient and better qualified for promotion, the association member would get his preference for promotion. The other's lack of social responsibility was sufficient reason to pass him over. And there was the clue to Fraser's stance—his puritanical brand of socialism that demanded demonstrable social responsibility.

Detective Bill Murray, the man the police approached to be first president of the association. *Earle Andrew*

Fraser also faced opposition to allowing an association within the higher ranks of the police and government. He told Parliament that when he became Minister of Police, there were difficulties in the way of granting the police the concession to form their own association. He was warned the association would not work; it would tend to insubordination and it would threaten the discipline of the force. His concession to such fears was to restrict membership to police below commissioned rank. By compelling a voluntary organisation he could test the strength of desire for an association. Willing voluntary members would make the association work.

The Solicitor-General confirmed to Fraser that there was no bar to the association being registered as an incorporated society, and this was duly done on 28 October 1936. In the November Fraser sent the association his message of welcome. This was followed by the commissioner's Circular 6/1936 of 24 November giving the association permission to hold meetings 'when such are considered necessary'. Each district secretary was required to notify the officer in charge in good time of the date and hour of the meeting, so he could relieve as many men from duty as possible.

The association was now quasi-legal. Fraser, however, had kept an ace up his sleeve. The association was not a statutory body. The regulations had been amended to permit its formation, but they did not create the association or recognise it specifically. At any time the association could be rendered null and void by a political withdrawal of recognition. If it became too aggressive, a government could disband it. Such a drastic step was doubtful while the association demonstrated almost total voluntary membership. It does, however, differ from the Police Federation of England and Wales, a body created by statute. Every member of the force automatically belongs to it, meetings and related expenses are part of police duty and provided for. British bobbies have a union under the thumb of their employers, while their New Zealand counterparts enjoy a tentative freedom, which in recent years has been seen to pay off.

Fraser also denied the association affiliation with any other organisation, although this was later overruled and the association voted in 1988 to become affiliated with the New Zealand Council of Trade Unions.

In permitting the association, Fraser explained that, whereas you could not run an army with a trade union organisation, a police association 'can be justified up to the point that it differs from the Army, or the Navy or the Air Force'. What weighed with him in agreeing to the associa-

Back Row: Det. A. Jenvey (New Plymouth); Const. Bowick (Napier); Const. H. Shields (Palmerston North); Const. F. H. Healey (Nelson); Const. F. W. Edwards (Wanganui); Const. G. A. McCurrach (Gisborne); Sgt. D. I. Tocher (Whangarei and Auckland).

Front Row: Sgt. J. Isbister (Greymouth); Const. T. Smith (Wellington); Chief Det. J. B. Young (Dunedin); Sen. Sgt. D. J. Hewitt (Timaru); Const. W. Calwell (Christchurch); Sgt. T. Kelly (Hamilton).

tion was 'a request that was made for many years by members of the Police Force at varying intervals and with varying intensity and persistency' that the police 'are not aggregated together in regiments' but rather 'distributed all over the country, sometimes in very lonely places'. He would certainly have seen this in the case of Constable Thom at Ross. Fraser went as far as he felt he could—to the point where there could be a danger to morale, discipline and loyalty.

The political ace has been invoked only by Fraser himself, when he used it to threaten the association's first professional secretary Ian Campbell. In those early years, the late 1930s, the Auckland district of the association was making strong criticisms of the department through the press, ignoring or defying the more muted Wellington-based management committee. Campbell got a phone call from Fraser telling him the government had consented to the formation of the association and could 'if it felt it necessary to do so, withdraw its consent'. Fraser added that, if the management committee could not control its members, 'such action would be considered'.

Campbell says he was too inexperienced then to know whether this was entirely a bluff. In any case, he took the view that the most effective spokesmen for the police in industrial matters were those who had come up through their ranks and had years of experience as negotiators—men like Bill Murray, first elected president of the association, whom Campbell characterised as one who 'combined strength and calmness, great assets in negotiation'. It was Murray who was charged by his fellows with uniting 15 districts to present a coherent case for the association.

Murray was born in Kirkystephen in Cumbria, the border county in the north-west of England, on 25 April 1896. He attended the local board school between the ages of four and 14, before having one year of secondary school instruction at a private school run by Dr Nicholson. He followed his father into the local post office, working as a clerk and telegraphist. In World War One he served as a sapper or engineer, returning briefly to his job as telegraphist before emigrating to New Zealand in 1919. He says the army had given him 'itchy feet' and he could not settle back into a staid job.

On the ship out he lent money to a man who could not repay, but promised his sister at Napier would. The debtor proceeded to quarrel with his sister over his drinking habits, so they left to find work on the West Coast. Murray worked as a sawmill hand at Ruru, but he had a hankering to see Auckland and did so, leaving job and debt behind.

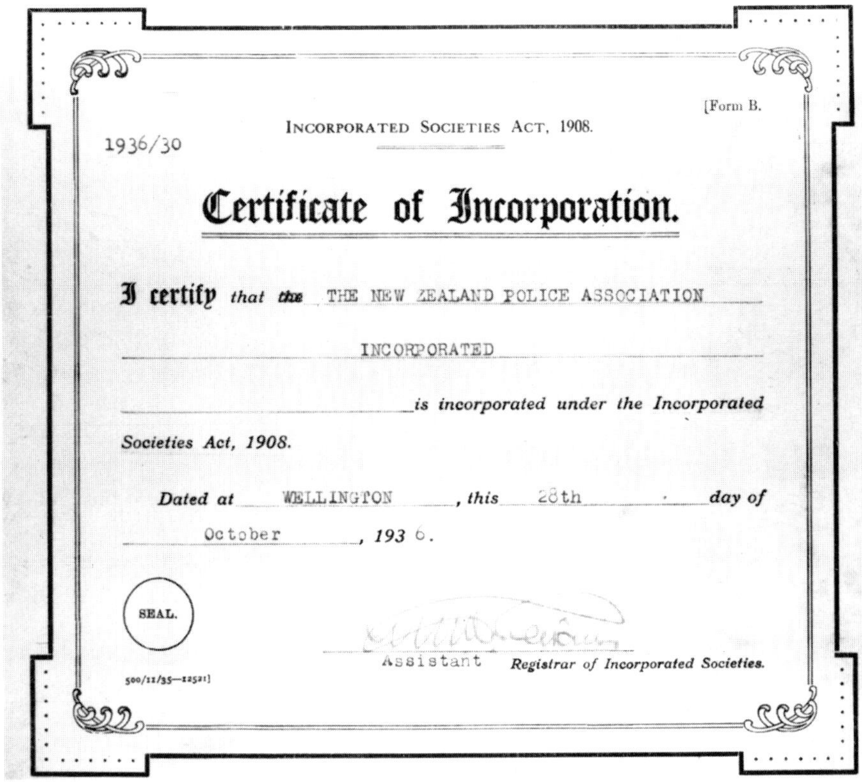

[Form B.

1936/30

INCORPORATED SOCIETIES ACT, 1908.

Certificate of Incorporation.

I certify that the THE NEW ZEALAND POLICE ASSOCIATION INCORPORATED is incorporated under the Incorporated Societies Act, 1908.

Dated at WELLINGTON, this 28th day of October, 1936.

SEAL.

Assistant Registrar of Incorporated Societies.

500/11/35—12521]

The association document of incorporation

There was no work in the city so he took a farmhand job at Elstow near Te Aroha, slept in a wood hut, learned to milk by hand and ride bareback. At the end of 1921, with no prospect of buying land on his wage, he returned to Auckland and joined the police because it was well paid. He planned to stay 12 months and save enough to get to British Columbia. Instead he stayed in the New Zealand Police for 38 years.

It was a rude beginning, living in army barracks at Mount Cook in Wellington he thought little different from a prison, the soup full of cockroaches and the cook berating the recruits as softies. Training was drill, first aid and lectures on the Police Force Act, the Police Offences Act and some of the Crimes Act. You learned by heart such matters as definition of a public place and powers of arrest.

Bill passed out top of his class, but got no recognition for it because numbers were awarded alphabetically. Promotion was strictly by seniority and progression through the numbers. He worked beat and point duty, chasing sly groggers and fortune tellers. Back at the station he scraped dirt off brown linoleum floors and cleaned lavatories in structures that dated back to the Armed Constabulary days.

After several years he was told to join the detective office, although he was not keen. He made suggestions for change, and was ignored. The officers took the view that suggestions from the ranks reflected badly on them, because they had not thought of them. All his superiors wanted was unquestioning obedience. He was not impressed with their administrative abilities; there was no training for such work. The commissioner aimed to run the department more cheaply than his predecessor.

In 1924, when Murray went home on leave to see his dying mother, he visited Scotland Yard and asked to look at their index system. He realised then how poor the New Zealand name-only index was. At the Yard they had also broken down the professions of burglary, arson and so on, had records of criminal work preferences, such as entering by window or picking a lock.

On his return Bill was careful not to put in a report straightaway, lest he be thought a smart guy. Instead he got on with the job of chasing a woman who was going around Wellington department stores getting costly credit. He told Kirkcaldies, James Smiths, DIC and C. Smiths to be on the lookout for her. She gave a different name at each place and was a tricky operator. Eventually he caught her and found that she had a long list of convictions for false pretences. Had he known that, he could have distributed her photograph to businesses and prevented a lot of damage. Murray put in a report based on this case, suggesting indexing under crimes as well as names.

The report moved from chief detective to inspector to superintendent to Commissioner William Bernard McIlveney, whom Murray described as a clever but unstable man. The commissioner acknowledged that there might be some merit in Murray's system, but the time had not yet come to adopt such a scheme in New Zealand.

Murray remembers another case, in which a gang of larrikins were breaking and entering in the Wellington suburb of Island Bay. They had got the idea from films screened at the local picture theatre. The report Murray put in on the influence of cinema on youth was filed. There was no interest in it.

As a result, he says, his own interest waned. There was no incentive to do well in the job. This went for everybody; the force was in the doldrums. Promotion was known as 'dead man's shoes' because that was the only way to climb the ladder. Murray was finally promoted to detective sergeant after 16 years, and even then the powers that were thought his batch too inexperienced! Some had to wait 20 years for promotion.

By now the criminals were motorised but the police were not. Transport services were generally not available to constables and detectives working on enquiries. It was possible to get a train or rail pass for city work, but where there was no public transport the police had to find their own. Murray says it was often a case of walking until you got there. Stuck at Heretaunga after the last train had gone, he was asked by his boss what was wrong with walking—it was downhill all the way. He hitched to Wellington city and walked home to Hataitai.

Departmental parsimony was distinguished. Murray was once dressed down for having the audacity to put in for something not in the regulations. He had spent a departmental shilling on unauthorised pillow hire when travelling by train from Wellington to Auckland. A refund was demanded from him. Meals were another problem for the department. If a meal cost more than half a crown, you were asked why you did not use the barrack facilities, regardless of where you might have been.

It was not unusual for police in the 1930s to work seven days a week. There was no assistance to travel from home to station. Housing was difficult. Promotion and/or transfer brought with them the anxiety of where a policeman would find a home for his family.

Murray sums up that authoritarian era in the person of Commissioner McIlveney, who served from 1926 to 1930, a man so vain he had a new uniform made for himself decorated all over with gold braid and tassels. Murray remembers the first monthly pay day parade when the 'troops' had to step up and salute McIlveney, who told them, 'I am the master of you all, every one of you.'

Murray was not impressed with McIlveney's successor W.G. Wohlmann, commissioner from 1930 to 1936, who was not very brilliant and got into trouble for using a police car on his honeymoon. After an inquiry he had to pay money back.

Murray saw a lot of the new Commissioner Denis Cummings (1936-44), who was not keen on the association. Murray was known to be very much the opposite. When the delegates from each police district gathered in Wellington, they came out to Murray's house to ask him to be the first president, who had to be Wellington-based.

Murray remembers the first meeting in the old gymnasium at the Waring Taylor Street station, on the ancient brown lino among a few dumbbells, vaulting horses and weightlifting bars. He was elected chairman; the meeting's secretary was Willis Brown, later to become commissioner. The old gym was packed, with men standing outside. Murray addressed the meeting.

'The atmosphere was absolutely electric,' he recalled,

> because never before had anything like this been dreamt of amidst the rank and file. They were held under so much by men like McIlveney, who impressed upon us he could dismiss under Section 9 any man not fit to be in the police force. He was very keen on quoting Section 9. He sought to drill the spirit of fear into men, so you would do everything as set out in regulations. The sudden breakaway from this impressed the men and some were revolutionary in what they wanted.

Murray felt he had to be careful what he said, for 'Cummings would have his scouts there to tell him how the meeting went'. He told them the rank and file had been given a voice: 'Let us use it sanely and wisely to try to work in co-operation. The deadmen's shoes system of those who got to the top had lost all contact with the desires of the men. Now we had a voice and we could work in co-operation with the Department.'

The meeting elected a management committee, extracted subs and made use of a real estate agent Bill Murray knew to get an office in the downtown T & G Building, at least a few hundred metres from the central police station and so giving the members some feeling of independence. A lawyer called W. P. Rollings was hired to see to the procedure of registering the association. Murray himself copied the rules of other associations. As secretary Tom Smith handled the subs and finances, while Murray wrote to police forces in Britain, Australia, the United States and Canada to learn of their pay, hours of duty and general conditions. This, he says, gave him some idea of what he could talk about in negotiations.

While Tom Smith, proposing his association in isolation from Meiklejohn and Belton, was typical of the rank and file unaware of activities outside their station, Murray was for that time and place a unique strategist. He had learned in the army how vital communications are, and as a former telegraphist he set about establishing lines of communication. He proposed a journal to inform members, using a friend's British journal as a model. He located the cheapest printer, the *Hutt Chronicle*, and got him to copy the British model.

In his 15 June 1936 letter to Meiklejohn in Auckland Murray explained how he had run the Wellington meeting and suggested that no district in New Zealand attempt to make up rules and a constitution before the association was formed. He stated bluntly that 'here in Wellington we are on the spot, and we think other parts of the Dominion look to us to do our part in bringing this matter to a head'. He outlined a six-point plan the Wellington delegation intended putting to the minister and wished 'Meik' every success with his Auckland meeting. Murray was determined to avoid the chaos of 15 sets of proposals for regulating an association that was not yet formed.

He did not, however, manage to reassure all districts. Timaru protested about only Wellington members waiting upon the minister. A memo dated 13 July 1936 and signed by Willis Brown, honorary secretary of the Wellington committee, was despatched to all district secretaries of the proposed association. It quoted the minister wishing to meet initially with Wellington representatives, and defended this against Timaru protest on the grounds that the police were unorganised and without funds, so surely it was up to those in Wellington to see to arrangements. The memo laid out the steps needed to achieve amending legislation that would allow the formation of the association, and to seek funds to bring delegates to Wellington.

On 22 July the Timaru police met and approved the Wellington action. Hamilton police had done so the previous week. Districts were beginning to get the hang of having meetings in their own police stations and sending other districts memoranda of their meetings. The cyclostyled, foolscap-sized memos began to whizz around the 15 districts.

On 21 October Murray briefed the district secretaries on the meeting with the minister. He explained that when Fraser claimed there was nothing to prevent them going ahead, he had replied that a large number of men had not paid their dues because they were waiting for the association to be legally established. Murray suggested that Fraser get on with the legislation, and Fraser promised it would be done within the week. Murray made a play for compulsory membership; Fraser declined, saying he wanted to see the association start on a voluntary basis.

Sergeant McHolm pressed for compulsory membership as the only way men would join because they 'liked to please the bosses'. Fraser acknowledged the argument. When Smith repeated the call for compulsion, Fraser said that they could not expect a 'primrose path'; the voluntary system must be tried first. If it was a failure, he promised he would accept compulsory membership. He was surprised that they anticipated any lack of support; he was confident that every man in the service would give the association his support. He promised to publish his support in the *Police Gazette*, and did so. Fraser's confidence was well founded when all but six of the 1200 eligible joined the association.

TO THE POLICE OFFICERS AND MEN OF THE POLICE FORCE OF NEW ZEALAND

Gentlemen,—

As you all know, an Association of members of the Police Force has been formed. The regulations under the Police Force Act have been amended to permit of its formation. It has been registered as an incorporated society. The Government has not only recognised the Association, but has encouraged it.

The Government is very anxious that the Association should be successful, and has asked me to further its interests in every possible way. I, therefore, convey to each and every member of the Police Force, other than commissioned officers, the Government's earnest wish that he should immediately join the Association.

In furtherance of the Government's policy I urge every man to do so.

The sooner the full membership of the Association is built up and ascertained the soonest will an agreement regarding working conditions and remuneration be arrived at, with benefit to all members of the Association. It is clearly the duty of every member of the Force, other than commissioned officers, to join the Association.

I expect that out of a sense of loyalty to the Government, to the Service, and to his colleagues, every eligible man of the Force will do so.

P. FRASER,
Minister in Charge of the Police Department

The next months weighed heavily on Murray. His management committee was Constables W.S. Brown, J.M. O'Connor, A.J. Johnston, C. L. Spencer and G.W. Gilmour, and Detective Sergeant L. Revell, with Constable A. Hardie as auditor. The committee would, he found, attend meetings but it did not do much else. As a result the association was occupying every spare minute of his time, and Tom Smith's. He proposed a fulltime permanent paid secretary to run the business side, and put part of the subs into a reserve fund to get the association on a sound financial footing, envisaging that it would one day own its own building. Meantime he called a meeting of all district delegates in Wellington on 8 December 1936 to appoint a fulltime secretary, overhaul the rules, consider remits and publication of a journal.

The meeting began at 9.30 am in police headquarters. Present were F.W. Edwards, Wanganui; J. Isbister, Greymouth; A. Jenvey, New Plymouth; F.W. Johnson, Dunedin; D. Hewitt, Timaru; A.B. Meiklejohn, Auckland; W.R. Murray, Wellington (acting chairman); C. Peterson, Nelson; H. Russell, Wellington; H. Shields, Palmerston North; F. Sinclair, Christchurch; G. Sivyer, Napier; T. Smith, Invercargill; T.F. Smith, Wellington; E. Wigmore, Gisborne and T. Kelly, Hamilton. Murray also welcomed Fraser, Commissioner Cummings and New South Wales Police Commissioner McKay to what was effectively the first annual conference of the New Zealand Police Association.

McKay addressed the delegates, warning them not to let every Tom, Dick and Harry 'invent some idea and then demand that the Association broadcast it throughout the length and breadth of New Zealand', as had happened in New South Wales. The result had been embarrassment for the government, which could not meet unrealistic demands. He warned of avoiding dissension publicly, to avoid press interest.

After this sage advice, the first item of business was a debate on whether a general secretary was needed. Smith of Invercargill thought not. Meiklejohn felt that there was such a need, and noted that in 1921 the Queensland Police, with 1300 members, employed a secretary at £500 a year. Murray told delegates that if they did not accept a paid secretary, there would be nobody to do the job, for he and Tom Smith would not be there.

Debate on a general secretary went into the second day, but most discussion now centred on whether outside applicants should be accepted. It might have helped Murray's position that the commissioner was against a paid secretary and wanted Murray to stay on, promising it would not affect his promotion. Accepting outside applicants was voted on 14 to 10 in favour. Murray had anticipated this by placing an advertisement for a secretary; applicants would be interviewed by the delegates. Murray moved that barrister

Sergeant Frederick William Edwards, left, with Constable W.A. Calwell, was not only a delegate to the first association conference, but, two decades later, would incorporate the Officers' Guild

Ian Campbell, an outside applicant, was the 'only satisfactory candidate in view'. This was carried and Campbell was appointed at £350 per annum.

There was no disagreement about accepting the Auckland draft of association rules, a journal and the desirability of a 40-hour week.

Murray produced statistics to show that New Zealand was bottom of the police barrel, its 1211 police at 5s 6d per capita lower than 11 other cities or countries, its one policeman to 1279 citizens the highest ratio. Ahead of New Zealand were six Australian states, Vancouver, Transvaal, Scotland Yard and, best of all, San Francisco, its 1298 police costing $4.53 per head at a ratio of one to 580.

Other matters canvassed included superannuation, leave, meals, travel and house allowances and retirement at 60. The conference sought abolition of the hated Section 9, allowing dismissal without appeal. Many more improvements were sought. The fourth day wound up with Murray warning delegates not to ask for the moon.

The warning was ignored. Fraser was sent submissions for a 40-hour, five-day week, an extra day's leave each week in addition to Sunday, retirement at 60, abolition of Section 9, fortnightly pay at present rates and civil rights 'in the same way as any ordinary citizen'.

Murray had the job of presenting this wish list. Fraser told him he would not change things just for the sake of change, that he needed to be convinced by facts.

Murray offered the case of the 64-year-old Te Kuiti sergeant called out of bed in the early hours of the morning to deal with a man who had gone berserk. In the course of the struggle the sergeant was kicked in the stomach and died soon afterwards. It could not be established that the kick was the cause of death, but it was an example of why earlier retirement should take place.

'Are you seriously suggesting, Mr Murray,' said Fraser, 'that the Commissioner and myself are too old for the job?'

Murray naturally replied no. His point was that the frontline police were in the special situation of having to be physically fit.

It took until the eve of Murray's own retirement, at the age of 64 in 1959, for this remit to be implemented by the authorities. He did, however, learn quickly not to go before Fraser and Cummings with too many remits and without ammunition. Fraser and Cummings would gladly waste time on silly remits. When Murray made a plea to have a member of the association alongside a commissioned officer and a magistrate on the Board of Appeal, Cummings was against the idea. Murray took it to Fraser on the grounds that it would give members more confidence in the board. Fraser replied that he had representation. This, Murray pointed out, was from the department, not the men. Fraser asked for an illustration where an injustice had resulted. Murray could not provide one. Accepting Fraser's sound logic, and the cunning of his reply, Murray concentrated on important remits that had facts to back them up.

Fraser did not argue about the need for urgent changes to pay and hours of duty. It was the commissioner who caused trouble on this issue; Cummings was 'very much against early retirement'. Fraser had told Murray to settle the administrative question of hours worked with the commissioner. Murray argued that detective hours of seven days a week, 13½ hours a day were too much. Cummings conceded half a day a week and every other Sunday off, if convenient. Murray said it practically never was convenient, and went on to publish his own roster in the *Police Journal* to prove what could be achieved. Cummings then agreed and hours improved, with every other night off.

Murray was the ideal man to draw all parties together, his own fellow officers as much as those with whom he negotiated. He preferred the informal chat, whether it was with the minister or commissioner, an MP on a tram, another policeman. He was the ideal frontman to foster a sense of what police historian Graeme Dunstall calls 'occupational community'. For too long the police had been working in isolation from each other. The association ended the isolation, and Murray focused collective feelings. It was the end of the era of anonymous complaints through the press, of mass resignations by dissatisfied men. At last the police could share in the most basic civil right enjoyed by the rest of the community—the right to express their complaints. The police had a voice, the warm, strong frontline voice of the calm man from Cumbria. The association had its house up and framed. What it needed now was somebody to attend to the back rooms, the furnishings and the fittings.

Chapter Seven

The Legal Eagle Who Led the Police

Professor Ian Drummond Campbell recalls his introduction to the police. 'I was led into the interview room by Detective Murray, to face a group who could readily have provided the front row of a scrum. But I survived the examination and can now only recall one of the questions I was invited to answer—"Do you have any strong political leanings?"'

Campbell attended the opening of the Service Organisations' Willis Street office in mid-1991, a good stone's throw from where he first encountered the police. Many were now less than half his age, but Campbell still cuts a tall, lean and alert figure. The association continues to play by virtually the same rules he redrafted back in 1936.

He was a young barrister and solicitor then. He joined the firm of W.P. Rollings in May of 1936 and was delegated to prepare the incorporation of the Police Association and redraft its rules. After six years as a junior clerk, he had become a barrister and solicitor in 1933 and the following year taken his master of laws with honours in contracts and torts (law that deals with private or civil wrong), company

Ian Drummond Campbell

law, international law and conflict of laws, at what is now the Victoria University of Wellington. Along the way Campbell had edited the university magazine *Spike* and was founder and first secretary of the university literary society. He had written articles for the press and for educational and legal journals. He was founder and first vice-president of the Wellington Legal Employees Union, and had acted as adviser to the New Zealand Educational Institute, the primary teachers' union, on legal interpretations and in appeals by members. Campbell declared himself 'thrilled' to get the job of Police Association secretary, which seemed far more satisfying than continuing in legal practice with a succession of clients. The police scrum, too, were well pleased to get this 26-year-old who had such an awesome array of legal qualifications and such broad union and journalistic experience, and was not a raving Marxist.

Campbell started from scratch. He had to furnish an office, find a typist, establish records, chase advertising for the new journal. He hired an exceptionally qualified typist, who promptly wanted a large pay rise and he had to let her go.

Murray and Campbell overlooked the need to make a courtesy call on the commissioner and at their first meeting Cummings was ropable. He preferred, in any case, to deal with the president, a real policeman. Campbell says he often felt he was up against a brick wall, but he made allowances. It was the first time a Commissioner of Police had had to cope with submissions from his non-commissioned officers, in a period when the country was coming out of a depression and heads of departments were required to keep down costs.

Campbell estimates it took 12 months to get the office up and running. He had to obtain members' views on matters on which they wanted redress, and see that those submissions were placed in the right quarter. He organised the conference, arranging the presentation of remits and ensuring that they were properly prepared. He went with delegates to see the minister and commissioner about submissions.

His principal task, though, was setting up the *Police Journal*, and he was lucky to have a first-rate advertising canvasser in R.E. Owen, later to be Government Printer. The first issue of the *Journal* in February 1937 greeted members with the news that all but a handful of the police had joined the association. Campbell invited members to use the new magazine to express opinions.

The *Journal* briefed members on the inaugural delegation to the minister and commissioner pressing for change. On 26 and 27 January Senior Sergeant Dave Hewitt,

The New Zealand Police Association (Incorporated.)

MANAGEMENT COMMITTEE, 1937.

President:—Mr. W. R. Murray.

Vice-President:—Mr. J. W. McHolm.

Committeemen—Mr. E. Burnett.
Mr. A. L. Downes.
Mr. F. H. Healey.
Mr. A. Johnston.
Mr. J. M. O'Connor.
Mr. T. F. Smith.

Auditor—Mr. J. H. Ward.

Official Organ—"The New Zealand Police Journal."

General Secretary, and Editor of Journal:—I. D. Campbell, LL.M.

Registered Office:—Room 120, T. & G. Building, Lambton Quay, Wellington, C.1.

All correspondence on Association business and M.SS. for "The N.Z. Police Journal" should be addressed to The General Secretary, N.Z. Police Association (Inc.), P.O. Box 928, Wellington.

DISTRICT COMMITTEES.

AUCKLAND—Messrs C. M. Francis (Chairman), H. J. Olsen (Vice Chairman), A. T. Gillum (Secretary), F. C. Solly (Treasurer), A. Bisset, M. F. Miller, J. Needham, G. Rushton, E. A. Stevenson, H. C. Murch, C. D. King, T. W. Allsopp, D. O'Carroll, F. Wakelin.

CHRISTCHURCH—Messrs F. Sinclair (Chairman), A. H. Barnes (Vice Chairman), R. Hill (Secretary), W. J. Dobson, G. Innes, J. McLeod, F. T. Pool, W. A. Shepperd, R. M. Walden.

DUNEDIN—Messrs J. B. Young (Chairman), G. Taylor (Secretary), W. S. Boyle, F. W. Johnsen, R. S. Rusbatch, A. E. J. Stark, J. Tither.

GISBORNE—Messrs H. Hunter (Chairman), E. Wigmore (Secretary), L. M. Allan, J. R. Gedye, J. F. H. Macnamara, G. A. McCurrach, G. A. McWhirter, G. Neale, R. T. Thom, G. Wap'e.

GREYMOUTH—Messrs E. J. C. Hay (Chairman), H. E. Knight (Vice Chairman), W. Tumilty (Secretary), A. A. Baynes, E. M. Best, C. George, J. Isbister, G. S. Murray.

HAMILTON—Messrs A. J. White (Chairman), A. A. Gudsell (Secretary), G. C. Donnelly, T. Kelly, M. H. Kirby, C. H. Maisey, D. A. Maclean, V. C. Naylor, G. P. Spence.

INVERCARGILL—Messrs H. J. Thompson, J. Robertson, A. White, E. S. Summers, W. A. Cromie, A. Webb, and T. Smith (Secretary).

NAPIER—Messrs G. Sivyer (Chairman), S. Tucker (Secretary), J. Gartly, E. J. Gibbs, P. A. Hardy, H. Nuttall, R. J. Sutherland.

NELSON—Messrs C. Petersen (Chairman), J. Jackson (Secretary), R. Audley, J. McLeod, A. C. J. Rush, W. H. Simister, E. F. Smith, W. J. Theyers.

NEW PLYMOUTH—Messrs E. T. C. Turner (Chairman), F. Longbottom (Vice Chairman), A. H. Canning, A. Jenvey, A. J. Mills, J. O'Donovan, E. E. Strawbridge.

PALMERSTON NORTH—Messrs J. Bickerdike (Chairman), W. O'Donnell (Vice Chairman), G. T. Beadle (Secretary), W. R. Evans, A. McCowan, C. McRae, O. S. W. Power, H. Shields.

TIMARU—Messrs D. J. Hewitt (Chairman), T. E. Johnston (Secretary), A. Leckie, D. B. Murray, E. M. Thomas, M. L. J. Thyne, D. Vaughan, M. J. Watt.

WANGANUI—Messrs H. Mackintosh (Chairman), F. W. Edwards (Secretary), L. R. Capp, W. Fleming, J. Fletcher, H. Hedley, J. J. Murray.

WELLINGTON—Messrs H. H. Russell (Chairman), J. H. Ward (Secretary), R. Anderson, F. Banks, N. W. Baylis, L. Gordon, H. Hudson, A. McLeod, R. Trask, I. R. Wilson.

WHANGAREI—Messrs E. Finch (Chairman), J. H. Dennehy (Vice Chairman), P. Geraghty (Secretary), J. V. Bell, J. Dawson, H. J. Harrington, J. King, P. J. Nalder, J. Norris, H. H. Smith, C. Snow.

Printed and published by The Hutt & Petone Chronicle, Sydney Street, Petone, for The New Zealand Police Association (Inc.), 120 T. & G. Building, Wellington, C.1.

Sergeant Tom Kelly and Murray and Campbell met Cummings. The first matter discussed was hours of duty. The association wanted a 40-hour week; this was government policy, and police was the only government department that had not received an improvement in hours of duty.

Detectives were leaving home at 8.30 am and getting back at 11 pm, which had a detrimental effect on their health and efficiency. Members usually worked public holidays and got only about 12 Sundays off a year. This system led to such extremes as a chief detective in charge of 30 men possibly earning less than a country constable. The low cost of New Zealand Police per capita merited the improved conditions sought, and these would be in the interests of the force.

The commissioner opposed the 40-hour week as impracticable and considered two days off a week would be fatal to detective enquiries. He thought some improvement might be possible.

The delegation urged a maximum 48-hour week and 3s per day extra in lieu of overtime, with two days' leave a week. The commissioner was presented with detailed charts of how, with staff increases, a roster could achieve a 47-hour week. The commissioner objected that 100 extra men would cost £104,000, but the delegation did not think that much compared with the £17,000,000 dispensed for public works and asked for an extra 175 men. Other departments asked for more money and got overtime and penal rates, while the police received no extra for such filthy and dangerous jobs as handling dead bodies in advanced stages of decomposition, bailing out septic tanks and cesspools, searching persons suffering from disgusting diseases. The commissioner repeated his cost argument. Agreement was reached on the principle of the 48-hour week.

The delegation argued for retirement at 60 or after 35 years' service, which was equivalent to other public servants working 40 years. The aim was to bring New Zealand in line with the British Police. Then 97 per cent of the force were below commissioned rank, most constables. The average age for joining was 25. By 60 most were no longer fit for active duty, yet were called out night and day. These men had entered the force above average physically, but broke down at an age when other government employees were still vigorous because they had to work in all weathers for long periods and were subject to injury and disablement. The aim was to achieve a younger and more efficient force.

The commissioner, however, was against a proposal that would disadvantage officers not in the association, so the delegation agreed to exclude officers and provide a graduated scale of retirement, reducing to 60 over five years. The delegation also asked for repeal of Section 9 but the commissioner insisted on retaining the right to discharge inefficient men. The delegation also discussed appeal board costs, motor car allowances, regulations and other matters.

At 3.30 pm on the 27th the delegation met Peter Fraser. Murray was spokesman, telling the minister that Cummings had a difficult job because of the long-standing policy of commissioners gauging their success by their ability to run the force more cheaply than their predecessors. This had led to an understaffed force that maintained efficiency at the expense of men working long hours under poor conditions. He asked for a 48-hour week and 3s a day extra. All the men, he said, expected improvements in hours and pay. The minister was pleased to help in improvements and would place them before Cabinet. The details must be worked out with the commissioner.

Campbell might reasonably have expected members to be impressed with this first publication of negotiations where the commissioner's former godlike status was reduced to exchanging views with the ranks. On the contrary, as Campbell toured the country many members told him they thought the association representatives were too timid, or were involved where they should not be. Campbell says they wanted in a fortnight what could not be achieved in a decade.

On his travels he followed his own *Journal*'s exhortation to 'patronise our advertisers'. Many advertisers were hoteliers and several times he was told he had visited establishments of which his members disapproved in their line of duty. He had to be careful where he stayed.

The second issue of the *Journal*, in May 1937, was able to broadcast the good news of a six-day week, 125 extra men and an increase of 10s a week. It had been many years since any government had announced such improvements for the police. Murray welcomed these advances in his mid-year presidential address, which also demanded loyalty to the association, the approved means of representation and expression. Murray called for a halt to 'harmful and unauthorised statements' from branches. He praised Campbell as capable and efficient and doing more than enough work for one man.

Campbell found that the *Journal* alone took many hours of unpaid overtime. He found time, too, to fulfil Fraser's request for facts. He prepared a paper on the association's major policy issue of early retirement, quoting at length from the 1920 Desborough Report on retirement at 55 for British sergeants and constables, and citing the superior retirement provisions in Canada and some Australian states. He produced statistics to show how few New Zealand policemen lived to enjoy full superannuation, adducing the support for a 60-year retirement age from the last annual conference of the New Zealand Justices of the Peace.

For the 1937 conference Campbell had to process over 100 remits, many new ones. The most prominent were those dealing with early retirement, and superannuation provisions, forwarded by nine districts. Other prominent remits concerned pay and allowances, particularly the inadequate car allowance, and repeal of Section 9.

Campbell was also publishing more ammunition for the association battles in letters from members, even if most still felt safer behind pseudonyms. 'Association Member' claimed that the injustice of those denied promotion by the present late retirement structure cost a constable £57 by being denied the sergeant's chevrons, a sergeant who never made senior sergeant £64, the senior not making sub-inspector £62, and the sub not making inspector £30. 'Jay See' and 'Pioneer Pete' joined A.G. Quin in commenting on the disincentive of the painfully slow promotion system. An anonymous correspondent called Section 9 'a blot on the Constitution of our Force' that 'suited the old hard school of disciplinarian'. The forthright A.B. Meiklejohn reported how the Scottish police did better with the appeal procedure.

MPs were not going to miss out on the changes. In the 21 September session of Parliament Hamilton MP C.A. Barrell praised this government for doing something about the disgraceful hours and low pay endured by 'as fine a body of men as it would be possible to find in this world' who had 'been made the Cinderella of the Service for far too long'. On 13 October A. Campbell of Chalmers was specifically pleased that 'instead of a thousand members chasing the Minister', now one man, his namesake, did the chasing on their behalf. Other MPs claimed credit for promised new police stations at Palmerston North, Mount Cook in Wellington, Whangarei, Wanganui, Nelson, Greymouth and Timaru.

Political flannel was no use to the association. Fraser had made it clear that he had complete confidence in his commissioner, and they must first make their case to him. Fraser would not move unless Cummings recommended change. On 3 December 1937 Murray and Campbell met the commissioner to discuss remits passed at conference.

They asked that all members of the force be compulsorily retired at 60, except, of course, for the commissioner. Cummings objected that quite a number of country policemen had told him 'that it would be an extreme hardship to them' and they were 'bitterly opposed' to the association's proposal. If they had to go at 60, they would have nothing but an inadequate pension. Campbell had been around the stations; this was news to him. Murray responded with a rhetorical question: 'Do you not think we are behind the British Police Force in regard to our retiring age?'

The commissioner said a number of men were better at 60 than recruits because the public had confidence in them. He preferred them to recruits. Murray argued that they were not physically able to cope. The commissioner acknowledged that a man over 60 should not be on wharf duty, but he believed that, through tact and experience, an older man would avoid what a young constable might provoke through inexperience.

The commissioner thought superannuation was better left alone because the actuaries who worked it out knew best. It was not a good time to ask for concessions because the fund was bankrupt. That, Murray said, was so because the government had not kept up contributions.

The deputation wanted to do away with the probationary period for sergeants, but the commissioner responded that he had to find if a man was suitable to be a sergeant. Murray and Campbell wanted remote station service restricted to five years; the commissioner did not want unnecessary transfers. Cummings also rejected a claim for a plain clothes allowance, suggesting that any who were dissatisfied should go back to uniform duty. The deputation wanted drill, parades and classes in department time, but the commissioner saw no hardship in the present situation.

Cummings was conciliatory on sick pay and leave being changed to that enjoyed by London bobbies. He acknowledged that a circular aimed at malingering was 'probably too drastic'. He was not, however, impressed with the 'hardy annual' of not deducting car allowances from members on leave, as they did not supply the department with a car; if benzine went up, the allowance would be reviewed. He allowed for crediting of passes in some examination subjects, assuring Murray and Campbell that the statutes on which men were to be tested would be made available in all stations.

Campbell argued against an officer involved in a case against a member also having a part in deciding its outcome. The commissioner did not agree, and nor would he have an association representative on the Board of Appeal. He would not allow appeal against Section 9 dismissals because the force was a disciplinary one and he must have the same right as any private employer to deal with men considered unfit. Campbell pointed out that, in some industries, a man had a right of appeal. Not in all, said the commissioner, and not in a disciplinary force. He would not hand over the final say on whether a man should serve to a civilian appeal board that knew nothing of the inner working of the force. Campbell said Britain allowed appeal. Cummings asked for an instance of hardship in the last 18 months. Murray and Campbell had none, and were given a lecture on the need to produce evidence for change. Not liking a section of the act, he told them sternly, was no justification for its repeal.

The commissioner had held back the tide. He let through a trickling concession—district secretaries of the association could handle local activity officially; he would look into overtime for hours involved in getting to a brief court appearance.

Murray had hopes of his long-awaited promotion and was planning to resign the presidency, but he saw that Campbell needed help on the negotiating front. He suggested he write to Sergeant Tom Kelly at Hamilton, who had been at the original delegation to see the commissioner and the minister. Kelly responded with a number of laboriously typed letters, which in themselves indicated that police needed a better deal, for they were written at 3 am after he came off night patrol. On 2 March 1938 he urged that the association not wear the bogey of a bankrupt superannuation fund. The fund needed rehabilitation. Kelly advised accepting the argument from Cummings that other departments would object to the police receiving superannuation after 35 years of service. And if the minister rejected the argument that police, in 35 years, worked what an ordinary public servant did in 40, 'fight for the other dog to work the same period as you'. Kelly refuted the commissioner's claim that country cops were opposed to the association stand.

Campbell replied to Kelly, telling him how exasperated another member was about the commissioner's stance. On 17 March Kelly wrote that the commissioner should be forced to give a reason why he denied the association a member on the Appeal Board. He concluded by saying he would now return to his modest home, where he hoped his wife would have breakfast ready. Campbell thanked him for his 'individual flavour' and encouragement.

Then came the bombshell that the government intended to make everybody pay a shilling in the pound to fund superannuation. The police were already paying 5 per cent of their salary. Campbell told members in the April 1938 issue of the *Journal* it was 'neither reasonable, logical nor equitable'.

In June Fraser made the vague promise that if the government were returned to office, it would give full consideration to representations on earlier retirement and superannuation, but he would not repeal Section 9 or allow change to the Appeal Board without evidence of the need to do so. Fraser claimed to be well disposed towards the association, but it seemed to members that this was mere rhetoric, and that the commissioner was an immovable barrier between members and minister.

Members complained that the association was doing nothing. Campbell countered that the association had definitely started to fulfil its proper role as an organisation 'to maintain the rights and advance the welfare of members'. He listed nine cases where members were helped, as in an assurance from the commissioner that a certain superintendent would no longer give district committee members on his patch a hard time, and the association paying for legal assistance for members. One member in financial difficulty received £50 from the association.

In his final annual report Murray was upbeat about the association being vigorous in negotiation and the *Journal* now being published bi-monthly. The management committee had had to censor some contributions to the *Journal* on the grounds of 'decorum'. The office had moved to a bigger and more up-to-date site in the New Zealand Insurance Building and there had been purchases—card index systems, filing cabinets and a Gestetner duplicator. Murray could not praise sufficiently the valuable work of the general secretary.

At the third annual conference of the association the commissioner concentrated on praising his inanimate achievements such as wireless in cars and the latest fingerprinting and ballistic instrument. He warned members to keep out of party politics. Detective Charles Belton had applied for permission to stand for Parliament as an independent. He received a negative reply four months later, when the election was over.

Murray welcomed Peter Fraser with the theme song for this conference, 'One more river to cross'—'and that river is earlier retirement'. Fraser told them he had encouraged their formation when there had been hesitation and fear of incurring official displeasure. 'I believe that as a result of your activities,' he crowed, 'the Police Force today is more contented than it has ever been in the past, and I do not think we have ever had a higher state of efficiency.'

New Zealand's standard of living was, he told them, probably the highest in the world, but it could only be maintained by higher productivity. He hoped Mr Murray's case for earlier retirement did not include himself, but he left that decision to Wellington Central voters. The association had received the bouquet of its existence from Fraser; now it had to endure his bromides.

Most members appeared to have put all their energies into remits. Three days were spent ploughing through the big familiar ones and a raft of lesser ones on remote station status, witness fees, transfer expenses, torch supplies, car insurance, heating, registering of bicycles, the need for police, in the interests of efficiency, to take over traffic control, deferring a death benefit fund because of impending social security legislation, whether they should follow the government lead and approve policewomen. (They passed on this one, although another remit agreed to continue the Women's Page in the *Journal*.) The permission to confer had quickly become a Tower of Babel.

A great deal of conference time was taken up with what association words should be said or seen by whom. Murray would not agree to anything being published in the *Journal* that discredited the force or opposed conference decisions, while Charles Belton called for the greatest freedom of expression in its pages and Auckland's A.T. Gillum accused the management committee of being dictatorial in debarring the minority from having their say. Campbell told him there was no unity unless the minority accepted the majority verdict. Auckland objected to a remit making it illegal to speak to the press without district committee, management committee or conference permission. This was passed after the illegal bit was removed. A move to make the *Journal* confidential to members, to prevent it appearing in

Entries in the Journal Cover Competition. . .

In 1937 association members were invited to design a cover for the *Police Journal*, entries to be judged by the management committee, the winner to receive goods to the value of 2 guineas. It was three decades before the *Journal* cover and contents received their first revamping

Office holders, 1937

hotel bars, and to discontinue advertising was lost on the grounds that hotels provided most of the advertising that stopped the magazine running at a loss. Unlike the Women's Page, a remit to have a dissenting correspondence page in the *Journal* was defeated 14 to two.

Incoming president John Bruce Young, who had now transferred from Dunedin to Wellington, went with Campbell and Murray to present the 1938 remits to the commissioner. The positions were restated on the big issues, such as early retirement and superannuation, but the manner changed. Campbell interrupted Cummings to ask him to deal with roster arrangements before going on to another matter. The value of lectures was questioned, Young noting that one on photography was far above the audience and irrelevant when they needed only to know about its value in criminal investigation. The commissioner, however, saw value even in dry lectures. When he was challenged on the need for drill and lectures on days off, he bit back that he was surprised to hear of men on their day off seen 60 miles away at the races.

The men were more willing to challenge the commissioner than in past years. Murray told him two hours of compensation for attending court was half what it was in Britain. Campbell asked him bluntly what his objection was to late leave to 1 am, for single men in barracks. The commissioner replied that he could not understand why anybody would want it.

'Surely,' said Campbell, 'any member of the community wants one night out in his life. Some do not get out of barracks for months at a time.' Cummings replied that he would tell any man wanting to stay out until 1 o'clock 'he had better seek another job'.

Campbell said 11 pm was a pre-war hour and Young asked if the commissioner would consider midnight. Cummings did not think he could go that far.

The commissioner was asked for increments for those who had served 25 years, given that a constable or detective stayed on the same wage for the second 20 years of service.

Some examples of the advertising that kept the *Police Journal* solvent through its first years

Cummings did not want to express an opinion until he had worked out the cost of the proposed £9 2s annual increment. Campbell told him they considered the request justified.

Although the commissioner was not budging on most issues raised, Campbell was beginning to hit his straps in terms of generating debate. In his last year in the job he hammered away at several major concerns, including run-down stations, staff numbers, shiftwork and the association position on thwarted promotion.

In April 1939 he picked up on a local newspaper story about the Hutt police station being a two-room adjunct of the sergeant's residence, which accommodated two police officers when the borough population was 5000. Now a sergeant, a detective sergeant and eight men served 19,000 people out of the same two rooms. Campbell argued from this that, whereas some countries saw the police as a branch of the political machinery of state, here they amounted to 'no more than a necessary evil'. Last century canvas stations were often built by the occupier; this century buildings were still 'extremely inadequate'. If police were to move from being mere gaolers' assistants to making the more positive contribution Fraser envisaged, then the stations had to be better than in the Hutt, where the police were sent into the street when the mayor or a JP came to confide in the sergeant, and where recovered bicycles lay against the wall. Such conditions would not be tolerated in any other industry subject to trade union conditions. Short-sighted, tight-pursed policies left 10 major centres from Whangarei and Auckland to Timaru and Dunedin hopelessly inadequate.

In the August *Police Journal* Campbell blasted the commissioner and Parliament for not bringing the force up to strength. There had been additions in 1937, but still not enough to allow the 48-hour week. In the last year 25 staff were approved, only 11 appointed. This year districts were asking for 61 and the commissioner chopped the number to 30. Meantime the population had increased by 20,000, which meant more police duties, and on top of that the extra work handling the new benefit applications under the Social Security Act, the Centennial Exhibition and the impending visit of the Duke and Duchess of Kent. New Zealand had three policemen for every five in South Australia. Local police protection cost a quarter less than in Australia. Campbell called for the minister to authorise increased numbers.

The same issue carried a long letter from 'Nine to Five', describing how creeping in from work at 5.30 am and tripping over chairs did nothing for domestic bliss. The writer suggested ending the shift at 7 am, so that the two-

A Message From The President

TO THE MEMBERS OF THE NEW ZEALAND POLICE ASSOCIATION.

I desire to take this opportunity of conveying to you all a message in this the last publication of our Journal for the year and at a time which marks the beginning of the fourth year of the Association's activities.

I will first tender to you my sincere thanks for the honour your delegates conferred upon me in re-electing me unanimously to the position of President of your Association. This is a very responsible and arduous position and is one that was not sought after by me, but having decided to accept it I have no hesitation in saying that I will give of my best in an earnest endeavour to further the objects of the Association to the utmost, by improving the feeling of amity and goodfellowship throughout the Police Service and seeking to raise the prestige of the service in the eyes of the public. Ours is an honourable calling, requiring as it does at times, the highest degree of courage from its members. We should be proud of the service and do everything in our power as members of the Association to see that nothing is done to besmirch it. Loyalty should be the watchword of every member. In return for my services, I ask for nothing more than the loyalty and hearty co-operation that was accorded me last year.

The Empire is again in the throes of a great war. No one has the remotest idea how long it will last, but we do know that every member of our Association will do everything in his power to assist in the successful prosecution of it, and do nothing which may embarrass the Government in its gigantic effort.

We are peace officers and it is our duty to preserve for civilisation the priceless boon of peace. Police officers will carry out that duty to the end of time. We are always on active service fighting the law breaker in the interests of peace. Every hour of the day, every day of the year and every year of the century we render to the community a service as essential as that of the armed forces. We fight the enemy within. Our fight never ceases.

To those members who have joined the Special Force and to the sons and relatives of members of our Association who have joined up I send my sincerest best wishes and an earnest prayer that you will be spared and returned to your loved ones in perfect health. While you are away we will take a live and active interest in protecting your interests.

Now to you all—particularly those members who are serving in distant parts of the Dominion and of whom we in the cities see but little—I send you my very best wishes for a Happy Christmas and a prosperous New Year.

Yours sincerely,

J. BRUCE YOUNG,
President New Zealand
Police Association (Inc.)

Wellington, 9/12/39.

N.Z. Police Journal, December, 1939. 513

Chief Detective John Bruce Young, association president 1938-43

thirds of staff who were married could take trams home instead of walking or bicycling, and have breakfast with their families before going to bed. Campbell did not leave it at that. He told readers that the commissioner did not believe men were required to do consecutive terms of night duty and was not aware that this was caused by staff shortages. Double night duty was discontinued soon after this.

Campbell was developing strategies. In the April 1939 issue he published the news that 187,000 of the 250,000 workers in New Zealand industry now enjoyed the 40-hour week and that Minister of Labour Paddy Webb was promising its rapid introduction for the 54,000 doing an extra four hours, apparently unaware that 1200 policemen were doing 48 hours and more.

That was one issue for the conference. Another was the commissioner changing from his 1937 position that commissioned officers must be excluded from earlier retirement to opposing it for everybody under him.

In February Campbell had warned members to think about another issue and decide on it at the conference—the association position on defending members with promotion grievances. Sergeant Holt had claimed to be disadvantaged by the promotion of other sergeants and sought association assistance over this threat to his seniority. The management committee had been reluctant to intervene, not just because doing so would challenge the commissioner's decision, but because it meant defending a member against fellow members. Then the committee decided that a question of principle was involved, that the association was formed to protect the rights of the individual. New Zealand did not have the British prohibition against making representations regarding discipline and promotion. Campbell called on members to decide whether they risked losing members and creating a numerically weak association or whether, by never taking a stand on a principle, the association would become morally weak. The Christchurch district committee specifically challenged the association to keep out of departmental decisions on promotion.

Paddy Webb stood in for Fraser at the conference, but the tradition of not putting the minister under fire at a conference left the field to him. Police, he told delegates, were no longer looked down on as they were 20 or 30 years ago. He told them they were comparatively inexperienced as unionists. Indeed they were, to let him deliver a few bromides and then depart without being questioned.

The conference called for a better superannuation deal and a retiring age of 60 through a five-year changeover period. Then came the promotion debate, in which Sergeant Holt explained how he lost seniority by failing to be credited with five of the 11 months he had served as acting or probationary sergeant. Five others had suffered similarly. The minister had promised to rectify the situation in May 1938, but had not. He could not afford to take the matter to court himself, which is why he asked for association help. Christchurch delegate C. McRae said he, too, had suffered, having passed his exam and seen at least 20 men promoted over him.

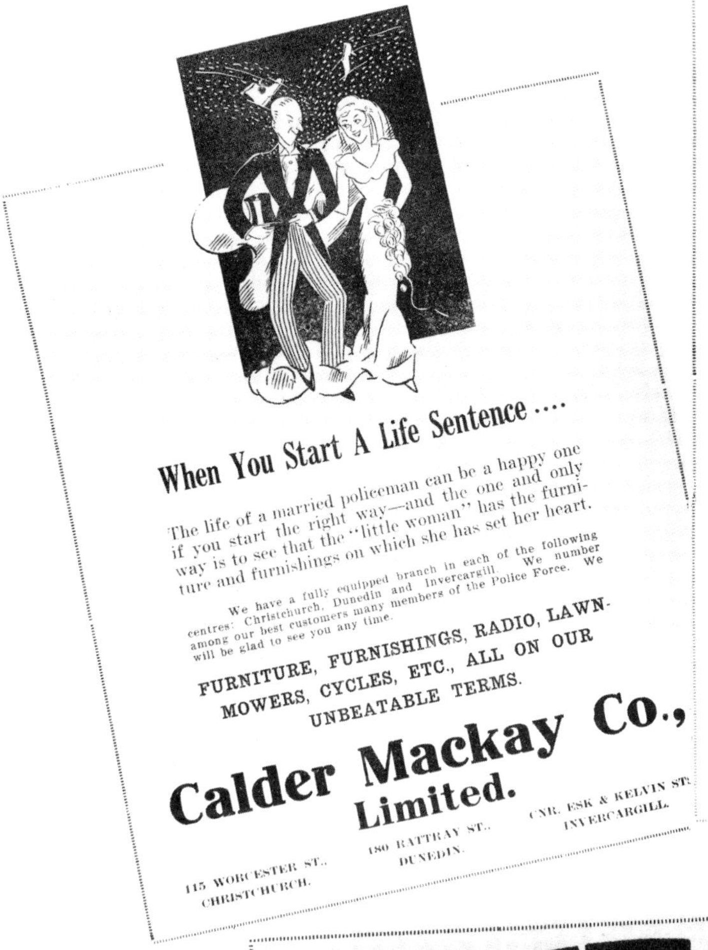
When You Start A Life Sentence ....
The life of a married policeman can be a happy one if you start the right way—and the one and only way is to see that the "little woman" has the furniture and furnishings on which she has set her heart.
We have a fully equipped branch in each of the following centres: Christchurch, Dunedin and Invercargill. We number among our best customers many members of the Police Force. We will be glad to see you any time.
FURNITURE, FURNISHINGS, RADIO, LAWN-MOWERS, CYCLES, ETC., ALL ON OUR UNBEATABLE TERMS.
Calder Mackay Co., Limited.
115 WORCESTER ST., CHRISTCHURCH.
180 RATTRAY ST., DUNEDIN.
CNR. ESK & KELVIN STS. INVERCARGILL.

PORTABLES for POLICE WORK
Remington
To-day's best typewriter bargains —Remington and Imperial Portables! Designed to give just that speedy, accurate, dependable service which police work demands. Sturdy, compact models, easy-in-action and built for long life.
REMINGTON, MODEL 5. Streamlined Portable with new operating conveniences. Complete with carrying case.
IMPERIAL 'GOOD COMPANION.' The only British Made portable with Standard Four-Row Keyboard. Complete with carrying case.
ASK FOR DEMONSTRATION AND DETAILS OF EASY PAYMENT TERMS.
Armstrong & Springhall Ltd.
Sales and Service
Throughout New Zealand.

STOP!
MAY WE ARREST YOUR ATTENTION AND CHARGE YOU TO INSPECT OUR VERY UP-TO-DATE SHOW-ROOMS
FOR ALL FURNITURE and FURNISHINGS
WE SHALL BE VERY HAPPY TO ARRANGE EXTENDED TERMS.
SEE
CHRISTIES'
RUSSELL ST., HASTINGS.

Minhinnick, in the *New Zealand Herald*, connected the German measles attack on Auckland barracks policemen with Walter Nash signing a trade agreement with Germany in November 1937. *Courtesy* New Zealand Herald

The conference agreed that Sergeant Holt and the Auckland branch should petition the minister to institute a committee of inquiry and come back to the association if the outcome was unsatisfactory. The management committee was judged to have acted in good faith. The implication was that it should not get into such situations again, but only involve itself in assistance where a clear principle was involved, not a conflict between individual members.

No other matter stirred such controversy. Remits from previous years were reaffirmed. War had just broken out. A late Wellington remit proposing the issuing of a press release on the police being ineligible to enlist was carried; police wished the public to understand why they were not signing up. An Auckland remit that those who resigned to enlist be reinstated to due seniority was lost 10 to 12 in a north/south split; it appeared to conflict with another Auckland remit proposing 200 more police, which did not square with this suggestion of wholesale resignations.

In addressing the conference, the commissioner was able to use the war as a valid reason for why the building programme was slowed. Campbell himself wrote in the October issue that all such work would have to be put aside in the war effort.

Campbell wrote one more editorial in the December issue, before resigning to take up an appointment at his old university. The association, he said, had won the 48-hour week, a pay increase, more staff and promotions, car allowances, extra leave, abolition of meals in doorways, improved rosters, increased travel time, acting sergeants were no longer losing seniority through another member passing the sergeant's exam in the period of probation, sick leave no longer meant docked pay. He looked forward to renewal, in calmer times, of the pressure for early retirement.

He told members he was better suited to the university and was not cut out for the combative trade union advocacy they needed. He would settle, he said, for getting the association established. New Zealand police enjoyed a right their British counterparts did not have—to hold meetings and exchange views. These meetings, the conferences and the *Journal* had welded the force into a more united body promoting good fellowship.

Campbell was overly modest. Even Cummings, who had no time for an outsider in the job, praised the *Police Journal*, once it had ceased publishing skits and articles by ex-members. He did not approve of the magazine being circulated in bars, where his replies to remits were on show. President Young hailed the *Journal*'s success, evidenced in the large extracts from it reprinted in other journals.

Campbell received 10 testimonials to his work from district secretaries, the Hamilton one memorable for appreciating the 'zeal and ability he had displayed in placing the Association on a sound and solid foundation. The *Journal* has been built up under his editorship to the best publication of its kind in the Dominion.'

The next secretary was very much more of the combative kind. Campbell went on to a distinguished career as a professor of law at Victoria University, taking with him the credit for quietly, quickly and thoroughly putting the association on a businesslike and democratic footing. The grudging praise from the commissioner at the last conference showed that he had won some concession from the association's most unyielding critic. With Campbell's successor any concessions were out. Cummings was soon to lock horns in a protracted battle with General Secretary Jack Meltzer.

Chapter Eight

A Hectic Honeymoon for the Feisty New Secretary

President Young and Vice-President Murray played their private and public parts in the selection of the second general secretary. The job was advertised through January 1940 and 49 applications were received. Both men favoured Jack Meltzer, Young because he knew him personally, Murray because, like many local police, he had seen Jack Meltzer in court action.

'We had a case against a Miramar man on an indecency charge,' Murray recalled.

> Micky Myers the Chief Justice was on the bench, and never hesitated to criticise the police—an arrogant man. Meltzer defended this case and asked if I had warned and cautioned the accused. I said "no" because I had not made up my mind to arrest him. Myers asked Meltzer if he wanted to cross-examine. Meltzer said, "No, your Honour, I have discussed the matter with my client, who had nothing but praise for the way he had been treated and had no complaint whatever about the detective." I thought that a great thing to say against the Chief Justice.

Lawyer Jack Meltzer upon his appointment, aged 41, to what would be a generation as general secretary of the association

Meltzer was a small, neat man of 41 who had begun as a clerk in the Customs Department before taking a law degree and becoming a partner in the firm of Burton and Meltzer. A shrewd and feisty fellow, he spent his first four war years as secretary pushing the parameters of the job to their limits. The commissioner, emphatically against an outsider speaking on behalf of his troops, shoved back just as hard. Out of this push and shove came a clear idea of the possibilities and limits of the association.

Meltzer came into the job as acting secretary until the September 1940 conference confirmed his appointment, at a time when the gains in manpower were being lost to the armed forces and long hours with loss of days off were again the norm. Men were being held back past 65 as recruiting for the armed forces increased. Equipment and buildings suffered even more neglect; the development of communications and motorised patrols ceased.

Carping letters to the *Journal* claimed that the commissioner and the minister were unsympathetic to the association. In the February 1940 issue 'Articus' complained that the 'roseate vision' of four years before had faded to 'a drab grey', as a 'self-satisfied Department', knowing the men were loyal to their oaths, was determined 'to disregard our pleas for reform, until such time as more strenuous efforts are made to force reform upon it'. 'Articus' wanted the association to publish articles in the press, circularise MPs, appeal to the organised labour movement for help. 'Articus' did not simply rant, but made the reasonable point that, while the commissioner compared the experience of men on the shady side of 60 with raw recruits, it would be fairer to compare them with those on the sunny side of 60, five years or so younger and raring for promotion. The minister forgot, he pointed out, that policemen in 35 years paid as much to the superannuation fund as did civil servants in 40 and that no other government department asked staff to provide their own cars and run them for the department at their own expense. At present there were 1300 men with 31,200 days of leave earned annually and accruing beyond the ability of reduced staff to deal with it; it was a problem that would keep recurring.

Meltzer replied, agreeing with the 'Articus' suggestion that membership should be compulsory, but saying that he should note the association's success with the 48-hour week and increased pay.

Commissioner Denis Cummings where he was most content, amidst a well-turned out group of his men, at the opening of the new Rotorua station in 1940. He was not at all happy about the association appointing another lawyer, another non-policeman, as its secretary that year. On the commissioner's left are Detective Sergeant J. White and Inspector G.B. Edwards, on his immediate right Inspector E.J. Carroll, then Sergeant O.I. Tocher. Middle row, from left to right: Constables J. Richardson, A.T. Kelk, J. Patterson, Te Whaiti District Constable Bidois, M. Egan. Back row, left to right: Constables J.J. Quirke, R.O. Nixon, G. Donnelly, G.W. Kilgour and W.M. Riddle

Meltzer replied at length to most correspondents. When several Palmerston North constables resigned because the management committee did not grant a small loan to a fellow member, Meltzer accused them of behaving like small boys refusing to play. When G.W. Hunt accused the management committee of being high-handed in appointing Meltzer, the acting general secretary explained how punctilious they had been with all applicants.

Meltzer joined Young and Murray in delivering the conference remits to the commissioner on 15 March 1940. Young asked Cummings to set up a committee of inquiry under Section 25 of the Police Force Act in regard to the dispute about seniority involving Sergeant Holt and others. Cummings rejected this as but one complaint, from Holt, who had had a legal opinion that he had no case. Holt had not passed this embarrassing news on to the association. Cummings used the occasion to berate former secretary Campbell for having gone to South Island districts and talked about two cases the commissioner had already dealt with directly. Cummings objected to this back-door behaviour, vowing 'I am going to have discipline at all costs'.

Cummings was at his most bullish. Young asked him to change the seniority system from an alphabetical one to one based on the date a constable joined so that Annis would not be senior to Ross simply by virtue of the first letter of his surname. The commissioner shrugged that off as having been the policy for years.

The commissioner rejected as costly or unnecessary such issues as leave and pay, motor car allowances, clothing. He would not allow departmental co-operation with the *Journal* in such matters as legal articles while the magazine was available around the pubs and other places where he deemed it should not be found.

All Young, in his presidential report to members, could claim conceded by the commissioner was a promise to write to a fellow departmental head to ease unnecessary work with police registration of Maori births and collecting small debts for Marine and Railways, Cummings personally seeing to the provision of gymnasium and recreational facilities in new stations, the consolidation of regulations and circulars, counsel as a right and not a privilege for a member charged with a breach of regulations. The commissioner had got away with a few vague promises.

Cummings might have modified his remarks about Campbell's back-door trips if he could have seen the whistle-stop touring undertaken by the sociable Jack Meltzer. On 6 May 1940 Meltzer began his touring at Palmerston North, where he met his old Wellington mate Inspector H. Scott, saw a spiffing new station, but was amazed to find none of those recreational and gymnasium facilities the commissioner had promised to see to. Meltzer was told the gym would go in when funds were available. He spoke to those who had resigned from the association, and was sure they would soon rejoin.

At Napier Meltzer discussed with members the reasons behind those Palmerston North resignations, early retirement, better mileage allowances, pay and gyms, telling the men it was important for them to keep fit. Meltzer himself was fighting fit, having been a boxing blue at university and in 1916 champion shot in the Auckland Military District.

At Gisborne the men told him they wanted more legal articles and departmental lectures in the *Journal*. At Opotiki he spent hours round a log fire with another Wellington friend, Sergeant Isbister, and other members, mulling over the anticipated new station, early retirement and better car allowances.

The irrepressible Meltzer was on the road at 6 am heading for Whakatane, where they wanted better mileage allowances. The same message came as he clocked up the miles through Tauranga, Thames and Whangarei. He was nervous of Auckland, the lion's den, but soon had his fears allayed, as he was taken on a guided tour of suburban stations, visited sick members, saw the police rugby team in action. Members suggested a £25 death benefit and leave pay. Hamilton had suggestions on communicating the problems of distressed members to the management committee; New Plymouth received his acknowledgement that Pukekura Park was the country's finest and that a man from Internal Affairs should not be doing fatigue duty at police stations; Hawera told him of their concern at junior men being appointed to country stations over the heads of senior men. At Wanganui he met another old friend and delivered his longest address to members, almost two hours. Back in Palmerston North he teamed up with Bruce Young, who delivered a spirited address on the constitution and goodwill of management. They welcomed back a resignee who was rejoining the association.

Spring-heeled Jack had won over the North Island in two glad-handing weeks. It was little wonder that Meltzer was confirmed as secretary at the September conference, on £520 per annum. The conference had to swallow the commissioner's message that the war had put everything on hold, but the £25 death benefit scheme was approved.

In the November Meltzer won from Fraser, who had become Prime Minister in April, recognition that the Police Association would be included in government consultations with other public service organisations in matters affecting the Police Department. This came about when the Minister of Marine called representatives of other public service organisations into his office to hear the government announcement on the cost of living allowance. Meltzer told Fraser on 14 November that, although his association had no affiliations with other organisations, because of its special nature, he 'did not wish this to be the cause of being overlooked'. Fraser agreed.

It was all he was agreeing to. In mid-year Sid Holland claimed in Parliament that the police were 'shockingly underpaid'; the Commissioner of Police, on £1,000 a year, earned half the salary of the Director of the Internal Marketing Division. Fraser thanked him for his appreciation, but said the police had their own association, and it was working well. He answered another Holland question with the news that advertisements for policewomen would soon appear.

On 17 November Meltzer took the ferry to Lyttelton to start his South Island membership tour. He met old friends in the Christchurch superintendent and inspector, heard from the men how seniority and intelligence were not rewarded. Ashburton members were pleased at the restoration of tyre purchases at government contract rates, something the association had lobbied for. At Timaru he met an old friend, Detective Sergeant Thomas, and the widow of Constable King, coping with nine children, including two sets of twins and a 21-month-old baby, and very grateful for the death benefit. At Oamaru he was questioned about superannuation provisions, and promised more information in a forthcoming *Journal*.

Dunedin's barracks were converted prison cells barely improved by electric heaters, but Meltzer was warmed by the welcome of old friends Chief Detective Holmes, Detective Sergeant Hall, Sergeant Johnsen and the matron, Mrs Mahoney. The men wanted to know about mileage allowances and whether they received the extra allowances given to Railways.

Travelling through Central Otago, Meltzer was struck virtually blind and had to spend a month in Invercargill Hospital. He fought this affliction for the rest of his quarter-century in the job, and the quantities of *Journal* material and reports show just how successful he was. His special love, however, was acting as counsel for members, something he was denied in that month when W.P. Rollings was hired by the association for the committee of inquiry held after the Chief Justice criticised conduct of a case where police allegedly failed to caution a young woman who admitted to having an abortion. The police were cleared of any misconduct in this first case where the association was represented.

Boosted by his membership tour, Meltzer wrote to Fraser on 5 February 1941; members were dissatisfied that the 14 remits on which the minister had promised action eight months ago had still not been dealt with. Later in the month Meltzer and Young met the commissioner over the next batch of remits and were once again knocked back for the all-pervading war cause. When Meltzer rang Fraser, the minister dismissed his 'tiddlywinking' remits and, as for retiring at 65, Fraser was 'concerned more with the age at which we might be dying'. Meltzer did wring from him agreement to legislate the appointment of an association representative on the Appeal Board.

Meltzer lobbied all MPs and got support from 14, including Opposition leader Sid Holland, for association stands on dilapidated stations, abolition of Section 9 and earlier retirement on full superannuation.

On 10 October 1941 Fraser made a heartfelt statement of sympathy for the wives and families of the four policemen killed at Koiterangi by the unbalanced Stan Graham. Despite the war, this tragedy cast a gloom over the 1941 conference. Fraser made a stirring speech praising Commissioner Cummings' organisation of the capture of the 'demented' Graham. He also noted the value of the association for men who had been scattered about the country with no representation; the association had now won representation on the Appeal Board. He agreed with President Young that the association had a role to play in exchanging and pooling ideas about the efficiency of the force.

Fraser had given the philosophical green light to association involvement in the running of the force. The commissioner, however, saw red over this, and much of the conflict during his last three years in the job stemmed from this attitude. For Cummings the discipline of the force hinged on his maintaining total control.

Meltzer printed Fraser's speech in full in the February 1942 *Journal*, saying it indicated there was scope for more consultation between department and association, 'when any legislation or regulations are in contemplation. If the view of the Association was obtained beforehand it would, we believe, be to the advantage of all.' The association had, in Meltzer's view, moved from the bad old days of 'existing on sufferance' to being 'officially sanctioned' by ministerial statement and 'inferentially sanctioned' by amendments to police regulations.

Meltzer found fault with the commissioner for gazetting the regulations dealing with election of police to the Appeal Board without consulting the association. 'We think we should have been,' he wrote, 'and, moreover, we believe the Minister would have favoured such a course. We hope it was merely due to oversight and that in future we will be taken into the confidence of the Department.'

If Cummings thought that was provocative, things got worse. With his promotion and move to Hamilton, Murray, praised by Young as the association's most valuable founding member, resigned as vice-president. He was replaced by Senior Sergeant G. J. Paine, who became acting president when, in 1942, Young was promoted out of the association. The commissioner expressed his displeasure at a lower ranked man speaking as president over those of higher rank, regarding this as bad for discipline. Murray had taken the view that the president spoke for the association, but in this period Meltzer began increasingly to speak on its behalf. An outsider speaking for the police was deplored by the commissioner.

There was no stopping Meltzer. In the *Journal* he quoted Professor Harold Laski on the need for government to consult its citizens and H.G. Wells on the desirability of an international police force. Already he was looking ahead to the post-war possibilities of international law and security, something about which the Labour leaders were passionate, and Commissioner Cummings was not.

Meltzer brought the tone back to earth in the April 1942 issue, when he reminded Fraser of his statement that he would be pleased to consult the association in matters affecting members. Here was just such a matter. Wages were lagging behind the cost of living to the extent that policemen with growing families 'are faced with the spectre of debt—a state of affairs that is, you will agree, undesirable in a police force'. His members were particularly disadvantaged in comparison with other workers because overtime pay was unknown to police in New Zealand, although it was being paid overseas.

Meltzer at the same time made representations to the commissioner for an increase in pay to meet the rising cost of living. A small overtime allowance was granted, but time

THE NEW ZEALAND POLICE JOURNAL

Official Organ of the New Zealand Police Association (Incorporated) Wellington, N.Z.

Published Every Second Month
June 1940, Vol. 4, No. 3
Registered Magazine

GROWTH OF POLICE DEPARTMENT

DURING the visit of the General Secretary to the North Island districts, great interest was shown in certain figures quoted by him during the course of discussions.

The following are amongst some of the references made by him:—

Percentage of Officers and Non-Commissioned Officers.

In 1878, the total strength of the New Zealand Police was 458, consisting of
25 Officers,
90 Non-Commissioned Officers,
343 Detectives and Constables.

In 1939, the total strength of the New Zealand Police Force was 1,439, consisting of
27 Officers,
148 Non-Commissioned Officers,
1264 Detectives and Constables.

It is to be noted that although the total strength of the Force increased from 458 to 1,439, the officers increased only from 25 to 27 and non-commissioned officers increased from 90 to 148.

Expressed in percentages, these figures become even more striking:—

In 1878, the percentage of Officers was 5.4.

In 1939, the percentage of Officers was 1.8—**A DECREASE OF 3.6 PER CENT.**

In 1878, the percentage of Non-Commissioned Officers was 19.6.

In 1939, the percentage of Non-Commissioned Officers was 9.7—**A DECREASE OF 9.9 PER CENT.**

The sociable new general secretary began visiting members in May 1940, and the next month's editorial hammered out conclusions. He laid at the commissioner's door the decision as to whether there would be an increase in officers and NCOs. If there was not, achieving the association's major platform of retirement at 60 or after 35 years of service would not lead to quicker promotion. Sergeant Tanner farewelled friend Sergeant McHolm's 40 years with warm fuzzies and perhaps the hint that he was hobbling off with little more than he could carry in his battered old suitcase. The station he left behind depended, the cartoon suggests, on the tender loving care of its staff

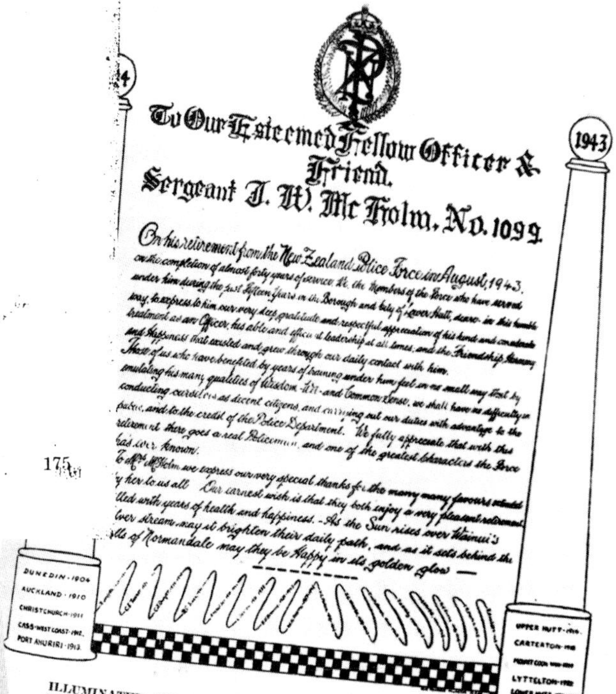

ILLUMINATED ADDRESS PRESENTED TO SGT. J. W. McHOLM ON THE OCCASION OF HIS RECENT RETIREMENT BY MEMBERS OF THE FORCE WHO HAD SERVED UNDER HIM.
(Printing by Sgt. C. T. Tanner who was associated with Sgt. McHolm for many years.)

LOWER HUTT CITY POLICE STATION.

FOR THE BENEFIT OF THOSE MEMBERS WHO HAVE NOT HAD THE PRIVILEGE OF VISITING THE CITY OF LOWER HUTT, WE PORTRAY OUR STATION AS IT APPEARS AT THE PRESENT TIME.

'Eureka', one of the regular correspondents to the *Police Journal*, delivered just what the editor wanted

A POLICEMAN'S PAY

(By "Eureka.")

Being a member of the New Zealand Police Force, naturally I am interested in the pay and allowances. I don't suppose that anyone outside of the Force is interested in what we receive. It has frequently occurred to me that we are very poorly paid, right from the top to the bottom, in comparison to the responsibility that we have to carry, and the hours that we have to work. Take men in other walks of life, with equal responsibility, and you will find that they are far better paid than members of the Force.

It is frequently suggested to me when I mention this subject that we have very little to complain about, and, to a certain extent, I agree, but in respect to pay and allowances I do not agree, and it is only by complaining that we are ikely to receive any improvement.

I would like to attempt to draw a comparison between the pay received by a man of my service and a man whom I know, who is employed in a business house where I am stationed. This party, in my opinion, and upon his own adission, has about half the worry and responsibility that I have.

I have 12 years' service and I receive £327/2/6 salary and £39 house allowance annually, making a total of £366/2/6. By way of deductions (I am only referring to normal times) I pay £36/12/3 by way of superannuation, and Social Security tax, leaving me a balance of £6/6/9 per week or £329/10/3 annually.

My friend receives the sum of £6 per week, or £312 per annum, and has deducted the sum of £15/12/- for Social Security tax only, leaving him a balance of £296/8/- annually, or £5/14/- per week.

I am called upon to work a 48-hour week on shift work, both night and day, while my friend works a 40hour week, with no shift work, and practically every Saturday, Sunday and holidays free. If he is required to work on any of the latter-mentioned days he receives overtime at the rate of time and a half, which works out at £1/14/3 per day overtime.

I am compelled to work a 6-day week against my friend's 5-day week; but for the 6th day I only receive £1/1/1. Therefore my friend, with admittedly about half of my responsibility receives £1/14/3 extra when he works a 6-day week, while I receive £1/1/1, or 13/2 less for the 6th day.

Work it out another way—My friend receives £5/14/- per week for a 5-day week, while I receive £6/6/9 for a 6-day week. Without requiring a mathematician to work it out, it is plainly seen that for the 6th day I receive the magnificent sum of 12/9, or 1/9 per hour, whereas if my friend works on the 6th day he receives £1/14/3, or 4/3 per hour.

My friend has every night in the week at his fireside. I work the "fortnight about," and have nine nights in the month at my fireside—this is counting in the day off per week. My home is two miles from the station and I have to cycle to and from work in all weather, while my friend who lives near me, can make use of the bus in bad weather. I cannot obtain a house closer to my work, and owing to the hours worked it is necessary for me to use a cycle at all times.

Another factor which must be taken into consideration is this. My friend is fortunate enough to have his own home, which he built in the depression. He has the place free of mortgage, all of the money being saved from his wages. He values his house at £1000. He therefore has no rent to pay, his total outgoings being about £20 per year for rates, insurance and upkeep.

Now take my side of the picture. It is well known that it does not pay a policeman to purchase a house, for more reasons than one. Through no fault of my own I am compelled to pay 30/- per week for a house that is worth about two-thirds of the value of my friend's house, and I have to put up with the inconvenience of having the house sold over my head or the owner wishing to reside in it himself, or of being transferred.

If I was fortunate enough to have £1000 saved up and in the Post Office, this being the value of my friend's house, what would it be worth to me? At 3 per cent. I would receive £30 per annum interest, less £1/10/- Social Security tax, leaving me a balance of £28/10/-. Let us work it out and see how much better off my friend is with his house in comparison with me with my £1000 in the Post Office. He has house rent free, less £20 odd for rates, etc., and less £28/10/- interest which he would receive if he had the equity in his house invested in the Post Office, this making a total of £48/10/- per annum. This works out less than £1 per week rent. As stated, I pay 30/- per week rent, less £28/10/- for my £1000 invested in the Post Office, this making a total of £49/10/- per year rent. Therefore I am £1 per annum better off than my friend, that is providing the Income Tax Department does not catch me for income tax on my interest from the Post Office. The fact still remains, however, that I do not, and never will be able to own the roof over my head.

It is plainly seen that I am far worse off than by friend. Under the circumstances, no one can convince me that we are over-paid, or even well paid. Different members of the Force, when I have mentioned this matter to them, have suggested to me that I should leave the Force if I am not satisfied with the pay. I contend that this is not the point. In other walks of life when men are not satisfied, they do not walk off the job, but they ask for more. Therefore I suggest that we should do the same.

N.Z. POLICE JOURNAL, AUGUST, 1942. 259

off for attending court after night duty was cancelled, justifying the complaint that the department gave with one hand and took away with the other.

The commissioner rejected most of the 1941 remits on the grounds of wartime restrictions. Meltzer argued that vacancies should be advertised because this method worked; when Commissioner O'Donovan did so in 1920 for allegedly unpopular stations Denniston and Blackball on the West Coast, the stations were readily filled. The advertisements would help the commissioner to ascertion whether men were willing to go to such stations. Cummings insisted that the men would go where they were sent.

He also reminded the association that complaints should be submitted first to a superior; he could never approve of men going behind the back of officers. Meltzer restated the association position that, where a complaint affected all members, it was proper for the association to take it up.

Meltzer had now to signal a constitutional change he did not support—proposing to replace the Wellington-only management committee with representation from all districts. He had rounded up local trade union and overseas police association opinions that such a move was cumbersome and expensive and would only place more power in the hands of the general secretary. It was a constant gripe of the other districts that the management committee was a Wellington operation, but the conference voted against the constitutional change. The costs in time and travel determined that there would be no change for some years yet. At the same time Meltzer took over more and more of the association operation, as the elected representatives showed great reluctance to take on the tough commissioner.

In his farewell address in 1942, Young told the police not to expect too much in these war times, but leavened his remarks with reminiscences about what life used to be like for a country cop. During a seven-week stint at Wairoa he found himself being best man as the sergeant married a local couple, as well as handling potato sales, stamping possum skins and investigating a storekeeper selling chewing gum at 1½d, 50 per cent above the proper price.

Meltzer paid tribute to this man, large in physique and outlook, a methodical man distinguished as a student of police law and practice, as seen in his *Journal* articles on criminal investigation. Meltzer referred particularly to Young helping recruits and those sitting examinations. It would be a few years before the force as a whole would benefit from this broad sympathy when Young became commissioner.

Both Fraser and the present commissioner promised to help with the urgent housing problems, but war was still the problem. Parliament aired some of the grievances. Mrs Dreaver of Waitemata said Mount Eden prisoners appeared to have better amenities than the police barracks. Acting Police Minister Paddy Webb said £3,000 was spent on Auckland barracks. Answering questions about those police who had resigned to serve in the armed forces before the law was amended to prevent them doing so, he said ex-policemen would be given consideration after discharge. There was no official reaction to Otago Central's William Alexander Bodkin regretting that police who had resigned subsequent to the legislation were being prosecuted for joining the armed forces. They were casualties of war.

In the August 1942 *Journal* 'Eureka' had succinctly expressed the policeman's unequal lot when he wrote of a friend owning a freehold house from a job with half the worry and responsibility, while he spent a quarter of his salary on rent for a house he could be turfed out of at any time. He identified a salary increase as the priority.

So did Meltzer, writing to Fraser on 23 October about the four pay increase remits passed at the conference. He got a letter back from an official telling him to wait and see. When the government announced a pay offer of time and a half for working over 44 hours to those public servants earning under £565 a year, Meltzer wrote back asking how this affected police. A reply promised a reply.

It was too late coming. On 9 December 1942 the *New Zealand Herald* carried an item about a meeting of the Auckland branch of the association asking for an increase in pay after being told they could not take on extra work outside the force. Young men, unable to support their families on police pay, were working on the wharves, unloading American ammunition and stores. The commissioner had told them if they could work longer hours, they would work them on police duties to make up for shortage of staff. These were men working on their Sundays off, earning 17s 6d a week when casual labourers took home £2 18s 8d. Whereas seven years ago a general labourer and a constable were on equal pay, now the labourer earned 25s more a week. Young constables, unable to resign in order to enlist, were resorting to the time payment system to buy the necessities of life. Hamilton and other towns had association members meeting to request up to 5s a week increase.

The press, and notably *Truth*, publicised the unrest. It was the *Auckland Star* of 30 December 1942 which noted that two cost of living increases since 1937 had not reached policemen of more than nine years' service with growing families, working long hours on extra wartime duties. They were unable to seek redress from the Conciliation Commissioner, as private employees could, without the approval of the Commissioner of Police—and that was not going to be granted.

Meltzer got his meeting with the minister on 18 January 1943. He emphasised the way in which the police differed from other public servants as a powerful argument for a pay increase. He quoted the 1920 British Desborough Report on the extra responsibilities of a constable and asked for pay to reflect that status. He argued that law and order and public confidence were threatened by his members' 'sense of injustice based on an opinion that they are underpaid'. If conditions drove a policeman to the moneylender, then the moneylender had a mortgage, body and soul, on the policeman and on the law and order system. A constable should not have to add the anxieties of inadequate pay to the temptations to which he was already exposed. A policeman was vulnerable to special dangers. After the Graham

A typical joky gossip page beloved of the man who edited the *Journal* for over 26 years, but infuriating to those who thought it should be a serious and focused union mouthpiece

GUESTS OF THE LICENSEE

(Dedicated to the Wanganui Police)

Of our annual dinner a tale we can tell
The guests of the licensee
We had a fine crowd and enjoyed it well
The guests of the licensee.
We drank and ate, from glass and from plate
Beer and whisky, and chicken and skate
The only thing wrong was the finish was late
The guests of the licensee.

You never saw such a spread of food
The guests of the licensee.
The room was cosy the beer was good,
The guests of the licensee.
During the night we drank many a toast
With an extra special one for Mine Host
Our song in his honour reached ships off the
coast
The guests of the licensee.

When all was done and each had his fill
The guests of the licensee
We went to the office and settled our bill
The guests of the licensee.
Mine Host said "A pleasure 'twould be
And finish the night most fittingly
If you all had 'one for the road' with me
As guests of the licensee."

And so we all went to the private bar
As guests of the licensee
A cosy room and a nice warm fire
For the guests of the licensee
We ordered drinks as quick as we could
Some from the bottle and some from the
wood
This, of all drinks, would be really good
For the guests of the licensee.

Then who should come in but a man in blue
On the guests of the licensee
What did we do? Well, what would you?
As guests of the licensee.
He asked us questions and details untold
And then he flung us out in the cold
And we never had that one for the road
As the guests of the licensee.

And so we were bundled off to Court
The guests of the licensee
And there the famous case was fought
Of the guests of the licensee.
We said that all we went there for
Was to have one drink Oh! no, no more
And what on earth did they summons us for?
We were the guests of the licensee.

The Magistrate said the case was clear
We were the guests of the licensee.
We were fully entitled to have a beer
As guests of the licensee.
"For the life of me I cannot see
That any crime was done," said he
I discharge you all—honest and free
Guests of the licensee.

An so we went back to the private bar
As guests of the licensee
With its cosy room and nice warm fire
For the guests of the licensee
We ordered drinks as fast as could
Some from the bottle and some from the
wood
And these of all drinks seemed wonderfully
good
TO THE GUESTS OF THE LICENSEE.
—"ANON."

SOUTHLAND COMMUNIQUE

RENEWED ACTIVITIES ON BOTTLE FRONT. MUCH BOOTY CAPTURED.

X.X.X.X. by L. C. ORR.

The shades of night were falling fast,
When through a Southland city passed,
A sergeant with his band of cops,
Well weighted down with bottled hops,
EXELSIOR.

While in the clubs from whence it came,
The members all devised a name,
Describing Harry Hogg, we wot,
The alias he got was not,
EXELSIOR.
(With apologies to a fellow bard.)

DRAWN BY SGT. C. E. TANNER, WELLINGTON CENTRAL.

...occasion of the retirement of Sgt. J. W. McHolm from the N.Z. Police Force. Sgt. Tanner also prepared by hand an illuminated address which was presented to the popular retiring Sergeant. The artistic work of Sgt. Tanner was the subject of many favourable comments.

Who was the constable who, on recently returning to the watch-house after a particularly dreary shift of beat duty, was heard to say: "If Hitler wants more territory, he can have mine!"

318

The Product of New Zealand Breweries Ltd., Speights Branch, Dunedin.

158

N.Z. POLICE JOURNAL, APRIL, 1941.

Booze played its part in on- and off-duty police lives. Over the years members worried about the *Journal* accepting liquor ads, but the association agreed that it could scarcely afford to reject them shootings a paper had written: 'Not often are we personally aware of their activities ... In a shattering moment it is revealed that they walk with death.' As Commissioner Wohlmann had said, a policeman is 'a civil soldier always on active service'.

Meltzer quoted the 1898 Royal Commission on how men came into the force superior in physical development, but broke down earlier than other government employees. He quoted a 1932 study showing that, in a four-year period, 22 police died and 52 retired, none completing 40 years' service. Police were always on call, had holidays cancelled, handled dirty and diseased bodies. They got no overtime or special rates.

It was a splendid outburst, but it fell on stony ground. Fraser would make no exceptions to the Cabinet's economic stabilisation policy, which fixed wages, salaries, rents and prices. Any increases would be illegal. All he would grant the police was the equivalent of the overtime paid to the rest of the public service, and he muzzled any publication in the *Police Journal* of discontent over pay and conditions.

In Parliament on 3 March 1943 Holland attacked this denial of a fundamental right, in a democracy, for public servants to make a case to the government that employed them. Schramm replied that the police had an association. This, Holland said, was 'hamstrung and hogtied'; he would give them the right to say what they liked in their own house journal. Fraser stated that it was 'impossible to tolerate' any agitation from the police in wartime, because they were part of the defence of the country. Discipline must be maintained. The police were not underpaid. Walter Tomes Broadfoot, MP for Waitomo, said that 100 of the 350 Auckland police worked on the wharves. Webb replied that this had been stopped, and a case of a policeman delivering bottles of beer after 6 o'clock 'was not right'.

Meltzer carefully spelled out in the April 1943 issue of the *Journal* that the overriding consideration was to assist and foster the war effort, but that those running the association had the constitutional responsibility to 'improve conditions for the men'. This need not conflict with public interest. All representations to the government had emphasised that 'a satisfied Police Force is a good public investment'. The *Journal* aimed to pursue the principles enunciated by its British counterpart: 'By cultivating the self-respect of the Constabulary of this country, to raise them in the esteem and regard of all their fellow citizens' and 'to give its members increased facilities for gaining proficiency in their own department'.

In June Meltzer pleaded with members to become more active at district level. He quoted the British experience that the management committee drew its degree of authority in representations to government from the strength of branch support.

At the annual conference Paddy Webb and the commissioner talked about improving police buildings, and Cummings said the newly inducted policewomen were doing a good job in the main centres. The association asked for a 20 per cent pay increase, early retirement and full superannuation rights. Their requests were promised early consideration. Nothing had changed. It was a wartime standoff.

And then there was a drastic change. The commissioner refused to meet Meltzer, deciding to keep this pesky outsider at letter's length. Meltzer's mettle was tested severely during this latter period of the war, but it was a time when he developed the research that ultimately won the association its major plank of early retirement on full superannuation.

Chapter Nine

The Secretary Versus the Commissioner

In March of 1943 Commissioner Denis Cummings refused to see Meltzer any more. Neither publicly announced this, and Meltzer tried to maintain business as usual by letter and memorandum. By March of the following year, however, the situation had become impossible.

In the February Meltzer had pushed hard for two changes. On the 10th he had written asking whether a country station member promoted to the city could leave his wife and children in the country residence until he found accommodation in the city. On 29 February the commissioner replied no, it could lead to country house vacancies being unfilled for indefinite periods.

Meltzer had also asked the commissioner for an extension of the conference from two to three days. Back, on the 29th, came another no, because the conference wasted time on remits the minister had already indicated would have to wait until after the war. Meltzer attempted a letter debate, saying no time was wasted on remits already dealt with, but the first day was wasted on speeches. The commissioner refused any extension.

On 24 March 1944 Meltzer managed to arrange a meeting with the commissioner. Meltzer asked for an informal chat to clear the air, but Cummings insisted on a police representative being present. Vice-President Paine came along, and the commissioner had the meeting recorded.

'It hardly creates the atmosphere one would like to feel,' Meltzer protested.

Commissioner: 'What have you got to be afraid of?'

Meltzer: 'I have not come to talk sedition.'

Commissioner: 'You started it and then you followed up by sending out a circular all coloured in your own favour with an attempt to discredit me—that's my view of it—in the eyes of constables and non-commissioned officers.'

Meltzer asked if Cummings would accept his assurance that he had done nothing to break down discipline. 'Not in view of your own activities,' came the reply, 'I could not.'

After a further exchange of accusations, Meltzer insisted that he did not make personal attacks but represented the association. An example was reporting on temporary constables, to which the majority of sergeants and senior sergeants were opposed. It was inevitable, he reminded Cummings, that the association would criticise certain of his decisions. The commissioner's response was by letter, a 'curt way of telling us that we were more or less interfering in something which was not our business'. Meltzer respectfully questioned his attitude, and suggested submitting to an outsider for a decision. Cummings asked who he had in mind. Meltzer said the minister. Cummings felt this was wrong. Meltzer challenged that, asking again that he ask a higher authority whether objecting to reporting on

On the left, Secretary Jack Meltzer. On the right, Commissioner Denis Cummings. And never the twain met through 1943-44, when the commissioner refused to meet with the secretary

temporary constables was out of the association's scope. The commissioner refused.

Meltzer: 'How am I to know where our scope begins and ends?'

Cummings suggested that the man with him, Vice-President Paine, was his answer, while he, as commissioner, was the final authority on police administration, not the minister. Meltzer said he was not questioning his vested authority, but whether the matter came within the scope of the association. He said there should be a ruling from the minister.

Commissioner: 'I would not be worth my salt if I was going to be dictated to by the Association.' In that case, Meltzer countered, 'we will have to get a ruling from the Minister'.

Cummings challenged that Meltzer had not put the matter to the management committee. Meltzer said he had done so at the last meeting and if the commissioner took that attitude, the association would be guided by what it thought right.

The reddest rag to the commissioner was Meltzer's circular published in the October 1943 *Journal* headed 'Temporary Constables and Superannuation: An Association Success'. It stated the association claim that, under Section 30 of the Finance Act 1928, temporary constables could pay into the Superannuation Fund and thereby, upon permanent appointment, avoid having to pay back a large sum under the Statutes Amendment Act 1941. The association had been told that Section 30 did not apply to the Police Department, but now the official view had changed. At the 1937, 1938 and 1939 conferences the minister and commissioner had claimed special legislation was needed to allow this.

Worried by the large numbers of temporary constables taken on during the war, the association chose a temporary member as a test case. The commissioner said that because Section 30 'was not free from doubt' it was not desirable to use it. The association continued to press the case, its 1942 conference proposing that temporary constables be granted the right to contribute to the Superannuation Fund. On 2 September 1943 Fraser advised that temporary members of the force might join the Superannuation Fund.

'It is extremely gratifying,' wrote Meltzer, 'to know that the views always held by the Association, have been upheld.' The commissioner was not gratified. He had egg on his face, and Meltzer was rubbing it in. This circular was held by Cummings to be bad for the discipline of the force.

The commissioner had stopped Meltzer attending depots to enrol members in the association. In the 24 March interview Meltzer asked why. 'Unfortunately,' Cummings replied, 'the General Secretary has lost my confidence recently.'

When Meltzer objected to this as a personal attack, Cummings said the job was one for a policeman. Meltzer said it was not. Cummings responded that Meltzer had started it when he went to the press and undermined the discipline and prestige of the force. Meltzer asked for the association to have the right to differ from the commissioner. Cummings agreed, but not through the press.

'The Association was made,' Cummings reminded him, 'so that you could come to the Minister or me, but instead of that the General Secretary goes to the press and condemns us bell, book and candle and challenges Regulations. It is a frightful blow at discipline, you buoy all the young men up with false hopes and that sort of thing. A young police official would not dare do a thing like that. He would be dismissed. So why let the General Secretary of the Association although he is a civilian do it?'

Meltzer: 'Is the Association to be governed by Police Regulations?'

Commissioner: 'Police officials are.'

Meltzer said the commissioner had not had much to complain about over the last four years, to which Cummings replied that it was one of the worst things he had seen since the association was formed. When Meltzer objected to the commissioner saying that the men were badly led by him, Cummings claimed Meltzer had been going around New Zealand putting matters in an untrue light.

Meltzer: 'You are accusing me of dishonesty?'

Commissioner: 'No. I am telling you what I am told.'

Cummings spoke of being upset about his men going to work on the wharves, where one had had his leg broken. Meltzer replied that the British Police allowed their men to work outside the force. His concern, however, was that the association and the commissioner should be able to have differences of opinion and not fall out.

The commissioner returned to the circular Meltzer sent out attacking the Prime Minister. 'Where are you going to stop?' he asked. 'Discrediting him is a most discrediting thing.' Meltzer said he would not be worth his own salt if he did not protect his personal integrity from an attack by the Prime Minister.

Cummings further objected to a sergeant at the last conference saying that the Police Department 'looked around to see where they could filch something away to balance it'. Such comments affected discipline and the chairman should have stopped it. In another case when he dismissed a man for carrying on with another constable's wife Meltzer published the opinion that he had 'dealt with the man harshly'.

Meltzer apologised and assured him it was not his intention to undermine discipline. Could they start again as they had four years ago, as the best of friends?

Commissioner: 'If you publish that to the Association.'

Meltzer: 'To crucify myself.'

Commissioner: 'I used to tell you things confidentially ... I lost all confidence in you after publications in the press and when the Prime Minister showed me the circular about himself, and the one where I was supposed to be silenced by you.' Cummings added how appalled he was at the recent insubordination in the force, which was 'never known to happen in the old days'.

Cummings was the old broom resisting the change swept in by Fraser. Meltzer had conceded he may have raised too much dust, but it was nothing compared with what some of his members wanted. After all, many of the police had seen or knew of the success Peter Fraser and his colleagues had enjoyed in confrontation and trade union barricade behaviour. Meltzer appreciated that the association had limits, and that these did not include the right to strike. He also accepted Fraser's insistence that the commissioner was the conduit for change, and was thick-skinned enough to seek another meeting with Cummings, in an attempt to resume normal relations.

Cummings saw Meltzer on 4 April 1944. The general secretary asked for retrospective appointments to be dated back nine months. The answer was no. He asked for reconsideration of three days for the conference. No. He asked if the commissioner thought he had the right to make representations on temporary constables; Cummings said he did not.

Meltzer cited the case of Constable Williams, who had chased a man who had assaulted another constable with a bottle of wine in Ghuznee Street, Wellington. He caught the man in a boarding house. He was charged over an alleged incident there. The charge was later withdrawn, yet Constable Williams incurred legal costs for something he had done in the execution of his duty. The principle concerning the association was whether he should pay. He would like to hear the commissioner's reply. Cummings said he had had a cold. That was the end of that.

Meltzer managed to see Associate Police Minister Paddy

Constable Blodger's Lament.

TELL me, Blodger, are you happy,
Said the Sergeant on the street,
To the gangling, knock-kneed Bobby,
Who was ambling round his beat.

Is that long and mournful outlook
Stretched across your vacant "dial"
Caused by pains beneath your tunic,
Or by evil thoughts,—or bile?

Do you harbour thoughts of murder,
Has promotion been denied?
What is it that ails you, Blodger?
Speak up, mon, and let's decide.

Now the Cop takes up the story.
Look here, Sarge. I'm sick and sore
Of this bleedin', one-eyed outfit
That does naught but raise yer gore.

Forty years of blinkin' service,
Then a wheel-chair, or a "bin"
In the bone yard round the corner
When you sling your "darbies" in.

Take a "decka" at our pay sheet.
Not a rise in fifteen year.
That's the sort of stuff they hand yer;
Not enough to buy a beer.

Scrounge a car to do yer duty.
Some may think this just a "frost."
And the service will recoup yer
Not a cent towards the cost.

And the cash they grant for mileage
For the bally work you do,
Wouldn't run a blinkin' scooter
With the gas at three and two.

Do your work in some old office,
Freezin' cold in winter clime.
Why should District "heads" be worried
If the coal is not on time.

When the kiddies need some schoolin'
Send the John away "out back"
To some lost, forsaken station,
Where the road is but a track.

If he sends his kid by transport
To a distant City school,
It will cost him all his earnings,
And they say,—the bally fool.

Never mind about vacation,
Why should Cops have any leave?
Leave is for the higher mortals,
Men with braid upon their sleeve.

Should you act with indiscretion,
Regulations,—by the score,
Loom before your startled vision
To make life a cursed bore.

There is rules and Acts and what not
Just to keep a policeman coy.
They were printed by the ancients
When old Grand-dad was a boy.

Oh, the life's one lasting pleasure.
You enjoy it—day by day,
As the "heads" think up the tit-bits
To relieve you of your pay.

Take it all, and ask for nothing
Buy your type and other gear.
That's the "motto" of the Service,
Do I make my story clear.

And you ask me—why so mournful?
Why my "clock" is grim and set?
In the light of such a future
Dear old Sarge—you priceless pet.

Now the Sergeant ponders deeply,
P.C. nine, I think you're right.
Did you learn all this from study,
Or a brain storm through the night?

Not a doubt, you've cut your eye-tooth,
And you have the story pat.
We must send you to the City,
Where the breezes blow your hat.

Then again,—why worry trifles,
What's long service mean to you?
You'll not stay with us to see it.
I can tip you that in two.

When a fizz-gig puts your weights up,
And the Chief gets on your track,
You'll be going down the skid-way
With your kit bag on your back.

You may get your cranium punctured
By a stone or piece of brick,
When the "wharfies" go out striking,
Or a miner swings his pick.

And just think of all the honour
To "pass on" that pleasant way.
We would "plant" you as a hero,
And then confiscate your pay.

There are fifty things may happen
In a policeman's life—so gay.
Section nine is still a nightmare.
You may get the "sack" to-day.

Now then, Blodger, 'tend to duty,
Tho' I think you may be right.
It's against the Third Commandment
For a Cop, like you, to bite.

So come now,—get a move on,
It is work we need for you;
And leave grousing to the Sergeants,
That is all they're paid to do.

And for hatchin' thoughts of trouble
We will have to settle that.
So, for slanderin' down the Police Force
P.C. nine you're on the mat.

—Makouta Bill.

N.Z. Police Journal, April, 1944. 111

The war years and the private war between the commissioner and the secretary meant frustration for association members, and Makouta Bill lampooned their sorry plight

Webb in early July. Webb proved as tough as Cummings, ruling that the association should not have interfered in the matter of temporary constables. He also declined to allow association representation before police matters were gazetted by the commissioner.

On 7 July the commissioner stated that he was against retirement at 60 or after 35 years. It was not in the public interest to have all the officers from the commissioner down retired and replaced by sergeants and senior sergeants with no administrative experience. Cummings indignantly pointed to men of 70 such as Prime Minister Winston Churchill and General Smuts, men over 70 such as American Secretary of State Cordell Hull and the New Zealand Minister of Works. 'It would be a bold man,' he growled, 'who would suggest that they should be scrapped for young men.'

Meltzer wrote to Cummings on 20 July protesting at the delay of a month in the Appeal Board telling Detective R.S. Smith that his appeal was successful. It caused the member anxiety over whether he would have to seek other employment. Meltzer asked to be told where the delay was and what system was adopted in such matters, so the association could ensure there was no delay in future. On 28 July the commissioner replied that he was not prepared to give any information about this isolated example of unavoidable circumstances.

It began to look as though, whether by accident or design, the government was siding with the commissioner to sideline Meltzer and clip the association's wings at a time when its elected leaders were in a weakened state. Sergeant Thomas Evan Johnston had been only a few months into his term as presidential replacement for Young when he had to resign because he was transferred from Wellington to Blenheim. (This was in the days before improved communications enabled Alan Monk to act as president from Blenheim.) Paine had had to stand in again as acting president.

At this low point in Meltzer's job Paine delivered the mid-year presidential report. He listed achievements as time off for court attendance required on a member's day off or when on night duty, no longer having to attend lectures or drill on days off, temporary police permitted, after 12 months, to sit the written section of the police examinations, a new scale of disability pensions, women

The Superannuation Board, that stern government quango to which Meltzer made, during the low point of the war years, perhaps his finest pitch for improving his members' lot

3rd. Nov. 1944.

The Rt. Hon P. Fraser,
Minister in Charge of Police,
Parliament Buildings,
WELLINGTON.

Dear Sir,

I have been directed by my Executive to communicate with you with reference to recent communications made by the late Commissioner of Police to separate Districts in the South Island during his recent visit there. We understand that at a number of Districts he called the men together and indicated to them that he wanted their decision on twomalternatives as to suggested changes in present pay and conditions.

Irrespective of the merits in such proposals the Management Committee o onsiders that the method adopted by the Commissioner was not in accordance with our understanding as to the status of the Association and did not appear to be in our view, a very happy interpretation of the desire for co-operation between the Association and the Department.

We are mindful of the fact that you have approved of the Association and its constitution which makes it "the official channel of communication between its members as a body and (1) the Minister in Charge of the Department (2) the Commissioner of Police."

In view of this, it is strongly felt that if proposals are in train involving a consideration of pay, conditions or other similar important matters, such should be communicated to the Management Committee of the Association who could, in turn, advise the Commissioner officially of the views of all members.

We think it therefore opportune at this stage to raise the issue and we desire to ask whether steps could not be taken to ensure that this policy will be carried out in the future. We confidently feel that this is just as you would wish it to be and that nothing but good can come out of the closest co-operation between the Department and this body.

We would be obliged to have your views on this matter at your earliest convenience.

Yours faithfully,

J. MELTZER.

JM/PMcL. GENERAL SECRETARY

DOMINION OF NEW ZEALAND

Office of the Minister in Charge,

Police Department,

WELLINGTON.

29th November, 1944.

The General Secretary,
The New Zealand Police Association,
P.O.Box 928,
WELLINGTON, C.1.

Dear Sir,

With reference to your letter of 3rd November relating to ex Commissioner Cummings discussing matters of pay with members of the Force in the South Island, I have now to inform you I have had inquiries made, and it would appear that any action taken by Mr. Cummings was in consequence of his having been asked by several members of the Force as to the possibility of getting an increase in pay.

I do not consider there are any justifiable grounds for criticism of the course taken in the circumstances. It is surely outside the province of your Executive to question the propriety of the Head of the Department, or any of his officers at his request, obtaining from members of the Force assembled on parade their views on matters upon which representations had been made to him direct by individual members.

While appreciating the desirability of co-operation between the Department and the Association, I regret that I cannot give effect to the wishes of your Executive as indicated in your letter. It would be improper for me to interfere in any way with the legitimate function of the Commissioner in meeting assembled members of the Force and discussing with them matters of interest.

It is to be regretted that your Executive should authorise the sending of a letter which amounts to a suggestion that I discipline the Commissioner.

Yours faithfully,

P C Webb

Minister in Charge of
Police Department.

The final exchanges between Meltzer and the outgoing commissioner culminated in Meltzer's 3 November letter appeal to Fraser against the way Cummings had circumvented the association. Fraser wanted nothing of this row, leaving it to his sidekick Paddy Webb to tick off Meltzer. Note Meltzer's block script signature, that of a man with severe eyesight problems. These, however, did not cause him to give an inch in his struggle to establish association status police allowed to join the association, and all 33 doing so. He noted that the management committee was not always successful in convincing the commissioner and minister, but it had confidence in the strenuous labours of its general secretary. He singled out Meltzer's particular effort, the extensive submissions to the Government Superannuation Committee. These 14 pages of submissions were perhaps Meltzer's most significant contribution to the association's development. In his darkest hour came his finest flowering. He brought together every possible argument he could find for introducing early retirement and full superannuation rights for members retiring at 60 or after 35 years. It was to be the basis of submissions for years to come, until success was finally achieved.

In his first section of submissions presented on 6 to 8 June 1944 on behalf of the association, Meltzer covered the history of superannuation. The Police Provident Fund Act 1899 established the first superannuation fund in the New Zealand public service. A decade later, without the consent of police contributors, the government merged it into the public service, including the monies members had contributed. Thus the police moved on to a retiring allowance, after the age of 65 or 40 years of service, that would not exceed two-thirds of salary, with the military pension scale in respect of death or disablement.

Meltzer's first submission for retirement at 60 or after 35 years, with seven years of service to count as eight years of the public service scale, was that it was in the public interest. He defined the strenuous nature of the job, which did not suit men of advancing years, the special moral, mental and physical qualities required, the need to be on call at any time, the handicaps retired police endured. He also pointed out the effect the proposal would have—a younger and more efficient force enjoying earlier promotion and more incentives. He quoted, in support, the Royal Commission of 1898, the 1920 British Desborough Report in which local police surgeons spoke of the stresses to which police were subject. Meltzer demonstrated that the proposed system would not place police in a favoured position because they were disadvantaged by poor overtime return and no compensation for night, Sunday and holiday work, or other work of an unpleasant type. Over his career a policeman paid approximately £150 more into the fund than the public servant, and then did not enjoy as long a retirement. Walter Nash had proposed a special retirement fund, and this was justified as part of a police budget that was, in per capita terms, 30 per cent smaller than that for most Australian states. He provided comparisons demonstrating that the British, Australian and Canadian situations were more favourable.

Meltzer was as persistent as he was thorough. On 2 August 1944 he wrote to the commissioner asking yet again for an extension of conference time to three days. He now claimed the extra day for the exceptional circumstance of discussing the sickness benefit Cummings himself had proposed at the 1942 conference. This time the commissioner said yes.

Cummings was not without his own brand of shrewdness. Before he retired in October he visited Christchurch, Timaru, Dunedin, Invercargill, Greymouth and Nelson making an all-out assault on the main association plank of the 40-hour week. He told South Island police the notion was impractical because of its effect on efficiency. He suggested instead an extra day's pay, and a house allowance. On 29 September he wrote to Fraser that this extra day's pay would go a long way toward settling the men's complaints.

His memorandum to the minister described Meltzer as 'a very bad influence on young constables in particular' because the general secretary discussed the actions of the minister, commissioner and officers and 'boasts of his own ability and how he deals with them ... He is really the management committee as well as the General Secretary. He has such a plausible tongue that he is able to twist and distort words to suit his argument and purpose.'

Cummings went on to claim that the conference had voted 20 to one to dismiss Meltzer, but Meltzer had written his own contract of employment which did not allow dismissal for anything except misconduct. He claimed members were not told that the commissioner refused to see their secretary and that the management committee ignored the nomination of two sergeants for the office of president and instead appointed a constable, who had not qualified for a country station or passed any examination for advancement. This was not, Cummings grumbled, in the interests of discipline and 'cannot be allowed by the Department'.

Fraser initialled the memo and noted it for discussion with the commissioner. He had already chosen Cummings' younger brother James as the new commissioner, and wisely left this old can of worms unopened.

In Parliament on 15 September Fraser had defined the limits on a police officer approaching an MP as housing conditions, wages, standard of living, opportunities for recreation. Hawke's Bay MP Edward Luttrell Cullen had provoked this definition by claiming that a police officer should be able to approach his MP just like anybody else in the community. Fraser went on to define discipline, promotion and transfer as administrative matters where the police were strictly prohibited from approaching MPs. He warned that if the association militated in any way against the discipline and efficiency of the force, 'there would be a case for abolishing the Association'.

In answer to Holland's question about whether the argument between the government and the *Police Journal* over the publication of certain matters had been resolved, Fraser claimed relations were 'very happy'. He added that they had to be careful not to retire men 'in the full flush of their ability' simply to suit others. The public service was not, he said, run for the benefit of members, but for the benefit of the public. He would never be a party to reducing the retiring age of 'still useful members of the Police Force'. Nor did he see anything wrong with police applying to the commissioner for consent to marry. The commissioner was getting the increases in police numbers he needed.

At the association conference Fraser praised the

outgoing commissioner for his humanitarianism, saying he had appointed him because he was impressed with his conduct during the 1931 Napier earthquake. No police force anywhere had ever had a more competent head.

Fraser then told the conference that the go-slow and strike were the language of 30 years ago, and were not for the police. The association was the outlet for their grievances, aspirations and ideals, but they were still semi-military and without the ordinary principles of trade unionism. He praised them for coming through the war second to no other government department.

Cummings told the conference that his first job as commissioner had been recommending the 48 hour week and a pay increase. In his 45½ years in the police he had come through from bottom to top and knew what it was like to spend a fortnight without a break on night duty. He was against the 40-hour week because a detective could not drop a case for two days then pick up the threads, and a country constable could not stop work for two days. He had approved allowances for typewriters, bicycles, cars, travelling and overtime, and hoped for more from building programmes. Meltzer joined in the congratulations.

On 3 November Meltzer wrote to Fraser that the commissioner pitching to the South Island men was 'not in accordance with our understanding as to the status of the Association' as the official channel of communication on pay and conditions. Webb answered on Fraser's behalf on 29 November that it was improper for the minister to interfere with the legitimate function of the commissioner in meeting assembled members of the force. Webb regretted Meltzer had sent a letter 'which amounts to a suggestion I discipline the Commissioner'.

Meltzer wrote back to Fraser again, on 11 December, saying he had no intention that the commissioner should be disciplined, but wanted the status of the association preserved in accordance with Fraser's desire, expressed at the formation of the association and at two subsequent conferences.

While Meltzer was trying to prevent any future commissioner going over his head, or that of the management committee, to the men, trouble was coming from the other direction. The association conduit, the management committee, was ignored as Auckland police officers took direct action.

DOMINION OF NEW ZEALAND

PRIME MINISTER'S OFFICE,

WELLINGTON.

CONFIDENTIAL TO OFFICERS AND MEMBERS OF THE EXECUTIVE OF THE NEW ZEALAND POLICE ASSOCIATION.

22 FEB 1945

Dear Sir,

I have to acknowledge the receipt of your letter of the 20th February, and in reply have to state that your reference to dissatisfaction in the Police Force carries no weight with me whatever as, if such dissatisfaction is so fomented as to affect discipline means will be found for dealing with it speedily and effectively.

An announcement has already been made that amounts corresponding to the decision of the Railways Tribunal will be paid to all Public Servants, including the Police Force.

That decision has been endorsed by Cabinet and no further announcement is required except the payments to the men and women concerned. These will be made retrospective to the 30th June, 1944, as agreed to.

This amount will be a very substantial increase in the remuneration of the members of the Force.

When this matter is adjusted the question of whether there is any justification for a further review in regard to house allowance or general remuneration will be given careful consideration.

Yours faithfully,

P. Fraser.

J. Meltzer Esq.,
General Secretary,
The N.Z. Police Association (Inc.)
P.O. Box 928,
WELLINGTON, C1.

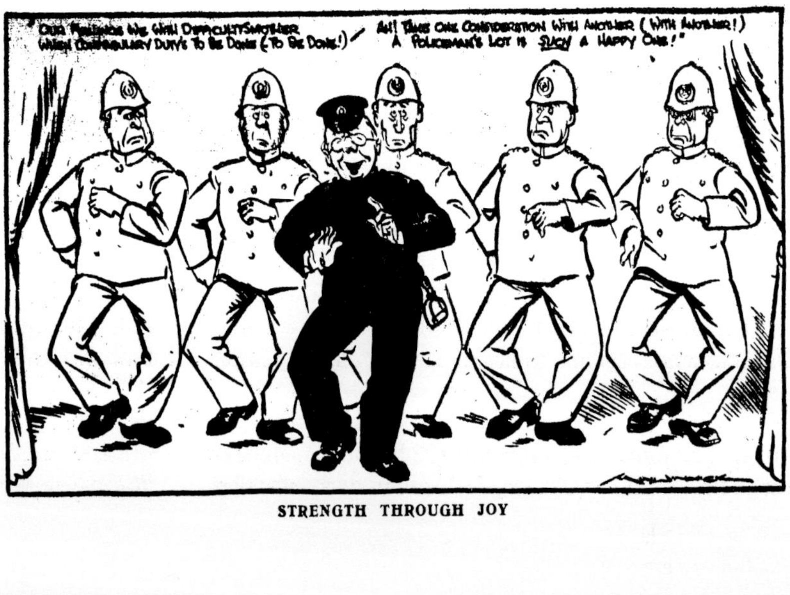

STRENGTH THROUGH JOY

Like many of his colleagues after the war, Peter Fraser was unable to ease up. In terms of grievances, he kept the police in gaol and reacted belligerently to the pleas of their appointed counsel, as indicated in the 1945 letter. Minhinnick had the measure of the unhappy policemen's lot. *Courtesy* New Zealand Herald

Chapter Ten

The Unpacified Post-war Police Force

On 16 February 1945 the *New Zealand Herald* reported over 100 members of the Auckland branch of the association expressing strong dissatisfaction over pay, housing and other conditions. The branch called for a Royal Commission to investigate pay and conditions, its recommendations to be mandatory. The meeting wanted no further transfers to Auckland until decent accommodation was available, and those in Auckland without accommodation to be supplied through the Housing Department immediately. The meeting claimed that the men were underpaid and overworked; the constable's pay cited as £282 15s per annum deterred recruits and some had 84 days' accumulated leave they could not take until extra staff were recruited. Technically, this was mutiny in time of war, a hanging offence. The newspaper reported the Prime Minister saying that men who were not satisfied could leave the force.

Three days before this hit the newspaper, Meltzer had tried to prevent the meeting taking place. He had telegraphed Auckland district secretary Constable C. O'Brien, asking for a postponement of the meeting because he was convinced moves on pay and conditions were imminent. Nobody else was. It was rather surprising that Meltzer said this, since he had been writing regular reminders about promised pay increases to Peter Fraser since April 1942, when he had quoted the Arbitration Court ruling that wages had dropped behind an increase in the cost of living, and the British police had received a 13s a week war duty bonus.

The situation had been worst in the north of New Zealand. Ruby Watson had written in the *Auckland Star* of 25 March 1944 that taxation ensured the police received the same pay they did 20 years ago, but everything cost more and more was demanded from the police, some of whom were working 60-hour weeks. In August 1944 Hamilton Opposition MP F. Findlay called the government the largest and meanest employer in the country and asked if any big union would put up with working overtime and not being paid for it. Paddy Webb had replied that New Zealand's was the best paid police force in the world.

The Cabinet would have had this belief to themselves. On the day the *Herald* reported the meeting, the superintendent at Auckland was reporting to his boss that eight married men were having to live apart from their families in barracks with single men because of their inability to get houses.

While *Truth* informed its readers that in the last year 29 members had joined the force, but 102 had left it, Meltzer wrote to Fraser on 20 February 1945 about dissatisfaction in the force and urging an immediate statement and a complete revision of the salary scale. Fraser was unrelenting—dissatisfaction in the force 'carries no weight with me whatever and if such dissatisfaction is fomented as to affect discipline, measures will be found for dealing with it speedily and effectively'. All he offered was the same as every other public servant would get from the Railways Tribunal. Meantime the new commissioner, James Cummings, told Meltzer on 14 February he would decide the adequate allowance for each temporary transfer. Neither minister nor commissioner would cave in to direct demands.

Fraser was, if anything, closer to the younger Cummings. He had recently taken him on his trip to Britain, where the then superintendent had studied Scotland Yard methods. Cummings had had a rapid rise through the ranks. Born and bred in Lawrence, Otago, he had joined the permanent artillery at Wellington and then the police in 1907. He was the youngest man to reach chief detective rank. Shorter and more rugged-looking than his more groomed older brother, he had preferred to stay in touch with his men while Denis had moved more in administrative circles. James Cummings was combative, countering association media pressure with newspaper articles of his own on his efforts with the force. Like the tough little Jewish Geordie Jack Meltzer, he was an expert in police law. Both, too, were nuggety men who liked company.

Cummings threw his energies into practical improvements, and had the *Evening Post* of 2 November 1945 tell its readers so. Now there were motorised night patrols and experiments with two-way radios. He met with Meltzer and the association president and vice-president a number of times and promised a better deal on housing. The force was, he estimated, 140 under strength. His problems were the same as those of the association and they could only be solved by a political solution, namely, an increased budget.

The principal problem was that the politicians in charge were finding it difficult to cope with the outbreak of peace and an end to wartime restraints on complaints. Fraser put a benign face on things, telling Parliament on 28 November 1945 that any police dissatisfied with their conditions had only to make representations to the commissioner; it was 'undesirable that the impression should get abroad that the Police Force was discontented'. Any indication of discontent was 'misrepresentation' and 'a serious reflection on the Police'. When Hauraki MP Sutherland said it was disturbing to see so many resignations from an understrength force with unattractive pay and conditions, Waimarino MP Frank Langstone claimed it was humbug to say there was much discontent in the police.

Such bromides could not contain the problem of an underpaid, underhoused, understrength and unhappy force. The *Auckland Star* of 6 December 1945 reported Police Association meetings in Auckland, Hamilton and Dunedin passing resolutions in favour of improvements in the conditions of employment. If a 40-hour week was necessary for the rest of the community, the *Star* thought it was equally necessary for the police.

On 11 December the *Star* noted the reality of an understrength force with 'hopelessly outdated equipment, and irritated by a sense of injustice' unable to cope with the crime increase. In the last month there had been a rash of shopbreaking and theft of radios, jewellery, cameras, liquor, tobacco, clocks and clothing in the Auckland suburbs of Remuera, Epsom, Grafton, Grey Lynn, Sandringham, Herne Bay, Mount Eden and Mount Albert. Vandalism, particularly of state houses, was increasing. Juveniles were the prime suspects. In this situation four to six constables were handling what 10 to 12 men did when the force was at full strength. The accumulation and frustration of overwork had led to the unrest, which was spreading to Wellington and Christchurch.

The *Star* was kind enough to suggest that Mr Fraser was wrongly informed when he denied in the House that there was unrest in the police. He had a golden opportunity, as the men of the Second Division returned, to assure them that conditions in the force would be comparable to those in other avenues of employment and so attract recruits. The newspaper also advised him to take the opportunity to confirm temporary constables, some of whom had been five years in this position. The paper concluded that the longer the dissatisfaction continues, 'the greater must be the encouragement to the lawbreaker'.

In Wellington the *Dominion* weighed in on 11 December along the same lines, suggesting that New Zealand follow the recruiting drives in the armies of Britain and Australia to combat this wave of vandalism and crime. More police were the only answer, and this was only possible by improving pay and conditions.

The 'police discontent' headlines raced through the country. Even the *Westport News* of 14 December ticked Fraser off for rewarding the loyal police who worked long hours in wartime without being allowed to complain with the vague comment that 'he had no knowledge of discontent within the Force'.

The government had all the good advice it needed. Unfortunately, however, the habits of a secretive war Cabinet and sluggish departmental procedures would not respond quickly enough to the crisis.

Sutherland had already commented in Parliament about the commissioner not accepting all applicants for the police, but sifting them, seeking only the best. Meltzer tried to encourage Cummings to offer more material inducements. He told him how much men in barracks appreciated the Christmas dispensation of staying out until 1 am, suggesting he permanently revise late leave restrictions because they 'discourage recruits'. In his February 1946 editorial Meltzer called for more publicity about police conditions and what the police were thinking.

The press accentuated the negative. The weekly National Party magazine *Freedom* led the attack on 13 February 1946 with an article headed 'No Arrest of Policemen's Long Term Grievances'. It claimed the understrength force was further depleted by resignations of men tired of the hours worked and general conditions compared with those in other sections of the community. It called for immediate improvements in conditions and wider opportunities for promotion. It quoted one former policeman saying that the force was like the army in Kipling's day in requiring recruits to be taught to drive, regardless of whether they already could. Another former policeman talked of the soul-destroying knowledge that you could pass your exams and still wait 10, 20 or even 30 years for promotion. *Freedom* claimed that nothing had happened since the war and that government indifference could result in the force declining to a point where 'it is inadequate to ensure the community's safety'.

The *New Zealand Herald* of 27 February cited 124 men leaving the force in the last year and only 43 joining. It quoted the Auckland branch of the association saying that the 40-hour, five-day week would halt resignations and encourage recruits. The commissioner had visited Auckland and listened to grievances. The men blamed the minister for their problems, not the commissioner.

Meltzer had already refused to comment to *Freedom*. Now he dissociated the management committee from the Auckland comment, saying the minister had never refused them a hearing. He, too, was finding it difficult to adjust to the more open criticisms from the post-war community.

These included comments from the conservative south. On 1 March Dunedin's *Evening Star* ran a long article on police resignations representing 'wholesale discontent in the ranks' and a public danger, with insufficient police to cover city beats—only three or four where 14 were regarded as essential. The commissioner was still refusing to employ temporary wartime constables on a permanent basis. According to the *Star*, a constable or detective averaged 17 years before being promoted, a senior sergeant 25, an inspector 30. This meant that administrative work was done by men set in their ways and caused the force to stay in a rut.

With over 200 resignations, the force of 1239 was 15 per cent under strength. The *Star* could not understand why the authorities did not use the Rehabilitation Department to recruit returning servicemen who were trained in modern methods and well used to discipline and correct deportment. The one occasion on which this had been done—an address by police to demobilised airmen—had resulted in half a dozen recruits. Instead the government shrugged its shoulders at the resignations. Prime Minister Fraser claimed that those resigning were going on the land, but resignees in Dunedin were painters, plasterers and grocers.

The commissioner countered with his story in the Labour-oriented *Southern Cross* newspaper of 5 March saying it was not resignations that were the problem but attracting recruits. It was not practicable to fill some posts until the wishes of former constables serving overseas were known. The coming of peace had greatly increased police work, but it was becoming increasingly attractive and promotion on merit was occurring.

On 11 March Meltzer called for introduction of the 40-hour week and the setting up of a commission of inquiry to overhaul regulations, circulars and memoranda. He was certainly getting the publicity he had called for and he had a more responsive commissioner in the younger Cummings. What they both lacked was the attention of their minister, who was overseas producing resounding rhetoric for a brave new world at the inception of the United Nations.

Cummings suffered tragically from his department's outdated equipment when his 34-year-old nephew, Constable Andrew James Cummings, was killed when his police car struck a telegraph pole in Auckland in late April. He was being driven by a police driver, to whom no blame attached. The car, the second oldest in the fleet, had 129,000 miles on the clock and had never had an overhaul. Some police had refused to ride in such vehicles because they regarded them as unsafe, but Superintendent J. Sweeney required that the oldest cars be used first. Police told the *Herald* they wanted the system changed so that cars had six-monthly examinations, as with other cars. It was a bitter reminder to the commissioner of the need to upgrade equipment and administration.

In May Sweeney led an Auckland administration deputation to Wellington to discuss the serious staff problems with the commissioner. Back in 1939 the detective strength had been halved from 39 to 20, and at present 11 were trainees. Since Christmas seven detectives had resigned. Only five constables were available for 15 night beats from 9 pm to 5 am. The Press Association report on this deputation noted how reluctant police were to talk because of the rigid censorship of their superiors. The report challenged Cummings' claim that recruits were coming forward in satisfactory numbers, but that those who did often resigned. A returned soldier who had been awarded the Military Medal did not relish mowing lawns, scrubbing dormitories and doing other menial tasks for six weeks while the government fiddled about letting contracts for uniforms to various tailors. Meantime Auckland was so bad that in the five weeks up to 9 May 19 firms had been burglarised and there was talk of establishing a vigilante committee to do the job the police could not. After the theft of tapestries from the Prince Edward Theatre foyer, the stealing of suits and coats from Violette Gowns in Vulcan Lane and four burglaries in Anzac Avenue, one businessman called for the return of the cat-o'-nine-tails.

The 40-hour week was not possible at present, Cummings told the Press Association, and the existing 45 hours would stay. Conditions were good and pay never better. He said he had released a memorandum that a constable could move up to sergeant after 13 years. He claimed there was no crime increase in the Dominion.

It was as well he made these statements in Christchurch and not in Auckland. It was too much even for Meltzer. He told the *Dominion* on 15 May that the men worked not 45 but at least 48 hours, often more, and that they wanted pay for the extra hours as long as the 40-hour week was not there. They knew nothing of any memo about promotion.

The press had taken Meltzer's call for publicity to heart. On 11 and 13 May respectively the *Herald* and *Star* carried extracts from Meltzer's April editorial in the *Police Journal* on the 40-hour week negotiations between the association and the minister, who accepted the principle.

The government finally cracked under the press pressure. After the association deputation met the minister on 17 May, its application for the 40-hour week was referred to the Stabilisation Commission, and the association would meet the commission the following week. The next day Cummings told the press he had the Prime Minister's authority 'to get more men and whatever equipment is needed'. Those temporary constables who had passed the exams would be appointed without delay. He acknowledged that Auckland was more under strength than Wellington and that there had been an increase there in breaking and entering. He promised a substantial increase in staff and a steady improvement in salaries.

On 3 July 1946 *Truth* finally gave the commissioner a good press, hailing the prospect of promotion for constables after eight years as no longer stifling enthusiasm and ambition. It also approved his encouragement for police to use planes, and the teleprinters and radio he had introduced. He recognised, the paper said, that this was the day of the young man.

Cummings was doing no more for others than had been done for him. *Truth* might not have been so impressed, however, at the behind-the-scenes Cummings. On 8 August 1946 he declared to the Secretary of Treasury that he was against retirement at 60 or after 35 years, and against seven years counting as eight. He repeated his brother's objections to these major association platforms—they meant bringing inexperienced officers into administration, it was 'wrong for people in the zenith of life to become idle' and, if the police got what they were after, other organisations would want similar concessions. There was no justification for his third objection; on 26 July the association had informed him that the Combined Service Organisations were not opposed to special consideration for the police, accepting that they were recruited at a higher age and had restricted promotion potential.

Meltzer did well out of this month at his meeting with the Stabilisation Commission, which was run by Fintan Patrick Walsh, Vice-President of the Federation of Labour. Walsh recommended that police be paid time and a half for an extra five hours a week until staff strength was sufficient to allow for the 40-hour week. Men could take cash in lieu of accumulated leave.

Fraser was able to come before the 1946 conference in a relaxed frame of mind, telling them that when he came into the job constables were on £267 a year, and now they were on £466. He confessed to being in two minds about early retirement, which facilitated young men's progress but forced men of 60 to become dependent on the young. He supposed it was a natural thought for a man over 60, and he would soon learn what the voters felt about him. This, he thought, might be his last appearance at an association conference.

Vice-President F.H. Healey and management committee member S.T. Lush accompanied Meltzer to meet the commissioner on 10 December 1946. Meltzer asked for sergeants to receive seniority if they passed their examinations within three years, because they had not been able to sit exams in the army. Cummings thought he had given enough concessions but asked Healey and Lush what they thought. They thought what he thought. Meltzer, however, insisted that this did not cover those men who had done five or six years in the police before the war. Cummings promised to look into the matter, which would have lapsed if left to the police representatives.

Meltzer returned to his old advocacy of advertising vacancies to give the men the feeling that they were not being kept in the dark. Cummings pointed to the teleprinters he had so fulsomely praised at the conference as the way of avoiding being uninformed. Meltzer told him advertising was in the National Party policy. Cummings agreed to look at this again.

The commissioner was sympathetic to an increased boot allowance but not to shifting expenses, where he had to be on the lookout for false claims. An indignant Meltzer said the association would not stand by a man who did not play the game.

Lush told the commissioner the men did not object to lectures on their day off so much as attending parades. Meltzer, no doubt wishing Lush had remained silent, said the men should be free to do what they liked in their time off, and a lecture destroyed the day.

The promised rapid promotion was coming about, but it had bumped against the housing shortage, with five men promoted to Auckland in July still without a home. The commissioner told the deputation state housing was being looked into, but he did not approve of policemen living next door to each other in state houses. Meltzer wanted the mileage rate increased; it had been the same since 1931! Cummings promised to look at it.

As at most such meetings, the commissioner made vague promises. The second half of the 1940s was dominated by the association repeating requests and trying to push the pace of the commissioner's promises becoming practice. Cummings was in a Catch-22 situation, as the post-war boom times did not include the police. Other jobs were better paid, and the force could not be made more attractive with a 40-hour week until it attracted enough staff to make such hours feasible.

The commissioner was slow in resolving the status of temporary constables. Meltzer spent 1946 hammering at him on this issue. In February he asked Cummings to declare his intentions. In May he said an early decision would do much to increase contentment. In June he told the commissioner those temporary constables over 30 found their status belittling. The standard reply was that, if they passed their exams and were reported on favourably,

Honest John Pointon, president of the association 1944-47

they would become permanent. The commissioner's determination to maintain his standards and his administrative slowness meant it took a year to resolve the matter of 400 temporary constables.

The next few years were spent resolving the rights of district officers of the association. The superintendent at Dunedin was moving police out of the district office if they served on the local association committee. In April 1947 Cummings told Meltzer it was not desirable for an officer who handled confidential material to be on the district committee of the association. Meltzer protested that this was a reflection upon his members. In August a member resigned from an executive position on the association after a Christchurch superior officer told him it was contrary to the commissioner's memorandum.

A more serious problem blew up in April when the Auckland branch held a meeting to discuss poor housing and the decrease in staff. They invited the press to hear Meltzer speak to them, despite his protesting at the press presence. Cummings was informed that the local secretary, Constable Kirk, was gloating over the press coverage. Cummings and the Prime Minister were concerned about admitting the press, lest they learned of criminal investigations and methods used to detect offenders. Kirk and Senior Sergeant F.W. Edwards, the chairman of the meeting, were carpeted by the commissioner, although they claimed Sergeant Ernest Strawbridge had been the prime mover in getting the press there. When Kirk told the commissioner that the will of the majority was expressed, he was told he would be sacked if it happened again.

Meantime Meltzer was seeking full reimbursement of legal costs for two Christchurch detectives acquitted of using unnecessary violence. The department would only reimburse the Crown Prosecutor's fee, not the extra £14 5s. Meltzer spent a year lobbying the commissioner and Fraser until, on 16 July 1948, Fraser finally ruled in favour of the commissioner on this and on district secretaries of the association not being employed on confidential departmental matters.

Meltzer also lost his objection to a constable on crutches, and on sick leave, being used to trap a bookmaker, because the constable had agreed to it. The commissioner ticked Meltzer off for acting on representations apparently inspired by a disgruntled member of the force, before ascertaining the facts. The disgruntled member was the same Sergeant Strawbridge who had got the press to the Auckland meeting. Meltzer gracefully regretted his mistake.

These losses did not help Meltzer's cause. He had been under fire from association members since the 1944 conference over whether he should be hired as counsel, or do it as part of his job, and indeed over whether he enjoyed too cast-iron a contract. Meltzer survived a close ballot. The matter of revising his contract was raised in 1945 by Constable W.A. Calwell of Palmerston North, and lost two to 12. Meltzer, meantime, had defended a member not given his sergeant's stripes, protesting that the capacity to detect erring publicans should not be the criterion for promotion. The appeal succeeded, and this was a further setback for Meltzer.

Calwell retired but replaced Denis Cummings as police representative on the Superannuation Board, inheriting his predecessor's distaste for an outsider in the job of association secretary. In 1948 Palmerston North sought a meeting with other districts that circumvented the national office to replace Meltzer with a secretary of police experience, and proposed Calwell. The president, Sergeant A.G. Quin, heard of this, and told Meltzer, who reminded Palmerston North that correspondence should be sent through his office.

Meltzer's salary was questioned at the 1948 conference. He had originally been paid at a sub-inspector's stipend, but had fallen behind. Through the 1940s he had won three salary increases for the association, but had had none himself. Among testimonies to his ability Wellington delegate Constable C.W. Naylor said Meltzer was a great fighter and worth every penny. The association was lucky to have the services of a lawyer who could earn four times as much in his own profession. Furthermore, Meltzer had not written his own contract, as Denis Cummings had suggested; his boss at the time, Rollings, had done so. The clause that he be secretary for an indefinite period was approved by both Young and Murray, the two men appointed by the management committee to scrutinise the contract. It was agreed that Meltzer would receive a senior sergeant's salary of £709 per annum.

His achievements were acknowledged, as counsel and with deputations, in negotiations such as the approval in principle for a 40-hour week on 4 July 1946, his representations to the Minister of Finance on superannuation amendments, acceptance that injuries sustained to and from work were eligible for compensation, his overcoming the objections of other public service organisations to an earlier retiring age for the police. In 1947 he achieved an increase in overtime, policewomen being made eligible for permanent appointment, a correspondence coaching scheme for police law examination candidates, an extension of the meal break and clarification of the terms of the day off. Through the *Journal* he had promoted a more liberal and lowered age recruiting policy.

Quin made a point, in his 1949 presidential report, of saying that Meltzer and his assistant Mrs E. Urquhart never 'study their own convenience when our interests demand otherwise'. The association had gained considerably from Meltzer's modest counsel fees in such cases as his successful defence of two Napier members accused of receiving gifts of liquor.

A more celebrated case in which Meltzer was involved could not be referred to at that time because it was sub judice. This involved a crisis generated by the outgoing commissioner's policy of offering others the rapid promotion he had enjoyed. New Auckland district secretary Sergeant P.P. O'Boyle raised the matter in a telegram dated 16 June 1949. He asked the management committee urgently to consider the effect of the accelerated seniority of Senior Detective William Raymond Fell to sub-inspector over 50 other association members. He had been advanced four years in seniority 'for special aptitude and consistent zeal', notably in connection with a murder case.

Meltzer initially favoured the idea that individuals who felt they had been adversely affected should apply for a committee of inquiry. O'Boyle, however, claimed it was a matter of principle, for 'preferential treatment of members of a union is scorned by all respectable unionists'. He cited a parallel objection in the Tramways Union. O'Boyle said it was a clarion call to use the reserve fund, which had emerged from its wartime loan to the government. Meltzer accepted the call and went to Auckland to confer.

On 20 June Cummings was served with an injunction to stop the promotion. Plaintiffs included 10 from Auckland, 10 from Wellington, four from Christchurch and one each from Palmerston North, Ashburton and Lyttelton. The injunction succeeded.

Meltzer spent the next months gathering 54 statements from men who felt they had been passed over. He called for any future merit over seniority system to be decided by a board of three superintendents, with right of appeal before a properly constituted judicial body with mandatory powers, instead of the present report to the commissioner at the discretion of the minister.

On 5 August Crown Solicitor J.M. Tudhope informed Meltzer that the present regulations did not authorise such advancement and it was withdrawn. There was considerable newspaper comment, most of it disapproving of seniority blocking merit, of the entrenchment of the Constable Plod tradition.

Meltzer denied this was so, claiming that merit was provided for under certain circumstances, but not on this occasion. He now had his hands full, however, getting the

The 1949 association conference, and Dum Dum's 1950 doggerel about the personalities involved. By this time the association had won improved conditions from the outgoing Labour administration

Who's Who

By DUM DUM.
With Apologies to Debrett.

"A" stands for Aitchison
  Who puts in reports.
They always come back
  With suitable retorts.
"B" stands for Birse,
  Whose car ain't so hot.
It's silencer's gone,
  And it's shy of a pot.
"C" stands for Cross,
  Who's Courier too,
He's asking right now,
  For a grid that is new.
"D" stands for Dilberry,
  Alias the Earl.
He's put in his papers,
  To give farming a Burl.
"E" stands for Edwards,
  The son not the boss,
He gallops around
  Like an overworked hoss.
"F" stands for Fitz,
  With a face like a spade,
He never shouts tea,
  But drinks it when made.
"G" stands for Gordon,
  Who's on a good lerk,
He rings up the Doctor,
  To shy off hard work.
"H" stands for Hughes
  Who makes out the roster,
And causes the Sergeants
  Hard feelings to foster.

"I" stands for Irving,
  who's up witth the Dees'
When he looks at street lighting
  It's tail lights he sees.
"J" stands for Jensen
  Who loves lifting weights,
And annoying the Watch-house
  With the prisoners he takes.
"K" stands for Kelly
  The world's greatest lover,
If you can't get a house Ned,
  Just live with her Mother.
"L" stands for Lissette,
  Who weight lifts as well.
He'll be yelling out "Key Please,"
  When he's transferred to Hell.
"M" stands for Malcolm,
  Who made out this verse,
And if ever it's published,
  Get pipe band and herse.
"N" stands for Naylor,
  Who takes all the snaps.
His printing is awful
  And his subjects are saps.
"O" stands for O'Donnell,
  Who's on his way OUT.
How's the watch going Simon?
  It's a cheap one no doubt.
"P" stands for Parsons,
  Who knocks out the dents
And mucks up the wiring
  And putties the rents.

RECRUITS ARE NEEDED FOR THE NEW ZEALAND POLICE FORCE. THE N.Z. POLICE ASSOCIATION URGES ALL MEMBERS TO HELP IN THIS OBJECTIVE.

N.Z. Police Journal,—October, 1950,

department to revoke its *Police Gazette* notice in favour of Fell. Losing patience, Meltzer accused the commissioner of trifling with the Supreme Court decision. Cummings told Meltzer he had passed the matter to the Solicitor-General. The latter said he would get the Prime Minister's signature. That, Meltzer replied, was not necessary. Finally the Solicitor-General spoke to Cummings and the notice of revocation of Fell's promotion was rushed into the next *Gazette*. Meltzer had won a significant case. The press did not appreciate it, but his members did, particularly those who had seen his large file that included details on the close relationship between Fell and the commissioner's family.

On 24 November 1949 Meltzer received a personal note from G. Taylor at Pukekohe police station appreciating his excellent work on these injunction proceedings and superannuation. Although Taylor himself would not benefit from the injunction, on which the last shot had not been fired, at least Meltzer had beaten the commissioner to the draw and 'it should have a very salutary effect'.

What the injunction achieved was to draw the police in behind Meltzer, who expressed the view that there was greater harmony than existed before. One reason was that now most members of the police had passed through the association. Although commissioned officers had preferred to let the department decide whether they could join, the association had offered them honorary membership and entitlement to the sickness benefit.

Meltzer felt confident that past membership of the association 'more than anything else will ensure proper treatment of the men by the commissioned officers' in this country with no class distinctions where 'Jack can be civil without being servile' and 'his master can be tolerant as well as efficient'. In this happy combination the police could work as a team; the 'old school' had been poor prophets in predicting that the Police Association would

The smiling policeman in this ad in the *Police Journal* reflected the more upbeat times being promised by a new National Government

weaken discipline in the ranks.

It was appropriate that the guest speaker at the 1947 conference should be ex-president Inspector John Bruce Young, who promised he would be willing to help the association in any way he could. He was in a prime position to make good his promise when appointed commissioner on 14 March 1950. The association by then had a new National Party minister, W.H. Fortune. Now it was the commissioner who was the liberal, the minister who was the constrainer.

On 6 October 1949 Fraser told the conference that the life of the association had been almost the same as that of his government—14 years for Labour, the 14th conference for the association. The government and association, said President Quin, might not always have seen eye to eye, but on the whole relations with the minister and commissioner had been quite friendly. He did not think the government had any cause to regret consenting to the formation of the association. He could not, however, understand why this association, alone in the Commonwealth, could not have retirement at 60, and he urged safeguards in any changes to promotion to include merit.

Fraser was conciliatory about balancing seniority with the commissioner's view. You could not pay a policeman enough, for the police looked after lives as well as property, but he could not justify more pay at present, not until the community produced more. As for early retirement, the man well into his 60s held to his view that 'you were not too old at 60 to do work'.

In the case of his ageing government, the voters did not agree and turfed Labour out. It was the end of that first great era for both 14-year-olds. That it was also the end of the paternalistic commissioner era was emphasised the following year when an association member successfully appealed against now ex-Commissioner Cummings' refusal to allow him to marry. The association had perhaps come of age in Meltzer's successful injunction proceedings. Now it was a force every commissioner and government would have to reckon with. In the 1950s that reckoning came soon enough.

Part III

The Seesaw Years

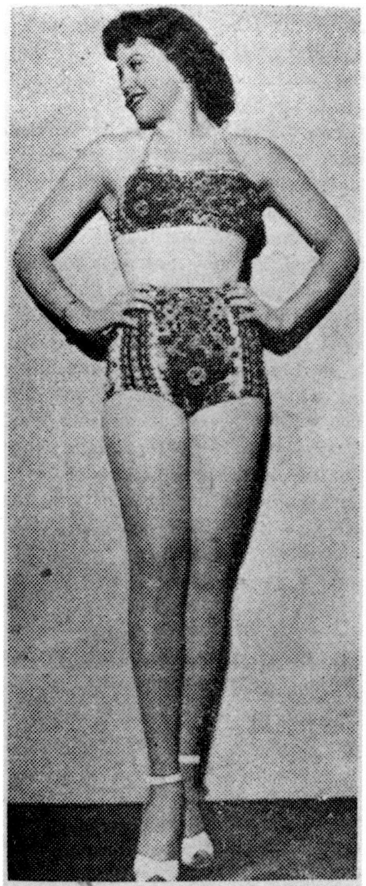

SEEN here is Suzi Crandall, whose natural charm and beauty is the envy of many girls, and the object of admiration of thousands of young men who have seen her in the movies.

The one pin-up to appear in the *Police Journal*, celebrating, in Meltzer's cheery fashion, the arrival of former association president John Bruce Young as commissioner. Meltzer took the opportunity to have some fun with the newspaper that never failed to sensationalise police news

Chapter Eleven

The Case of the Three Sergeants and the Compton Crisis

In April 1950 Meltzer was full of such good cheer that he published the only pin-up ever to grace the pages of the *Police Journal*. Bikini-clad movie star Suzi Crandall was in the *Journal* because she had had to be removed from *Truth* at the last minute to make way for the announcement of the new commissioner, John Bruce Young. The *Journal* felt it only fair to offer this quid pro quo.

The early 1950s were full of promise, starting with the new Police Minister, W.H. Fortune, delivering a former association president as commissioner. The association had a brochure ready to promote its main plank of early retirement direct to the public. The country was entering boom times of full employment under a new government dedicated to capitalist expansion. The forecast looked fine for association and country. Unfortunately, the former was out of political luck.

The first unlucky strike was Holland changing his mind about taking the police portfolio, giving it instead to Fortune, the second lowest ranked Cabinet member. Meltzer took the blow on the chin, his February 1950 editorial welcoming the 'depth of experience and wisdom' of this Paeroa-born former teacher with an arts degree.

The next *Journal* was over the moon about the appointment as commissioner of a man who was in the first association deputation to Peter Fraser, had an unparalleled understanding of the police since he had joined up in 1910, and had served in every rank. Meltzer looked forward to an era of 'free acceptance'. It was left to the two Auckland newspapers to wonder whether a man with three years until retirement could achieve much. In fact, Young had only two years, interrupted by illness, dying prematurely at 64. The *Free Lance* magazine said 'his kindly outlook and humanity are well known throughout New Zealand'. The irony of this was that it helped to mask the true nature of the association's political masters. The press observations that the politicians, in choosing Young, lost an opportunity to move away from promotion by seniority, prepared the way for the most disastrous appointment in New Zealand Police history.

Young did have time to make the force a better organisation in which to work. A more liberal interpretation was given to the provision dealing with police wives working. Employing civilian cleaners for fatigue duties was favoured. Car mileage rates were increased. After years of hanging fire, new Regulations and General Instructions were published. On uniforms lapels would replace stand-up collars.

Then Young and his force were plunged into the trauma of the 1951 Waterfront Dispute, 151 days of unpaid extra duty, the worst confrontation the police had had to cope with since the Depression. Young was credited with keeping the dispute under police control—there was no repeat of the 1913 uncontrolled attacks by Massey's specials—and with maintaining the police role as peacemakers between opposing factions. All he could get out of Cabinet for his officers was one cash bonus of £20.

By this stage the association was aware that Fortune was full of promises, but kept them to himself. He had expressed himself appalled at the conditions under which the police lived and worked. The bare floorboards in Auckland Central meant night duty staff got no sleep as day men moved about. The Paekakariki constable's home had not been painted in 40 years. Water poured through the Timaru station ceiling. All this would be rectified, Fortune promised. After 50 years of penny-pinching, there was to be a new era.

The early retirement brochure was taken from Meltzer's 1944 superannuation submissions; he was ready to cash in on the promise. His first item of business in 1950 was to circularise districts for their reactions to the brochure while the management committee put its arguments to the new administration. It presented an irresistible case. Here were men having to serve until at least 63 to get the full pension, men incapable of handling violent offenders half or a third their age, men whom police surgeons such as Auckland's Dr C.H. Tewsley said were worn out in feet and frame, suffering, after years of exposure to all weathers, from high incidences of bronchitis, sciatica, lumbago, rheumatism, and burdened by stomach troubles after years of irregular meals. Certainly, they had a commissioner who knew the score. In fairness, the management committee decided to defer publishing the brochure until the minister had been sounded out. It was a fatal hesitation.

Fortune listened courteously to the early retirement argument, to recruiting needs, to other conference remits about giving the men what the previous commissioner had secretly at the last minute offered the officers—amalgamation of pay and conditions. He promised to consider early retirement 'as soon as conditions permit', but first recruitment had to go up.

The 1950 conference elected Detective Sergeant Fergus Oliver Scott as president and voted to postpone the brochure in favour of the management committee concentrating on the recruitment the minister wanted and on accommodation. Only one district voted for immediate publication. The association decided to place its trust in the government.

Meltzer meantime had been finding it increasingly difficult to see the minister. When he learned officers would have their pay and allowances gazetted, he telegraphed Fortune on 29 June 1950 asking him to postpone this until negotiations established that association members received the same rights. Fortune replied that gazetting would not interfere with negotiations, but 'pressure of sessional duties' would have to postpone an interview with Meltzer.

In July Fortune reassured Meltzer by letter that he did not regard the police, to use Meltzer's words, as the Cinderella of the state services. He said the government was 'seized with the necessity for ensuring that its employees are adequately housed'. In August he replied to Meltzer's fears by promising him that police housing would go ahead, despite the government discovering an overcommitment on construction in the public service. Later in the month he thanked Meltzer for offering to help with recruiting.

A recruiting campaign was started, the focus the current film about the brave, unarmed British bobby, *The Blue Lamp*. The *Police Journal* carried ads urging recruitment and listing where and when you could see this inspirational movie.

The chirpy coppers in these ads illustrated the optimism of the force and the nation entering the affluent 1950s. The perky *Police Journal* got right in behind the pitch for more recruits with messages and urgings to see *The Blue Lamp*

THE BLUE LAMP

In our last issue we referred to the outstanding British film "The Blue Lamp," which created a very favourable impression with the Wellington public. It was noted that the Commissioner of Police took the opportunity of linking the screening of this Police picture with the Recruiting Campaign, and the Police Journal hopes that officers in charge of districts will do likewise. For the benefit of readers we set out a list of bookings made which are believed to be definite, although some alterations may be made:—

Dunedin—Century, approx. November 10.
Wanganui—Regent, October 13/18..
Lower Hutt—King George, October 19/21.
Petone—State, October 23/26.
Nelson—Majestic, October 28/31.
Hamilton—Civic, November 24/30.
Gisborne—Kings, December 15/21.
Hastings—State, December 22/28.
Palmerston North—State, Dec. 29/Jan. 4.
Masterton—Regent, January 6/9.
Feilding—Regent, January 12/15.
Timaru—State, Dec. 29/Jan. 4.
Waimate—Arcadia, January 6/8.
Invercargill—Regent, January 19/25.
Greymouth—Regent, February 2/5.

The advice of the Police Journal to all readers is "Don't Miss It." It's definitely "something different."

N.Z. Police Journal.—October, 1950. 335

In the June issue a warning note from 'Lucky to be Alive' claimed that the problem was not recruiting but resignations because of irregular hours and sudden transfers that cost a police family dearly. At the annual conference Fortune expressed himself amazed that there had been 400 resignations over the last four years, but having toured the stations he knew why—for 'too long in the past you have been the Cinderella of the Departments'. Although he got nothing from the commissioner but lists of things for approval, he did intend to improve things. They must, however, realise that he had six or seven departments to look after himself. Meantime he did not want a defeatist attitude in the force; he wanted police to sell their job and avoid mentioning any disadvantages.

In Parliament, too, Fortune made the right noises. He said there was a need for earlier retirement because so many senior police suffered illness from the strain. The rank and file should have amalgamation of pay and overtime just like the officers. He agreed with Grey Lynn Labour MP Fred Hackett about the need for brighter stations; he did not comment on Hackett's call for equal pay for women police. Fortune said he wanted 200 more police and had the matter of an assistant commissioner in hand.

On 11 December 1950 Fortune uncharacteristically came clean on where he stood, rejecting amalgamation of pay and conditions as paving the way for demands for a 40-hour, five-day week involving augmented overtime rates. He seemed to ignore the fact that the association had been paving this path for some time. In the same letter he announced that he was rejecting 'the existing practice of the Police Association approaching the Minister direct'. In future the association could appeal through the commissioner.

The management committee sought and won a brief meeting with Fortune, who backed down slightly, saying he did not intend to deny them the right ultimately to meet him on any question. This, however, was effectively what happened. Meltzer recognised this when he wrote in the October 1951 editorial that the association had 'lost touch' with the minister over some considerable period.

It was apparent how out of touch Fortune was when he spent the October conference speech railing about the communist menace. Young, praised by President Scott for his 'excellent leadership' in the waterfront dispute, tried to bridge the gulf between minister and members, telling them he and Fortune had worked to double retiring allowance to six months' leave after 40 years, despite Treasury objections.

Fortune had written a letter objecting to Meltzer saying that he was out of touch. Several Wellington association members passed the letter on to *Truth*, which was happy to print their anonymous comment that the minister was 'touchy' and objected to freedom of speech. The minister appeared more worried about the anti-democratic nature of communism than about his own attitude.

In its 2 January 1952 issue *Truth* also ran a lengthy article by an anonymous writer on the irksome regulations that discouraged young men from joining the police and caused them to resign, particularly because these regulations were interpreted by too many bullying dictators among the commissioned officers. The commissioner's job was too big for one man, and *Truth* proposed an outsider such as a lawyer or retired magistrate to administer the police and free the commissioner to move around among his men. Inefficient commissioned officers needed to be winkled out; there should be less emphasis on examinations for promotion; a tribunal should be established to investigate all resignations, complaints and dismissals.

Parliament had approved the need for an assistant commissioner under the provisions of the Police Force Amendment Act 1951. It had not made such an appointment, and Meltzer, in the June 1952 *Journal*, regretted this. The need was specific, for Young was off the job ill and *Truth* quoted senior officers talking about the rudderless state of the department. The paper repeated the call for an outsider to run the police, questioning that there was anybody in the force who could do the job well, particularly if the policy persisted of giving the job to somebody close to retirement.

Young was still on sick leave when the association finally got an interview with Fortune on 12 June 1952. Young had provided written support for early retirement. Meltzer put the case for introducing it in a staggered fashion over five years. This would have little effect on the executive staff but would bring in younger men and rectify the problem of the high percentage of sick senior members. The association also asked for more money, particularly for sergeants, so there would be an incentive to apply for a job that at present involved financial sacrifice and stifled ambition, and for the penal pay that was a third of what the previous commissioner had promised.

Fortune told them they had put their case well and he was not unsympathetic. He promised to look into all points, and suggested a committee to investigate everything. He was prepared to accept a formal application from the association for a Royal Commission, a committee of inquiry or a tribunal. As usual he had deflected any decision, leaving the association to discuss with Acting Commissioner Paine such matters as travelling and relieving allowances that

A TRIBUTE

[The Editor has received the following verses from an elderly lady admirer of the Police in Christchurch, and as an expression of thanks we publish them hereunder. Thanks, Jeanie Borthwick.]

TO THE POLICE

Have you ever lived with men of the law?
Stay a few years then you would want no more;
You would go looking for another house
Where you may sleep as quiet as a mouse.
His nights are spent guarding each shop and street,
While citizens are resting in their sleep;
But a night at home with telephone shrieking
Would send you for sleep some other place seeking.
So keen is he and strong; he gets his man,
In twos and one by one they come to hand,
Those men who waste their lives in crime so deep,
While wives can only stand aside and weep.
Thank God for brave men of integrity,
Who guard our homes and lives and property,
And are always ready at one's request
When danger threatens to give of their best.

JEANIE BORTHWICK.

TO THE POLICE WOMEN

I passed a lassie of the law
Strong and perfect, without a flaw;
Lovely her face and calmly sweet
In uniform she walked the street.
Women nearby standing together
Were not just talking of the weather;
Their eyes were full of anger and hate
As they gazed at that lass of the State.
Probably their husbands were, I thought,
Some of those men by the Police sought,
And I felt proud that women so sweet
Were not afraid to walk a hard beat.
So I smiled at one so fine and tall,
Who performed life's hardest duty call,
And wore her fine uniform with grace
While walking calmly each lonely place.

JEANIE BORTHWICK.

were below the public service scale.

Young was able to attend the annual conference, where he made what he called his swan song speech that recapped his long 'association with the Association' and his support for earlier retirement and amalgamating pay with overtime.

The association debated which kind of investigating body it should have. With no agreement on the first day, a sub-committee of three members and Meltzer was formed to consider the matter overnight. The next day the sub-committee reported back a refinement of what Meltzer had already proposed—an independent police council appointed by the minister and made up of a magistrate and representatives of the department and the association. The council would recommend to the minister, who would be guided by its decisions. This recommendation was adopted by conference, and the minister promised to give it consideration.

Two months later Fortune appointed 50-year-old Sub-Inspector Eric Henry Compton Assistant Commissioner over the heads of most of the commissioned officers. He had decided that promotion based on seniority had resulted in men reaching the top who only had a few more years to retirement and this was not in the best interests of the force. He wanted men at the top while they were still at their best.

A week later Compton was at the top, when Young died on 28 December. Full police honours were accorded at the funeral, the Auckland Police Pipe Band under Senior Detective Fell travelling to Wellington for the purpose. A large attendance of police and public paid their respects to this much-loved man, survived by his wife and five sons and two daughters. The association mourned the passing of a founding member who died with his hopes for the department and association intact. His passing only hastened the crisis generated by a dilatory and dimwitted minister, whom Holland should have been arraigned for appointing, and a commissioner allegedly chosen on merit but not fit, by any stretch of the imagination, to fill Young's boots. The National Government, and the baying press, learned the hard way that promotion on merit did not only mean younger men in the top jobs.

Compton was the prototype and protagonist for the new policy of promotion on merit. When he was exalted over the heads of more than 30 senior officers, the minister broke a convention going back to 1912 that commissioners were chosen from among the most senior officers. Born in 1902 in Hastings and educated there, Compton entered a solicitor's office before joining the police. For most of his career he was a detective, catching the eye of another former detective, Commissioner Young, who brought him to headquarters in May 1950. Compton had a reputation for being tough on bookmakers at a time when it was rumoured that police were on the take from bookies. Fortune, a fundamen-

Just the best — his honoured name
On finest records e'er will stay;
His character and work won fame,
No straighter man saw light of day.

Brave and fearless in his work
Righteousness his cherished goal
Until complete, no job did shirk,
Calm and steadfast was his soul.
Eternal joy God give to him.

Your mercy please on him bestow;
Observe his soul must never dim
Unless Thou say it shall not glow.
New Zealand's Police have lost a friend
God's will be done unto the end.

Superintendent John Bruce Young, District Commander, 1949 to 1950 and Commissioner of Police from 1950 until his death on 28 December 1952. Acrostic from *Invercargill News* 15 January 1953.
Invercargill News and S Young

The new Minister of Police, W.H. Fortune, was most unfortunate for the police. Two years later the greatly respected Commissioner Young died, a disaster for the police that ushered in the worst three years of maladministration and corruption in modern times talist Christian, was pleased to see that Compton attended the same Open Brethren church. He liked the look of this officer who would shake up both the bookies and a sluggish department. He would be an inspiration when there were severe recruiting problems—a man of 50 who had reached the top.

The newspapers agreed. The *Auckland Star* said it was a bold government decision to change the precedent, and Compton might now have some changes to propose himself. *Truth* welcomed promotion by merit, but warned that there needed to be careful safeguards and a complete overhaul of the promotion system to establish the right yardstick for measuring merit. The present system of promotion largely by immediate superior reports could count against a constable who did not see eye to eye with his senior sergeant. The police needed an independent board that could assess country coppers as well as city slickers solving flash crimes.

The newspaper had a good point about the way in which merit was assessed. If Compton had proved an even competent administrator, he could have surmounted much of the flak about merit promotion. From the beginning, however, he made arbitrary and insensitive changes. In March 1954 he changed the long-standing policy that had allowed re-employment of policemen who had resigned. One much-publicised victim was Detective Sergeant Kearton, for 22 years official police photographer. When told that he was being transferred to the beat at Nelson, he resigned, but thought better of the decision and withdrew his resignation. Compton would not accept it.

Eric Henry Compton, promoted to commissioner on the new merit system, leading to objections in virtually all ranks

The commissioner decided he would not allow policewomen who married to stay in the force. He refused an association request to have Sergeant Matheson of Invercargill, who had contracted tuberculosis, put on full pay and allowances. The milk of human kindness flowed thin through Compton's avowedly Christian veins.

Promotion policy caused most dissatisfaction. Compton ordered all personnel to be medically examined before they were promoted. Some were passed over. Others were passed over because Compton preferred younger men.

Compton had wasted no time recommending promotions. The February *Journal* reminded readers that the legal provision for any vacancy remained the same—it was filled from the next lower rank or grade. Physical fitness, educational qualifications and merit being equal, preference must still be given to seniority. The commissioner could make accelerated increments for special aptitude, consistent zeal or meritorious conduct, but this did not affect seniority status. The *Journal* took the view that exams tested merit already. Any assessment of conduct, efficiency, intelligence, zeal, temperament, practical experience and capacity to direct subordinates must be a uniform assessment of relative merit, and that should be done by a promotion board, made up of administration and staff, with right of appeal to a judicial body.

When Meltzer began dealing with Fortune in early 1953, he was referred to Compton. He went to the commissioner and was told that the association had to go to the minister about the police council and amalgamation of pay and allowances. From the beginning the Fortune/Compton team proved evasive.

Frustrated, the management committee used for the first time the right conferred by the 1952 conference in the event of stalled talks and called a special conference for 22 and 23 April. Promotion by merit was the big issue, and the conference eventually voted to approve a police council to adjudicate on differences between association and administration. Constable A.C. Osborne of Gisborne said any change to the present harmonious system would cause dissension in the ranks. The conference also passed Senior Sergeant O'Boyle's amendment that the government immediately set up a committee to investigate causes of dissatisfaction in the force. O'Boyle explained that his Auckland members were a new generation who did not want to work six days while their mates were having the weekend off. The association had passed through its adolescent stage. The present system in the force would not attract recruits and would lose those it had.

During the conference word arrived from Auckland that Compton was dismissing matrons and that policewomen would do the job. The management committee was delegated to challenge this. The conference stiffened its resolve not to have what Constable J. Molloy of Greymouth described as this 'so-called promotion by merit' which had created such discontent and jealousy when a member was promoted over 30 more senior members in 1921 and when Fell was promoted in 1949. The conference set another precedent by releasing its own press statement calling for an appeal board available to all members passed over for promotion. The association had moved from gentlemanly private requests to the commissioner and minister to the area of open public debate. Its press statement also called for a police council, a government committee, retirement at 60 and compensatory superannuation.

The flashpoint came when the association was involved in negotiations for amendments to the Police Act and regulations dealing with promotion. On 30 July 1953 Fortune announced the promotion of three sergeants at headquarters by three ranks to inspector, over the heads of more senior NCOs and the sub-inspectors; one of them was association President Scott, who had to resign as he rose to commissioned rank and understandably incurred the ire of his former association fellows. When association members read in the press of this promotion of their members—Scott over 69, Joseph Saunders over 73 and William McGuire over 85—the reaction was probably the most spontaneously hostile in association history. Meltzer was peppered with telegrams. Christchurch district expressed 'dismay and disgust at the cavalier fashion in which the Minister and Department have treated the Association' whose 'elementary rights have thus ruthlessly been swept away' by 'a naked display of power'. This was to be 'a do or die test' of the association. Hamilton, Greymouth, Hastings, Whangarei, Dunedin, Palmerston North, Nelson, all fired similar missives at Meltzer. Auckland, as usual, went one better and announced a protest meeting. Meltzer sent out a telegram suggesting that other districts might do likewise. Association members found the unity that their executives had been pleading for over the years. All that was needed was the right cause. The association claimed that the promotions were a breach of faith and took the cases to the Supreme Court to test the validity of the appointments.

While the association waited for its court appointment in the November, Compton went to Australia in September, leaving behind an unexplained delay in dealing with the police council and other matters the association was concerned about. Both the association and Detective James

Fergus Oliver Scott was president of the association when he was one of three sergeants promoted to commissioned rank by Commissioner Compton over dozens of more senior colleagues. It was the beginning of the end for Compton, provoking the most spontaneously hostile reaction in association history

Stanley Wrigley of the Special Branch made appointments to see Prime Minister Holland in September, while Assistant Commissioner Nalder approved full pay and allowances for Sergeant Matheson, suffering from tuberculosis.

Holland hoped to resolve association complaints by offering them a special Cabinet committee to consider their grievances. Wrigley was not so easy. He told Holland he had made a statutory declaration to the *Truth* solicitor about private work he had done on the commissioner's house and lent *Truth* the telephone he claimed Compton had used for illegal wire-tapping. Holland did not approve of pimping and he was aware that Wrigley had been rejected for promotion under Police Regulation 24. He could not, however, ignore the serious allegations that *Truth* was about to make public.

Fortune pre-empted the problems and effectively destroyed himself and the commissioner by going public himself, calling for a Royal Commission to inquire into serious allegations of misconduct in the police, including telephone tapping, work done on the commissioner's house by police technicians, opening of examination papers, hush money from bookmakers to police, laxity in police administration of the licensing laws. On 30 September *Truth* enlarged upon the minister's brief, asking why Compton needed two tall radio masts at his private residence and hinting that the telephone tapping might be in pursuit of communists.

That afternoon MP Fred Hackett gave notice of questions for Fortune. Holland chimed in first, telling the House that he had spoken to Assistant Commissioner Nalder in charge of Special Branch and made it clear that any opening of correspondence or telephone tapping would not be tolerated. Fortune said he had spoken by phone to Compton in Hobart. The commissioner denied issuing instructions to tap telephones; he had the radio masts to maintain contact with police patrols. Fortune then told the *Dominion* newspaper he favoured a Royal Commission into police misconduct. A week later Holland announced that Fortune was ill in bed with congestion of the lungs and that he was taking over the police portfolio.

Holland allowed Compton to return and offer his explanations before announcing a commission of inquiry three weeks later. The papers and the Labour Opposition wanted a Royal Commission, but Holland preferred to exclude any investigation into police morale, which could lead to loss of public confidence in the force. On 23 October he appointed retired Supreme Court judge Sir Robert Kennedy to inquire into five matters: whether, as a senior detective, Compton had tapped telephones while investigating bookmakers; whether he had improperly had work done by police at his private residence; whether there had been bribes by bookies to police; whether there was any laxity or irregularity in the administration of the licensing laws, whether some members of the police had criminal records. Sir Robert was given two months to do the job. There would be no immunity for pimps. There would be no investigation into the internal administration of the police, as the association wanted.

The government hoped by these means to achieve damage control. Sir Robert was not concerned about that. He took a year to do the job, releasing his findings in stages. Meltzer was association counsel at Kennedy's hearings, to protect association interests. At one stage he informed the retired judge that, when Wrigley had sought his advice about suing *Truth* for libel, he had opposed the idea.

Kennedy delivered three answers by 17 December. As a detective sergeant Compton had tapped telephones before this was made illegal in 1948. He had had police improperly do private work on a radio, fluorescent lights and shelving. The cost was £7 18s, for which Compton had made restitution. Kennedy accepted Compton's claim that the radio masts were to monitor patrol car communications rather than Wrigley's evidence that, as detective in charge of radio communications, he believed Compton had the masts for private use. On the matter of police with criminal records, Kennedy found only one.

The Kennedy inquiry was put on hold while the Royal Tour went ahead in late December. That month, however, the Supreme Court heard the case brought by Sub-Inspector Joseph Henry Dennehy of Masterton on behalf of 89 members with more seniority than the three sergeants promoted. Chief Justice Sir Harold Barrowclough found for the plaintiff, as he was bound to. Regulations 107 and 108 required promotion from rank to rank. The Chief Justice made a point of saying that his conclusion did not reflect on the three men promoted, and even suggested that they could have lawfully been accelerated through the intervening ranks of senior sergeant and sub-inspector. This may have helped Scott's cause when he appeared apologetically at the next association conference and survived a suggestion from Senior Sergeant O'Boyle, one of the senior men who had already stated his intention to give way to younger men, to have him thrown out of the association.

Barrowclough concluded with the obvious remark that the minister had been unwise to accept Compton's recommendation. Holland must have wished Fortune had resisted it, although the decision itself had the very effect Holland had feared from a Royal Commission. The police were seen to be in open conflict with their commissioner and minister, the Opposition and the newspapers were baying for blood, police morale was in tatters, resignations were increasing.

In this active December Meltzer met the Prime Minister and his investigating Cabinet sub-committee, telling them that the association had lost confidence in the minister and commissioner because of their breaches of faith and failure to carry out decisions they indicated were definite. There were also general actions by the commissioner which the association had successfully opposed, including the sacking of matrons, the three sergeants' promotion, appeals against non-promotion caused by injury. Holland told Meltzer and later the postponed annual association conference held the following February that the Cabinet subcommittee would be fair and just to them. Fortune and Compton spoke briefly to members, Fortune insisting that seniority was a dead hand, Compton saying that other government departments suffered from resignations. The delegates seized the time to vote for a substantial salary increase, despite Holland telling them they could not 'just name your terms'.

Kennedy resumed his inquiries in April, looking unsuccessfully into administration of the liquor law. Nobody was giving evidence, not without immunity. Sir Robert satisfied himself with saying that the licensing law needed tightening up.

Meantime the newspapers were claiming that the police were not getting a fair go compared with the rest of the community. This was why, as the *Auckland Star* pointed out, there was one day when there was no policeman on duty in Queen Street. The police were resigning. The system needed an overhaul. A business consultant would help.

Compton announced that promotion would revert to the old system, but the resignations continued. In 1953 there were 67, but 115 in 1954. Police were leaving for better paid jobs with better prospects.

At the end of October Kennedy investigated the matter of bookmakers paying hush money to detectives. Compton's counsel, H.R.C. Wild, called him to the witness stand. He testified that he kept his savings parcelled up with the money his wife earned from eggs. 'I am an individualist,' he told the court. 'I feel most people live their lives upside

THE SOUTHLAND DAILY NEWS

The very essence of a FREE PRESS lies in its right to be the sole judge of what it prints.

SATURDAY, DECEMBER 18, 1954

THREE-MAN COMMISSION SUGGESTED TO CONTROL POLICE, BUT MR HOLLAND HAS A STICKY PROBLEM

NEWSLETTER FROM THE CAPITAL
— by The News Parliamentary Correspondent

WELLINGTON, Today. — Definite action to resolve the problems agitating the police force has been promised by the Prime Minister. The width of the administrative changes contemplated will not be known until the Government's plans are announced but, broadly speaking, it can be said that the Police Association has won a victory.

The association has been at odds with the Commissioner of Police, Mr E. H. Compton, almost from the time he assumed office, but most decisions in the various clashes went to Mr Compton and his then immediate chief as Minister, Mr Fortune.

Probably the tide began to flow the other way after a Supreme Court ruling that the appointment of three men to commissioned rank in specialist roles breached seniority procedure established over a long period of years.

In resuming the responsibilities of Police Minister, to which he delegated Mr Fortune for a period, the Prime Minister has accepted unpleasant duties.

He knows that his departmental chief, Mr Compton, lacks the confidence of the Police Association, representing the non-commissioned officers and other ranks in the force. But he is also cognisant of the fact that the Government has endorsed some decisions, unpalatable to the association, advanced by Mr Compton as considered advisable for the added efficiency of the force.

Any plans the Government contemplates for administrative reorganisation of the force must spread down from the post of Commissioner. But the problem and its solution bristles with thorns.

The Commission of Inquiry set up to investigate specific allegations gave Mr Compton and other named officers a clean bill of health. So there can be no question of the Government dismissing Mr Compton for any misdemeanour.

It is probable also that Mr Compton, with 10 or 11 years of potential service still ahead of him, will be grimly determined, as a matter of principle, not to resign his post.

Ultimately it is thought, as was mentioned in this column last week, that the Government will adopt the London Metropolitan Police practice of appointing someone outside the force to the post of Commissioner.

In the meantime, the suggestion is that a three-man commission might be appointed. Sir Howard Kippenberger has been mentioned as a likely choice for chairman. His duties as editor of war histories have slackened off considerably; he is a qualified lawyer, with considerable practising experience before the recent war, and in the army and since he has been conceded to be a good administrator.

Ticklish problems

Presumably Mr Compton would be a member of the Commission also, but the choice of a third man poses ticklish problems. The present administration eliminated employee representation on the Public Service Commission, so a decision to give the Police Association membership on any commission set up would be inadvisable.

MR HOLLAND IS PLANNING POLICE REORGANISATION

WELLINGTON, Friday. — The Minister of Police, Mr Holland, in the course of planning the administrative reorganisation of the New Zealand Police Force, had talks today with representatives of senior police officers in the Wellington district.

It is expected that a further series of talks will begin on Monday with the officer representatives of districts outside the capital.

Mr Holland, it is thought, will announce the scheme he is preparing early next week.—PA.

MR COMPTON
Has been at odds with Police Association.

SIR HOWARD KIPPENBERGER
Could be chairman of three-man commission to control force

Press publicity about association disagreements with the commissioner had never been so widespread down.' His nest egg was about £2,000, including the egg money. Kennedy concluded that it was not impossible to have accumulated such savings from hens and salary, and found no evidence that any police had received money from bookmakers.

Truth was not impressed. The inquiry was, it said, hamstrung by the lack of immunity for witnesses and Sir Robert had made light of the telephone tapping and the work done on Compton's house.

The newspapers had, however, been publishing detailed reports on the hearings for several months, with headlines such as that in the *Evening Post* of 28 October, 'Denials of Dealings with Bookmakers'. The *Dominion* of 13 December said it was the sole topic of conversation in the country, whether in Parliament, on a train, in a factory. Even a hamstrung commission was realising Holland's worst fears.

The government passed an amendment setting up a Police Council to advise the government on pay, promotion and general conditions. Holland confirmed himself as minister, having lost Fortune in the general election. Holland promised to consult Meltzer before any legislation was introduced, but the annual association conference still vowed to seek publicity for its views. Holland's big concession was to promise a change in police administration, leaving the papers to speculate, over the silly season, what this might be.

Compton did not modify his administrative habits in the interval. A new regulation was that members off duty because of sickness must be certified fully recovered before they returned to duty. This eliminated the practice of convalescent members being assigned light duties, introducing half pay until recovery was certified. The association objected strongly and took the matter up with Holland. The regulation was dropped. The police were returning to being administered at political level. *Truth* reported rumours of no confidence votes in Compton.

The rumours proved true when an administration conference of senior officers in mid-January 1955 passed a vote of no confidence in Compton on the grounds that he had told the Prime Minister he had not tapped telephones when he had, had improperly used police labour and materials and had illegally promoted three sergeants.

Holland left for England, leaving behind a three-man commission made up of Compton as chairman and his two most senior officers, Nalder and Munro. Not legislated for, the commission was illegal while Holland was in Britain.

MR. COMPTON REJECTS VOTE OF NO CONFIDENCE

A VOTE of no confidence was passed in Mr. E. H. Compton, chairman of the Police Commission, by 22 of New Zealand's 28 senior police officers when they conferred in Wellington last week, and at least four of them are reported to have refused to shake hands with him. Twenty-three officers were present when the vote was taken, the members of the three-man Commission being among the absent.

No hint of this discord was contained in a statement issued to the daily press which said that, after a 90-minute address by the Prime Minister and Minister in Charge of Police, Mr. Holland, the conference "unanimously passed a vote pledging loyalty and assistance to the new Police Commission of three members." Actually the vote of confidence was passed "in the Commission as constituted."

AS soon as the senior police officers' conference opened with Mr. Compton in the chair, a vote of no confidence was moved in the chairman. It was pointed out that the officers could have no confidence in the chairman because:

- He had assured the Prime Minister by radio-telephone from Australia that he had not tapped telephones when, in fact, he had.
- He had improperly used police labour and materials.
- He had illegally promoted three specialist police sergeants.

Mr. Compton overruled the motion on the grounds that he had been appointed chairman of the Commission by the Government. At this, a point of order was raised that the conference was a conference of senior police officers and not a conference between the officers and the Commission.

The agenda was headed: "Conference of Police Officers" and the notice of the conference contained nothing to suggest that it was a conference between the officers and the Commission. Mr. Compton declined to accept the point of order.

It is understood that an effort was then made to pass a motion ... adjournment, 22 of 24 officers passed a motion of no confidence in him. One police officer was not present when the vote was taken and another did not vote. Mr. Compton was informed of this resolution when the conference resumed, but overruled it.

After that, conditions at the conference are reported to have worsened and when Mr. Holland and his

AT LEAST FOUR OFFICERS DECLINED TO SHAKE HANDS WITH HIM: Mr. E. H. Compton, chairman of the Police Commission.

Minister-assistant, Mr. Halstead, arrived the following day there was a distinct air of tension in the room.

The vote of no confidence in Mr. Compton passed the previous day was handed to Mr. Holland in the form of a letter. After reading it, Mr. Holland told the officers that, under ... makes no provision for the establishment of a Police Commission.

Any necessary validating legislation to establish the Commission in law would be brought down, said Mr. Holland. It was a fairly frequent occurrence for the Government to introduce measures which required validating legislation. The pre-Christmas increases given social security beneficiaries was an example of an act which would need validating legislation.

He said it was high time police officers kept their troubles to themselves. He would welcome the formation of a police officers' guild to promote welfare and efficiency within the force. Complaints about police organisation should be made through their own organisation instead of through the Press.

WELL RECEIVED

In reply to a question, Mr. Holland said that the chairman of the Police Commission had no vote as chairman so that the votes of its three members would be equal. This statement was well received by the conference.

One officer told the Prime Minister that promotion other than by seniority would not be acceptable to police officers. Mr. Holland said that view was unacceptable to the Government. He added, however, that any promotion out of order would be considered with the greatest care before it was made.

According to the hand-out issued to the daily Press, Mr. Holland said that, while in Britain, he hoped to discuss with Scotland Yard authorities the establishment of a temporary exchange scheme for police officers of both countries.

He outlined the functions of the newly-appointed Commission, said it was hoped to give a greater degree of administrative responsibility to the police districts, and added that he

THE other two members of the Police Commission, Mr. J. P. Nalder (left) and Mr. P. Munro, have equal voting powers with the chairman.

General may, from time to time, appoint a fit and proper person to be Commissioner of Police "who shall have general control of the force."

The Act makes it plain that superintendents and inspectors in charge of districts are all subject to the control of the commissioner. He is the only person who can initiate disciplinary action against a sergeant or carry out disciplinary action recommended by an officer against a constable.

The provisions of this Act remain in full force and there is certainly nothing in it providing for the establishment of a three-man commission. Equally certain, Mr. Holland's statement that the three members of the commission are of equal status has no foundation in law.

Mr. Nalder, as assistant commissioner, can legally only do what Mr. Compton delegates to him and M[r.] Munro, as a superintendent, woul[d] be subject to the authority and con[]trol of Mr. Compton as commissione[r]. As an assistant commissioner—th[e] post to which he was recently pro[]moted—Mr. Munro is in the sam[e] position as Mr. Nalder.

The fact that Mr. Compton ma[y] have agreed to hand over his author[]ity to the commission cannot affe[ct] the legal position until it is validat[ed] by Parliament. If the commissio[n] appoints, promotes or dismisses ser[]geants or constables or takes an[y] other disciplinary action, it will b[e] void in law until the law is amende[d].

Legally the Commissioner of Polic[e], Mr. Compton, still remains in fu[ll] control of the force and nothing ca[n] alter that fact until legislation [is] provided.

This is the extraordinary situation in which the police force is left. Mr. Holland, now also Minister of Police, will be out of the country for several weeks and Parliament is not expected to meet, at the earliest, until April and possibly later.

The famous *Truth* article that precipitated Compton's downfall

It was rumoured that Holland was trying to attract a senior Scotland Yard administrator, but he did not bring one back. While he was away the commission met an association delegation headed by President Mick Rodgers. Nalder accepted that amalgamation of pay and allowances would go a long way towards restoring confidence in the police; at present he was seeing prospective recruits and he could offer them no reassurances on overtime. The result was they did not seek enlistment. He proposed agreeing to support the amalgamation, but Compton dissented, saying he did not think it would help recruiting one bit. End of discussion.

Just over a week later, on 9 March, Holland returned without much to say to the press. He called in the commission and allegedly told Compton that he had had his chance and failed. On 19 April Holland told the House that Compton had retired voluntarily, agreeing to accept £6,000 in lieu of the £24,000 income he was forfeiting. It was a golden handshake. The Opposition and the press objected.

In Parliament Compton was defended as a good Christian. This did not, however, seem to square with what he had told the Cabinet investigating sub-committee in regard to Meltzer's claim that Sergeant Matheson of Invercargill had contracted TB through his police duties. Compton told the committee you could not 'definitely say when TB was contracted' and he was not prepared to commit the government to what might yet be a large sum of money. Compton noted that Meltzer consistently opposed him in matters of the welfare of association members.

Meltzer had good reason. Heretaunga MP Phil Holloway told the House on 5 May 1955 that, following the death of Commissioner Young, his widow went into hospital. She had an invalid son and lived in a police house, paying a weekly rent of £2. Her superannuation was £300 a year. Compton had sent a Labour Department representative to the house to have it assessed for increased rental. Later Compton wrote to Mrs Young saying that if the higher rental of £3 10s a week was not paid he would seek a magistrate's order. It was then that Mrs Young asked her MP Phil Holloway to raise the matter. It was arranged that she would not have to pay the increased rental.

When Compton accused Meltzer before the Cabinet investigating sub-committee of 'half truth and very malicious', he was really talking about himself. Meltzer had protested at Compton's non-promotion of two senior sergeants and a sergeant, saying the commissioner had made a mistake. This led to Compton's attack. Yet the commissioner had chosen not to tell the sub-committee the full background, that these three police had made the first successful application to the Promotion Board made up of a magistrate and two policemen. They were vindicated, yet Compton refused to allow the department to pay their court costs of £94 10s.

It was Inspector Bill Murray of Gisborne, former president of the association who, as a member of the Promotions Board, had dictated that the men be promoted. Murray took the view that Compton was promoted out of turn and 'thought he was the big smoke and the Association much subservient and a concession to even listen to them was his general attitude'.

The vital factor for the association was Meltzer. Had past moves to replace this shrewd lawyer with a policeman as secretary been successful, it is quite likely a serving or even retired policeman would not always have stood up to the commissioner so staunchly. Yet Meltzer, with a lengthy legal career behind him, had no qualms about fighting Compton on every occasion. When Meltzer objected to the non-promotion of Senior Sergeant F.W. Edwards of Auckland, Compton pointed out that a bad heart had kept him off duty for 293 days. Compton had introduced the policy to have all men medically examined, because of the very point the association made, that there were so many sick commissioned officers. The doctor examining Edwards had not recommended his promotion. Meltzer, however, kept pitching for Edwards. Other medical certificates were acquired. Finally Edwards got his promotion, and the commissioner lost once more to this jack rabbit of a secretary. Little wonder Meltzer was the focus of Compton's complaints to the Cabinet sub-committee.

Holland's problem was to decide who and/or what should replace Compton. On 29 April 1955 the Police Force Amendment Bill had been introduced, proposing a commission of five members. Happily this hydra-headed team did not eventuate, but what did emerge from all this trauma was the realisation that the question of the pay and conditions of 1600 police could not be left in the hands of one man, particularly such a man as Compton.

Compton was an aberration. He continued to defend his promotion of the three sergeants to the Cabinet sub-committee, as part of the worldwide trend towards giving 'younger and more efficient men the executive positions'. He could not see that his entire force, including his officers (perhaps with the exception of the luckless three during their temporary promotion), were vigorously opposed to his policy. Commissioners since have learned from this and acknowledged that they cannot stay in the job without the confidence of those under them.

Compton was not even consistent in seeking out the younger and more efficient. Superintendent G.H.L. Holt of Hamilton was one of those specified by Compton to the sub-committee as 'joining forces with the Association against the Commissioner in the recent injunctions'. A letter from Holt dated 28 August 1953 to Meltzer indicates why. 'Dear Sparring Pal,' it began, 'The Brains Trust [Compton] has been up this way and in his usual boyish way went round amongst the cops at the out stations and promised them all sorts of things unbeknownst to his Officer-in-Charge.' Consequently a constable Holt reported on as being too old for promotion 'sold himself horribly expensively to the Trust'. As a result Holt received a memorandum from Compton saying that the constable should fill a vacancy at headquarters and that Holt's report on his unfitness for promotion was 'irrelevant as the constable had not yet had the opportunity to sit for an examination'. From his personal interview the commissioner considered that the constable 'would make an excellent sergeant'.

Compton was the worst commissioner in New Zealand police history, by a country copper's mile. He also forced Holland's National Government to give the police a better deal before the voting public consigned them to the political dustbin now occupied by the former Minister of Police. As for the association, the traumas of the last few years had united it as it had not been in its tentative adolescent years. On the verge of its majority it was geared up to fight for the 40-hour, five-day week the Labour era had bestowed on everybody else. It seemed as though a chastened National administration was ready to deliver.

Chapter Twelve

The Outsider Who Brought the Association in From the Cold

The Police Force Amendment Bill was introduced to an unprecedented outcry from the Opposition, the press and the association. If anything, the association was the most vociferous opponent. The days of discreet lobbying were over; the association made sure the press heard what it wanted. And above all else it did not want an outsider in the commissioner's job.

The bill still proposed a five-man commission, but nobody believed for a moment that an unwieldy extension of the unsuccessful three-man commission would be introduced. While the Labour Opposition sought to get Holland to admit that new Secretary of Justice Sam Barnett was the choice, the press took punts on such contenders as Assistant Commissioner Nalder and Brigadier J.T. Burrows. The new status of the association in the minds of the press was reflected in the rhetorical question asked by the political gossip column of the 2 May edition of the *Dominion*: 'Could the Prime Minister be awaiting the views of a meeting of the executive of the Police Association to be held in Wellington today?'

At 8.30 am that day Meltzer was busy on the phone giving the hurry-up for answers from district secretaries to his telegram: 'Wire urgently district view outside head police force Management Committee meeting today two o'clock.'

At 11.40 am the first telegram came in: 'Nelson District

Controller-General Samuel Barnett, far left, was the choice of Police Minister Sid Holland (centre) to run the police force in 1955. Alongside Barnett is Peter Munro, the assistant commissioner whom Walter Nash (far right) proposed should be commissioner. On Holland's right is the other assistant commissioner, Jim Nalder, whom the association wanted as commissioner. High-flying bureaucrat Barnett was an inspired choice to sort out the sorry administration of the police

NEW ZEALAND

Prime Minister,

Wellington.

6th May, 1955.

Dear Mr. Meltzer,

The Police Force Amendment Bill has now passed through Parliament, so that there is little I cansay in regard to the representations of your letter of 2nd May except to thank you for writing and to assure you that what you had to say on behalf of your Management Committee was seriously considered.

The Government's decision was taken with the welfare and efficiency of the Police Force firmly in view and we think that the new legislation will lead to this result.

I am glad to be able to point out that the Bill in its final form does meet the principle of one-man control, as suggested by your committee. The appointment of a Controller-General from outside the force was decided on to meet the needs and circumstances of the present position of the Police Force. I think it will be generally admitted that there is a need for administrative reorganisation and that the present system does not provide adequate facilities for training members of the force in general administration. I would not for a moment say that the force has not produced good administrators, but I do not think this has been a result of conscious design in organisation. I am sure that the new Controller-General will give early attention to devising a better method of administrative training within the force.

None of the decisions implemented in the Bill are derogatory of serving members of the force. They will merely make it possible to introduce systems of administration which will lead to better things for the force.

I thank the Management Committee for its assurance of co-operation and loyalty. With those I think we can make a real success of the new scheme of things.

Yours truly,

S. G. Holland

Mr. J. Meltzer,
General-Secretary,
The New Zealand Police Association
(Incorporated),
P.O.Box 928,
WELLINGTON, C.1.

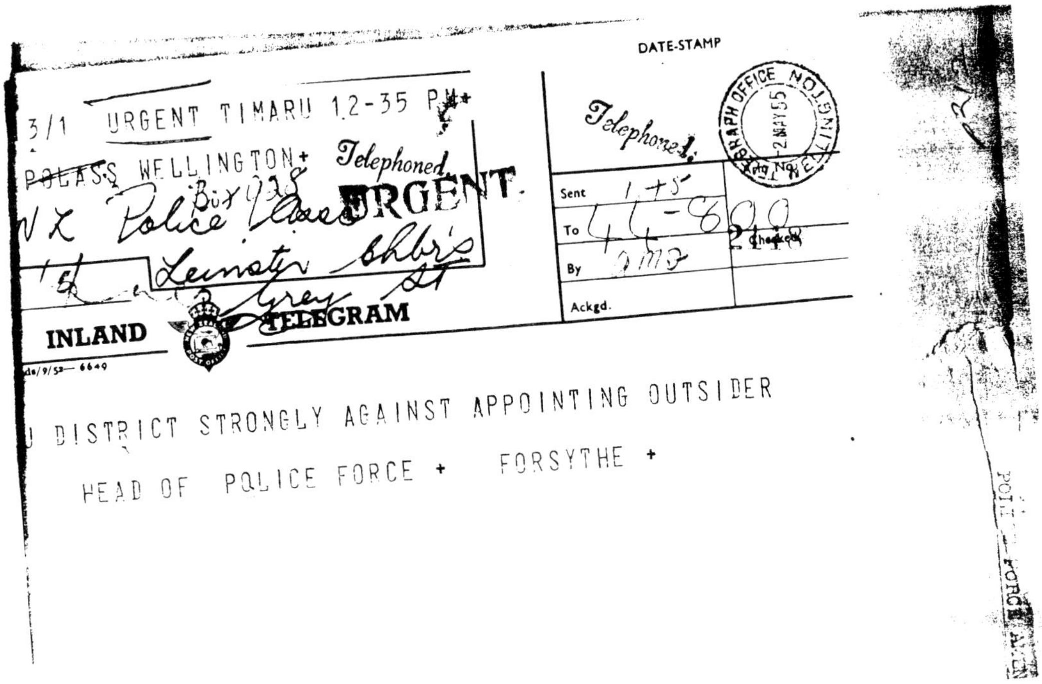

3/1 URGENT TIMARU 12-35 PM+

POLASS WELLINGTON+ Telephoned

URGENT.

INLAND TELEGRAM

DATE-STAMP

TELEGRAPH OFFICE WELLINGTON 2 MAY 55

Sent 1.45

To 44-800

By

Ackgd.

Checked

DISTRICT STRONGLY AGAINST APPOINTING OUTSIDER

HEAD OF POLICE FORCE + FORSYTHE +

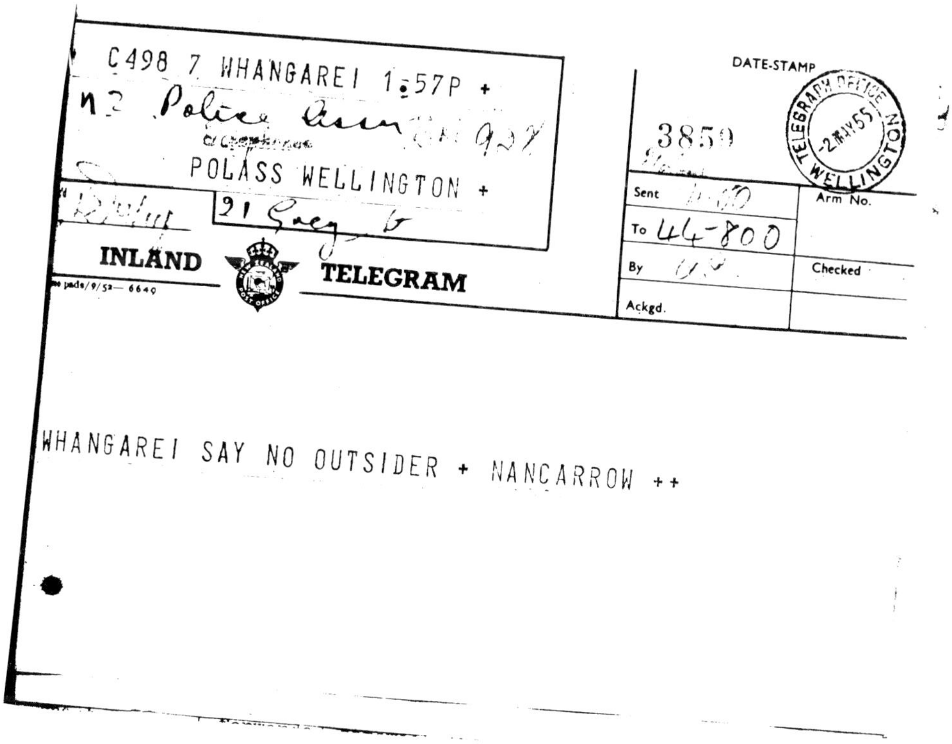

C498 7 WHANGAREI 1.57P +

POLASS WELLINGTON +

INLAND TELEGRAM

DATE-STAMP

TELEGRAPH OFFICE WELLINGTON 2 MAY 55

3850

Sent

To 44-800

By

Ackgd.

Arm No.

Checked

WHANGAREI SAY NO OUTSIDER + NANCARROW ++

Two of the majority of district telegrams opposing any outsider running the police. Holland passed the legislation appointing an outsider before he responded to the association's now obsolete lobbying against it protest suggested appointment Barnett without consultation officers and Association.' At 12.47 pm: 'Outside appointment of head opposed. Scally, Invercargill.'

Christchurch District Committee, 1.30 pm: 'This district feels very strongly that the Permanent Head of the Police Force should be recruited from the ranks of the Force.'

Throughout the afternoon the telegrams came in. Greymouth was opposed to an outsider; New Plymouth thought an outsider an 'insult to officers and lack of confidence in Force'; Gisborne, Auckland, Whangarei were opposed too. Then came Napier not opposed to an outsider. Hamilton was divided, one view being that an outsider for the next term 'would probably result in us getting earlier retirement and other anomalies the Association have been after, whereas, the appointment of a commissioned officer would not likely have the same result owing to the way it could affect him'.

It was none other than F.W. Edwards, for whose promotion Meltzer had fought, who, as secretary of the emerging guild of 100 commissioned officers, wrote to Holland on 2 May stating that his group 'considers that the Force and the country as a whole would be best served by a return to control by a Commissioner. Such Commissioner to be chosen from the New Zealand Police Force.' Hamilton was wrong about commissioned officers fearing for their employment, but correct about the outsider.

The management committee of the association told Holland on 2 May that 'there is a deep rooted antagonism by the Force to a Commissioner or Head who is not a trained member of the Force'. The letter was signed by Meltzer, himself a bugbear to two past commissioners for the same reason—that he was not one of the force.

The letter harked back to the tradition established in 1897 and canonised in 1920 by Commissioner O'Donovan when he said, 'Literally every constable now potentially carries the Commissioner's baton.' The letter warned that any departure from this venerable tradition would be strongly resented and 'conducive to a lowering of morale'.

The next day the bill got its second reading and Holland told the House that Barnett had the job of Controller-General; Nalder would be his deputy. Opposition leader Walter Nash responded that Assistant Commissioner Munro should have the job and it should be that of commissioner; it would be as soon as Labour got back in. Holland claimed the support of Nalder and Munro, the latter did not want the job because he had only two years until retirement and the former had good prospects in his nine remaining years of service. It was intended that within three years Police, Justice, Prisons and Probation would be under one departmental roof—an idea that remains ahead of its time, although the time is now approaching.

Parliament sat continuously from Wednesday at 2.30 pm. At 2 pm on the Thursday the management committee met and drafted an eleventh hour letter to Holland asking him to drop the proposal to appoint an outsider, suggesting instead an administrative adviser to Nalder as Commissioner, with Munro as Assistant Commissioner. Meltzer took the unprecedented step, for him, of informing the press first, although the story came out in the *Dominion* next morning, after the bill had passed at 10 minutes to midnight on the 5th, at the end of a 36-hour sitting. Holland had triumphed. There was little, he told Meltzer, that he could say about his letter except thank you; the present system in the force did not provide adequate facilities for the training in general administration it was generally admitted was needed.

In his 70-minute summing up in the House, Holland had said a new day would dawn bright with the uniform, crime and security branches under one man; it was now up to him. The man in question was a public service success story. Born in Dunedin in 1901, Sam Barnett joined the Department of Lands and Survey at 17 and went on to became the first superintendent of staff training in the public service. A solicitor, he rose from assistant undersecretary in Lands and Survey to be Assistant Director of Education charged with overhauling education administration, before becoming Undersecretary of Justice in 1949. The next year he was awarded a Carnegie Fellowship to study penal and criminological developments overseas. He observed British and American police forces in operation, and served on the five-man international committee set up by the United Nations to investigate the prevention and treatment of crime. If Holland could not get a Scotland Yard expert, Barnett must have seemed the next best thing. Even the *Police Journal*, in its April/May issue, managed to call him 'a proved and capable administrator'.

Barnett was appointed on 16 May. He started with a tour of the country's police stations as the newspapers pondered whether one man could manage both the justice and police departments. *Truth*, on 15 June, picked up the story of advertisements in the *Police Gazette* carrying stipulations tailored for two of the three sergeants the association had challenged in the Supreme Court. The Auckland branch of the association was waiting to see Barnett, and not just to shake his hand. The ads were withdrawn shortly afterwards. *Truth* said his prompt action averted revival of the case.

On 23 June Barnett ended his tour in Christchurch amidst an indignant rumour that he had ordered the police to march to hear him talk. Barnett condemned the story as 'mischievous and untrue'; the order had come from Superintendent Denis Sugrue, and he later rescinded it. By now the newspapers were firmly on Barnett's side. It was not hard to spot a new and flexible mind ready to talk about shaking up a soporific police administration.

Housing was his first target, for both married and single men. It was so poor that it was restricting recruitment and prejudicing promotion. He decided a new training school was needed, and not at Lyttelton, but probably in Wellington because specialist staff were available there. Believing the force was 20 per cent below efficient strength, he proposed turning over routine clerical work to civilians, although he recognised this was not a popular move.

Barnett was not by any means all good news for the association. The 40-hour, five-day week was 'an impossibility' because the very nature of police work meant members must work when required. He would not commit himself on overtime, earlier retirement on full superannuation or adjusting meal and travel allowances in line with other public service departments.

Over the next month, however, the association executive successfully lobbied Barnett and the Prime Minister to amalgamate pay, overtime and allowances into a higher consolidated wage. On 1 August the press relayed the good news that Holland was developing a new pay scale and looking at the possibility of introducing the five-day week. President Mick Rodgers put out a press release the next day welcoming this as 'the greatest step forward' for the association. He praised Barnett for being ready to discuss problems at all times in an atmosphere of goodwill.

The newspapers gave Holland a good press, welcoming his putting the police on the same pay and conditions as the rest of the community. With starting pay of £15 a week it was expected the force would soon move from 1694 personnel to the desired 2000.

Holland announced that a new National Police School would open at Trentham the following February. It would use 11 of the immigration hostel buildings in the military camp to house 200 recruits, and would also offer facilities for cadet, specialist and refresher courses.

In Parliament, during discussion of the Police Estimates, Holland basked in the pleasant atmosphere. He had, he told the assembly, become very fond of the police force. They now worked without limitation on hours of overtime and each man was going to try and get more recruits so that they could do their job in a five-day week.

Even the *Police Journal* joined in the congratulations, its September issue hailing Holland's vigorous approach and his bold stroke in appointing Barnett. The department joined in the new togetherness by taking two pages of the *Journal* to brief members on departmental doings, such as Nalder explaining the recruiting campaign on radio and in the cinema and with posters, leaflets and pamphlets. Nalder observed the improved morale in resignations being down to 35 in the last six months from 73 in the previous half-year.

Holland launched the recruiting campaign with a folksy radio broadcast. He mentioned the good new pay scale, the intensely interesting job in a happy and contented force. He spoke of talking only days before to General Secretary Meltzer, who told him how things had improved, how keen members were on their work, how he could get on with helping to build the force instead of spending all his time arguing over regulations and disputes. Every member of the police was now keen to recruit.

Every tuning knob was turned by an ebullient Holland. He told youngsters of 17 there was provision for them coming into the police. If you belonged to a sports team, you would be right at home in the force. It was 'a grand team, with some fine sportsmen in it, men who have been sports champions, like Assistant Commissioner Peter Munro'. Barnett was presently in England looking into the work of the famous London bobby everybody admired for his friendliness, and that was what was wanted here.

Cabinet had generously given him extra money, he told listeners, so he could spend it on houses, barracks, better uniforms, equipment and a training centre, to get the police on the march again, together with the government. He told his national audience that he was introducing police dogs and, although some might think it old-fashioned, he hoped to be able to bring back the mounted police, because 'everyone admired those smartly turned-out Mounties on their wonderfully trained horses'. This amount of Kiwi schmaltz has not been poured into the nation's ears by a leader before or since. And it worked.

Meltzer did find he could attend to small social duties for which he had had little time in his first 15 years in the job. 'Greetings and salutations,' he wrote to Senior Sergeant C.E. Tanner at Napier on 19 August. 'It is a long time since I have heard your sweet dulcet tones, but one of these days we must meet up with each other again.' He asked Tanner to send him his booklet on 'Motor Law, as dealt with by the Police'. It was to be part of Meltzer's drive to 'equip the office with informative data'.

Later in the month Meltzer had the sad duty of paying tribute to former Vice-President F. H. (Tim) Healey, one of the original 1936 deputation to Fraser, who had died suddenly. Steps were being taken to appoint life members, and Healey was intended to be the first recipient.

Meltzer wrote to new police widow Mrs Moore of Ongarue telling her he had in his personal capacity sought housing for her, but the association could not help because it only handled matters of principle.

Meltzer carried out the humdrum chore of congratulating every retiring member. In November Constables E. Christmas of Manurewa, W.S.B. Phillips of Wyndham, P. Slattery of Christchurch and H.E. Hollinshead of Warkworth finished their service. He told each he could continue to receive the *Journal* for a modest 6s 6d per annum.

At the 20th annual conference in November Holland told delegates he had not received an illuminated address for appointing Barnett, but now they had confidence in his decision. Barnett said he had accepted reluctantly as his public service duty, but now found the work absorbing and was satisfied by his association with the police. He had observed the effect of the English bobby as a model for the national character, and he could not see why the police here could not fulfil the same role, as the All Blacks and the New Zealand fighting forces did.

Barnett accepted that the improved pay and conditions were a lift and after the honeymoon they would have to go on living together. One thing he had noticed in his trip around the country was how pleasant and rewarding consultation was. The police had not, he imagined, had a great deal of that from their leadership. He rated pay well behind good supervision in getting the best out of employees. He reminded association members that they carried the burden and responsibility of supervision, especially of the recruits. They must show personal interest in every member of their team, expecting a good job to be done but remaining concerned about welfare and being sure to praise everybody.

Six months after Barnett's appointment to run the police, the association joined the chorus of praise for the police saviour. Left to right: Meltzer, Holland, association president Mick Rodgers and Barnett. Again, at the association annual conference, these four sit happily in the same order in the front row

'The day has gone altogether,' he told delegates,

when men can be treated as robots. We will never build a Police Force in New Zealand by housing men like animals, as we have been doing in some of our barracks, and putting them to work in shabby offices—throwing them off the wharf to teach them to swim, and then, the final humiliation, using them as charwomen.

It is simply not good enough to say, "That is how they treated me, and look at me—I survived!" "It made a man of me," I heard one say, "so these fellows can take their medicine." Well, maybe we did grow up to be men—in spite of it. Maybe we would have been better men if we had been treated reasonably.

He then gave his audience some mildly nasty medicine, reminding them they would not get the five-day week until they recruited 200 more men. And they would have to accept civilians, and make better use of staff, including policewomen, and vehicles. Despite their blood pressure problems with the three sergeants, he wanted them to rethink their position. He proposed temporary rank for specialised positions, particularly the commandant of the Police Training School, who should be of officer rank.

After the stick, the carrot. At an international conference in Istanbul he spoke to members of 15 police forces. None required men to work 40 years to earn the maximum pension, or to work until they were 65. The force needed a better superannuation scheme, although the law at present was against it. He suggested they devise a better scheme themselves.

Barnett wanted a review of policewomen's salaries. He also promised 100 houses in the next year, 100 the following year, and less use of the police residence on call every hour of the day.

Consultation was his approach, so who had questions for him? Delegates took advantage of this precedent. Auckland's Sergeant H.C. Richardson asked if Barnett intended applying the promotion on merit policy to other appointments as well as to that of the commandant.

He would not at present, he replied, but he would keep talking about it until they came round to recognising the merit of merit promotion. Police in Britain were well used to it and were scathing of the New Zealand system based on seniority. Delegates must appreciate that some constables were better than others, some sergeants better than others.

'Of course,' said Mick Rodgers, 'one reason is that we have had no safeguards.' Barnett warned them that, whatever they were used to, he would be telling the incoming police to expect advancement on the basis of merit. He could not understand why good men should sit down and abide by the rules of seniority, but he accepted their resolute opposition for the time being.

Meltzer suggested amalgamating the house allowance into a basic salary package. Barnett agreed. Sergeant C.D. Taylor of Hamilton asked about traffic work done by the police. Barnett proposed a joint Justice/Police committee to reduce the bailiff work. Sergeant J.W. Thompson of Dunedin asked if Barnett favoured the monthly parades so long an irritation to shift workers. Barnett did, because they required senior men to see and meet their men.

Barnett was asked about textbooks and statutes being available at stations. He said the police were shockingly short of the tools of their trade, but now there was more money, they would get more tools. When Constable L.J. Brazier of Invercargill mentioned poorly tailored uniforms, Barnett agreed that, if stock did not fit, then a tailor could be used.

President Rodgers thanked Barnett for this unprecedented consultation. It would, he thought, have solved many problems in the past.

At this one gathering Barnett had broken down the iron division between the departmental head and his men. He went further, offering himself as a go-between if they had any complaints about officers denying them privileges.

In six months Holland and Barnett had turned the police around, creating harmony and high morale. Rodgers called it, in his annual presidential report, 'the most momentous year in our history'. Politicians of all persuasions, press and police in association, guild and administration were agreed that the force was back on an even keel. After a dodgy start, National had dipped into the consolidated fund, got its top personnel right, and was setting the association fair towards achieving the aspirations of men such as Constables Smith, Thom and Smyth and the reforming Labour leader Peter Fraser. The police were getting less of the lash and more of a fair crack of the whip.

New initiatives created new problems. Meltzer wrote to the new president, Cyril William Naylor, on 31 January 1956 briefing him about the one serious problem worrying Barnett—a shortage of sergeants. It was possible there would be 400 recruits coming in the next year, which would require 40 more sergeants. Where would they come from? Every qualified member of the force had been promoted. Meltzer suggested permanent sergeants, or making suitably regarded senior constables permanent sergeants before they passed their exams. It was a novel problem, but it did indicate the success of the recruiting campaign.

Barnett announced in April that staff were at 2041 and resignations down to a trickle. Two months later he was able to introduce the 11-day fortnight, the prelude to the five-day week. He was not, however, satisfied with this. He still worried that the new amity between administration and association would founder on the promotion by merit issue, and said so in his first annual report to Parliament. One change he had achieved with the approval of members was that exams were no longer tests of memorising law, but included an oral interview with a bench of examiners designed to assess personality, character and leadership qualities.

Barnett continued to be concerned that the police were alone in this or any public service, in clinging to the seniority system that promoted a man with a bare pass after 10 years of trying over the man who passed at first attempt. A personnel system had been set up and a training course for 26 senior officers, but the system did not identify the best. In his view, the state could not afford such a force when police work was becoming more intricate and its responsibilities increasing. The *Dominion* shared his concern. Its 30 August 1956 editorial wondered if the association might be seen by the public as the impediment in the path of Barnett's ideas of reform.

At the association conference that year Barnett told delegates there should be no more complaints about pay because the management committee had stretched him 'to the point of breaking'. He regarded their pension as their biggest problem now, and repeated his advice that they design their own scheme and fight for it. He insisted on the power to make temporary appointments for several months to circumvent the cumbersome system and to meet the urgent need for more sergeants. He would persist with oral examinations, despite President Naylor's objections, because the department wanted 'men, and not fellows who merely can acquit themselves in a written examination'.

At question time Meltzer led the objections to the oral exams, which, in at least two cases, had failed candidates who had passed the four written exams. He wanted a return to written exams, local superior officer assessment and the personnel branch opinion all placed before the Promotions Board.

Barnett disagreed. He had spoken to the three examiners, and was convinced that the written exam was getting worse as a means of testing a man's fitness for promotion. Accordingly, the written exam would count for less in promotion.

Meltzer hit back that young men were nervous about a set-up to which they were unaccustomed; it was unsatisfactory. Barnett was not sure whether a man aspiring to be sergeant should become upset. Meltzer pointed out that the standard of oral interviews varied. It only got tougher, Barnett replied, with candidates who were doing well, so examiners could see how good they might be. Meltzer asked for the results of written exams to be given to candidates before the oral, and a statement of what was expected in the interview. Barnett agreed to the second, but would not prejudice a sporting chance for everybody.

What was different about this exchange, apart from it signalling that the honeymoon was over for Barnett, was that delegates heard for the first time their general secretary in action. They could report back on his performance. It helped to dissipate the long-standing friction over the value Meltzer gave.

The press was more worried about the Prime Minister announcing at the conference a new pay scale that gave 19-year-olds joining the police £790 a year, when graduates entered the public service on £640. The *Dominion* rated the Police Association 'the most influential pressure group in New Zealand today'.

Meltzer replied that in Britain 40 years ago the Desborough Committee defined a policeman's special responsibilities and obligations which distinguished him from other public servants in regard to pay and pensions. A policeman's pay had to be high enough to prevent his succumbing to temptations that came his way. This was the formula on which all association representations were made. Meltzer had prepared 22 reasons why police were different. These included the risk of injury, liability to action for damages for wrongful arrest or other excess use of police powers, the call to duty at all hours, high standards of private conduct, restrictions on where an officer could live and what an officer could wear, denial of participation in politics, having to apply for permission to marry if below sub-inspector rank, restrictions on other employment for police and police wives. The PSA had agreed some years ago that the police had a special case for earlier retirement. The *Evening Post* obliged readers by publishing Meltzer's list on 15 October.

PSA President J. Ferguson was provoked to reply that Meltzer knew the improved pay was to get more police, not because the force was different. Ferguson noted other public service occupations with dangers and restrictions, and quoted Barnett, a few years before, saying that the job of a prison officer was 'infinitely more difficult' than that of a policeman.

Opposition speakers on 25 October attacked the government for allowing other youngsters in the public service to earn too low a salary by comparison with the police. None, however, took up Holland's challenge to say that the police were paid too much. Holland claimed that if you took out the average unpaid overtime of £200 worked by a police officer, the salaries were comparable.

When teachers demanded the same conditions as police, Holland wrote to them and to the press that police worked an 11-day fortnight of unlimited hours. If you took out overtime and a house allowance of about £525 some 19-year-old government tradesmen earned more. The teachers responded by inviting Holland to become their minister and spread some of the financial largesse their way.

There were claims in the press that the police pay caused a breakdown in armed forces pay negotiations and that public service clerical workers wanted comparable salaries to the police. The *Dominion* noted attacks on Meltzer for implying that the police had to have a higher standard of integrity than other public servants, but he was rated 'the most successful trade union secretary in New Zealand' and the association was acclaimed as 'shrewd enough to know that politicians are more amenable than an independent wage-fixing tribunal'. The *Public Service Journal* for November 1956 grumbled that Meltzer had done no service to his members by pretending the increases were due to special features of police work; he had made invidious comparisons in seeking to justify an increase that all state employees deserved.

Holland had had enough of being Police Minister. On 6 December, disregarding association pleas, he handed the portfolio over to Dean Eyre. The outside controller experiment had worked, he said, because of Barnett's personal qualities in creating a modern force. He left Barnett to complete the job.

On 25 March 1957 Barnett announced that the force was up to 2230, with 70 more recruits to reach full strength. He hoped to increase policewomen numbers. Meltzer defiantly repeated his view that the police must be considered in a special category different from all other government departments. A sub-committee would work with Barnett to ensure the 'hard won conditions and systems are not lost'.

In the August/September issue of the *Police Journal* Meltzer reminded all the new young readers they were reaping the benefit of 'much blood, sweat and tears by older members' such as the recently deceased former president Mick Rodgers. Now the push was on for a more favourable retiring policy.

Dean Eyre told his first association annual conference that the tidying up of pay scales which saw a constable move from £638 in 1950 to £1,000 today was fair relativity

Prime Minister Holland finally gets to inspect the thin blue line, a role, as their minister, the association had hoped he would have filled from the start of his administration

compared with other public servants if the public realised that 27 per cent of police pay was penal rates. Earlier retirement legislation was, he explained, still being studied. President Naylor expressed his disappointment at this but praised Barnett for giving the public an efficient force. He still had doubts about the oral exam, which was failing men who had passed the written test.

Barnett gave perhaps his most reform-minded address to the conference. He began with a eulogy to the late Mick Rodgers, an utterly decent man after whom one of the recruitment intakes would be named. He confessed he had taken his first licking over not getting earlier retirement through, but it was only the first round. He noted that Meltzer had now increased his list of differences between police and public from 22, when Barnett arrived, to 39 now. One difference was the unusual hours worked by police, isolating them from society and throwing them on their own resources more than most citizens. He was worried about the lack of healthy resources. Bowls, beer and idleness were not enough; department and staff must work together to make police leisure more useful. He was concerned that, apart from his work with Meltzer on the earlier retirement bill, there was so little contact between administration and association. He regretted that the management committee regarded every administration proposal with suspicion.

The single major difference between department and association remained promotion—the association wanting a man promoted unless, in Meltzer's words, 'his inefficiency is glaring'. Barnett did not think this attitude had a leg to stand on or any sympathiser 'outside your own ranks'. He believed in disposition of the force according to the usefulness of a member for a particular post. He wondered if the association was 'becoming somewhat reactionary' thinking it needed only the five-day week and 'a few trifling matters' to round off the programme of reform. He regarded it as a tragic mistake to raise young police officers in the old ways. The force must be dynamic and virile, able to adapt to change.

The conference dealt with its 'trifles', such as pre-focus torches, the return of tailor-made tunics, the purchase of welfare cottages and better boot allowances. Barnett returned for consultation time. When Meltzer again raised the subject of oral exams, Barnett said that somebody like himself could swot for the sergeant's exam, pass it and then be a sergeant!

Barnett then introduced Dr Blin Bull, recently retired from directing Army Medical Services, who was to set up a police medical service. When Meltzer asked Bull if he was introducing army standards, the doctor replied that there was no uniform standard throughout the country—a man could pass in Auckland one year and be turned down elsewhere. Men could serve 20 years without a medical check-up. The force required better medical supervision, but it would not be according to army practice. Good colour vision was essential, but standards had been allowed to drop in this area. The proposed three-year medical examination was to see if an officer was fit for duties, but it would also allow for early treatment of such conditions as a developing hernia, diabetes, even the impact of bunions and ingrown toenails, or the effects of hastily snatched meals. He hoped to introduce a chest x-ray. Barnett added that if there had been regular medical examinations, Mick Rodgers might be alive today. These checks represented not a rejection of individuals, but concern about their wellbeing.

On one day the conference adjourned to Trentham Training School for a conducted tour and to learn about the modernisation in police communications, notably in telephones, teleprinters and search and rescue equipment. The department would soon, Barnett announced, have a scientific officer.

Barnett's reforms were too frequent and too fast for the management committee, which shied away from him. On 18 April 1958 he wrote to Meltzer asking why there had been no visit since the last conference. Meltzer replied offhandedly that there was 'no particular problem to discuss' other than the five-day week, earlier retirement and injuries received while travelling to and from duty.

What Meltzer did not have to say was that the month after the conference the Labour Party returned to power and Barnett's days were numbered. His appointment was withdrawn in June so that departmental control could revert to a police officer, as promised. Superintendent Willis Brown of Dunedin was promoted above more senior officers due to retire, initially as Controller-General. At least there was promotion by merit at the top.

Barnett and the management committee did have a pleasant final meeting on 18 June, before Meltzer, too, was off—to Cardiff as New Zealand manager at the Empire Games. His *Journal* editorial that month was brief and cheery. He had checked Barnett's approach to promotion in the Supreme Court before Judge Hutchison on 14 and 15 May and got cancellation of Promotion Board recommendations for four commissioned appointments on the merit basis. Because district reports on these had not been maintained and referred to the Promotions Board under Police Regulations, they were invalid. Once again Meltzer had won by applying the letter of the regulation laws.

This, the culmination of months of association protest, was another reason why Barnett was kept at arm's length. Most vociferous had been Wellington district, which asked newspapers to publicise their dissatisfaction at Barnett's four merit promotions. The newspapers naturally concurred, but also editorialised that such lack of restraint put the force offside with the public. It smacked of militant unionism and an attempt to intimidate the administration.

The association perspective was more one of anxiety, at least among the present majority of members. Barnett had declared in the December *Police Bulletin* that promotion by merit was inevitable, the chief assurance of a competent police force and the greatest incentive 'to good and keen young men' who represented one-third of the force. It was the other two-thirds of older men, left out of Barnett's plans, who, naturally, protested at this perceived threat to their careers. Meltzer had taken their case to court, and the management committee representatives wasted no time telling new Police Minister Phil Connolly of their concern at promotion on merit as practised by Barnett. Meltzer went off to Cardiff saying he had his fingers crossed, hoping for the best.

With Meltzer away, the *Journal* published a short presidential report from Naylor looking forward to 'some stabilisation of the promotion system', as well as providing the five-day week and earlier retirement.

Former association president Bill Murray was Chief Superintendent at Auckland when he typed up for Barnett a brief history of the police from the days when commissioners ran the department at less cost than their predecessors. He rates Barnett as bringing in new ideas, rejuvenating buildings, replacing brown lino with carpet, changing the uniform from the lion-tamer braid days and bringing in a lighter summer outfit for the men, adding the ranks of chief inspector and chief superintendent, increasing wages and allowances. 'He was,' says Murray, 'the greatest reformer the police ever had.'

Perhaps Barnett's greatest achievement, from the association perspective, came after his quiet exit, when members' eyes were fixed firmly on the upcoming Police Bill on which Barnett and Meltzer had worked. Labour had changed little about the legislation, which introduced the eagerly awaited earlier retirement. One of its first beneficiaries was A. Carlyon, who wrote in the June 1959 *Police Journal* that it had taken a civilian administrator—Barnett—to win them earlier retirement, the amalgamation of pay and allowances and the 40-hour week. Carlyon credited Barnett with putting new life into a force that had for some time 'suffered sadly from lethargy'. Barnett had seen the need for houses to prevent constables from settling for a secure nine to five job instead of promotion and no house for 12 months. Now young constables crowded the exam rooms, while recruits learned in a first-class training school established by Barnett. The only problem for Barnett was promotion by merit.

Rob Butler, who joined the police in 1951, recalls the Compton era and those officers aligned with him remaining under a cloud. He remembers Barnett coming in with an open chequebook from the government. Butler says he brought a refreshing change to the top administration and got the police cracking, but was not accepted because he was an outsider. He was a hard case and enjoyed life, but he was a top-line administrator who gained the police recognition as people with whom the government had to be concerned rather than 'a necessary evil' who 'boxed on with the pittance they were being paid'.

Barnett eclipsed the association in the reform stakes, then the association eclipsed him in its reactionary resistance to promotion on merit. In the process the profile of Meltzer and the association expanded from being a minor domestic part of the Police Department to a major player on the industrial relations stage. Barnett had got them most of the pay and conditions they had sought for years. The police had needed the outsider more than the outsider needed them.

December, 1958 N.Z. POLICE JOURNAL 285

The New Zealand Police Journal

Official Organ of the New Zealand Police Association (Incorporated), Wellington, N.Z.

Published every Second Month
Registered Magazine.

Vol. 22.—No. 6

DECEMBER, 1958

Editorial

We are privileged to publish the following message from the Commissioner of Police (Mr. W. S. Brown):—

"The past year has been one of remarkable progress for the Police. With the introduction of the ten day fortnight and the provision under the Police Act for retirement at the age of sixty we have at last achieved our major objectives. However, much still remains to be done to improve conditions and efficiency.

The service is attracting a good type of candidate, we are now almost up to full strength, and morale is steadily improving.

It is most gratifying to know that the administration is assured of the goodwill and co-operation of the Association, which, since its inception, has proved its worth and more than justified its existence. We can now face the future confident in our ability to fulfill our duties and responsibilities to the public and the Government.

I send Christmas greetings to every member of the Police, and may the season's spirit of goodwill remain with you all throughout the New Year."

W. S. BROWN,
Commissioner

The next commissioner was Willis Brown, who was on the association's first management committee. Labour had kept its promise to bring back the commissioner, and the police were content once more to be run by one of their own.

Chapter Thirteen

The Pumped-Up Public Profile for the Police

The Police Act 1958 fulfilled the association's original aims—to a five-day, 40-hour week was added retirement at 60 on full superannuation. New Minister Phil Connolly invited association delegates to Parliament for a social hour, which Meltzer said was 'very favourably received'. Indeed he thought the police 'look to be in good shape, and the barometer seems to be set fair'. On 1 December Willis Brown assumed the title of commissioner. A member of the original management committee, he ushered in the same kind of stable few years Young had brought the police in the early 1950s.

Meltzer and the management committee sub-committee had worked closely with Police Solicitor Jack Dwyer in preparing the legislation. The association got exactly what it had always asked for, defined so extensively by Meltzer in his 1944 submission to the Superannuation Board. Seven years of service in the police would count as eight years for superannuation purposes. Every police officer who had joined at 20 would have each year count as a year and a bit, not exceeding one-seventh, to bring the officer up to 40 years' service at the age of 60. A person who joined at 22 would have each year rate as one year and one-nineteenth of a year, to make up the two missing years. Someone joining at 25 would have the appropriate mathematical adjustment made. All police were required to join the scheme. The new arrangements would, Connolly told the association conference that year, cost the government £200,000 out of the Superannuation Fund over the next 20 years.

Other major changes included simplifying promotions to one right of appeal against any recommendation of the Promotions Board; abolition of the Police Council, which had never been in session; merging of the Board of Appeal, which heard disciplinary charges, with the Police Force Promotions Appeal Board; injuries received journeying to and from work to be considered as having arisen in the course of employment, an area where the police led the public service. And police could stand for Parliament, provided the candidate took leave during the campaign and resigned if elected.

Brown's value as an experienced policeman was apparent at the 1959 association conference. He said statistics showed that most offences were committed between 4 pm and midnight, but staff disposition did not reflect this. An example from one country station was four staff rostered from 1 pm to 5 pm and only one staff member on duty after 5 o'clock. The five-day week would mean the end of one-person suburban stations as manpower was used to best advantage. There would be an amalgamation of stations and the public would have to get used to the mobile station, the patrol car. Medical examinations had justified the association push for earlier retirement; one-third of constables over 60 had been shown to be unfit for duty.

The conference was concerned about civilians in the police not being under the commissioner's control. They were chosen by the public service, passed through and were promoted out of the police. Such a situation was not conducive to harmony and efficiency. There was, said new President Gideon Tait, a problem of divided loyalty.

Sneaking into this conference was a harbinger of the 1960s climate, when Wanganui delegate G.R. Gillespie referred to adverse press publicity. He was concerned at the press habit of naming former members of the force as such if they were brought up on a charge, so bringing the police into disrepute. It was sniping at the force merely for news value. Meltzer said the commissioner was to address the Newspaper Proprietors' Association shortly and he would raise the matter. It was to no avail. Press interest in any police connection, particularly where force was involved, coincided with the 1958 act eliminating the word 'Force' from what was to be henceforward the New Zealand Police Service. Meltzer wrote an editorial on the subject, tracing the line from Astynomi city police of ancient Athens controlling flute girls and female harp performers, through the tythingmen, the watchmen of Shakespeare's time, the Bow Street runners, peelers and cops, all fulfilling the same role of preserving law and order. He personally liked the name 'Police Force', although he recognised the sinister implications of the modern 'police State'. The difference, he concluded, was that there was now a vast improvement in the conditions of the guardians of law and order.

Meltzer concentrated, in these mellow times, on bolstering the conservative association stand on promotion by merit. He filled the *Journal* with dire warnings from abroad of junior personnel placed over seniors, with consequent breakdown of morale. It was conceded that the Promotion Board was not unduly disturbing, since few juniors were preferred. The commissioner was not sure that the Promotions Board was 'quite sure of itself'. Brown indicated that an improved personal reporting system was needed to make promotion on merit work, but he carefully acknowledged that the administration would have to earn the confidence of members.

As the 1960s were about to dawn the minister confessed he did not know, until the association told him, that policewomen got no further increments after three years; the matter would have to be looked into. He also shared the president's view that newspapers tended to headline anything which reflected unfavourably on the police, such as handling of arrested persons. Two Christchurch cases had been particularly disturbing to the association. In one a defence lawyer wished a civil claim in which a constable was involved to be heard before a parallel criminal charge; in another the complainant had lost a tooth while being arrested for obstructing the footpath. In both cases the press had had a field day, in both cases the complainants had not proceeded with claims for damages. The police were regarded by the press as a cheap means of gaining public attention. There was much worse to come.

In 1960 the association repeated its concern about members being passed over by the promotion system and civilians being employed in a job that could be done by a member. However one-term president Gideon Tait summed up the association position as one of high morale following the major reforms. Meltzer must have agreed, for he accepted the departmental offer to write a history of the New Zealand Police, later having to withdraw because of his bad eyesight, and took accumulated annual leave of six months to travel abroad from April to October 1961. Connolly announced a new pay scale and Meltzer, too, got a rise, moving up to the salary level of an assistant commissioner with one year of service. The fighting fund or reserve fund was dropped, reflecting the calmer waters in which the association found itself.

The mild nature of 1961 was further suggested in the shortest presidential report yet by new incumbent Senior Sergeant Harry Richardson. It noted deaths, membership, finances, regretted the appeal lost by a Christchurch policewoman against her fitness for duty, which the association had supported. Sadly, Richardson died during his second term.

The conference that year was delayed until Meltzer's return. The three November days were dominated by the new go-getting commissioner, Les Spencer, another of the original management committee, but now eager to continue the Barnett reforms. Brown had been a solid policeman with a heart of gold, well liked by everybody. Spencer was more interested in modernising and improving efficiency than in making friends.

Meltzer wanted to know if the rumour was true that Spencer would not allow right of appeal against appointment to the rank of superintendent, even though it was not strictly association business. The association was jealous of appeal rights for which it had fought so hard. Spencer replied that he did not want any restrictions on choosing the best man and that the guild had not objected. When Meltzer reminded him of the only recently repealed Section 9 denying right of appeal against dismissal, the commissioner said he would retain his right until a personal reporting system was established in about three years' time. Meltzer challenged him to revoke the measure before he retired. Spencer said he very likely would.

Meltzer was still in dogged mood, a terrier where a serving police officer might hesitate to worry at the commissioner. He snapped again when Richardson asked about acting sergeants and Spencer said he could not see one going to a station ahead of a qualified sergeant. Meltzer pointed out that there was one, at Tauranga. Spencer denied it was his decision.

Early in 1962 rumours were published in newspapers of police concern at sudden dismissals and transfers. Spencer was quoted denying this. *Truth*, on 14 March, cited three Canterbury police and another in a small North Island town who were dismissed, and an East Coast policeman claiming 'Gestapo' tactics in police surveillance of other police. A plain-clothes 'stranger' was allegedly moving around reporting on 'dud cops'. *Truth* said Spencer was new in his job. Investigations within the police established that there was no truth in the rumours published by the paper.

The 1962 conference was a low-key affair. Through the year Meltzer had been promoting a compulsory subscription to the Sports Council so that the police would cease to be the 'poor relation' in services sports organisations. Not enough members were as keen as Meltzer, who said the words 'police' and 'sport' should be synonymous, so the conference declared that the sub would be levied but a refund would be available. At successive conferences this compulsory sub continued to be unpopular. Rob Butler believed its effect, overall, was to wake the department up to the value of sport, which had previously been left to the individual, providing a police team identity and giving those who could not afford sport on their own the opportunity to participate instead of lolling about in barracks.

Auckland delegate Senior Sergeant A.J. Johnston brought up a request from two women members that they get equal pay as women in the public service did. Constable J.J. Charnley of Hamilton said policewomen did a good job there on patrol, enquiries, race duty, hotels (in the company of a male sergeant) and with female prisoners arrested at night. Delegates voted, however, to leave the women's pay at 80 per cent of male pay unless the department advocated equality.

Auckland continued to hammer this message at the next conference, pointing to policewomen with 21 years' service earning £45 less than a 21-year-old first year constable. There was sporadic support. Wanganui delegate Constable H.T. Surgenor said that two of his district's women's division did the same work as men for less pay. There were too few women, however, to win over the association, and it was left to the equal rights legislation to bring them equal pay.

Spencer told the conference that he wanted to introduce into the service advances he had seen abroad. One was information, for which he wanted to bring over a man retired from the New South Wales Criminal Registration Branch. He was also after a supply transport officer experienced in ordering and preparing reports for Treasury, something nobody in the police could do. He agreed to Meltzer's request that the jobs be advertised here too but, like Barnett, he suggested that the association not be suspicious of those in administration, who were workers in the same show.

Meltzer signalled his intention to stand down once another secretary was found. In the meantime he had to

OLD BILL BLODGER SAYS FAREWELL

Well, my shift is nearly over, and I'm headin' out to pastures new,
Where I'll buy myself a shade in "strides" that's not for ever blue.
No more heart aches. No more head pains.
No more nagging please explains.
And I'm leaving all behind—with no regrets.

I have worked with many "cobbers." I have had my ups and downs.
I have seen good men succumber, to the bark of bumptious clowns.
I have signed my last report sheet.
Had my last turn 'round the street.
And I've closed the office door with no regrets.

It's many, many years ago, I signed those dotted lines.
I've had my brighter moments, and I've had my moans and whines.
I've hung my hand-cuffs on the bracket.
The old 'phone has ceased its racket.
And I'm walking out the gate—with no regrets.

Through forty years of duty, I think I've earned my 'screw.'
I've rarely trod on many corns, and my enemies are few.
I've dragged the streams. I've searched the ranges.
Witnessed good and "other" changes.
And I'm signing off today with no regrets.

I've seen my share of criminals, and booked in quite a few.
But have never changed my theory, that in crime there's little new.
And of times an act of kindness
Will assist and help the spineless.
Though it leaves an empty cell—with no regrets.

No more mileage sheets and vouchers, no more trips to run and take.
On fabricated figures, that the so-called "experts" fake.
No more roads of endless rubble.
No more pot-holes, slush and trouble.
For my car is now my own—with no regrets.

No more hunting down a debtor, like an evil, stalking ghoul.
To execute a Warrant, for a debt collecting Pool.
No more Judgment, Writs and Orders,
No more notes from Court Recorders,
For my Process Book is closed—with no regrets.

No more delving in the cob-webs, for Gazettes of ancient dates,
To record, another luckless Sykes, has reached the Pearly Gates.
Information most important be assured,
But the kind of Sunday pastime, most abhorred.
I have thumbed my last Gazette—with no regrets.

To all those who seek promotion, this old Cop extends his best,
May you climb the Jacob's ladder to that golden chair of rest?
But make sure your seat is stable,
And your grip is firm and able.
For the others climbing up—have no regrets.

When you reach the age of sixty, and are on your final round,
Just think of all the "pals" you've made, and all the friends you've found.
They'll remind you how they'll miss you.
Then they'll wrangle for your pew.
And some may even see you go—with no regrets.

Not all are superhuman. Some may fail to make the grade.
But rest an easy conscience, son, if you've earned what you've been paid.
Forget your problems, woes and sorrow.
Keep your eyes fixed on the morrow.
And you'll look back on those years—without regrets.

You are in a fine old Service, but of new ideas beware,
For no man can police a district, from his padded office chair.
There are times you'll tread the border,
To maintain good law and order,
If you wish to end your time—with no regrets.

MORE RECRUITS ARE NEEDED FOR THE POLICE

A more amiable line in doggerel for a more relaxed period in association history

THE WOES OF CONSTABLE BLODGER

(Years ago "Makatua Bill" delighted readers with his Constable Blodger contributions. He has suddenly sprung to life again.)

Seated in his station office
Old Bill Blodger ruminates
On the wrongs and rights of policemen
And all things that, agitates.
Strewn across his ink-smeared table
Are reports and forms galore
And the one on—Superannuation
Seems prominently to the fore.
It is clear that Bill is worried
Scraps of paper strew the floor,
And he mumbles to the ink pot
As he tries to add the score.
Now, two-thirds of what I'm gettin'
At a thousand quid a year
With PAY-E and "perks" extracted
Hum—not much is left I fear.
Now if four and three are seven
And that seven and one make eight
Bill adds a couple of figures—Grunts,
And shakes his old bald pate.
Well if that's me flamin' pension
After all these years of strife,
It leaves nothing for the barman
And darn little for the wife.
Many years have passed since Blodger
And the old Sarge on the beat
Used to amble down "gay" Queen Street
To the measured tramp of feet.
Now the old Sarge has passed onward
To that berth—good policemen—fill
But his portrait near the window
Still stares sternly down at Bill.
With one final last erasure
The papers go back in the drawer
And Bill turns to face the photo,
As in years, he's done before.
Well, Sarge, 'tis getting near the finish
And my "shift" is nearly through,
It has had it's knotty problems
But we've "made it"—thanks to you.
We "flogged" the beat together
We reformed that backblock town,
And tho' you didn't last the distance
Your advice was worth a Crown.
They can have their forty hours,
Their statistics, facts and time,
But they'll find out in the long run
It's the Cop that solves the crime.
Writing memo's in some office
Till a man has writer's cramp
Will do naught to catch the forger
Or detect the sexual scamp.
When we tramped the streets at midnight
Ne'er a Teddy Boy was there,
For a baton 'round his breeches
Taught him how to cut his hair.
And the cow-boys" at the milk bar
With their female "hangers-on"
Did not need a Braille translation
When they heard your . . "Come, Move On!"
But those old ways now seem altered,
Perhaps we're getting too much pay.
That, I suppose would change our outlook,
Make us sort of coy and gay.
Old Bill leans back in his armchair
Thumbs the warts upon his ears
And his thoughts dwell on the by-gones
Of those long forgotten years.
When the "screw" was near a fiver
And you worked the clock around
But although the "perks" were scanty
A policeman stood his ground.
Sarge . . . The old days are forgotten
When we kept the peace by night
And if the effort raised a "shiner"
Well, no questions came to light.
When the Stokers oiled their boilers
And Big Shine came off his boat,
You hadn't time to thumb the text book,
It was swing your right . . . or float.
But now the old order changeth,
The pen is mightier than the sword.
Sarge, I think the job has had it,
And a Cop's not worth his board.
Did the eyes in that portrait twinkle?
Perhaps it just seemed that way,
And the light distort the features
As if the Sarge, was trying to say.
Blodger—You contentious old humbug,
Will you never cease to growl?

run hard to keep up with the commissioner, who was using the press directly to get across his message about police presenting a more pleasant and polite public image. In 1963 Meltzer went with Spencer to a United Nations seminar in Canberra, where the commissioner presented a paper on 'Human Rights and Police'. Spencer argued against politicians being involved in the police, and police in politics. Meltzer clashed publicly with New South Wales Commissioner of Police Allan over his denying the police federation there any political affiliation.

In August 1963 Meltzer successfully appealed against Spencer's dismissal of three Palmerston North policemen involved in after-hours drinking and brawling. Spencer had not gone through Police Regulations procedures, denying the men the basic right of defending themselves.

Spencer was bypassing the association in other respects by inviting suggestions from police for improvements. Over 60 were handled by the Research and Planning Division, one of his modernising thrusts, along with the Criminal Registration Bureau, the Welfare Section and an in-service training scheme to improve standards in the uniform branch.

One of Spencer's techniques was to tell conferences that he used to feel the same as them until he joined the administration. When Sergeant L.F. Smith of Invercargill told him he thought exams were conducted only to find out what you didn't know, Spencer said he had felt like that, and had once taken carbon copies to prove it, and given them to Meltzer. The general secretary said they were good answers, but not to the questions asked. Spencer's concern was low pass rates suggesting that the exams were too tough. He wanted to see if in-service training raised standards. He also reassured members that the Welfare Section was 'not a Gestapo'; on the contrary, it was there as a confidential place to discuss any official or domestic problem. The *Police Journal* published the role of welfare officers as counsellors and visitors of sick staff. Rob Butler said the department was at last taking from the association some responsibility for welfare concerns.

Spencer promised to support the association's 1963 claim to Treasury for a 10 per cent pay rise, but he wanted them to know it would be a tough claim to achieve.

A week after the conference the first anti-vice squad was set up in Christchurch. According to the Christchurch

Commissioner Les Spencer, left, took over in 1961 dedicated to continuing Barnett's administrative reforms. On this occasion he appreciates Jack Meltzer's remarks, at the farewell for Chief Superintendent Jim Graham, right

Press, its first major haul was five constables, instead of the anticipated US servicemen. The Greymouth branch of the association protested to Meltzer about 'unwarranted' publicity in the *Press* when the commissioner had announced that no laws had been broken. Meltzer promised to pass the Greymouth letter on to the commissioner, but said there was little he could do about the newspapers. Spencer was concerned to find the member in Christchurch who tipped off the media. He was never nabbed.

The police got a much better press out of their 20-man peace-keeping force in Cyprus. Meltzer was right behind this preventive action as 'the greatest historical achievement of Sir Robert Peel's British Police' concept. Once they were there, Meltzer had to push the commissioner to get the men a special allowance to cope with the excessive costs of local beer and soft drinks; it was necessary to drink 8 pints of liquid a day and the local water was unsafe. He gained the Australian contingent's per diem allowance of 30s for married men and £1 for single, despite arguing that both should get the same allowance in this unprecedented situation.

The 1964 conference passed a remit that a constable entering the police at 19 could retire after 35 years instead of waiting until the age of 60. This was intended to set up the push for retirement at 55.

Although Auckland delegate Brian Mooney thought this a little too radical, he revolutionised proceedings with his 18-page Auckland sub-committee review of the pay scale. Tables showed that the police had once more fallen behind, that the special nature of the police had again been lost sight of, that police were resigning for better paid jobs and that the wrong kind of recruits were coming in. The commitment the association made over a decade ago not to seek overtime or penal rates in exchange for the amalgamation package did not mean, he argued, that it could not make representations about pay and conditions. He called for a committee of inquiry into pay and conditions following the rejection of their 1963 10 per cent claim. His remit, one of 21 dealing with pay scales, was passed.

The conference welcomed the new personal reporting system it had largely designed but got in a huff about the commissioner vowing, in the press, to weed 'bullies and brutes' out of the police. He had, however, subsequently regretted the remark and Constable Kelk's remit taking exception was lost.

The association this year demonstrated its more outward-looking posture by making friendly contact with the International Police Association, founded in Britain and counting 25 branches. It aimed to promote friendship between serving and retired members of the world's police.

The *Journal* was trimmed from six to four issues in 1964, but Meltzer claimed that this did not indicate 'a state of seeming inaction'. He was proved right the next year when the association call for a committee of inquiry was met by the surprise government announcement that instead they would have a police tribunal. Police Minister Percy Allen told them he did not want recommendations from any body with two police on it and no government representation. He also did not want toing and froing between police administration and Cabinet.

Spencer had been bypassed by the association, so he told them not to blame him for now having to put the employer's case against the association and guild claims. Allen gave Meltzer all the credit for proposing and pushing through recognition of the police as a special category, in that this tribunal was only for police. Meltzer advised members to be extremely cautious in accepting this major change that put the association at the crossroads. He suggested there should be no hurry.

The year was another busy one for Meltzer, smoothing down ruffled association feathers about rough publicity. The 7 April 1965 *Truth* billboard, 'Detective's Affair with

New Zealand Police as part of the peace-keeping force in Cyprus, in Meltzer's view the flowering of the British police model followed by New Zealand

Members of the Sixth Contingent.

Butcher's Wife', upset Timaru members. Both Meltzer and Spencer went to see the editor of *Truth*, who defended the article as dealing with a man on the police payroll during the court case and one who still called himself a detective, in a private capacity. Meltzer argued that the editor had the same duty as every citizen 'to protect the dignity and reputation of the Police'. The editor promised to consider this and in the next issue printed a small item informing readers that the commissioner and the general secretary of the Police Association wished it to be known that the detective concerned had resigned from the police. The department renewed its efforts to have legislation passed that private detectives be registered, and Meltzer joined in.

On 7 May the Christchurch branch met to deplore Spencer being quoted in the Christchurch *Press* as saying detectives were underpaid. This, it was felt, created disharmony between the detective and uniformed branches, and was typical of the unwise publicity emanating from the commissioner's office which undermined morale and damaged the public image. This time the commissioner denied some of the statements attributed to him. Meltzer told the Christchurch branch that Spencer regretted any ill feeling engendered, but he reminded the commissioner of 'the necessity for greater care when talking to reporters'.

On 23 June 1965 *Truth* came out with its infamous billboard, 'Cop Took Stripper to Park After Dark'. *Truth* had a field day reporting on this lower court hearing. An undercover constable on assignment in a Wellington coffee bar was found by colleagues 'clutching a pair of woman's tight black slacks'. The charge was that a coffee bar assistant procured a woman to have sexual intercourse with a male, namely the undercover cop. The damage was done in the opening paragraph: 'Constable lost stripper's panties, but held on to her slacks.'

Palmerston North branch informed Meltzer that the constable, aged 40, married with a teenage son and daughter, had done his duty. He was not called to refute the evidence of the unnamed stripper that he touched her private parts. The constable was made to appear in the article a philanderer, the billboard suggested he was in serious trouble, he was referred to as a 'cop', the matter was humiliating and degrading and 'directly affects his wife and family'. The branch wanted the matter referred to the commissioner and an endeavour made to prevent the paper publishing billboards connected with police doing their duty.

Meltzer replied that the commissioner was making representations, that he too objected to the word 'cop', that there was no love lost between him and the publication concerned. If it was a true account of court proceedings, however, it was doubtful that anything could be done to prevent its publication. Spencer was seeing the Crown Prosecutor to ask him, in the Supreme Court proceedings, to call the woman before the constable, so that he could contradict her evidence. It would give the policeman the opportunity to assert his own dignity. The commissioner was pursuing similar cases and in others, such as where a policewoman was used to trap an abortionist, he sought court suppression of the officer's name. On 10 July *Truth* reported the Supreme Court case, naming both constable and stripper and giving their different versions. The prosecutor had called the stripper first. The commissioner informed Meltzer later in the month that he was issuing instructions that police seek name suppression in such cases.

New association president Rob Butler paid tribute at the conference to the 'remarkable dedication and exceptional service' of Jack Meltzer, who would retire at the next conference. Minister Allen referred to Meltzer as a hard man to bargain with, but none could be straighter in pressing claims and fighting for what he believed was just and right. He had always found Jack amiable and forthright, and he left behind a solid organisation.

The conference proposed changing a journal that had not altered its cover since the first issue. Meltzer declared himself attached to it, and Constable Kelk argued against Meltzer having to change format in his last year. A remit was passed to consider changing the format.

This conference was dominated by dissatisfaction over exams, particularly the 17 per cent pass rate in the Police and Detective Duty paper. Delegates called for a committee of inquiry, but Meltzer argued that this would antagonise the commissioner, counselling instead courteous and restrained discussions.

Spencer later defended these exams as necessary to meet changing conditions. He justified Meltzer's warning by saying that he regarded being challenged about those he appointed to deal with exams as a reflection on his integrity. He had the examination board run by a lawyer to avoid any suggestion that he was influencing promotion. To him the exams were of the same difficulty as School Certificate and police should regard themselves as extramural students. Success boiled down to how much work members did and how well they applied themselves. However, the association pressure resulted in the March 1966 *Journal* printing examination answers supplied by the department to indicate what failed, passed and achieved high marks. At last members had some kind of examination model.

In this March issue Meltzer began his last year by advising members to take one or two specific salary claims to the Police Tribunal rather than any overall salary claim. Auckland agitation was so bad, however, that in April Meltzer and the management committee executive went there to hear Mooney make a case, then sought a £2 10s a week increase from the tribunal. Meltzer reminded the tribunal of its statutory obligation to regard 'the special conditions of service applicable to the police'. He was bowing out with his long campaign to have the police recognised as a special case legislated for and in practice.

Meltzer signed off in the September *Journal* with the comment that the 'Police Service is the bulwark against a deterioration of our standards'. He had realised the hopes expressed in his first edition of April 1940 for 'happy cooperation between members'.

At 5.30 pm on 12 October 1966, the second day of the 31st annual conference, in the National Party Centre in

The *Truth* poster that confirmed the press fascination with any news involving the police, no matter the personal consequences to those publicised. The association fought hard to protect its members from such unwanted and unwarranted attention

Hunter Street in Wellington, Jack Meltzer was farewelled. Prime Minister Keith Holyoake and Opposition leader Norman Kirk were among the guests. The association and Meltzer 'have become synonymous', said President Butler, and that was why he was being retained as a consultant. Meltzer had seen the association grow from 1400 to 2700 members. He had led the fight for the 40-hour, five-day week, been mainly responsible for the Sickness Benefit Fund, had drafted police legislation culminating in recognition of the special conditions of service. His visits to police establishments in other countries had brought a fresh approach to association thinking. His visit to the office of the Danish Ombudsman was followed by representations to Parliament to establish a local Ombudsman. His prowess with a pistol was reflected in the Meltzer trophy for pistol shooting at the Police Training School. He had received an MBE in 1957, and this year an OBE for services to the association and other community work, including secretaryship of the Crippled Children Society. He had put his heart and soul into his job.

Justice Minister Ralph Hanan said he had been waiting 15 years to take back a remark that Meltzer was 'driving the Government up the wall'. He had said Meltzer only wanted a pay increase for the police because his own was based on that of a sergeant and he stood to benefit. Since then the police had gone from strength to strength. Meltzer had done a tremendous job in improving relations with successive governments.

Meltzer replied that after such encomiums he was brought down to earth by a letter recently addressed to 'Police Ass, Wellington', which had no difficulty in reaching him. He paid tribute to the women in his life, who included that remarkable band, the country policemen's wives. He had served under four Prime Ministers, six ministers, seven commissioners and 14 association presidents. He had always felt that the door was open and recalled no rancour, not even towards Hanan.

Assistant Commissioner Urquhart mentioned the time in the early 1950s when a lesser man would have gone to the wall. Meltzer acknowledged that he had been thrust into a leadership role—'if I had wiggled my finger one way instead of the other this country could have seen something happen which one would not want to think about'. He paid tribute to Prime Minister Holland's tact, kindness and wisdom in bringing them through that difficult period. During that time Mrs A. Meltzer used to tell friends she almost had to make an appointment to see her husband. Asked if she had ever considered divorce she said no, 'but murder, often'. The couple were two months away from

Meltzer a few years before his retirement, speaking at a 1963 United Nations seminar in Canberra. He upset a local police chief by challenging his right to deny his men political affiliation, yet back in New Zealand Meltzer was urging caution and conciliation in all dealings with the administration. Meltzer, warmly farewelled at the 31st association annual conference, in reply judged that he was leaving a well-contented and efficient service—and it had been far from that when he arrived their 40th wedding anniversary.

Meltzer had written in 1943 that the post-war world could hope for success only if police preventive principles were adopted in international relations. This was happening in Cyprus, and the New Zealand Police Association was playing a part. He saw it as our 'most valuable contribution to civilisation'. His own fulfilment was in seeing 'an efficient, happy, well-contented and well-orientated Police force, morally clean and comparable with world standards'. He said he would always have 'a love and affection for the members of the New Zealand Police Association'.

Jack Meltzer had made a considerable contribution to the Police Service he described, even if he preferred the old word 'force'. After an astonishing 27 years in the job, the assembled members and guests applauded off the stage the little big man in association history.

Chapter Fourteen

The Triumphs of the New Tandem Team

David Clifford Lee took over as general secretary on 1 November 1966, the first former policeman in the job. He was brought in to achieve radical changes in association style and housekeeping, but the change had begun a few years before when Rob Butler was elected president. Butler and Lee worked in tandem to shake up and streamline the association through the mid-1960s.

Butler had grown up in Palmerston North keen to be a physical education teacher. He missed out on that when he failed the required University Entrance exam by a few per cent in one subject. When he was in Auckland on holiday his uncle, with the wharf police for many years, suggested that the boy try his profession. Rob agreed and was accepted.

There was nothing radical about his politics. Like many police, he always voted National, and believed capital punishment should have been retained when it was abandoned in 1961. He was, however, a different breed from the old-style liberal Jack Meltzer and, indeed, from most of the management committee. When Butler became a committee member he characterised the dozen men serving on it as a cross-section of go-getters and figureheads from suburban and country stations and the plain-clothes branch. They were happy to let Meltzer run the association, and by now Meltzer was running it in low gear. Butler remembers that Meltzer, above all else, wanted things to run smoothly; it was difficult to sway him from this approach. The secretary spent a lot of his time going around the country helping members with legal aid in disciplinary charges such as being held accountable for prisoner monies going astray or being involved in traffic accidents.

Typical of Meltzer's cautious approach, in Butler's view, was the situation, in 1960, when a Tauranga citizen wanted to show his appreciation of the police by giving them some land. Meltzer and the president went up to see the man.

The three secretaries of the association, from the left Jack Meltzer, Ian Campbell and new 1966 secretary Dave Lee, the first policeman in the job, although he aspired to the lawyer status of his two colleagues

Jack decided against accepting the land because it might be seen as the police taking a gift and that 'was not on'. Meltzer would not even countenance a token payment for the land, lest the police administration disapprove. The offer lapsed.

When Butler came on to the management committee in 1961, a lot of members were, he says, under the impression that the office bearers were quite ineffective and that Meltzer ran the association as he wished. It did not help that nobody had stayed long in the president's chair over recent years. Butler says that, in later years, Meltzer did not push too hard for better pay and conditions.

In 1964 Butler was urged to stand for president, a position that had had six incumbents in the last decade. Although Butler was in the CIB, it was the uniformed branch and Wellington district members of the management committee who wanted him to stand.

'There was discontent about the activities and the approach of the association,' Butler says,

> and I was getting vocal about a few things, especially the discontent felt that we were not being forceful enough in making representations over mainly better pay and better conditions of service. There was a move for new blood at the top, someone who might change our approach and make the Association become more recognised by the administration. I leapfrogged over the senior and junior vice-presidents, who are usually the stage to becoming president. It was thought Jack was not forceful enough, content to roll along, not pushing the Association views strongly enough. Members wanted office bearers to become more involved in representations to the administration, the Minister and the Prime Minister, if necessary. I came in on the head of that wave.

Butler was in charge of the Crime Prevention Unit, on the same floor as the commissioner. This cancelled the need for letters; he simply crossed the carpet to the commissioner's office. And Les Spencer would come out, tell him what he was going to propose and sound him out on what the association might think of it. Butler says Spencer was a direct man. They had a few verbal confrontations, but once they were done with, Spencer would suggest a drink.

In Butler's first year as president the administration introduced in-service training. Butler remembers this as the beginning of the modern organisation. The job was becoming more sophisticated and criminal activity more difficult to detect and handle, yet the supervising officers who had passed exams had no training and were sadly lacking. In-service training was ad hoc and many floated through the job without an adequate knowledge of their duties. The association welcomed the change. Butler could see, too, that the association itself must modernise.

The oppportunity came the following year when the secretary's job was advertised. Police Prosecutor Graeme Dallow had applied for and been given the job, but in October 1966 declined because it meant no better pay than he was already getting. Butler knew the man for the job, one of his staff in Christchurch. 'Dave Lee, obviously had the ability and his capacity for work was phenomenal.'

The pay was equivalent to an inspector's, and Lee had not achieved that rank. He doubtless would have done so soon, for he had quite an array of qualifications. He had been an Inland Revenue Department clerk, an army lieutenant, a member of the 1957 intake of 30 men recruited directly into the CIB and, after eight years in the job, was a detective sergeant and the first fulltime crime prevention officer in Christchurch. He had three commendations for courses passed and a murder investigation, and no marks against him. He described himself as an average detective, but a lover of administration. He had a law degree and units towards a bachelor of commerce in bookkeeping, secretarial practice and company law. A character reference from his Christchurch superior described him as 'a very competent organiser and a tireless worker', but the recommendation of his Wellington boss, Butler, coupled with his qualifications, no doubt swung the job for him. Thirteen of the 15 districts approved his appointment, only Auckland wanted wider advertising of the job.

Lee had his probationary six months through 1966. Butler recalls Meltzer as being fearful of the new Police Tribunal, preferring to carry on without additional hurdles. When Lee took over, Butler says, he quickly tackled 'all the prime problems of pay and conditions'.

Lee's first editorial in December 1966 set the tone. He referred to Meltzer's three eras of association history: the Taboo Period, when the very existence of the association was regarded with suspicion; the Tolerance Period; then the Togetherness Phase, when the administrators had all been members of the association and accepted its role in contributing to an efficient and contented service. Lee now added the Tribunal Phase, when salaries and allowances would be determined by a body independent of government, to whom the association could plead its case. This and editorials to come were longer than those Meltzer wrote, and they concentrated on pragmatic matters. They aimed to achieve what Lee concluded his first editorial by vowing to do—get on with the job.

It was an auspicious bull's-eye for Lee to target the tribunal as the key to a contented and full-strength police service. The old problem of increasing resignations had re-emerged—207 in the year to the 1966 conference, up 28 on the previous year. Recruiting intakes were not full either, and for the same reason—salaries were slipping behind those paid to the rest of the community. Cops were voting with their feet. The government solution was to build up numbers on the cheap, by trying to recruit at schools and overseas.

The government had finally accepted equal pay for policewomen, but churlishly required equal performance. Policewomen were to carry batons. Auckland district, at the 1966 conference, objected to this as a retrograde step in the view of policewomen past and present. Auckland delegate Brian Mooney noted that the commissioner had exhorted equal treatment for women officers, yet women police had not been assaulted in the past. If they carried a baton they would be subject to the risk of physical violence.

Meltzer made the most of his last hurrah. Not only did

President Rob Butler, fourth right, and Dave Lee on the other side of Meltzer. Lee and Butler formed a winning combination for the association, as they had already done in police crime prevention. On Butler's right John Kuzmich, Brian Toomey and Dan Ingram. On Butler's left Jim Fleming, Meltzer, Waho Tibble, Steve Rusbatch, Lee, Bernard O'Shea, Ian Mills, Bill Brien, George Gilmour and Peter Gentry

he talk the delegates out of voting to reintroduce capital punishment, but he made an impassioned speech against the baton risk to women. This was the old High Tory liberal in full cry. Most districts were with him on this. Mooney suggested that the administration had been too literal about equality and was not being practical. Eventually the administration did retreat from its position.

Lee proceeded apace with his practical approach, he and Butler taking his submissions on penal rates and overtime to the Police Tribunal. On 17 February 1967 the tribunal formally approved the association application to increase the built-in overtime allowance. This resolved the arbitrary nature of the allowance from as far back as 1948. What was paid now reflected actual working conditions. The government agreed to over 90 per cent of the association application.

With Lee providing the expertise, Butler says the association had simply to prove its case to the tribunal's satisfaction and the government was bound by the decision. Under the old system it had not mattered how strong a case the association mounted; the administration presented its case, with the idea always in the back of its mind that the government could not afford what was being requested.

Butler also credits Lee's solid research with winning the association the extra week of leave and something he was personally grateful for in the CIB, the plain-clothes allowance. He remembers the commissioner telling him the association had no show on this one, but they 'bolted in'. Butler believes this was because Lee's arguments could not be countered.

It was as a number cruncher that Lee was most effective. It was time, he told members, to make a case for adjusting basic salaries, which did not compare favourably with rates in outside employment. This had led to the current crisis in recruiting and resignations. Methodically Lee set about assembling a case demonstrating that the increase since 1948 had been only 15 per cent for overtime and penal rates, when the true value of the increase was 23.5 per cent.

His statistical charts were new and irresistible. One chart, used again and again, compared a member on overtime allowance incorporated into salary with a member paid actual overtime worked. Lee listed A and B, both on a salary of £1,040 per annum, the same weekly £20, the same hourly 10s, the same overtime hourly rate of 15s, the same average 2.5 hours per week overtime worth £2 5s, total £117 per annum. The second comparative list showed the allowance incorporated with the ruling rate increase, £1,261 for A, but B earning £1,144 salary plus overtime. While A earned the basic hourly rate of 10s 10d, B earned 11s; overtime rates were 16s 4d for A and 16s 6d for B. The total earnings of B were now £1,272, which was £11 4s more than A.

Lee compiled similar charts for every rank and year of service. He made chart summaries of recruitment, resignation and wastage. In support of such charts, his first memorandum to the tribunal ran to 25 pages, to demonstrate that remuneration did 'materially affect the percentage content in relation to overtime'.

His research revealed that members averaged 2.57 hours of overtime per week, and that often the commissioner's recommendations were not met. The government of the day might decide to pay half the overtime, and there was 'no factual or actual basis' for such arbitrary decisions.

Lee's research was hampered by the department not having the information he requested; it had to go back to districts and seek out the details. Lee changed his calculations three times during his painstaking charting of rosters, finally coming up with the 23.5 per cent loading on basic salary as a mathematically established increase. As he emphasised, he was only asking for the same penal, overtime and night shift payments as the public service enjoyed, averaged out over all the police. If he had done beat constables alone, it would have been 30 per cent. He was making a police team claim, and he was the expert. Everybody had to wait while Treasury pored over these detailed figures. Finally the tribunal approved his case.

Lee began to shake up the *Police Journal*. Out went Meltzer's beloved articles on such discursive subjects as 'The Modern Wonders of Anaesthesia' and 'There is no Such Thing as a Dreamless Sleep', along with the reports on international advances in forensic science and law, the jokes, the gossip of the painstakingly compiled district notes on births, deaths, marriages, farewells and social activities. In their place were long editorials like the June 1967 argument against current recruiting practice. New Zealand used the Otis test long after it had been discarded overseas. Lee questioned whether police needed such a high academic level, whether the public wanted 'a veritable walking law library' on the beat, where common sense and fair play were more important. He advocated recruiting older men to solve the shortage. The previous month the academically oriented Les Spencer was replaced as commissioner by the gentlemanly Colin Urquhart.

During April and May 1967 Lee had travelled around the districts promoting his proposal to replace the death benefit scheme with a welfare fund. The idea of such a comprehensive welfare scheme had been around for some years. One reason for its lack of progress was the unwieldy, overconsultative way in which the association worked. The opinion of every member had to be canvassed because of what Butler calls 'that little bit of mistrust that delegates did something not directed by the district, irrespective of how beneficial'. So Lee did the consultative legwork.

Jack Craig, a Dunedin delegate to many conferences, was one of those opposed to this newfangled welfare fund. He thought Meltzer's death benefit 'one of the most humane things the association ever did', tiding a widow over the first six weeks when her late husband's assets were

Peter Thomas Isaacs, office manager, treasurer, secretary of the new welfare fund, all part of Lee's more professional approach to association administration

impounded and the family was reduced to pauper status. He could see no reason, however, to extend the benefit to an area dealt with satisfactorily by friendly lodges. 'We weren't out to pay a widow's mortgages,' he says. 'Our association did not set out to wet-nurse members. We were out to get betterment of working conditions.'

Craig was eventually won over. He was typical of most members, unable to see how far-reaching the benefits could be. Lee was not only far-sighted but, Butler maintains, possessed that rare ability and enthusiasm with ideas 'to make them a reality'.

The indefatigable Lee wrote to dozens of insurance companies, seeking quotes for a police group scheme that would insure lives. He sought cover of £1,000. The quotes hovered around the £5 per annum. Royal Exchange Assurance won the nod. After deductions, about 80 per cent of the premium was refundable. He proposed to invest this for other welfare purposes.

In the June 1967 issue he published on yellow paper a special eight-page report to members, including a pink slip questionnaire asking for a yes or no to his welfare fund proposal revolving around a £1,000 death benefit. He got 94.1 per cent approval, but less than half the forms sent out to 1300 members were returned. He expressed his disappointment about this at the conference, but proceeded to make out a good case and delegates agreed that a new welfare fund would be set up by Lee and the management committee, absorbing the Sickness Benefit Fund.

Lee tended to talk in numbers. When he was profiled by a newspaper in January 1967 he talked about a 12 per cent increase in violent crime but a police service 82 below strength. By mid-year that figure had nearly doubled, and the police available were having to cope with angry and aggressive crowds demonstrating against the Vietnam War, particularly the visit of South Vietnamese leader Air Vice-

Marshal Ky. The secretary talked figures but his members were getting emotionally involved, often reacting against this more permissive era.

Association members were still hypersensitive to any newspaper criticism. In May a Wanganui newspaper article set out to praise the police as among the best in the world, but its opening sentence made the mistake of saying that six years ago, before the public relations drive, the public image of the police was 'punk'. As Wanganui district secretary, Constable J.F. McGlynn wrote to Lee about his 40 years in the police and the strong exception he took to this word 'punk'. Six other Wanganui officers signed the letter and the 13 July agm in Wanganui passed a motion protesting at this article and at general press publicity.

It was not Lee's area of interest. Sending the district secretary the briefest acknowledgement, he passed the matter on to Urquhart, who tried to explain to Wanganui how the press operated. Lee told Wanganui he was not satisfied with the commissioner's response, but did nothing more.

Butler had more to say on the police image, telling that year's conference that, in a period of rapid social change, the police were losing touch with the community, particularly as mobilised forces replaced the man on the beat. The association, he told Minister Allen, was concerned that the public tended to hear only the sometimes extravagant minority views on such matters as narcotics, homosexuality, police powers, the rights of criminal suspects. The association wanted the department to take up issues and ensure that the community was informed on all aspects. Meantime the association, at its 32nd conference, would take stock of itself and ascertain whether 'we have moved with the times'.

The minister praised Butler for his work as director of Crime Prevention, in encouraging people to take personal and property precautions, and he referred to the 120 per cent increase in police search and rescue work over the last two years. Like the police, he did not address the problems of the Hell's Angels gangs, the anti-war demonstrators or even the 80 students in Wellington who occupied a public convenience until the police stormed them and arrests were made. Nobody seemed to have anything to say about coping with such change.

The tribunal overtime award had moderated rank and file resentments. Resignations were down and recruitment up, helped by 30 assisted British immigrant recruits and increasing the policewomen ceiling to 3 per cent, or 80 officers.

The minister asked the police to be aware of the disturbing number of allegations of assault made against them. Most proved groundless, but he was concerned at how the press seized on such stories, which did irreparable harm to the image of the police. Understandably, the delegates were more concerned at the almost daily assaults on their members, and the inadequate penalties handed down. With five deaths in the last four years, as well as some serious assaults, the conference asked the government to reintroduce the death penalty for murder of police in the course of their duty. There was no Meltzer around to argue against this in these more volatile times. His consultancy only lasted for Lee's first year, before the new secretary dispensed with the costly exercise.

This conference took action against one curious hangover from almost Victorian times, the so-called literary exam. It had escaped Spencer's modernising efforts, perhaps because its title satisfied his academic bent. As Sergeant L.F. Smith of Invercargill said, the exam had no relationship to police work; he cited, as a prime example, the question about the running of the Australian sheep and dairy industry. Delegates voted to abolish the exam, but it took a few further pushes before this happened.

The one innovative aspect of the conference was Hamilton delegate Detective Sergeant Harry McCombe proposing that the police get their own credit union. He argued that many young police resigned not because of the pay but because they were not skilled at handling the money they received. His proposal was endorsed.

That December the *Police Journal* ceased to be published. Lee was busy with the welfare fund the next year, and a continuation of his modernising programme that began with a move from Jack Meltzer's beloved, dingy, smoke-filled room to a new office on Jervois Quay. He kept members informed with circulars, finding time in one to tick off members, particularly the youngsters, who got into financial difficulties with car running costs because they saw the mileage rate as a perk and bought flash cars they could not afford.

Lee was not keen on becoming embroiled as Meltzer had in public controversy. When the teachers once more raised the question of a policeman starting on over $2,000 and a teaching recruit on $1,200, Lee wrote to the press saying this would only have some validity if teaching recruits worked shifts over 24 hours of a seven-day week and spent 18 evenings out of 35 at work in all weathers and with potential hazards that included being assaulted and being always on call to fires, floods and civil disturbances.

Lee had stoutly stood his statistical ground, but this was an exception. Usually he wrote to the editor privately asking for more care to be taken. One example was a headline in the *Dominion* of 10 February 1968 reading 'Ex-policeman guilty of threat to kill'. Lee pointed out that readers were two-thirds of the way through the story before they learned that the subject was a retired inspector from India!

As usual it was *Truth* that provoked the biggest controversy in this context, with its 5 March 1968 cover line 'Girls Grilled in Police Witch-Hunt'. The association was just as indignant about a departmental investigation of a pregnant woman who had brought a complaint against a constable and subsequently tried to withdraw it after resolving the matter with the man concerned. It happened to be on the patch of the now Auckland Assistant Commissioner, Fergus Oliver Scott. The investigation broadened to include the reluctant complainant's flatmate being asked for the names of other police visitors, and the investigating officer getting a certificate from the doctor concerned confirming pregnancy after pretending that the woman had given him permission. She complained to *Truth* about this 'hounding'.

Auckland district secretary A.F. Edwardson complained to Lee, asking him to tell the commissioner that it was high time he ended 'ideas that were prevalent during mid-Victorian times'. The matter was badly handled by the department and resulted in an article 'derogatory to all members of the Police', as well as causing strife between members working overtime and their wives. Lee duly passed on the message, which was rejected by a defensive Urquhart.

It was a year of articles from journalists, attacks by lobby groups such as the Constitutional Society and judges querying whether police had too many powers—the right, for example, to enter and search for suspected drugs and wide powers over meetings and demonstrations. One headline hitter was an Auckland housewife arrested on a charge of offensive behaviour for singing an anti-Vietnam war song while aboard an American warship. The magistrate acquitted her. 'Police State Here Just a Knock Away' said another headline.

The only countering public response came from one J. Meltzer, Wellington coroner, reported as telling police recruits that the police were 'a bulwark on which the public relied to protect their life and property and all they held dear in a democratic way of life'. In reporting his remarks, the *Dominion* of 29 April 1968 included the point that here the police adopted an attitude of 'tolerant neutrality' towards 'demonstrators who keep within the law'.

In February 1969 Lee offered members his short, sharp, eight-page glossy newsletter, one-tenth the size of Meltzer's rambling, newsprint magazine. Lee paid tribute to the *Journal* as a valuable record of association history and progress, but times had changed and there should be more on offer than 'a mere house journal'.

Lee rated staff shortages the most contentious item of business in 1968. The management committee or executive, as he called it, was in the driving seat, instead of being passengers steered by Meltzer. Lee stayed alongside the executive drivers as the map reader charting their course.

He provided the critical data to show why the executive was determined that the administration would not get complacent about the improvements since the tribunal order. The department, he argued, was not taking into account population increases, particularly in Auckland. From 1961 to 1966 the population there had increased 21 per cent, police strength 14.5 per cent.

The grim effects of this imbalance could be seen on 27 June 1968 when Constable P.J. Sheriff of Papakura was alone in his radio car because no officer was available to accompany him. He was set upon by four escaped prisoners and battered almost to death.

The association executive had written to the Minister of Justice about the increase in violent crimes. Add to this the extra commitment to search and rescue, security in the new large shopping malls, fishing protection duty, anti-litter inspection and demonstrations, and Auckland alone was 200 staff short, not 53, as the department claimed.

At a meeting with the commissioner and senior officers in Auckland on 16 August, the executive used a large-scale map to drive home their claim. The administration response was to say that such disclosure would cause alarm and encourage criminals, something no government would wear. There would be no extra resources in the current economic downturn.

The association response was quite a turnaround. The executive suggested that civilians be brought in to do clerical jobs and even radio despatch, and that more women be recruited. Earlier retirement could encourage more recruits and the department had the provision of Section 71 (3) of the Police Act 1958 to improve salary with 'inducement to recruitment'.

It was 10 months and much association lobbying after the attack on Sheriff before the government and administration relented and agreed that such one-man patrols would now be required to observe, report and await back-up.

Feeling they had been dismissed as alarmists, Butler and Lee had seen the minister after the last conference and told him that the association was at breaking point and would not co-operate unless there was swift and positive action. Allen promised more finance and civilian help. Then the national police survey confirmed the association claims, indicating that the service was 21 per cent or 600 officers below strength.

Once again Auckland proved troublesome. This time an Auckland senior officer told the *Auckland Star* on 3 October that they were 'not seriously short' of staff; the Auckland recruiting officer repeated the claim on 28 November. Some government advisers then suggested that the shortage problem could be overcome by two-way radios, a particularly silly remark given how few constables were left on the beat to use them.

There was talk of the association going public. Although Lee, characteristically, would not appear on the television current affairs programme *Gallery*, he and Butler met the minister again on 18 March 1969. The next month the commissioner briefed Butler and Lee on the new system with one-man patrols and other administrative plans. Allen promised finance for a new police college and increased staff.

On 27 September 1968 the welfare fund came into existence, with Lee as executive director. The following March he reported its rapid development of death, sickness, discretionary and home aid payments. Holiday homes for members were being studied.

In the May *Newsletter* there were letters approving the new glossy format and simple paragraphs, but a major complaint from Lee that his March questionnaire on members' conditions had drawn such a poor response. Out of 700 Auckland members only 50 had replied. Without facts, he explained, he had no case to take to the tribunal for a pay increase.

In the June *Newsletter* Lee allowed himself the luxury of a Meltzer-style editorial, except that he hammered the flag bearers of the permissive society. Such obscene, drunken,

POLICE SALARY SCALE

On 17 June, 1969, the Police Department (The Commissioner of Police as Applicant) filed an application to have the increases based on the 1969 survey of ruling rates in industry applied to Police Salaries. The application also sought the adjustment of the overtime/penal content to 23.5 per cent of the new basic salaries. For all ranks up to and including Inspector the ruling rate increase was $160 as from 12 August, 1968, but with the adjustment in the penal component, the increases for all ranks up to and including Senior Sergeant amount to $195 to $200 per annum. Matrons however were to receive 90 per cent of the new comprehensive salaries.

On 18 June, the Association filed its consent to the application, and on 20 June, 1969, the Police Staff Tribunal made an order granting the increases sought, but subject to abatement by the amount of the interim increase of $84 paid by way of allowance since 19 August, 1968.

The following is the new Police Salary Scale effective as from 12 August, 1968, showing the components of the comprehensive salaries:—

SCHEDULE 1

Ranks and Increment Levels	R.R.S. Increase from 12/8/68	New Basic Pay at 12/8/68	New O.T./P.T. (23.5%) at 12/8/68	Shift Allowance	New Actual Comprehensive	Normal Rounding to $5 to give Comprehensive Scale at 12/8/68
SUPERINTENDENTS	$	$	$	$	$	$
After one year	90	5,820	—	—	5,820	5,820
First year	110	5,640	—	—	5,640	5,640
CHIEF INSPECTORS						
After one year	135	5,365	—	—	5,365	5,365
First year	155	5,185	—	—	5,185	5,185
INSPECTORS						
After one year	160	4,890	—	—	4,890	4,890
First year	160	4,690	—	—	4,690	4,690
SENIOR SERGEANTS						
After three years	160	3,466	814	55	4,335	4,335
3rd year	160	3,371	792	55	4,218	4,220
2nd year	160	3,274	769	55	4,098	4,100
1st year	160	3,206	753	55	4,014	4,015
SERGEANTS						
After three years	160	3,090	726	55	3,871	3,870
3rd year	160	3,013	708	55	3,776	3,775
2nd year	160	2,938	690	55	3,683	3,685
1st year	160	2,888	679	55	3,622	3,620
CONSTABLES						
After 25 years	160	2,826	664	55	3,545	3,545
After 20 years	160	2,732	642	55	3,429	3,430
After 14 years	160	2,685	631	55	3,371	3,370
After 9 years	160	2,628	618	55	3,301	3,300
After 6 years	160	2,594	610	55	3,259	3,260
After 3 years	160	2,535	596	55	3,186	3,185
After 2 years	160	2,444	574	55	3,073	3,075
After 1 year	160	2,394	563	55	3,012	3,010
1st year after age 21	160	2,334	548	55	2,937	2,935
20 years of age	160	2,309	543	55	2,907	2,905
19 years of age	160	2,279	536	55	2,870	2,870
CADETS						
Under age 18	90	1,295	—	—	1,295	1,295
Under age 19	100	1,460	—	—	1,460	1,460
Under age 20	115	1,665	—	—	1,665	1,665

POLICE MATRONS PAY SCALE

Increment Levels	Matrons Scale at 11/8/68	New Scale from 12/8/68 for Constables	New Scale for Matrons Expressed at 90% of Constable Scales & Rounded off to $5
	$	$	$
After 25 years of service	3,015	3,545	3,190
After 20 years of service	2,905	3,430	3,085
After 14 years of service	2,860	3,370	3,035
After 9 years of service	2,795	3,300	2,970
After 6 years of service	2,755	3,260	2,935
After 3 years of service	2,690	3,185	2,865
After 2 years of service	2,590	3,075	2,765
After 1 year of service	2,535	3,010	2,710
First year of service	2,465	2,935	2,640

The new-look, glossy, brief *Newsletter* introduced the kind of number-crunched tables beloved of Lee, this hard-working and most pragmatic association secretary

SCHEDULE I — POLICE PAY SCALE EFFECTIVE 15 JUNE, 1969

(Providing for percentalisation of 1967 and 1968 Ruling Rate Surveys and recalculation of overtime/penal time content of base pay at 23.5%)

Ranks and Increment levels	Basic Pay at 1.4.68. (1)	Percent-alisation 8.78% (2)	New Basic pay at 15 June 1969 (3)	New O.T./P.T. (23.5%) at 15 June 1969 (4)	Shift Allow-ance (5)	New Actual Compre-hensive (6)	Rounding to $5 to give comprehensive Scale at 15 June 1969 (7)
Assistant Commissioners	$	$	$	$	$	$	$
After 1 year	7,070	620.74	7,690.74	—	—	7,690.74	7,690
First year	6,600	579.48	7,179.48	—	—	7,179.48	7,180
Additional salary for Snr. A.C. at National H.Q.	230	20.19	250.19	—	—	250.19	250
Chief Superintendents							
After 1 year	6,250	548.75	6,798.75	—	—	6,798.75	6,800
First year	6,050	531.19	6,581.19	—	—	6,581.19	6,580
Superintendents							
After 1 year	5,700	500.46	6,200.46	—	—	6,200.46	6,200
First year	5,500	482.90	5,982.90	—	—	5,982.90	5,985
Chief Inspectors							
After 1 year	5,200	456.56	5,656.56	—	—	5,656.56	5,655
First year	5,000	439.00	5,439.00	—	—	5,439.00	5,440
Inspectors							
After 1 year	4,700	412.66	5,112.66	—	—	5,112.66	5,115
First year	4,500	395.10	4,895.10	—	—	4,895.10	4,895
Senior Sergeants							
After 3 years	3,276	287.63	3,563.63	837.45	55	4,456.08	4,455
3rd year	3,181	279.29	3,460.29	813.16	55	4,328.45	4,330
2nd year	3,084	270.77	3,354.77	788.37	55	4,198.14	4,200
1st year	3,016	264.80	3,280.80	770.98	55	4,106.78	4,105
Sergeants							
After 3 years	2,900	254.62	3,154.62	741.33	55	3,950.95	3,950
3rd year	2,823	247.85	3,070.85	721.65	55	3,847.50	3,850
2nd year	2,748	241.27	2,989.27	702.47	55	3,746.74	3,745
1st year	2,698	236.88	2,934.88	689.69	55	3,679.57	3,680
Constables							
After 25 years	2,636	231.44	2,867.44	673.84	55	3,596.28	3,595
After 20 years	2,542	223.18	2,765.18	649.81	55	3,469.99	3,470
After 14 years	2,495	219.06	2,714.06	637.80	55	3,406.86	3,405
After 9 years	2,438	214.05	2,652.05	623.23	55	3,330.28	3,330
After 6 years	2,404	211.07	2,615.07	614.54	55	3,284.61	3,285
After 3 years	2,345	205.89	2,550.89	599.45	55	3,205.34	3,205
After 2 years	2,254	197.90	2,451.90	576.19	55	3,083.09	3,085
After 1 year	2,204	193.51	2,397.51	563.41	55	3,015.92	3,015
1st year after age 21	2,144	188.24	2,332.24	548.07	55	2,935.31	2,935
20 years of age	2,119	186.04	2,305.04	543.68	55	2,903.72	2,905
19 years of age	2,094	183.85	2,277.85	535.29	55	2,868.14	2,870
Cadets							
Under age 18		(No change on rates existing at 14 June 1969)					1,295
Under age 19		(No change on rates existing at 14 June 1969)					1,460
Under age 20		(No change on rates existing at 14 June 1969)					1,665

SCHEDULE II — POLICE MATRONS PAY SCALE FROM 15 JUNE, 1969

(Expressed as 90% of the Constable Salary Scale)

Increment Levels	Matrons scale at 14 June, 1969 (1)	New scale for Constables from 15 June, 1969 (2)	New scale for Matrons expressed as 90% and rounded off to $5 (3)
	$	$	$
After 25 years' service	3,190	3,595	3,235
After 20 years' service	3,085	3,470	3,125
After 14 years' service	3,035	3,405	3,065
After 9 years' service	2,970	3,330	2,995
After 6 years' service	2,935	3,285	2,955
After 3 years' service	2,865	3,205	2,885
After 2 years' service	2,765	3,085	2,775
After 1 year's service	2,710	3,015	2,715
First year of service	2,640	2,935	2,640

drug-dabbling students must suffer the consequences of blowing up Waitangi flagpoles. A follow-up came in the next *Newsletter* from 'Common Cop' W.D. Hall, who challenged any 'long-haired PhD' to go on the beat for a week.

On 24 June 1969 the association was vindicated in its stand on staff shortages when Allen announced that the government intended lowering the ratio from one police officer to 920 members of the public to one to 890, because staff were not keeping pace with the increased demands for their services. This month the tribunal gave police the ruling industry rate pay increase. First-year constables over 21 earned $2,334, first-year sergeants $2,888, superintendents, after one year, $5,820. It was quite a month for the association, and it included Dave Lee announcing his resignation. He was moving to New Plymouth to do what he had always dreamed of, being a lawyer. He had only ever intended to spend three years in this job, long enough to achieve what he wanted to.

And that he had done. The association now had a simpler structure that communicated better with the administration and its own members. The Police Staff Welfare Fund was in place, having already paid out over $6,600 in death benefits, $3,350 in sickness benefits and another $1,000 in hospital, home aid, discretionary, wife and dependant benefits. The fund was run solely by the association's board.

Lee was a doer, not a thinker. His August *Newsletter* repeated his attack on apathy in the association; less than 50 per cent of members had completed his 40-question survey so vital for a salary case. Members should remember that he had won them $3,000,000 in the last two years. If he did not get a 100 per cent response, there was no way he could build up an accurate statistical profile of the typical member, his or her age, marital status, dependants, housing, service and regular commitments such as superannuation and insurance. He had to know if there was a need to increase or decrease the death benefit. The British police pay report, he told them, ran to 1700 pages. Members must understand that pay applications were complex. This was the nearest he got to losing his celebrated cool. And still what he hit them with were figures, facts, statistics.

He did have an old Meltzer complaint, that members were not contributing to their paper. And he did have a sense of humour. A.F. Edwardson complained in the June 1969 issue that he thought he had seen the end of gossip until he read in the *Newsletter* that 'members baked and decorated a special cake for our birthday party'. Lee replied tersely that there was no other contribution from members to fill the space.

A less visible contribution from Lee was to defend the Police Staff Tribunal against public service attempts to abolish it. An amendment to the Police Act had been drafted to absorb it into a general tribunal for all state servants. It was typical of Lee that the joint submission by association and guild went beyond protest to propose simplifying procedures so that future applications were made direct to the commissioner. The tribunal would only be involved if there was any objection to the commissioner's decision. Urquhart was happy with this. The amendment was duly passed in late 1969.

New pay scales were also promulgated, an increase of 8.7 per cent that gave a 19-year-old constable a rise of $183 to $2,277; a sergeant of three years went up $254 to $3,154; an assistant commissioner after one year went up $620 to $7,690.

The November *Newsletter* praised the amendment as 'a great and personal victory' for Lee. The previous month's *Newsletter* had praised him for keeping members closely in touch with association matters, for a new office reorganisation with manager Peter Isaacs also acting now as secretary of the welfare fund, and for association numbers now being up to 2969, with only 20 officers not belonging.

At the conference that year affable Minister Allen praised Lee as 'uniquely qualified' for his job; he would be missed by both association and administration. Allen liked to talk, and he spoke at length about members needing to refrain from feeling that, in the changeover from foot to mobile patrols, they had lost touch with the public—it was essential to have a mobile police to catch mobile criminals. The conference was also addressed by Superintendent Ken Burnside on more efficient means of catching criminals.

It was not yet Burnside's turn, but Urquhart was retiring as commissioner, and Butler as president. Allen observed that he was fast becoming the old boy of the conference. He made no mention of the election in two weeks' time, which was threatening to retire him too, for Labour were expected to win.

A brisk era had ended for the association. Butler praised Lee for bringing about 'a new and heightened spirit within the Association'. Lee was crucial to the establishment of the welfare fund, which Butler called his crowning glory. His research back to 1925 had provided the case for the new pay formula and the extra week of leave, and he was responsible for the new, modern office and the pragmatic newsletter.

Butler spoke about the inadequate training college at Trentham, the need for earlier retirement and to sort out specialist positions so that they did not cheapen ranks and designations. He rated the tribunal as vital to the efficiency and harmony of the association. This year association and guild had had their first contested case, the claim for an increased plain-clothes allowance, but the tribunal had found for them. An optimist who emphasised the positive, Butler said he retired from an association 'in very good heart'; he would not be doing this job again.

That last bit was his only error. Butler was soon back as vice-president and as president again in the 1970s. He had restored the association's good heart in the mid-1960s. He would have to do so again in the early 1970s, when association support for its new 'secretary' proved far too faint of heart.

Chapter Fifteen

The Touchy Thomas Years

Hamish Stewart Thomas left behind the law to take on the job Lee had left for a law career. Thomas had accepted Governor General Cobham's invitation to establish the Outward Bound School at Anakiwa, and subsequently another such school at Singapore. After the break he felt he could not, at 47, return to his former position in his father's Christchurch law firm, and took up lawyer Brian McClelland's suggestion to apply for the association job. Thomas rated advocacy as his greatest strength, and he pleaded successfully for the job.

According to Rob Butler, Thomas was appointed because he was a lawyer and came highly recommended. Urquhart offered Butler three years' leave to take the job himself, but he felt he lacked the necessary legal experience. Other applicants were considered, some with a union background, but Thomas also offered continuity. As a practising criminal lawyer in Christchurch he had known Urquhart when he was chief of CIB there, opposing him in court and drinking with him afterwards. He saw the gregarious Jack Meltzer whenever he came to Christchurch. He not only knew Detective Sergeant Dave Lee in the line of work, but had been at school with Lee's sister.

Thomas saw Meltzer as a one-man band who also still worked as a lawyer. He watched Lee change the job from a secretaryship, with some counselling on the side, into a complete job, from an amateur ad hoc role to one of negotiating pay and conditions and building up welfare. When Thomas took over, he said the department was almost never the resister; that role was taken by the government and by Treasury.

One of Lee's last acts had been to write to the Prime Minister asking for an upgrading of the police portfolio, which had been declining in status for some years. This should not be so when there was a worldwide concern with law and order and the public were showing more interest in the role of the police. It was also time to increase numbers, both to improve morale and to increase contact with the public, who saw the police as the personification of the law. Surprisingly, Holyoake won the 1969 election, but he had never been one for philosophical game plans. David Thomson took over Police and Defence, roles Thomas said conflicted. The government did, however, increase police numbers, introducing impatient youngsters who had little time for the Thomas/Butler back-room advocacy style.

Thomas was interested in restructuring and advocated changes to association organisation throughout his seven-year stint. His first proposal was to bring another junior into the office so that manager Peter Isaacs could switch to doing more research on pay and conditions. At the time the office staff consisted of Isaacs and two women, plus another part-time woman. Thomas saw his job as deciding policy matters with the executive board and defining answers to legal problems, acting as secretary to the management committee, presenting its arguments and cases to department and government, making submissions to select committees. He extensively redrafted what he considered poorly

Hamish Stewart Thomas had all the legal qualifications Rob Butler thought were needed for the job

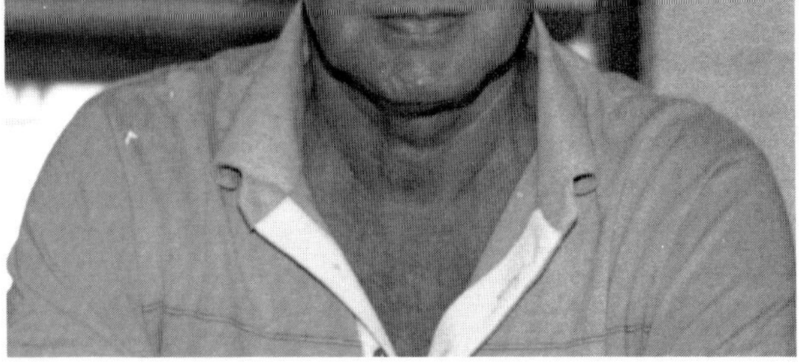

Rob Butler never went far from the executive table after his first presidential stint ended in 1969. President again in 1973, he spent a great deal of his second term defending Thomas to members

written association rules, including the legal assistance aspects, which he considered too restrictive. He professed a preference for working behind the scenes, swaying by argument and logic rather than by 'heavyweight tactics'. The new job definition of executive director suited him fine.

His first year in the job was spent in the laborious exchange of hand calculations on a pay review between the association and guild on one side and the department, government and Treasury on the other. He worked closely with another man he had known well from CIB days, President Harry McCombe. Thomas soon discovered that Urquhart could be sympathetic on such a matter as changing the heavy serge uniforms, but that Secretary of Police L.C. 'Snow' Hansen, one of the new breed of civilians in police administration and a bureaucrat through and through, would simply refuse the change point blank. Thomas had free access to the commissioner, but it was of little use when Hansen froze every remit put forward.

Thomas was able to change the way remits were presented. At his first conference in 1969 he saw how much time was frittered away on too many remits. In his February 1970 editorial he argued that the management committee could deal with many remit matters throughout the year, freeing up the conference to discuss policy. He wanted the conference to get away from what he called the infection of repetitive remits, such as the five on exams or the three on discipline. Thomas was in his element as advocate, but it was not the element of members, not all of whom appreciated being told by their employee how poorly they were performing.

In his March editorial Thomas expanded on the recruit theme. Exam remits, he said, were about specific difficulties, but exams were a complete problem that would only be resolved with a general policy on training, exams and promotion. Past remits were destructive, proposing no alternative. The new Police College would be the place to introduce examination for promotion.

There was no feedback, so Thomas took Lee's approach one step further. He left the back page of the *Newsletter* blank for members' contributions. When that did not work, he reduced the *Newsletter* to four pages. Some members took the view that he was paid to fill the *Newsletter*.

The 1970 conference decided that the national council rather than the management committee would decide policy. A management sub-committee reported to the conference that exams were unrealistic and improperly conducted. Pass marks as low as 6.3 per cent on criminal law compared with 50 per cent for School Certificate, and questions involved such obscure law as the definition of a firearm under the Wildlife Act, in which a boomerang qualified. The recommendation was for the department to set up an examinations section conducting fulltime correspondence courses and resident courses before the exams. The conference adopted this report instead of making its past repetitive objection to the literary exam. Several years later this was replaced by School Certificate.

Thomas and his staff had been busy in 1970 on a management directive to compare police pay with outside industry. The police had not only lost the margin over traffic and prison officers they had enjoyed since 1956, but they were falling behind the cost of living. Having determined that a 15 per cent increase was needed for each area,

CAL THE COPS

Police examinations continued to agitate association members

Thomas travelled around the association districts explaining this. In his 29 June letter to the commissioner, however, he asked for 45 per cent, a figure he said was set deliberately high so there would be room for manoeuvre. Unfortunately he had not told members of his strategy. When the department and Treasury offered 30 per cent and Thomas settled, members complained. Thomas rejected as illusory their complaint that the increase did not compare with that for tradesmen, because that was backdated whereas the police rise was effective from 1970. He believed his reasonable approach had worked but some members said the claim had failed and that Thomas had been dilatory in pressing it.

McCombe referred, at the 1970 conference, to police objections to being called 'pigs' and 'public utilities'. They might, he conceded, have been overzealous in a few incidents, but the police needed protection from assault as much as any citizen. There was a feeling that the police were on the back foot against accusations of bullyboy behaviour, and nowhere more so than from television. McCombe and Thomas went to see the new commissioner, Angus (Gus) Sharp, in late 1970 to express their concern about the television image of the police. Rob Butler, as immediate past president, went along, having had experience of the medium in his job as Crime Prevention director. They advised Sharp to insist that, in interviews, he be allowed to answer questions and not allow butting in with another hectoring enquiry.

When Sharp faced the most feared television inquisitor of all, Dr Brian Edwards of the *Gallery* programme, he refused to be sidetracked. He stated the police position and said he would leave it to the public to decide if there had been police brutality. Sharp's performance was a great morale boost for the beleaguered service. Thomas praised him in the December *Newsletter* for having 'placed himself in jeopardy on behalf of his men' and thanked him for his bravery.

Thomas did not, however, find the new commissioner as easy to deal with as his agreeable predecessor. Sharp was not only less inclined to accept submissions on face value as genuine, but was touchy about any criticism. He sent Thomas a strong letter claiming that he, the commissioner, had done all the work on getting the 30 per cent pay increase.

A stickler for the traditional appearance, Sharp resisted uniform change. He relented and decreed an unsatisfactorily inflexible change to summer uniform in October and winter uniform in April, regardless of whether it was a sweltering northerly in Kaitaia or a howling southerly in Bluff. Thomas prepared a paper on how uniforms should be neat and comfortable and not inhibit movement, as the present one did. The association advocated a uniform to suit the climate and the job, but Sharp would not budge. As another Christchurch man, Thomas decided that Sharp had developed his traditional taste when he was a chorister at Christchurch Cathedral, where the uniforms were not comfortable.

Uniforms had been a hardy annual at conferences for over a decade until the 1971 gathering appointed a subcommittee on the subject. A questionnaire suggested that officers were happy with the uniform, but fewer than 50 per cent had responded.

In the March 1972 *Newsletter* Sergeant J.A. Franklin of Napier claimed that the sub-committee had the wrong personnel—a policewoman, an inspector and a senior sergeant, those least affected by unsuitable uniform. Constables and sergeants spent most time in the field and in the heat. In 1965 he had produced evidence at the conference that the police were the only service organisation without a satisfactory uniform. The matter had been pigeon-holed at every conference since 1960. He was not impressed by the questionnaire. He knew, when he went into the field among 'skimpily and sensibly dressed holiday crowds' in his midwinter trousers, heavy boots and tie, with sweat-stained armpits, that he looked 'a silly big nit without even the brains' to dress for the prevailing conditions. He wanted association action.

What Franklin got was indignant sub-committee members Mrs Margaret Stebbings and L.E. Cooper saying that he was immature to claim they were less affected. Then Eric Bovey of Dargaville wrote that he would settle for just being allowed to undo his top button, and he had the endorsement of his wife and station colleagues for being tieless, with sleeves rolled up and lighter trousers, instead of 'a boiled down, wrung out glamour boy'.

The letters began to roll in, most favouring Franklin. Thomas at last had a response, an issue on the boil through the *Newsletter*. He must have been surprised at the 1972 conference to get the blame for pussyfooting around with the department over uniforms. Some delegates said they had been waiting 20 years for a sensible uniform. It was not good enough the commissioner saying he would allow shorts if there was 100 per cent support. It was not good enough Sharp banning short sleeves because some members had tattoos or arms that were too thin! Delegates demanded action.

They got it at the 1973 conference, which was attended by Mrs McDowell of the New Zealand Wool Board. She proposed long sleeves, long trousers. When delegates wanted to know where the difference was, she said woollen cloth breathed better.

Ian Sutherland of Palmerston North said they wanted what the Cyprus contingent had been given within days—open neck, short sleeves, shorts. They did not, said Hamish Beckett of Auckland, want something in which they would be mistaken for members of the Auckland Regional Authority.

When Mrs McDowell hit back that she did not like short sleeves and shorts, which 'spoiled the police image', Ian Paterson of Hamilton told her that, at the Ngaruawahia Festival, the police wore long-sleeved shirts with collars and ties and some collapsed from fatigue. Medical opinion blamed the long sleeves and done-up neck. Mrs McDowell was not amused. Shorts might be the thing in the Bahamas, but here they would make the police 'look like any beach bum'.

N. Shepherd of Nelson threw her a curly one. Given that the designation policewoman was soon to disappear into the all-embracing term constable, and he could not imagine a policewoman climbing a ladder in a dress, what thought had been given to slacks for female constables? Mrs McDowell said some thought had been given to this, but she did not think women police would be much better off climbing a ladder in trousers rather than a skirt, 'unless there was a man at the bottom!' She added that women were fashion conscious; present-day trousers were not suitable for climbing ladders.

Mark Penn reminded everybody that it got hot in Christchurch too; it was not just North Islanders who wanted summer uniforms. Furthermore, the uniform was hopeless in a scrap; it 'kept coming undone'. A zip was the answer. After further debate on Shepherd's point that the old uniforms were not colour fast, Mrs McDowell was, surprisingly, thanked by acclamation. Some might have thought her a commissioner plant.

The following 29 March summer and winter uniforms went on parade. They were a lighter blue, with new open-necked shirts in terylene and cotton, soft epaulettes carrying the word 'Police', trousers of lightest polyester and wool in navy blue, with a zip.

Butler returned as president this year, and resolved the uniform issue. He knew districts would keep disagreeing, as they had for 14 years, about which bits worked and what should still be changed. Butler went to Wellington, Auckland and Hutt with the new uniforms, then straight to the commissioner with the news that there was a general consensus that it was a smart effort and, despite objections, would eventually be accepted. The uniform was introduced and was being worn by the end of the year.

Since his resignation Butler had never been far away. As immediate past president he was wanted in the pay negotiations. Although running the CIB at Wanganui, he was voted back as senior vice-president in 1971. Thereafter pay negotiations with the department and government had broken down and over the next few years President Dan Ingram had not been well.

Butler's return was, Thomas says, good news because he was a good cop admired by his superiors and a pleasant bloke who got on well with the commissioners. Younger members thought him too cosy with commissioners, but none challenged his skills as chairman. Butler was really the first president to share power with the secretary/executive director. Although he could not save Thomas in the end, he remained fiercely loyal to him throughout the long and ultimately successful destabilising of his performance in the job.

In his 1972 presidential report Ingram had warned against members using this quiet period to play politics instead of concentrating on policy. He had toured the districts with Thomas early in the year to try and get members more involved, reminding them that their executive could act only if matters were brought to its attention.

Ingram happened to be Holyoake's brother-in-law, but he said this connection had not helped him in the job. He told the government of the association's considerable concern about the proposed Springbok tour. He hoped they would consider the police position and provide enough finance for the police to cope.

There was also the continuing problem of the police image with the public. There had, Ingram told the 1972 conference, been allegations that police had overstepped the mark in handling the motorcycle gangs at the Alexandra Blossom Festival. Ingram was upset that the allegations came from gang 'brutes'. While he did not defend what some members did, he hoped the general public recognised the considerable provocation involved. The result of it had been the association's biggest legal aid costs so far. Ingram said the police looked to the department to minimise any problems in future.

The department obliged over the holiday period, as bikies descended on Timaru's Caroline Bay and there were fears that they would trash the holiday resort. The police presence was strong, and there were no problems except that the *New Zealand Herald* of 6 January claimed the police campaign against bikies was excessive; bikies were entitled to the same treatment as any other citizens. The *Tablet* disagreed, saying the police presence did not come amiss in 'our increasingly flabby society'. The *Herald* claimed the new Kirk Labour Government had whipped up the climate of semi-hysteria; the *Tablet* said the behaviour of bikies was a denial of freedom because it lacked responsibility.

The *Newsletter* published both sides of the argument, but the police knew the new government, and particularly Police Minister Mick Connelly, were on their side. Connelly promised a tougher time for those who attacked police with bottles and accelerated staffing to achieve a ratio of one to 800. The *Newsletter* noted the general relief at the cancellation of the Springbok tour.

The media made more accusations of police brutality in 1973, when Sergeant Paul Gilfedder of Christchurch was accused of manhandling a lad in a patrol car during a scuffle in which the boy lost some hair. Thomas said the family had a history of difficulties with the police. If a land agent had not decided to take up the defence of the police against the charges and flown Gilfedder to Wellington to face the media, he would not have made him a cause célèbre and Gilfedder might have been reprimanded rather than sacked.

The association was concerned principally with the unfairness of the commissioner being able to suspend a member without pay while the courts dealt with the matter, then dismiss the member without allowing any representations. The incident caused much heartache in the service, and Butler recalls how the media seized the chance to drive a wedge into the association. The commissioner did, however, agree to the association lobbying. The Police Act was amended so that the commissioner could suspend with or without pay and receive submissions on the question of dismissal after conviction in an open court. It had been another expensive and lengthy legal assistance case for the association, and it had been played out in the full glare of the media. In the end, it did serve to unite the

MARCH 1974 ● VOL. 6, No. 2 ● PART SERIES OF "N.Z. POLICE JOURNAL"

Editorial

WHICH WAY?

Of recent times there have been some stirrings within the Association indicating a tendency towards a rather dictatorial or even militant approach to problems. If this is happening, this could well be the right time to review the meaning of the objects of the Association, and how best these can be achieved.

Rule three of the Association reads as follows:

The objects of the Association shall be:-

(a) To maintain discipline, increase the efficiency, improve working conditions and promote the general welfare and contentment of members of the Police of New Zealand.

(b) To constitute the official channel of communication between its members as a body and
(i) The Minister in charge of the Department.
(ii) The Commissioner of Police;

(c) To foster a feeling of amity and good fellowship throughout the Police Service;

(d) To provide assistance (other than financial assistance) to members, and to provide assistance to their dependents in need thereof and where necessary to bring their claims before the Department;

(e) To print and publish a magazine to be known as "The New Zealand Police Journal" and such other literature as may be considered conducive to promoting the objects of the Association;

(f) To take such action, consistent with the above objects and the constitution of the Association, as shall be deemed advisable in furthering the interests of members.

Let us now look at these more closely, and especially the language in which they are couched.

Surely the first object must indicate a respect for authority and discipline, coupled with a real concern for the well being, not only of members of the Association, but of all Police in New Zealand. Had this not been the case, the words used must have been very different. One can invisage such terminology as "to ensure that the Police Department improve the pay and conditions of members of the Association", but no such words are used; in fact the very words of the objects demonstrate a basic unselfishness within the Association and Police generally.

This is reinforced by the words of the third object which talks about the fostering of a feeling of amity and good fellowship throughout the whole Police Service, and not just the Association.

The second object sets out that the Association is constituted an official channel of communication between the members, the Minister of Police, and the Commissioner. Much is spoken today of the importance of communication between people, and all of it applies to this aspect of the Association. It is not enough just to state what our problems may be, or to make complaints, it is necessary to ensure that all information is given and that there be a full understanding of any problem. This requires on occasions some diplomacy, on others plain speaking, and yet again at other times quiet logic. But really, can militant or forceful action ever be necessary. Such tactics are best left for really desperate situations, or to the more dissident bodies, rather than this Association.

From the experience over the past few years in dealing with three separate Ministers of Police, it is clear that there is a ready acceptance of the role the Association plays in Police affairs, and all three Ministers have listened with interest and sympathy to any representations made to them. The rapport has been excellent.

This is too good to spoil by hasty and some times ill considered action. Not always do we win our arguments or get our way, but the success rate is extraordinarily high, both at Ministerial and Departmental levels. The times when a matter has not been adjusted in our favour are usually those where the matter is beyond the control of the person concerned, or where financial provisions make it impossible of achievement.

The fourth object specifies certain particular ways in which the Association shall help its members, but as with the other objects, there is an underlying humanity and understanding which indicates a reasonable approach.

The fifth object speaks for itself.

It is the final object which has really given rise to this Editorial. It states quite clearly that any action taken shall be consistent with all the objects of the Association. This must mean more than the strict interpretation of the words. It must mean the whole tenor of the objects collectively.

The Thomas editorial that incensed association members. Leading the attacks against the Thomas laissez faire approach was young Wellington member Alec Waugh. His newssheet, *Watchdog*, next page, unofficially told members what it alleged the *Newsletter* was failing to publish, notably the full story on the management committee meetings

THE WATCHDOG No.11

Editor: A.K.Waugh,
131 Major Drive,
Kelson,
LOWER HUTT.

696-810

WELLINGTON DISTRICT COMMITTEE PUBLICATION.

EDITORIAL: Apathy of police members is one of the biggest and most tragic aspects of holding back the effectiveness and development of the Police Association. This apathy shows itself at A.G.M. and local association meetings. The fault lies with all segments of the Association membership, and is often revealed by loud moaning at the ineffectiveness of the Association - while standing at the Police canteen. These moans may well be correct, but you never see these people attending meetings or putting forward their views. The result of membership apathy is far reaching. It leads to members well past their peak, not up to scratch, and plain socializers, achieving positions of responsibility in the Association, not on ability but because there is no one else willing to stand. Full credit to members willing to give their time, but willingness to stand, should not be the criteria for selection.

If you are one of these dissatisfied with Association police or achievements, put your nomination where your mouth is and stand for Committee membership.

Mick Connelly was a popular and supportive police minister in the Labour Governments of Kirk and Rowling in the early 1970s, proud to preside over increased police numbers and quite often a lone voice for the police view in a Cabinet inclined to liberal social legislation association against the unfairness of a member being suspended without pay pending court action.

The association honeymoon with the Labour Government lasted as long as Kirk did. Connelly promised the ratio would come down to one to 760, there would be more cars and housing, the government would listen to the association in drafting legislation to give adequate scope for dealing with young offenders such as the lad in the Gilfedder case. In these first two years the only clashes were with the Finance and Immigration Ministers. Finance Minister Bill Rowling proposed that the Superannuation Corporation Bill lock in all but 10 per cent of members' contributions. The association opposed this utterly, and eventually won back the right to retain 25 per cent of members' contributions. Immigration Minister Fraser Colman accused the police of conducting dawn raids on illegal immigrants in May 1974, when the police were carrying out their duty to suit his department's officials.

Connelly told Butler how he had moved heaven and earth on their behalf, even opposing Cabinet colleagues. For Butler, Connelly was the Police Minister who impressed him most, and he rated Kirk the most outstanding Prime Minister, even though he personally voted National all his life. During this period of restless Labour and bureaucratic legislators, the association needed these friends in high places. In late 1973 they objected to Kirk and Connelly about the provisions in the Children, Young Persons and their Families Bill that the police be restricted to arrest only in cases of manslaughter or murder. Association and guild insisted that this took away police powers at a time when it was unacceptable. The bill was rewritten, the section on arrest deleted and Youth Boards reduced from dealing with young offenders to advising the police.

One area that caused great frustration was the allocation of departmental cars. Each year the police watched everybody else get allocations and they waited, trying to cope with worn-out vehicles and feeble excuses about wharf strikes and delayed ships. Butler discovered he could get cars from Ford or from the Japanese instead of General Motors with whom the bureaucrats had a deal. Ken Burnside, who was now commissioner, told Butler he was wasting his time telling the Prime Minister. Butler did just that. The next thing a startled Connelly knew was Kirk telling him to get on with Butler's proposal. The police soon got their cars from General Motors.

Also worn out were the Trentham Training College facilities, where recruits shared makeshift World War One barracks and classrooms with the Army, Post Office and Transport. Thomas spent a good deal of time arguing with successive ministers about the poor conditions and the urgent need for the new police college David Thomson had promised in his first year as minister.

Meals were the biggest bugbear. Butler took the commissioner out to sample the food, which Butler said he could not bear to smell, let alone eat. 'I had never been an advocate of militancy,' he said, 'but we started to get quite militant over that.'

In March 1974 70 police college students were poisoned by the food. Thomas and the commissioner went to see the minister, Burnside pointing out that if something was not done the cadets and recruits would walk out. Something unprecedented was done. The police got a new contract with a private firm instead of with the Labour Department, with which the authorities had persisted until then because the college was part of the package involving the Department of Labour's immigration hostel. The manager of the kitchen was replaced, the police dining room was cut off from the rest of the facilities and the area was redecorated.

Ultimately, Thomas was the casualty of this incident and of an editorial he wrote the same month in the *Newsletter* entitled 'Which Way?', arguing against a militant approach in favour of his quiet behind-the-scenes style of advocacy. Butler thought his old school tie manner counted against Thomas; he may have appeared aloof from association affairs, but that was simply his nature. Thomas should, Butler believes, have defended himself more, particularly after he and Dan Ingram had had difficulty making any breakthrough on pay increases. At the end of 1972 Butler and Alan Monk, one of the active young members of the management committee, suggested Thomas write an editorial explaining that the delays in the pay claim were due to a slow-moving bureaucracy and government. Thomas said he knew what he was doing and did things his way.

The Thomas way had been to hammer into members every year the need to restructure the conference so that the management committee could get on with things, and leave the dispersed national council to decide policy. Some members from outside Wellington were more interested in having input into the management committee. At the 1973 conference there was a big debate about each district electing one member on to the management committee. At the time Auckland and North Auckland had 1200 members but one representative on the committee, the South Island had only two representatives. Whangarei delegate P.R. Haworth said the districts had been out in the cold for too long. The policy for the management committee had been formulated in 1936, when travel to Wellington took many hours. Most could now get there in under an hour. In proposing the change, Hamish Beckett of Auckland said the management committee was out of touch with the majority of members.

Thomas was among those who spoke against the remit, saying it was too costly. Six meetings in one year would cost $90,000, which was more than the equity they had in their newly acquired Manners Street building. What he wanted was a management committee that could react quickly. The remit was lost, which no doubt confirmed northern feelings that the numbers were stacked against them.

The outer regions had been checked for 1973, but their grievances had not gone away. Rebellion was in the air. Christchurch District Secretary P.J. O'Halloran went on television, breaking the rule that the management committee handled such things. He made an emotional speech about Gilfedder's dismissal, saying it would now be unsafe for policemen to help little old ladies across streets.

Agitation was taking place from within the Wellington

district. The fomenter was Alec Waugh, who had been a police cadet in late 1969 and, as a 19-year-old constable, went to a meeting of the Wellington branch of the association, where he was amazed at the age and gruffness of the people there. He walked straight into a row with district councillor, Rick Bos, objecting to the way the latter was dominating proceedings.

> Early in the 1970s it became clear the national executive of the association was rusty at best and incompetent at worst. Myself and Trevor Morley, who now runs his own security business in Wellington, and was then a detective who didn't like the slowness of change in the police, talked about how we could change it. We decided on writing this four or more pages of photocopied newsletter, *Watchdog*. I wrote it, distributed about 80, but got requests from round the country for about 200. There were 20 of them, every few months for about three years. We ran issues such as early retirement, rejuvenation of the police, merit promotion, professional pay and conditions. We targeted Hamish Thomas, though in hindsight we should have targeted Rob Butler as well. Butler called the shots and had a relationship with the commissioner that was too close. We wanted a paid professional who could negotiate for us.

Waugh received threats. One day in the lift his divisional commander decried his promotion chances, saying what he did was affecting policing. Waugh says Thomas wrote to Waugh threatening defamation proceedings.

Waugh was one of several in this ginger group of cops in their 20s and 30s. Others were Ken Burt, Brian Walkinshaw, Steve Brown and Robert Brown. Steve Brown is now a lawyer in Wellington. His contribution at the time was to tape a management committee meeting to demonstrate that what Thomas wrote up as the minutes was not what was said.

Butler says Thomas became the scapegoat for frustrations in the association, especially over lack of progress with pay negotiations. When Thomas went out to the college to investigate the food poisoning, he clashed with a group of detectives there, who challenged his version of events. When they walked out on him, he allegedly shouted that if that was how they felt, they could 'get stuffed'. This story spread like wildfire through the association, confirming the feeling that Thomas was being superior.

His March editorial 'Which Way?' claimed the association had been successful with the reasonable approach, but members were not convinced. R.B. McNaughton of Mount Maunganui said in the next *Newsletter* that the trouble was lack of communication between Wellington and the rest of the country. A letter from 'Action' said the editorial was a smokescreen for 'Association machinery rusted with conservative attitudes' and afraid of publicity and questioning, lacking vitality.

Throughout 1974 other letters claimed that stronger stands could have been made by the executive. C.F. Smith felt the information coming from the management committee was so sparse and brief 'as to seem to be given almost grudgingly'. Certainly what were written up and signed by Thomas were minute minutes.

Butler dismissed much of the criticism as the old suspicions, particularly in Auckland and Christchurch, that being in headquarters and on good terms with the commissioners meant you were in their pocket. He claims it was a distinct advantage to be able to resolve matters by walking into the commissioner's office. It was militant members who had not got their way over something who spread rumours that the president and executive director did what the commissioner wanted.

Communication in a more general area had been a problem in Sharp's strict era. Constable A.J. Picketts objected to Sharp saying he would have to employ civilians because there was no interest among police in the fingerprinting job advertised. The commissioner did not appreciate that police hesitated to give up a police house to pay twice the rent for a pool house in Wellington, the most expensive place in the country. Picketts suggested it would be more economic to set up a fingerprinting section and other sections such as a driving school in Rotorua. Then there would be dozens of applicants.

In 1974 Connelly announced that the two ratio improvements had resulted in the biggest increase in police history, with numbers now topping 4000. The large number of younger members in the association did not perhaps appreciate that government stabilisation regulations in the wake of the oil price rise prevented pay increases. All they could see was lack of action from their executive's softly softly approach.

On 14 August the Christchurch district held an extraordinary meeting and passed a motion that 'due to lack of aggressive pursuance of remits tabled by this and other districts, and the lack of major results during his term as executive director, this meeting expresses a vote of no confidence in Mr H.S. Thomas, in the hope that he will be replaced'.

Butler reacted swiftly. He circularised all national councillors and district secretaries saying that he had discussed the motion with the management committee and wanted Christchurch to send details of their complaint. He called a conference of national councillors to resolve the complaint. Invoking the rule that five was a quorum, he did not consider it necessary to bring councillors from outside Wellington. It took a few seconds to resolve that they still had confidence in Thomas.

Invercargill delegate L.F. Smith threatened Butler with a Supreme Court ruling on this view of the rules, but Butler, who prided himself on his knowledge of procedure, knew he was right. Smith suggested that the rules were 'a somewhat dented mirror'.

Christchurch gave notice of annual conference remits on Thomas, who lacked 'the necessary temperament, drive and initiative' and whose office was not cast in a positive enough role. Christchurch wanted his position abolished and the administration recast.

At the conference in October Christchurch delegate Mark Penn moved and Smith seconded a motion that Thomas be given three months' notice. Butler blocked this by saying the matter had been resolved at the special conference and the motion was out of order. Penn insisted that all the South Island except Timaru thought Thomas was not doing his job. His 'Which Way?' editorial indicated a man under fire, hiding behind the rules. He was not aggressive enough compared with his predecessor and had not achieved much in five years.

When Butler asked for specifics, Penn said Thomas had not done his homework on the benefits available from the Accident Compensation legislation and informed members. On a 1973 remit Thomas had said that only the Wages Tribunal could make orders, but the Labour Department in Christchurch advised that only an adjustment was involved, which could be made by the Police Staff Tribunal. Then there was the matter of claiming overtime on shiftwork, about which Thomas had given no information and no explanation. Concerning the food poisoning at Trentham, Thomas had told those affected they could 'go and get stuffed'. On pay and margins Thomas had written to the Minister and Prime Minister, who could do nothing. He should have pursued the provisions of the Police Act.

Hamish Beckett defended Thomas on the grounds that the government overrode all other tribunals with its Wages Tribunal, that Thomas had nothing to do with income tax, that it was not him but the management committee that should be censured over meals. If Thomas were not sufficiently forceful, it was because the members were not. They should tell him what to do. A.C. Harding also defended Thomas, but in the process said many younger members mistakenly thought he was the executive, whereas it was the president, national council and management committee.

D.A. Duffy of Wellington confirmed that his younger members, too, saw Thomas as the executive and thought he had done nothing. On the food poisoning issue, Thomas denied to the detectives at Trentham that he had been asked to communicate with Commandant Overton, who ran the college, but was challenged by one of the detectives who had been a witness. It was then that the detectives walked out on Thomas. His district agreed with Christchurch, except they would widen the no confidence vote to include the national council, president and management committee. Their solution to the lack of promptness was a fulltime president.

Ian Sutherland of Palmerston North drew attention to the slack service from the office. An application sent on 20 June 1973 was answered by Thomas on 28 May 1974, with the excuse that 'we have some file problems'. T.J. Owen of New Plymouth confirmed that they had not received replies to several items of correspondence.

Butler said he took some of the responsibility for the situation. He had accepted the presidency again because of the alleged lack of communication and the suggestion of a rift. Perhaps working from Wanganui was not as close as it could be, but he had worked more closely than anyone with Thomas and it was not true he dictated and did what he liked. Butler deplored the anti-establishment trend he had seen on his travels around districts. He did not know why he personally had been spared—he should be picked on, he was the top executive.

In his view Thomas had worked hard in a big job. He had already said they should spend more to ensure that the association operated efficiently. He believed the management committee and the national council pulled against each other because national councillors had not been present at monthly meetings. One or other body was superfluous. He did not accept that the association had lost its efficiency or esteem with department and government. He suggested that a representative from every district come together once a month.

Thomas then defended his editorial as part of his role as editor; it was one man's view, nothing to do with his job as executive director. He neither hid behind the rules, nor made them, but was controlled by them. As a lawyer, he advised members to obey government regulations, and so there was no application to the Police Tribunal. He did not understand why he had been called a liar over the Police College food poisoning when all the things asked for were being attended to. As for not answering letters, that happened everywhere and he apologised. He suggested that people write again. As for not being aggressive enough, he had access to the commissioner whenever he wished. Anybody who came into the commissioner's office thumping the table would be shown the door and only contacted thereafter by letter. Thomas had said years ago that the association needed restructuring; when it was, his own job could be dispensed with.

Penn said the association was in a mess. He was not after a table thumper, but a self-starter who got things done. Thomas was in a good position to be such a person, yet there was little change and no initiatives. Although Penn's motion was lost, it was agreed that a committee should be set up to study the restructuring of the association. Butler suggested the management committee, but he was defeated in favour of a committee of five national councillors representative of the country. Niven, Parfitt, Sutherland, Harding and McAvoy were elected.

The conference had decided on more special conferences for national councillors when proceedings were interrupted by Leader of the Opposition Rob Muldoon arriving for afternoon tea. He praised the police, particularly Sir Angus Sharp for the way he had nobbled Edwards on television. He said the public appreciated the way the task force had made Auckland streets safer. He said he would support rugby tours between South Africa and New Zealand, no matter what report he got from the police, because he would not allow organised dissident elements to take over.

In his farewell speech Sir Angus expressed his worry that the age of protest had entered the younger levels of the police. With the association as a channel for protest, the public should get no indication that all was not well in the ranks.

There had never been more dissatisfaction in the ranks with their elected and paid representatives, but it would be a few years before the dissidents had their way. Meantime,

Thomas had more to do as treasurer following the resignation of Isaacs. Retired Dan Ingram helped out in the office and continued to chair the welfare fund.

The sniping at Thomas continued. A.F. Edwardson of Auckland called for complete coverage of management committee minutes despite the conference voting against this. *Watchdog* No. 4 wrote ironically of recent attempts to oust the executive director, based on the misapprehension he was the association, when really he was its 'slave'.

There were calls for Thomas to come alone to meetings around the country, but Butler went instead, refusing to countenance Thomas being abused. He says Thomas became the focus of frustration over pay, but no headway was being made by anyone. He was told the police should not get more than others, but there was legislative validity for this, and the police did work twice as hard and faced twice the risk.

The association's relationship with the government soured after Kirk's death in August 1974. It was not simply money, but also liberal legislative proposals. The association was busy fighting rearguard actions with submissions. To the Royal Commission on Liquor they submitted that any law changes must consider policing. To the Crimes Amendment Bill they suggested 20 instead of the proposed 18 as the age for permitting homosexual acts between consenting adults because of teacher/pupil dangers, and that the definition of privacy not include public lavatories, hotels and the like. Justice Minister Martyn Finlay upset the association when he congratulated an Auckland group for setting up a sobering-up coffee shop for drunks who would 'otherwise be needlessly arrested'. The association felt he did not appreciate that their members had the dreary job of ensuring drunks did not cause personal injury or property damage. Connelly was on their side, but they knew he was on his own in Cabinet.

In October 1974 Burnside took over as commissioner. Butler knew Burnside was dedicated to new and better means of communication. As deputy commissioner he had pushed association requests, particularly for the lighter uniform. In the top job he sorted out a long running hassle for CIB and country members over cars. A Taihape detective under Butler's control had been promised a car. The unsealed country roads were atrocious and country cops invariably ran their own cars at a loss. The Taihape cop, furious at not getting a departmental car, was told that, if he did not like it, he could pack up and be transferred.

Butler saw Burnside. The commissioner chewed out his staff for misinterpreting his instructions and handed Butler his own second car for the Taihape detective. Butler was not popular with the headquarters staff who used the second car.

On another occasion a Constable A.L. Watts was paraded before Auckland staff and made an example of for allegedly having overlong hair. The association matched a photograph of Watts with a recruiting poster, showing both wearing hair the same length. Burnside, shown the photographs, resolved the matter in the constable's favour.

Butler led lobbying on earlier retirement, but the government would not commit itself to any pension subsidy for retirement at 55. Lobbying on the pay scale was jammed by the government not permitting any movement to the assistant commissioner's salary.

The Rowling regime was perceived to have switched from being hard to being soft on law and order. Association and guild opposed the proposed suppression of names until a case had been heard in court, fearing it would lead to acquittals and suppression of procedures. The association was concerned that senior government members were vilifying the task force.

Thomas wrote his May 1975 editorial on the government's softness on law and order, but it did not win him friends in the association. The restructuring committee reported back with some of his own proposals, such as remits dealt with as they arose by the national council or the management committee. It suggested a return to the title of national secretary.

Remits were already being referred back to initiating districts, and only four re-emerged at the annual conference. The conference concentrated on what really concerned it—the fact that there had been no salary increase since 1970. Smith said Thomas should have taken the pay case to the tribunal in 1972. Trevor Tozer, however, said there was an indication that the Higher Salaries Commission would be reviewing the salaries of commissioner and assistant commissioner soon, and then they could go to the Police Tribunal. The conference agreed.

National unexpectedly won a landslide victory and the new Police Minister was Allan McCready, who assured the association of the enforcement of law and order, but not of adjusted salaries and margins.

In May 1976 the government informed the police, through the *Gazette*, that no review of police pay would be possible before January 1977. The Butler/Thomas executive copped the flak from *Watchdog*. Butler said it was not the executive director's fault; the association and the department had had a case ready to go to government when the new regulations came out. It was too late. Thomas resigned, followed by Butler.

T.C. Gray wrote in the *Newsletter* that the bad old days were returning when police was treated as the Cinderella department by the government. The proof was there in traffic officers being paid $9,000 a year after three years compared with police on $8,200 after three times that length of service.

Butler suggested it was time to hire the best industrial lawyers. Alec Waugh and Trevor Morley had already been down that road, speaking to former police inspector and law lecturer Rob Moodie at university and at his home in 1975, trying to persuade him to work for the association. Moodie was not sure he was wanted. He had, after all, said a few terse things about the association and the administration. It did not matter. Both administration's Allan Galbraith and Rob Butler, who had worked with Moodie in the CIB, suggested that he apply for the job.

Part IV

The Moodie Years of Fulfilment

Dr Rob Moodie is remembered by most New Zealanders as the man in the dress. The man himself remembers the dress as a useful ploy in his high-profile advocacy on behalf of the Police Association. Here the *Dominion* photographer captures Moodie opening the men's boutique on the site of the Ingram Building, the former association-owned offices at 11 Manners Street named after Dan Ingram, the association president at the time of purchase

Chapter Sixteen

The Man for All Claims

Rob Moodie is remembered as the police spokesman who wore a dress. Rob Butler rates him a hot-shot negotiator in whose era the association made great strides. The dress was part of the negotiating strategy. His predecessor Hamish Thomas was, by his own admission, never a media man, but Moodie was a natural. After trying several lawyers who wanted to help the policeman's lot and a policeman who wanted to be a lawyer, the association got their choice absolutely right with a former policeman who was tired of the law and wanted a challenge. Moodie not only rose to the challenge but, over a decade, eclipsed every other union leader. In many ways Moodie brought as positive a change to the police as his ultimate political boss and opponent Rob Muldoon wrought in a negative fashion over a similar time span.

Moodie's agenda was ambitious—to change the political and administrative view of the police, to change the police view of society. It was grounded in a simple perception.

'The case of Constable Bob Fleming came up early on,' Moodie recalls,

> and was central to my approach to the job. He was a constable who was shot when attending a domestic dispute in the Hutt Valley. He suffered permanent damage to his stomach. I arrived on the scene seven years after the event. He was in a very bad way, almost desolate because he had been trying for seven years to get compensation for his injury. Nobody had done a damn thing for him, not the Commissioner, not the Welfare officer, not Butler as president or Hamish Thomas. In many people's eyes in the police Fleming was a malingerer. Half his guts had been blown away. Where was the true grit? They were a group of people who didn't know how to cry. By the time I'd finished we had built him a house.

People still talk about Rob Moodie's ego as much as his dress. Moodie himself prefers to talk about injustice put to rights. He saw that everybody had nice words to say, but that Fleming was not being helped, because nobody knew how to work the system. Fleming was caught between Accident Compensation and the War Pensions Board arguing over who paid what.

'I encountered the Fleming type of case again and again,' he says. 'Plenty of sympathetic words, but nothing happened. And 90 per cent of the reason was not because they didn't want to help, but because they didn't know their way round the system. When I arrived in 1976 not one person knew the rules for negotiating an industrial claim. There were no rules.'

Like the Fleming case, the police pay claim had been meandering on for seven years without any ground rules. Moodie saw that negotiation was based on what he calls the old pals' act. The first thing he was told was not to do anything, not to say anything to the media, not to make a fuss.

Moodie *did* make a fuss, go to the media, say a lot of things. He had begun the job on 22 November 1976 and was directed by the management committee to act 'under the guidance of the Executive Director'. He did not wait for guidance, but went on television that day to say that the police needed their pay claim settled.

'I decided we were going to rev this up. Hamish rang me and abused me and said I'd ruined years of work, blown away with my antics all that goodwill that he had built up over the years with the State Services Commission and the administration. Hamish never came back.'

The younger association members loved this. Keith Morrow was a newish national councillor from Gisborne. 'There was a certain excitement in the presence of Rob Moodie,' he remembers.

> You could feel things going to change. It was more business-like, there were issues starting to be discussed. As an ex-police

Moodie still wearing a collar and tie and about to get stuck into the pay claim that would make his name with association members

> officer he brought a fair amount of empathy to the police ethic and the rankling over injustices. He was like a breath of fresh air. There was a tremendous expectation of what was possible. I thought if the commissioner said no, that was that, executive power was absolute, you just didn't question it. It took awhile for me to adjust to a skilled negotiator who was going to call the police administration to account.

Robert Alexander Moodie was always a man in a hurry. Born at Port Chalmers, he ran away several times from an unhappy home life that eventually broke up. For two years he was a state ward. He was brought up by the Clyne family on their farm at Windsor near Oamaru and is still close to his foster parents. While with them he developed the love for the land that saw him managing a farm at 18 and led him to his present occupation as a fibre goat farmer.

Educated at Waitaki Boys High School, he graduated to the freezing works, contract fencing and farm labouring. His first encounters with the police were sharing a patrol car with the bobby bringing the absconding lad home, or ticking him off for nicking a bike or comics. He joined the police in 1959, encouraged into the job by local Senior Sergeant Fred Leadley. At 17 he had twice been asked by Leadley to escort Child Welfare absconders by train back to Christchurch. That led to discussion about police work. After two years of Leadley propaganda Rob joined up.

His independent streak soon became apparent. He arrived in Wellington to start work as a detective dressed in a charcoal suit, green suede waistcoat and green suede shoes. His grey-suited superiors initially refused to supply him with files, but his arrest record was soon so good that he won the sobriquet 'Ace' and his garb ceased to be an issue.

More importantly, Moodie's eyesight also ceased to be a problem, when he found an optometrist who prescribed the right glasses. The moment he discovered reading he would not stop. He studied part-time for a law degree, taking advantage of the more favourable study provisions available in the police. He also made the rank of inspector, but quit the police in 1972 to study law. That year he was senior scholar at Victoria University of Wellington, and accepted an appointment there as a lecturer in law. Over the next four years he read for a PhD, awarded in 1976. He published several articles on a wide range of legal subjects, his article in the *New Zealand Law Journal* 'The Gilfedder Affair—Another Perspective' winning the 1973 Rex Mason Memorial Prize for the best contribution to legal writing in New Zealand.

During these years Moodie became known as a current affairs commentator, particularly on police matters. By 1976 there were two teaching jobs on offer at Australian and Canadian universities. Moodie confesses that he had become bored with the police job; now he was bored with university teaching, but still interested in the police. An example was his article in the *Law Journal* attacking the police administration over whether they shot to wound or to kill. In an incident in Christchurch a man stuck a knife into a girl's neck to taunt her mother. The police hesitated to shoot him because the only target was his head. Moodie argued that they were allowing themselves to be distracted by this argument of whether they shot to wound or kill. The commissioner had responded to the situation by declaring that the police shot to wound. Moodie said they shot neither to wound nor to kill, but to achieve 'instant incapacitation of the target, because they were shooting to save lives. If that meant killing someone, that was tough. The police didn't create the situation.'

Moodie obviously impressed a few police. Allan Galbraith rang him to tell him that the association job was coming up. Moodie had some knowledge of the job already, because he had been consulted by the Wellington branch of the association, which was trying to get rid of Hamish Thomas. The cheques Moodie received were signed by Thomas. On a specific occasion Moodie represented Wellington member Lindsay Hunter on a disciplinary charge of abusing President Rob Butler.

Moodie had worked with Butler and characterised their relationship as one of mutual respect, although they had not got on well because of different work attitudes. Butler's approach, according to Moodie, was that 'you went down to the commissioner and had a few drinks'.

Moodie is remembered for regular office parties, but these were financed by the money the staff, including himself, saved by doing their own office cleaning. Moodie did not do association business over whiskies in the commissioner's office. As far as Moodie was concerned, the best place for Butler was using his skills as a policeman running the Wanganui CIB. Moodie took the view that any profession run by its members, like teaching, had to be a mess.

The Butler/Thomas era had believed in lobbying. They propped each other, but their armchair approach had provoked the dissident Wellington group that included Alec Waugh, Bob Bull and Lindsay Hunter. Alan Monk was one of the management committee who did not approve of Steve Brown recording the minutes to prove that Thomas was not publishing them in full. Monk admits, however, that he was dissatisfied with Thomas for much the same reasons. When he asked Thomas what he had done in the previous month, invariably he found it was nothing until a few days before the next meeting was due. 'Progressively,' says Monk, 'the message got across to him that he was not performing. He was reactive on issues as opposed to proactive.'

When Butler resigned, Monk was elected president because he was acceptable to Butler's supporters and to the Young Turks. Graham Butterworth, who became research officer in 1977, saw two important qualities in Monk—he was a good chairman and he represented the feeling of the average police officer, the thinking NCO, the long-serving career man who sets the tone and the attitude of the service. 'Alan was a very good lightning rod for the views of the others,' says Butterworth. 'You knew when his brow started to get furrowed you were going too fast, going too far. And he wasn't afraid to speak his viewpoint.'

Moodie liked having the president at a distance—Butler in Wanganui, Monk in Blenheim—well away from the office. The mild, gentlemanly Monk did not mind, for the one part of the job he did not like was the public speaking. He was happy to leave the media to Moodie.

At 34, he was the association's youngest president. He was educated at Hastings Boys High, where he was active in the school army cadet scheme. Through the army vocational guidance services he signed up for the police, with some awe, at the age of 19 in 1961. Monk passed through the primitive Trentham barracks and did the eight-hour beat duty for the first two years, just the half-hour meal break and a cuppa. He thought £915 a year an incredible salary then, but would not now because of all the night shifts and lack of allowances. He did two tours in Cyprus and drove for Commissioner Sharp.

His first experience of the association had been after he let a prisoner escape from the Auckland railyards and Jack Meltzer prepared his defence in the old Grey Street office. Nudged into association work, he developed an interest in police housing, establishing, after research, that it had got progressively worse over the years. He came to the fore with his reports for the housing sub-committee, became the highest polling member of the management committee, and senior vice-president under Butler, whose chairing skills he admired.

Monk and Moodie, only four years older, came into office together. Two resilient younger men were needed to cope with the high tide of feelings about the delayed police pay deal. Monk will never forget attending, with Moodie, an Auckland district meeting in a Mount Albert hall, with 800 angry coppers, two-thirds of the entire Auckland strength.

'I was overawed,' says Monk. 'Rob was in his element. It was a fantastic meeting. You could cut the air with a knife. We returned to Wellington, the publicity ahead of us. Within 12 hours of that meeting and our meeting with Minister McCready in Wellington, we had a pay claim settlement. The politicians could see that the level of discontent meant something was seriously wrong.' No politician wanted what Auckland district was threatening—a work to rule by police, public comment aimed at deterring recruits.

Moodie made sure they got the message loud and clear. 'The system,' he says, 'had always been that the association would prepare a claim and then put it to the commissioner. It was very gentlemanly. I insisted the association had a role.'

It took a little gentle persuasion to get his message through to the commissioner. At their first meeting, Burnside told Moodie he was there as a privilege, and Moodie replied he was there as of right. Burnside locked Moodie out of his office for a week. Moodie told him the office was not his; it belonged to the people of New Zealand and Moodie was going to tell them what was going on.

'We reached the point,' Moodie says with a twinkle behind his thick horn-rims, 'where I said to the president we either dump this turkey or he's going to do the job. He's not sitting there like King James and just dictating, or he'll suffer the same fate. It was a hard battle, and it still is. The commissioner still thinks he's God.'

Once the commissioner unlocked the door, Moodie charged through, on his way to see the people who got things done, Minister of State Services Peter Gordon in particular. Moodie knew it was not the Minister of Police

Moodie and President Monk tap State Services Minister Peter Gordon for the great pay hike

who made the decisions. His letters went to Gordon.

By the next management committee meeting of 20 and 21 December 1976, Moodie could report access to the State Services Commission and the Cabinet Sub-committee on State Services. Negotiations were underway directly between the association and the bureaucrats and politicians. There would be no more modifications of association claims by the commissioner.

At the 31 March 1977 management committee meeting Moodie announced that they had the 9.9 per cent pay increase, with penal rates and payment for night shifts on top of that. At the same meeting Hamish Beckett, Auckland vice-president, said little had been done about allowances. Moodie replied that if the exercise was to be done, it had to be done properly; the office was not equipped to handle it. Law student researcher Ross Revington was leaving and his position would be filled by 'people who can help with research and analysis and have general experience in the industrial area, so that we can make a movement in the area of allowances and conditions of service'.

Moodie had his strategy in place from the beginning. He began with a multifaceted pay claim. 'You don't go into a pay claim to resolve anomalies,' he said, 'you go in to create them. It's an ongoing thing. You resolve something this year, but you create an anomaly which you can go back and have a wee puddle in next year.'

So it was that Moodie told the May 1977 management committee meeting that the State Services 12-month salary rule required that a case for further salary movement must be prepared by this coming 11 October. If it was to be done properly, a research officer was needed now. He told them he had already placed an advertisement in the *Evening Post* to this effect. He also told them it was no longer possible for the association and the guild to go their separate ways on pay negotiations. Any future application must be a joint one. He and Monk had already made representations to the Officers' Guild, who agreed to make a financial contribution to the appointment of an executive officer.

Moodie acknowledged criticism that the executive was not fully informing members, or even this management committee and national council, of each step in pay negotiations. This was not possible. Such matters were confidential to the negotiators and would have prejudiced the case if revealed during negotiations.

In this frank fashion Moodie not only ensured that he stayed ahead of his employers, but also defused complaints by his directness. His style was to bring the rumours out into the open, where they invariably withered under the force of his obvious success.

On 1 July he told the management committee meeting that 36-year-old Graham Victor Butterworth had been appointed research officer. Furthermore, Butterworth had completed a report into the restructuring of the Criminal Registration Bureau, which was being evaluated by the police administration. Not only was Moodie steps ahead, but he had made a perfect choice. Butterworth and Moodie quickly became the most successful duet in union advocacy history.

Morrow describes Butterworth as the number cruncher and the man with the telling phrase, such as the 'rejuvenation of the service' that would so impress Deputy Prime Minister Geoffrey Palmer. Morrow rated Moodie and Butterworth without peer in any union or service organisation at the time because they 'had contacts, brains, determination and street brawling in the negotiating crunch for pay and conditions'.

Butterworth had been chief research officer at the Consumers' Institute. With an MA in history from Victoria University of Wellington, he had worked in the Department of Trade and Industry and the PSA and taught at Massey University. He says curiosity about social change attracted him to the job. He had dealt at Consumer with dollars and cents, but his real interest was race relations. His earliest publication was *The Maori in the New Zealand Economy*, which had involved major demographic and economic analysis. Unlike most historians, he liked the maths. His wife Susan, also an historian, told him that if he really wanted to know what was happening in New Zealand, the police were more likely to know than anybody else, since they dealt with the consequences.

Eighteen months into the job Moodie told Butterworth he had won out against some well-performed applicants because he was the one Alan Monk found hardest to stomach. Moodie wanted someone 'who would make operational cops think,' says Butterworth, 'and be a bit different from them, so we would always have another perspective ...'.

Moodie also emphasised that, for a union which could not strike, the quality of its material became crucial and so the research function became more important. Moodie did the advocacy, based on Butterworth's research, and a great deal of talking it through. They would spend two hours in the office every day reviewing problems and discussing solutions.

As with Moodie, results destroyed any complaints about Butterworth. Under the somewhat bumbling professorial exterior, as one member put it, Butterworth marshalled hard facts into irresistible arguments. His first major work was on allowances, which were being decided in a Mickey Mouse way. He looked for a logical basis, sorting them into categories and tying them to the appropriate points in the Consumer Price Index. He admits there was effrontery involved in marrying them into the general adjustments, but the exercise moved allowances from $300,000 to $1,200,000. Everybody, even the commissioner, gained from the plain-clothes allowance.

It was with the commissioner that Moodie and Butterworth started their campaign to raise the low status of the police. 'I think the major breakthrough for me,' Moodie says, was in the first two weeks in the job, with 'the decision based on de facto marriages for police officers. If a policeman was discovered living in a de facto relationship he was ordered to terminate it or he would be dismissed from the service. I waited for a case involving children. I wrote Burnside a 10-page letter pointing out how many homes the children had had, and asking if he wanted to play God.'

Burnside did not. 'It was the end of the commissioner's absolute authority,' says Moodie. 'And I think everything flowed from that. But it wasn't achieved without a great deal of resentment from senior officers.'

Moodie decided that he would speak out and attract controversy because his members could not, and because they did not have the ultimate weapon of the strike. His argument was not significantly different from Meltzer's—police officers' pay should be such that they can live in the community in a style befitting their position without the temptation to take another job or bribes. Moodie saw that Lee had successfully negotiated claims, but had set up no supporting structure. It is the same, Moodie says, whether you are running a farm or involved in industrial relations—you achieve something, then you must build something to maintain it. This had not been done. Moodie set about establishing an office structure and attracting a high profile.

When he arrived there was a research officer finishing a degree, two women working fulltime and another part-time. 'The women,' he says, 'had nothing to do. There was nothing happening—and there was a salary claim going! My recollection is Hamish wasn't very involved. When I started I used to get letters from people thanking me for answering their letters.' He was told the association could not afford to buy him a dictaphone. When he left a decade later the staff was up to 19 and growing, the police service organisations turning over millions of dollars annually.

Moodie made it a precondition of accepting the job that the old remit system be dropped. He knew well from his days in the CIB office how he would get boozed up and then go to the association and tie up the executive director with a few remit thoughts. Monk remembers how, apart from the legal assistance cases, the remits went round in circles. By the time everybody had had their say, there was no time left to do anything. Overnight it all changed, the management committee handling problems as they arose instead of waiting for remits, Moodie selecting what went to the commissioner. Out went the old chestnuts such as requesting that sirens be put back on police cars. The new system ended the slow round of the commissioner replying months later and saying no to remits, which were then resubmitted.

Secondly, Moodie ensured comprehensive minutes were written up and distributed to everybody, so that every member could understand what was happening. He encouraged branches to open at places such as Waipukurau, Wairoa and Blenheim, and made sure the minutes got there.

Moodie wanted a better newsletter, so after nine months a fulltime editor, Geoff Terpstra, was brought in to do the job. Moodie and Butterworth used the *Newsletter* to provoke as well as inform members. Butterworth wrote up big claims, but he also wrote about how gangs worked, and Moodie had a major speech on the macho Kiwi male published in the *Newsletter*.

Moodie reduced the 16-member management committee to a manageable size, at first six and then one more to give geographical balance. The committee did the day-to-day work and the national council was the association Parliament, where many a row was to be aired over Moodie's initiatives. He introduced more special conferences for the national council.

Moodie, Butterworth and the president made regular tours that reached every district at least once a year. On these trips policy initiatives were developed. Moodie remembers the pattern of early retirement shaped over such a tour; Monk recalls Moodie developing the association's own mortgage scheme, which the administration rubbished but is now an integral part of the association.

Moodie did not come into the job with a preconceived plan. The first thing to sort out was the pay. His philosophy was to establish the needs of police and their families. From his own experience he knew what an insecure job it was. 'If you wanted promotion, you were thrown to the four winds. Why couldn't a man be promoted in Wellington if he lived there? What the hell was the point of sending him all over the country? Promotion/transfer was the major issue, along with housing.'

Moodie began at the top, negotiating to have the commissioner's salary improved, so that all other salaries could be raised. Burnside had put forward a modest paper to the Higher Salaries Commission to raise his $24,000 by a few thousand. Moodie remembers items such as his wife's hairdressing bills and drycleaning for his suits. 'It was

Moodie's first battle was to confront Commissioner Burnside with his prejudice against de facto relationships causing resignations. As usual he made sure it was a publicly aired issue

pathetic, and nothing to do with what the Higher Salaries Commission was about, what factors they take into account.'

Moodie read the commission's constitution. The arguments should be about comparability with state and private managers of 5000 staff and similar budgets. Moodie and Butterworth made out a case for $38,000 15c. They failed to get the 15 cents, but getting the rest gave them the top rung of their margins ladder, from which they could argue the case for improving the pay for every margin of rank. It also determined Moodie's own salary. He had been one of the first to negotiate his own performance contract, and it was, he laughingly admits, based on earning more than the commissioner. Burnside persistently attacked Moodie over the claim, saying he would never get such nonsense through. It happened again with retirement at 55. Once it was achieved, nobody objected.

Moodie's next big effort was a paper, which took him a year, on how to change the promotion system. He was aware from his touring that the cost of housing meant many members lived in fear of transfers and promotions. The commissioner's solution was Regulation 15, barring members who turned down promotion from any further opportunity for several years. Moodie called for a joint committee with guild and administration to deal with 'the most unsettling issue in the police'.

He circularised his paper analysing how promotion would disadvantage a member who lost a low-interest mortgage when mortgage rates were rising rapidly. Regulation 15 was a narrow response that did not recognise why promotion was turned down. The paper was passed by the 1977 conference, and went to the commissioner, who accepted it; Moodie was providing the research that should have been coming from the department. From now on positions were advertised, applied for and could be considered in the context of the application and each person's situation. Housing was more difficult. Moodie first attacked those senior police enjoying police houses in the city and living in holiday homes.

Moodie spent the next three years nudging a reluctant government and bureaucracy into accepting more realistic margins between ranks and related conditions. He began by meeting McCready, Gordon and State Services Commission officers Dave Swallow and Ron Kelly to explain the situation. It was difficult to retain experienced staff. Four inspectors had resigned in one year; in one year the loss had been 7.5 per cent. He won their agreement that the police had lagged behind and that they were a special case, and he won it in writing. Thereafter he could produce it and say that the association was simply doing what had been agreed on, moving from upgrading to margins to hours of work, adequate insurance and related conditions. It was a grim battle of position papers, letters, meetings, pleas and occasional threats. State Services squirmed and wriggled, but was hooked and finally landed.

Butterworth did the research, analysing decades of salary scales back to 1937 to demonstrate that margins had been ignored and had slipped, particularly at the crucial NCO level. In 1937 the margin between a constable and a sergeant was 10.2 per cent, in 1977 it was 1.2 per cent. The narrowing margins were there too between sergeant, senior sergeant and inspector. Promotion could leave an officer only slightly better off, and worse off if he had to move house.

The result of this was little incentive to take promotion exams that led to transfers and little or no recognition of additional responsibilities. Many were resigning because they saw no future in accepting promotion. As one policeman observed, what other profession, after 20 years' service and every possible promotion, left you only $4,500 better off than a 19-year-old in his first week of training?

Moodie wedded this situation to the police taking the brunt of public criticism for, as he put it to Gordon in a letter dated 18 February 1977, 'increased street violence, an increased drug problem, serious racial and cultural conflicts, gang hooliganism and armed confrontations'. The public looked to the police for solutions to 'an apparent erosion of the social and political values ... the quality of the Police, more than any other single factor, ... determines the quality of life in any society'. The calibre of the police determined society's security, justice and equality. It was, therefore, a tragedy for the police and for society that 'many young highly qualified NCOs and officers' were leaving because they saw no recognition of their expertise and professionalism.

Moodie's timing proved excellent, for *Truth*, on 15 February 1977, published an article headed 'Top Cops Quit'. One was Detective Senior Sergeant Stapleton from the Auckland Fraud Squad, a 32-year-old qualified lawyer. Another was Inspector A.D. Orme, a 31-year-old criminologist majoring in economic history. Both were going into private enterprise.

In 1978 Moodie presented his 21-page Margins Review, which demonstrated how rare declining promotion was in the 1960s. In 1975 17.94 per cent of those considered for promotion declined it. In January 1978 it was up to 73.91 per cent. The crisis was accelerating. The guild and the association proposed to arrest it with a 9.5 per cent rise between each rank.

When Moodie and Stu McEwen from the Officers' Guild met with Gordon, McCready and State Services Commission officers Kelly and R. Green, Moodie stated that the attitude of the SSC was his biggest concern. He was incensed that the welfare fund had achieved the cheapest insurance in the country, yet the SSC kept emphasising the in-service implications of improving the insurance and an apparent instruction to the police administration not to discuss insurance with the service organisations.

Moodie also told the meeting he was concerned about the health and fitness problem. The Fleming case had given rise to the insurance scheme that more than doubled police cover from $15,000 to $35,000. Moodie pushed the quote he used in his submission that when the United States gave its police officers $50,000 cover, it said the sum demonstrated 'the esteem of a free society for those whom it entrusts with our public and personal safety'. Meltzer had liked to quote J. Edgar Hoover on the philosophy of the police officer, but Moodie liked to quote a more direct American contribution to police welfare.

Moodie pointed out that the police had established a precise actuarial base for their low insurance cover, 50 per cent less than Fire Service personnel could achieve. He was not prepared to forgo that, and he was unhappy that the SSC brushed this aside in favour of precedents set for public service groups who bore no relationship to the police.

Given the state of the economy, he had persuaded his reluctant members to relinquish the right to a general review of police salaries in favour of resolving this margins issue. He wanted it decided so there was an end to the present situation where three-quarters of those qualified for promotion to sergeant declined it. When Gordon pleaded for the Higher Salaries Commission to have more time to make its determination on the commissioner's salary, Moodie traded that for a commitment that the margins application would be negotiated to an agreement in principle by 1 October 1978.

Fighting on the social change front, Moodie continued to shake up the commissioner. He got the same spiel over policewomen in trousers that he got over de facto marriages, that it offended Burnside's Christian principles. Moodie told him, repeatedly and blatantly, that it was only his personal prejudices he could not come to grips with. Had he been on the board of Radio New Zealand or Fletchers, Moodie expects he would have been sacked. What he liked about the police was that you could say these things and there were no recriminations. Once Burnside saw the value of this collective decision-making, he was all for it, unlike a number of his senior officers. Moodie finally rated Burnside a good commissioner because, unlike his successors, he was in command of his service and did not tolerate incompetence.

Even so, Moodie was undoubtedly fortunate that a more liberal commissioner, Bob Walton, took over in mid-1978. The next year Walton indicated that the de facto regulation would be repealed. Although Moodie still gets called Bob, he favoured Rob, Butterworth says, because it was important to distinguish Bob Walton from himself. The latter became as much part of the team for change as Butterworth.

Bob's position was put to the test when Rob decided that the police were presenting the wrong image to the public, with too many imprisoned in their clothing. Moodie spent a lot of time sitting around talking to men in blue, braid-covered uniforms. He had begun to change from collar and tie, to no tie, to more casual dress such as a reefer jacket over a polo neck jersey and grey strides.

One day Moodie picked up a pearl necklace off his wife's dresser and wore it round his neck. He sat there fingering it in the meetings. About the second or third time he did this, Chief Superintendent Brian Davies said he would walk out if Moodie ever did that again. Bob Walton rang him to say there would be no trouble and Moodie could wear what he liked. So Moodie began to wear dresses, appearing on television first to say that he intended wearing a kaftan to work.

The dress was a deliberate technique. 'It was the way these people dealt with each other,' he says, 'that used to annoy me. The Fleming case was a major factor in this. Here was a man who was really hurting and they were doing nothing. All they could see were the reasons why something couldn't be done.'

When he first wore the dress, some members suggested he was queer. Moodie replied that he was not sure himself. When the subject was raised again, he told them it was their own fault for employing a transvestite. Jim Weeks from Paraparaumu, who had worked closely with Moodie, brought the matter officially before the management committee. Alan Monk was one of those who supported Moodie, saying that the important thing was he was doing the job well.

'Jim Weeks couldn't cope with it in his own mind,' says Moodie. 'That's what I was fighting in the police. It doesn't affect you so much in a normal occupation, but in a very rigid, disciplined organisation like the police everything like that affects you. A grown man of 27 has an inspector come along and tell him his hair's too long, would he get it trimmed. That was offensive, yet it was going on all the time.'

It soon became apparent to Moodie that the opposition to his dress came from the 'hard-nosed John Banks types, the ones people judge the police by'. Yet they were a minority. Most police did not open their mouths much, and they were as happy with Moodie's style as they were with Alan Monk, the lightning rod for the ordinary copper.

Moodie enjoyed the dress fuss, and soon recognised the way it liberated people who had been 'pushed in by prejudice'. It was part of the same reason why he had been passionate about Bob Fleming, who was fobbed off by the nice guys 'who drank booze with the boss and got a good job'. They were the people Moodie systematically peeled off the management committee, in favour of thinkers and positive people such as Monk and Alec Waugh.

Butterworth also saw the way Moodie used his dress to change the public cartoonist perception of the police as idiot monoliths with short back and sides haircuts. Butterworth thought it a good thing for senior officers particularly, who had been able to rest easy until then in their unthinking prejudices. They now had to come to terms with being represented by a man in a dress.

Butterworth remembers Moodie telling him that the national headquarters was too powerful, that district commanders and operational policemen needed to be able to function efficiently, to exercise their own judgement. He wanted the department to do its own research, to become more professional. He proposed it hired an industrial advocate, and it did.

The police were still, in Butterworth's words, resistant to formal education, 'a bureaucracy that wasn't really rational'. There was still the hangover from the military structure, of working by rule of thumb, hiding behind seniority. Moodie used himself and Butterworth as examples of what education could achieve. He demanded that police start thinking about their own role. In his address 'Violence in the Community', published in the July 1978

Newsletter, Moodie probed the causes of why one in five police were assaulted in the course of their duty, suggesting that the violence and excessive drinking were manifestations of high levels of frustration and anger in the community, particularly among young Polynesians.

Such behaviour, Moodie claimed, was a response to an uptight, macho, intolerant society that derided and abused anyone whose dress or habits differed from conformist norms. He rejected our claim to be a multiracial society because we allowed only European society to be acceptable. We demanded the Polynesian discard his culture for something 'we ourselves can't even identify'. The violent Polynesian was not our problem, 'we are his'. The European male in the grey flannel suit was threatened by cottons and checks. The booze barns were an illusory escape from an overregulated society.

His solution was for us to relax and enjoy different cultures, welcome the Polynesian emphasis on family and sharing instead of allowing only the European emphasis on possessions and status. He made sure that this red rag flapped in his members' faces—hence the kaftan. Subsequent editions of the *Newsletter* published criticisms of Moodie's thesis. The strongest and longest was an academic rejection of his viewpoint as cynical and superficial.

Butterworth joined in the challenge to the macho Kiwi and specifically police male image. In the January 1979 *Newsletter* he explained Maori gangs as 'a confused and erratic rejection of Pakeha society'. He reminded police that they must be seen as multicultural and supported Moodie's view on the need to break down European stereotypes, particularly in dress, and welcome Polynesian lifestyles.

Reactions were mixed. One correspondent suggested diverting gangs into sport, where their teamwork could have a more positive outlet. A woman objected to males being protected by police, when she was the one threatened by male gangs.

In April Derek Kirk probably summed up the 'hard-nosed' reaction. He objected to 'airy fairy huff and puff' dominating the *Newsletter*, which was 'not a platform for student sociologists to air their views'. He agreed that Moodie and Butterworth did a good job for the association, but suggested that they were far from the feelings of the working copper who sorted out the problems of society on the streets in the early hours of the morning, not in Parliament, at the university and on the marae.

Moodie and Butterworth, aiming for the silent copper majority, were achieving their aim of stimulating debate. Derek Kirk was probably right that, if the pair were not performing on the pay and conditions front, they would not

The upfront and very upbeat first years of the Moodie era

have a forum for sociological debate.

They continued to perform. In July 1977 they undertook a survey of police housing. Some 28 per cent of New Zealanders owned their own homes; fewer than 8 per cent of the police did. Police families were larger than the average New Zealand family, often with three or more usually young children. Many police families had short-term, high-interest mortgages; some said owning a house was only a dream they could not afford. Many older members were still in police houses. Present insurance would not save many police families if the breadwinner suffered death or disablement, which was increasingly likely in a more violent society.

Although the Moodie/Butterworth campaign moved on many fronts, it generally faced the same resistance from a reluctant government and bureaucracy. At the 3 August 1978 management committee meeting Moodie reported that the insurance proposal had become a long and protracted fight with the SSC. Instead of processing the police case on its merits, the SSC was engaged in 'a policy of procrastination and delay'. A complaint was lodged with the Minister of Police and a subsequent meeting with him and the Minister for State Services resulted in some progress.

At the 21 December meeting with the Cabinet Subcommittee on State Services it was Treasury that wanted more time. Moodie not only accused Treasury of 'procrastination as a way of life' but also objected to the 'element of dishonesty in the whole Treasury approach'. Treasury had argued that the death cover was unprecedented, when air traffic controllers and engine drivers had it, and firemen won it when they threatened strike action.

As Butterworth told the management committee, the main association argument centred on the police providing a 24-hour service with extensive overtime and often high stress and physical discomfort. In this context it was impossible to distinguish when a death was due to natural causes or related to police work. Death over the previous 10 years had been due mostly to heart attacks, which could be related to the pressures of the job, and particularly the high incidence of assaults on the police.

Alec Waugh commented that their well-prepared and reasonably presented case had been pushed aside. Other groups prepared to make threats of industrial action had their claims settled quickly. Similar dissatisfaction was expressed at the lack of progress in the margins claim.

Butterworth explained that the problem was the fact that State Services was in operational control of the system, Treasury in ultimate control. This meant the commissioner was effectively not in control of a large part of his operations. The result was a 'take it or leave it' attitude by the controlling departments and long delays in paying out agreed allowances, even in getting deductions for the credit union members.

In the 27 February 1979 issue of *Truth* Moodie went public with police frustration at the erosion of margins and the bureaucratic delays in a matter the government had promised twice in the previous year would be settled by 1 October last. He referred to another government organisation winning a settlement because it threatened industrial action. Police thought the government stalled them because they did not do likewise. It was a broad hint of what the police were considering.

At the 25 April meeting Treasury again delayed on the insurance proposal. Moodie expressed his anger at off-handed treatment that disregarded the feelings of police officers. The margins case was, however, going to the Higher Salaries Commission, presented by the administration's new industrial relations officer, Brian Mooney.

On 19 May Moodie wrote to Acting Minister of Police Colin McLachlan about police frustration and unrest at the procrastination in settling claims. Dunedin district members, he told the minister, had the week before sought an end to police issuing petrol permits under the Economic Stabilisation Regulations 1979. His members were

Rob Moodie. Chief Negotiator for both Service Organisations.
This negotiation marks the end of four years' hard work by Dr Moodie to restore police salary structure.

Graham Butterworth. Senior Research Officer.
Assisted Dr Moodie in the detailed work of preparing the case.

Four years on, Moodie and Graham Butterworth, the outspoken advocate and the behind-the-scenes number cruncher, were rated the most effective union team in the country threatening votes of no confidence in the government and other appropriate action.

At the same time this very morning, Moodie went on, he had to put up with a Treasury official arriving half an hour late for a meeting with the service organisations. The official was 'belligerent in his attitude' and 'stormed out of the meeting when the validity of his attack upon the Police Insurance Scheme was questioned'. He had threatened that Treasury 'would cut the Police off at the knees'. Moodie himself was always courteous in negotiation, Butterworth observed, never stooping to abuse.

Moodie called a special conference on 31 May 1979 to explain to the management committee and national council that the difficulties in negotiating settlements stemmed from the commissioner having to win the approval of the Minister of State Services before he could make any determination. The SSC and Treasury refused to treat the police as a special case, a union that could not strike. They thought the police were asking for more than they expected to get, and they had the procrastination habit. The present system did not work and was destructive of police morale. Moodie advocated establishing a government body that would continuously evaluate special police needs, including leave, sick leave, salaries, shifts, insurance and stress factors. The good news was that the government had agreed to subsidise the insurance scheme and the margins claim would be resolved later in the year.

Moodie and Butterworth went off to attend local association agms in the North Island. Mooney was told by the SSC that unless there was a decision by 16 July the police would miss out on the 10.4 per cent public service wage order. Commissioner Walton was advised that the SSC and Treasury did not support the margins case and that the Higher Salaries Commission would probably not make any change to the chief superintendent salary. Under this pressure, the new negotiator, Mooney, concluded an agreement with the SSC about some increases to ranks between sergeant and chief superintendent. Moodie had had the rug pulled from under him by the controlling departments.

Mooney had seen no point in informing the association and guild, as no negotiations were taking place. He would not admit what was patently obvious, that he showed a lack of experience with the machinery for negotiating police applications.

Moodie got an opinion from legal expert Don Mathieson that the service organisations for which he was agreed negotiator had an agreement with the government that entitled them to pursue the margins case after any general public service settlement. It was on this understanding that Moodie had persuaded his members to surrender a 1977 pay increase. Moodie claimed Mooney had negotiated in his own way and contrary to what had been agreed. Walton did not agree.

Moodie did not respond to Walton's defence of Mooney with the reaction that might have been expected. Instead of adopting a defensive posture, perhaps falling into the divide

The relaxed Moodie committee era

and conquer trap, he changed tactics. He wrote to the commissioner saying that both sides had learned from the negotiations. He praised Mooney for the 'excellent job' he did on police overtime and penal rates.

His subtle negotiating tactics and unrelenting pressure eventually yielded most of what Moodie wanted. In September 1979 the package was announced. On top of the general wage adjustment of 10.4 per cent and the 4.5 per cent general wage order, the police received the margins adjustments that had been an issue throughout the decade. A chief superintendent moved from $20,924 to $25,254, a superintendent from $19,328 to $23,713, a chief inspector from $17,861 to $21,983, an inspector from $16,367 to $20,252, a senior sergeant after three years from $15,134 to $18,621, a sergeant after three years from $13,818 to $16,602, a constable after 25 years from $12,905 to $15,209, and a constable in the first year from $10,952 to $12,734. At last there was an incentive for skilled and experienced officers to stay in the service.

Moodie did not pause. Now it was on to the survey of hours worked. The 23.5 per cent loading was based on the 1966 survey, and it was anticipated that a new survey would justify a loading of up to 30 per cent.

Although the police had to wait for their payout until the State Services computer came back on line, computers were making the negotiating much quicker. The service organisations and the administration were working together on a computerised survey of penal rates, overtime night rate and on-call elements or undertime worked. This would provide the objective base that would aim for the same impact Butterworth had achieved with his work on allowances. It would speed up future claims, as instanced by the first review of allowances taking over a year, the second about 30 minutes.

The Moodie/Butterworth strategy was to complete the pay and related claims by 1981, a five-year plan that would see a general survey of police salaries in place. Then it was on to early retirement, superannuation and sick leave.

What neither could anticipate was that their best laid plans would be interrupted by a period of unprecedented social turmoil surrounding the Springbok tour, the Arthur Allan Thomas inquiry and the overstayer issue. But the focus of the problem would not change and the service organisations would be locked into a fight with

The media loved Moodie's dress sense. Cartoonist Eric Heath contrasted Moodie's kaftan with other occupational dress habits. The letter from A.E. MacKay reflects the success of part of Moodie's dress intent, to get the macho cops talking openly about alternative behaviour

CORRESPONDENCE

Kerikeri.

The Editor,

Sir,

Regarding correspondence from I.J. Carr, Auckland. I can't help but agree with him most wholeheartedly. As a "front-line" member of the Police, I have, on many occasions been forced into the position, especially when making routine visits to hotels etc., to either shrug off or laugh off remarks from the general public about my "poncy boss" in his frocks. I make great haste to assure them that Dr Moodie is not, in actual fact, a policeman, but a civilian employee. This, I am afraid, goes right over their heads as he is closely associated to us, by the general public.

I too appreciate that Dr Moodie can garb himself however he chooses, especially in his own home, but I feel nothing but embarrassment akin to shame when he appears, representing us, looking like some fugitive from the Hari Krishnas.

The views set out above are entirely my own.

(Sgd) A.E. MacKay.

A man's a man for 'aw that —Ed.

Auckland.

The Editor,

Sir,

The letter of I. Carr which gained undue prominence and publicity does not reflect the attitudes of the membership of the Auckland Central District, as by now the National Secretary will be well aware.

Mr Carr's lamentable contribution to the New Zealand Police Association amounts to him being elected to the Auckland Committee and almost immediately resigning. He could ponder the words of J.R. Miller — "Every man has a larger chance in the world than he ever takes — here are three rules to avoid failure —

Worry less, work more:
Waste less, give more:
Preach less, practice more."

(Sgd) P.M. Hilt.

• • •

bureaucracy and government. This time the prize would be their souls as much as their salaries. In simplest terms it would be Rob versus Rob, Muldoon using the police in their traditional role of keeping dissidents in line, Moodie confronting this divisive samurai philosophy with an insistence on the human face of the service.

Chapter Seventeen

The Traumas of the Overstayers, the Thomas Commission and the Tour

The overstayer issue in late 1976 suggested the shape of the disruptions to come. Moodie was required, as he arrived in the job, to sort out the bitterness Auckland members felt at being ordered to make random checks and dawn raids on mostly Polynesians suspected of overstaying their work permits.

The crisis flared suddenly. The commissioner's Circular 1/1/450 dated 22 October 1976 ordered all districts to take more positive action to apprehend those from overseas overstaying their temporary entry permits, with two squads in place in Auckland, two in Wellington, one in Christchurch and all other personnel to assist. The *New Zealand Herald* of 22 October reported the overstayer 'blitz' beginning the previous night in Auckland, with 'Islanders' arrested in their homes and on the streets if they did not have a passport or proof of their identity. Bail was denied.

The *Auckland Star* of the same day printed photographs of two Samoans arrested, a story about a sobbing Samoan wrongly held. Auckland's acting police chief, A.G. Berriman, was reported as saying that anyone speaking in a non-Kiwi accent or looking as though he was not born in this country should carry a passport. The commissioner was reported as saying that the police had moved to a more 'positive' role in locating overstayers.

The next day Chief Superintendent Berriman issued a denial that there were random checks, the police were merely carrying out routine enquiries on behalf of the Labour Department. Berriman and Police Minister McCready repeated on the television news that evening that there were no random checks, Berriman explaining that Muldoon had just returned from a trip round the Islands, 'where he told everyone we would be reasonable about this'.

Police: If you don't look like a Kiwi carry a passport

Auckland and Wellington reporters

Anyone who speaks in a non-Kiwi accent or looks as though he was not born in this country should carry a passport.

This warning came from Auckland's acting police chief, Mr A. G. Berriman, today after a night in which patrols stopped hundreds of Polynesians in the streets.

In Wellington and Christchurch, too, police stopped Polynesians on suspicion that they might be overstayers or illegal immigrants.

Auckland police held 12 in cells overnight. They are expected to appear in Auckland, Otahuhu and North Shore courts this afternoon.

The Star was told today that one of those being held is legally here on a five-year permit, while another is a registered overstayer still waiting for advice from the Labour Department.

Mr Berriman, who said the random stop-and [illegible] tactic was a first for New Zealand, preferred to call the exercise an "emphasis on the immigration laws."

A small core team lead by Inspector Brian Middleton and supported by the majority of police on duty last night started work at 7 p.m.

"It was completely at random," said Mr Berriman. "They stopped anyone they suspected of breaking the Immigration Act."

He said there were a number of factors making people suspicious.

Asked if only Islanders were questioned, he said: "Naturally we'd look twice at someone we did not think was New Zealand born."

He said he knew of only one European questioned, a Canadian on the North Shore who was let go.

Asked if any attempt had been made to apprehend the

Two Samoans arrested in last night's police campaign arrive at Auckland Magistrate's Court today. Both were remanded on bail.

Switch to positive role

Police have switched to a more positive role in locating overstayers, Police Commissioner, K. B. Burnside said in Wellington today.

"This is a change in policy from the previous supportive role to the immigration division of the Labour Department."

The position had been reached when more positive action was required to restore the situation to a level where control could be exercised by immigration officials alone, Mr Burnside said.

The police operation would [illegible] resident Pacific Islanders.

He gave an assurance that the police would be as respectful and considerate as possible.

The police action in Auckland last night followed the end of the Immigration Department's "Operation Overstayer" when there was an amnesty to allow over[illegible] to register.

During the amnesty period, the Minister of Immigration, Mr Gill, warned that those who failed to register would be liable to prosecution and subsequent deportation as illegal immigrants.

[illegible] leaders in this country

He did not think the action would cause him any problems when he visited Tonga and Western Samoa in about [illegible]

The Minister of Police, Mr McCready, denied there was [illegible] which were highly emotive. Police carried out an investigation based on information submitted by the Immigration Department.

If people broke the law and there were warrants out for their arrest then the police took action.

That action was not con[illegible] tion Amendment Act, immigration and police officers can ask anyone suspected of committing an offence to produce his passport, produce his permit to enter New Zealand if he has one, and produce documentary or other evidence of his identity.

Anyone who refuses, or fails to do this without reasonable excuse, can be charged with having committed an offence.

Despite these powers Mr McCready denied any suggestion that there was likely to be widespread spot checks

Sobbing man wrongly held

Staff reporters

A young Samoan, wrongly arrested last night, spent hours sobbing in an Auckland police cell.

Iakopo-Tevaga Sio, a linesman with the Post Office spent almost 14 hours in custody after he was arrested while walking down a Grey Lynn street.

Sio was released at 9.30 this morning after immigration officials found out that he was here legally.

But his brother, Filipo Sio said: "There was no apology, no nothing from the officials after learning of their mistake."

"He was crying his eyes out when I saw him in the cells."

And this morning Tongan Government liaison officer Mr Liufau Saulala hammered tactics used last night by police.

"We don't mind them knocking on doors. But just picking them off the streets is not acceptable," he said.

"This is like South Africa where non-whites are asked for identification on the streets."

A short time ago the Prime Minister of Western Samoa, Mr Tupuloa Efi, said Pacific Island overstayers would become a "hat issue" again if police raids on overstayers continued.

Peni Taufa, alias Halangahu Niu, arrived from Tonga in July, 1974. He was remanded without plea on bail of $400 and a similar surety. Mrs Wallace added a daily reporting clause.

The *Auckland Star* for 22 October 1976 provided the police with perhaps their most negative publicity ever—and that was just a prelude to the Thomas Commission and the Springbok tour

1976/35
P.1/1/450

POLICE NATIONAL HEADQUARTERS
GENERAL BUILDINGS, WARING TAYLOR STREET,
WELLINGTON 1, NEW ZEALAND

Private Bag

22 October 1976

COMMISSIONER'S CIRCULAR

To All Districts and Police College.

IMMIGRATION : OVERSTAYING OF PERMITS

1. Commissioner's Circular 1976/9 dated 5 April 1976 refers.

2. The situation has been reached where more positive action is required by the Police to detect and apprehend persons from overseas who are overstaying their temporary entry permits. Accordingly all District Commanders are to give priority to the seeking out and apprehension of overstayers. Immediate action is to be taken.

3. In districts where large numbers of illegal overstayers are known to be living, staff are to be assigned full-time to the task. Squads, each comprising a Sergeant and three Constables, have already been established in Auckland (2), and Wellington (2) and Christchurch. All other personnel who are not engaged full-time on these duties must be briefed to accord priority to the detection and arrest of overstayers.

4. Enforcement action must be carried out in a reasonable and understanding way. Good Judgement must be exercised at all times. The Police must not only pay attention to suspects from the Pacific Islands, but must be alert to detect offenders of all nationalities. There is no restriction on the times that Police may visit private homes in the course of their enquiries but good sense must prevail in this regard. Every effort must be made to retain the support and goodwill of various community groups.

5. Police field operations are at all times to be conducted independently of Immigration Officers. The Immigration Division of the Department of Labour will supply information to the Police about overstayers but Police on their own initiative must seek out offenders. A close liaison should be created with officers of the Department of Labour in Districts. The Secretary of Labour has promised the closest co-operation and has alerted his District Superintendents. Immigration Officers will also continue their ov[n] independent enforcement action and when a request is made by them [for] Police assistance such aid may be given in terms of paragraph 9 of circular 1976/9.

2.

6. A review of the situation will be made in three months at which time it is hoped that effective Police action will have restored the situation to a level where control can be exercised largely by immigration officers alone.

7. Until further notice a daily Sitrep is to be sent to the Head of Training and Personnel advising the number of arrests of overstayers. Additionally, the following records are to be maintained and a return forwarded each week to the Head of Training and Personnel listing:

(a) A record of the time Police staff have spent on this duty.

(b) The mileage run by Police vehicles.

(c) The numbers of overstayers reported by the Department of Labour.

(d) The number of offenders detected by the Police.

(e) Brief details of any incorrect information supplied to the Police by the Department of Labour.

The above information should be dispatched every Monday.

(K. B. Burnside)
Commissioner

ALL STATIONS & OFFICES,
AUCKLAND DISTRICT.

Copy for your information and retention.

J.W. OVERTON
Assistant Commissioner of Police
88/76 29.10.76

TO ALL MEMBERS,
AUCKLAND POLICE DISTRICT.

Enquiries regarding overstayers who are
permits are to continue by individual members o
To assist in obtaining the true identity and st
offender, the attached guidelines are to be issu

Where there appear grounds to believe a p
in N.Z. an immediate arrest is not to be effecte
give information brings the person within the sco
Immigration Act 1964 which must be read and fully
members. Any such arrest must be subjected to cl
N.C.O. or Officer as soon as possible thereafter.

The questions listed are to be completed and
returned to Inspector Middleton's Office where a ch
out and a decision made as to future action.

Likewise any information regarding the probab
overstayers is to be forwarded by way of report throu
channels to Inspector Middleton's Office.

Until Immigration records are fully checked, a
to be made before clearance with Inspector Middleton's

Procedures regarding all other classes of illega
shall continue as in the past.

J.W. OVERTON
Assistant Commissione

---

r,

RE: IMMIGRANT..........

During Police enquiries the ...
following information was supplied by ...

Names (commonly known by)..........................
Names recorded in passport..........WHERE..........
Are you registered?.................................
If so, what names?..................Age:............
Address:..
Sex:..
Place of employment:................................
By what name employed:..............................
Date of entry to New Zealand:.......................
Period of permit granted. (Any extension):..........
By ship/plane/other:................................
Nationality:..
Passport or other documentation: (No.)..............
Who can verify Particulars Given:...................
(i.e. Solicitor, Church, Employer etc.)
Result of anonymous call:...........................

Sergea

The Officer in Charge,
Operation 'Immigration',
Auckland Central Police Station,
P. O. Box 40,
AUCKLAND.

Dear Sir,

RE: IMMIGRANT..............................

The records of the abovenamed person h
Departmental records and found to be correct/i

If incorrect, the following action is

1. Further Police enquiries are necessar
2. Records show that he/she is a registe
3. A Warrant to Arrest has been issued.
4. No record at the Department and ther
is required.
...med to be: (a) Cont
(b) Perm

Takapuna Police Station.
28 October 1976.

Const EDWARDSON,
Secretary for Police Assoc,
Auckland Branch.

Dear Sir,

I wish to put forward to the Association my views, and experiences from the latest situation in regard to the Immigration Act that we as members of the Police were called upon to enforce.

On Friday the 22/10/76 I was directed to arrest one Western Samoan woman who was suppected of having committed a breach against the Immigration Act. I duly arrested this woman after making necessary enquiries, at 0945 hrs and I transported her to the Auckland Central Police cells at 1100 hrs.

After placing her in the custody of the Central Police I thought that the matter as far as I was concerned was finished. However since then an allegation was made in the Herald of 28/10/76 that this woman was held in custody until the 23/10/76 and that during her stay in Police custody she received no food or water.

At 1100 hrs on 28/10/76 my mother recieved a telephone call from a const THOMPSON of Central Police. At this time I was in bed asleep after having completed night shift at 0700 hrs and I had been in bed asleep for only 2 hours. My mother informed const THOMPSON of this but he demanded that he speak personally to me. I was then awoken and spoke to const THOMPSON. He stated that Inspector MIDDLETON recquired that I immediately furnish a full report on the nature of the arrest I had made on 22/10/76. I was told that my report was to be forwarded to Auckland by early afternoon.

After recieving this telephone call I dressed and went to the Takapuna station where I typed out the report, and then travlled to Torbay in order to have the member who had been on patrol with me also furnish a report. This member was also in bed asleep after night shift. I then returned to the station where I handed in the reports and returned home at 1430 hrs. I was not able to get back asleep after this and I went on duty again at 2300 hrs having had only 2 hours sleep.

The reason given to me by const THOMPSOn for having the report completed urgently was that a reply was going to be press to the allegations made in the Herald of 28/10/76. I have not seen any such reply in the news as yet.

I fail to see the reasoning why I should have furnished such a report as the woman was in my custody only until 1100 hrs on 22/10/76, and this is well outside normal prisoners meal hours.

I feel that this whole situation that has resulted from the last few days has blown back to members of the police who work in the field. We are the members who have to deal with these people (Polynesians and other immigrants,) in the future, and it has become apparent to most members of the police that certain Senior officers in the Police will not stand by their orders that they gave us in the first place. The constables that took action are now the ones who are suffering and I feel are becoming implicated by what Senior officers are saying to the Press. To say the least, I am totally disgusted by what has happened in the last few days and if this is an indication of what is going to happen in the future, then I can only say that I want no part in it at all.

I would be most interested to here the reasons why Senior Officers have not admitted that they gave orders for random checks in the streets, Hotels etc.

Yours Faithfully
W.N.PAGE.

These documents on the overstayer issue indicate how quickly this crisis began and ended. The memorandum went out from headquarters on 22 October. On 28 October Eddie Edwardson was in the thick of members' complaints, mostly about their superiors. He calls it 'Operation Shambles', saying that the whole matter arose when District Commander Bill Overton was on leave and his stand-in Chief Superintendent Berriman 'decided that he would make a name for himself by having large numbers of overstayers arrested. He made a name for himself, but not in the manner intended'

There was nothing reasonable about the fears expressed in the media of several hundred Polynesians being stopped because of the colour of their skin, of fascist, racist police state behaviour. The Police Association was quoted on television as feeling that its members had been called on to take the bad press.

On 25 October the Auckland district of the association put out a press release claiming that its members were the meat in the sandwich and that 'the whole idea of stopping people on the streets to check their status under the immigration laws is abhorrent to say the least, as far as our members are concerned'. The release referred to the departmental memo ordering all police personnel to round up overstayers. This was perilously close to rebellion in the ranks.

The same day Auckland's Assistant Commissioner J.W. Overton assured the media that random checks had been stopped. Two days later Alan Monk circularised all districts to 'reject any temptation to make comments to the media regardless of what they personally feel'.

The departmental investigation that followed did not please Auckland district, which protested to Moodie that it had 'whitewashed' the local commissioned officers. Moodie replied that the management committee shared the Auckland view about serious errors in judgement by the senior commissioned officers there and that they were 'sheltering behind our members'. The management committee had decided, however, after Moodie had had lengthy discussions with the commissioner, that it was in the best interests of the service not to take the matter further, even though this did not satisfy members.

This was probably as mild as Moodie would ever be over a major issue. The fuss *did* die down and the Muldoon administration must have felt its wings singed, for there were no more dirty jobs for frontline police over the next few years. Things were still quiet enough for the June 1980 *Newsletter* to carry a lead article by Father Felix Donnelly saying it was not immoral to be gay, but it was immoral to be anti-gay. The introduction anticipated that this view would not receive unanimous approval in the police service, and the next two years of anti-Donnelly debate proved this so. The Moodie/Butterworth strategy of airing controversial issues was on target.

The August 1980 *Newsletter* carried two small paragraphs that presaged the major controversies to come. Moodie anounced the joint association/guild application on behalf of former Chief Inspector Bruce Hutton and Detective Len Johnston alleging bias and predetermination against the Thomas Commission of Inquiry. Below this an item expressed concern that the police would be labelled as responsible for whatever was decided on the Springbok tour; the association intended to seek representation on any planning team for the tour.

In the same issue Butterworth reported agreement between association and administration on optional early retirement at 55. The paper would go to Cabinet, introduced, it was hoped, in 1981. This would not in fact happen until the association executive had confronted and helped to get rid of the Muldoon Government. Butterworth believes the improvements they had won in the late 1970s fitted Muldoon's law and order strategy, until the service organisations began to grow too tall. The next few years were a testing time, but the end result was that Moodie and Butterworth wielded the poppy-toppers. They had little choice, because there would otherwise be no progress with this regime on early retirement and related provisions. Both Moodie and Butterworth perceive the social crises of the Thomas Commission and the tour as politically generated.

'The Thomas Commission was a disgrace,' says Moodie.

> We had the problem of evidence planted, but you don't solve one injustice by creating another. That's what the commission did. The association lost over $100,000 on legal assistance, but we did so because the whole thing was a fabrication. Arthur Allan Thomas was pardoned before it and the commission of inquiry constructed to deaden the blow to the government, which had done something unprecedented. It was also a marvellous distraction, which was why Muldoon got into it.

Butterworth remembers management committee member Barry Nalder bailing up Police Minister Frank Gill at the association Christmas party and demanding to know why the government had appointed a commission. Gill said feebly they thought it would make a lot of people happy. Nalder told him there was no way it made the police happy.

The government was not happy to see the police push successfully against their tide of cutbacks in departmental spending and a sinking lid policy of not replacing staff. Although Moodie had moved on from the margins success to win approval for a sick leave bank, it was restricted to each member's regular donation of half a day's annual leave. The association wanted to capitalise any leave left over at year's end and transfer it to the welfare fund. While the SSC objected to this, Treasury held up the claim for a year, and refused to accept any cashing in of surplus leave in case it caught on with other government departments. As usual Moodie argued that the police were a special case and there would be no flow-on effect. The bank was established, but any surplus monies were carried over to the next year.

In 1980 the push was for a salary settlement based on the results of the surveys of hours of work. Penal time, night time and overtime were translated into a percentage of the basic salary. One-person stations emerged as the hardest working, averaging over 10 hours of overtime. The survey established conditions of service in one package for the first time, so that members could refer to the award for their rights on meals, mileage, transfers and so on. Up until now police had never properly measured their time. The Agreement on Conditions removed the blur between on-duty and off-duty time. It got rid of the muddled management of staff that extended call-outs and hours of duty into off-duty time. The disciplinary provisions such as Regulation 46 requiring that you could not refuse duty had permitted this abuse of members' free time. Moodie brought some common sense and agreed positions to this situation, allowing fair allocation and evaluation of members' time.

Keith Morrow credits the good rapport between Moodie and Walton for this agreement going through. Some of the second stratum of administration did not, however, approve of Moodie or his good relationship with the commissioner. There were accusations that Walton pandered to him. Monk recalls the procrastination over publishing the conditions of service, resolved only when Moodie published a look-alike General Instructions format. There was a fuss and the administration published the conditions.

Monk said the survey and new pay scale were good for morale, but the year had been soured by the conduct of the commission chairman in the Thomas inquiry. The chairman Mr Justice Taylor persisted in the view that the pardon constituted a declaration of Thomas's innocence and the government refused to let the commissioner challenge this in the High Court. That was why the association and the guild took the case to court. The decision came too late to stop the damage done by the commission of inquiry finding that two former police officers had planted shell 350.

So the association and the guild took a case to the Court of Appeal, alleging a breach of natural justice and bias by this 'finding' of the commission, which had not been tested by the rules of evidence. The Court of Appeal did not say the commission was biased, but it was harsh on the commission's conduct.

The association and the guild were left with their largest ever legal assistance bill and a great deal of bitterness among members at the way the government had treated them. Even though Johnston was now dead and Hutton had left the service, they were committed by Rule 111 to give assistance in cases arising out of employment. The rule was changed in 1983 to allow the management committee discretion as to the amount of assistance rendered.

During the two court cases the association had had to keep the lid on restive members, particularly in Auckland. At the 3 August 1980 management committee meeting Ian Revell said his Auckland members were concerned at the mud being thrown and were prepared to make press statements. Monk warned against anything that could prejudice their case; Moodie told members to keep their mouths shut lest they play into the hands of the commission.

Moodie claimed at the October annual conference that the police came out of the High Court case with their reputation enhanced. They got the chance to present new evidence and the commission chairman's television outburst about Thomas's innocence and his direction to the DSIR scientist to change his evidence to say that the bullet could not have come from the Thomas rifle, coupled with the High Court confirmation that the commission had been on the wrong track gave the police a good result.

When the commission findings came out, Auckland district once again led the agitation. At the 10 December 1980 management committee meeting Ron Halpin read out the Auckland resolution recording 'extreme distress' at the findings and abhorring the Prime Minister's comments. Particular distress was felt at the late Detective Johnston being accused of impropriety 'on completely unsubstantiated speculation'. An anonymous Auckland letter in the March 1981 *Newsletter* deplored the damage done to Hutton and Johnston and their families and to all police. One day's leave should be taken by all police in protest at the findings of this ex-judge from Australia, a 'misguided crusader' who had 'set out to crucify an honest Police Force'.

Publicly, Moodie kept such strong feelings in check. The two court cases by the association and guild successfully challenged the right of a non-judicial body to bring down findings of criminal misconduct against individuals. The proof of this was that the Solicitor-General did not accept the commission of inquiry findings as grounds for instituting criminal proceedings against Hutton, who was 'found' by the commission to have 'planted evidence'.

Moodie also played a subtle game with the media. 'When it became obvious the way the chairman from Australia was working,' says Butterworth,

> Rob Moodie put into the media that if the commission was right in their judgement that a wrong had been done, then six figures wasn't enough to cure the wrong. He knew that would really hurt Muldoon where he lived, if the government had to pay a million dollars. Who knows the rights and wrongs of it ultimately, but that was certainly the oddest commission in my experience. The only way we were going to take it was to stop the government using the police as a political football and destroy the police reputation for some political game that Muldoon was playing. We wanted the cost to the government to be so high that they would think twice about solving their political problems again in that way.

Butterworth says they were well aware that the government was trying to break the association and guild with the costs of the case. The police, however, were united on this issue and a special levy on members paid the court costs. The only internal debate was over whether Thomas was innocent.

It was the same with the next big politically provoked crisis, the Springbok tour. The police were no different from the rest of the community in being split for and against.

Moodie's principal concern, before any decision was made about the tour, was that the police not be involved. He lobbied from mid-1980 to keep any report by the commissioner on the law and order implications of a tour completely confidential, so that it could not be an excuse for a government decision either way. If used as an excuse to cancel the tour, it would antagonise tour supporters. If it was used to approve the tour going ahead, the police could, as his circulated letter said, 'expect quite violent and vicious retaliation against our members' for performing their public duty.

Over the next 10 months the management committee debated at every meeting what it could expect. When it became obvious from what the Rugby Union and Police Minister Ben Couch were saying that the tour would go

New Zealand Police Association **newsletter**

August/September 1983 ★ Vol. 15, No. 8/9 ★ Part Series "N.Z. Police Journal"

"SHAME FOR OUR NATION" —says Association President

NOBODY'S FRIEND
(Photo Courtesy NZ Newspapers Ltd)

WHO PAYS FOR THIS?
(Photo Courtesy "The Dominion")

It was recently reported from the office of the Chief Ombudsman that investigation into complaints made to him on aspects of police conduct during the 1981 Springbok rugby tour have now been completed, and Mr K. J. Morrow, president of the New Zealand Police Association has endorsed the Chief Ombudsman's conclusions as the final curtain is rung down on the complaints against the police.

We place on record in this issue of the Newsletter Mr Morrow's words on that occasion. We republish also some random photographs typical of the scenes which occurred during those trying days, though to most events are still so fresh in mind as to make recall unnecessary.

Mr Morrow said—"The Ombudsman's Report should be read by every New Zealander because even a cursory reading will show that the next Tour will start where the third test in Auckland on the last Springbok Tour left off.

The Ombudsman's conclusions are an endorsement of the Police Service. The tour and the complaints were handled impartially, objectively and with only minor irregularities or individual lapses.

The clear conclusion to be drawn from the report is that any failings on the part of individual policemen and policewomen pales into insignificance when considered against the failing of our society when faced with the complex issues presented by a Springbok tour.

The Ombudsman's report vindicates the Association's confidence in the Service for the Ombudsman has upheld the integrity of police investigations into complaints and finds only minor irregularities or lapses which, when looked at against the totality

Published by R. A. Moodie, 11 Manners Street, Wellington, on behalf of the New Zealand Police Association (Inc.)

President Keith Morrow sums up the impact of the Springbok tour on his members. A sorry politicised chapter in police history ends and business can return to normal

the National Anthem and a lone protester moved into the no-man's land between the lines to lay down some tree leaves in a symbolic gesture."

The front ranks of the parade knelt down to give those further back a clear view of what they were facing. The sight was met with a barrage of jeers. The main body of the march then

t and later fragmented to spearhead

The 1981 Springbok tour was the most divisive incident in recent New Zealand history. The police were in the unique position of being the only people required to attend the games, there to keep the pro- and anti-tour forces apart and to maintain law and order. The campaigners, the photographers and the cartoonists had a field day. The police did not

ahead, Moodie began to plan police tactics. Long batons were the most frequent subject of discussion. They had been introduced from the United States following a gang incident in Moerewa on 3 August 1979. Moodie pressed for them as preferable to firearms in situations where police were not coping.

Moodie acknowledges that the long baton controversy which emerged during the tour, of the police as faceless thugs, 'has an element of truth in it—but that was because of the way they were used. Meurant wanted the tour resolved with the long baton. As it turned out, he got it. That's what Hamilton created.' Before the Hamilton incident, Moodie was against the tour.

Hamilton was where the mighty Springbok rugby tourists had been tamed in 1956. Crowds of perfervid rugby fans hoped and prayed for a repeat in 1981. Then New Zealand saw something else—protesters invading the pitch, and a pilot threatening to fly into a stand with the potential loss of many lives. Commissioner Walton's actions resulted in the calling off of the game and New Zealand seemed to descend into a civil war between pro- and anti-tour forces.

The July *Newsletter* had warned members that, come the 22nd of the month when the tour started, they would face 'one of the sternest challenges for many years'. The association had no opinion about whether or not the tour should go ahead, but the police must remember that the New Zealand philosophy of policing was based on overwhelming community support. By protecting strikers and their families in the 1951 waterfront dispute the police had avoided a legacy of bitterness. This would be another such testing time, and unwise conduct by any officer 'will be seized upon to hold the Police service collectively responsible'.

At this stage Moodie believed that about 40 per cent of the police shared his opposition to the tour. His meetings with Ross Meurant and Phil Keber did not convince him that they represented the average policeman. He regarded his working partnership with Walton as one where they used each other for the good of the service. 'When Walton got into trouble in Hamilton,' says Moodie, and 'Meurant led the vote of no confidence they wanted to pass in him—the first person Walton rang was me.'

Moodie and Butterworth drove through the night from Wellington to Hamilton and spoke to Walton in the morning. Moodie was alarmed that Walton was fluctuating between going ahead and telling the government that the tour could not go on. 'So I chartered a plane and flew back to Wellington behind him,' says Moodie, 'to make sure he didn't tell the government we couldn't go on with it. If the tour was cancelled because of what happened in Hamilton, the level of violence would increase. There was no turning back. The police took a softer line at Hamilton and I was proud of Walton for cancelling the game. It was a very dangerous situation. He didn't get a lot of thanks in the police service, but he did the right thing.'

Keith Morrow is convinced that Moodie did the right thing in talking Walton out of stopping the tour because he could not guarantee the safety of players or public. If he had done that, Morrow says, New Zealand police 'would never have been able to lift our heads again'.

Moodie recognised the elements in the police such as Red Squad leaders Meurant and Keber who were 'out to prove themselves and prove to the New Zealand society that the police could do the job'. He was also concerned about the element in New Zealand society which wanted confrontation. That morning in Hamilton he was abused everywhere by rugby supporters who felt 'licked'. He told them that if the plane had flown into the stand, Walton would be in gaol. Facing a fiery meeting of Hamilton members, he told them he was emphatically behind Walton.

At a special management committee meeting called in Wellington on 28 July, he proposed the strategy they should put to the commissioner. This included the police meeting the demonstrators outside the rugby grounds and ensuring that the police were better equipped and led than they had been at Hamilton; the riot police inside the ground had been well equipped, whereas most police outside had had only helmets and short batons. He proposed that games be moved from indefensible grounds and that semi-sedentary staff should not be deployed at games.

Walton attended the meeting to discuss Operation Rugby, where Moodie described his attempts to bring the protest movement leaders, the Rugby Union, the government and the police to the conference table.

Monk issued a statement to members reminding them that each was responsible for any excess force used. The public that was calling for a harder line now would be quick to condemn excess force. Monk, as president, from now on attended games in a welfare role, ensuring that staff committed to an operation were adequately housed, fed and looked after. Morrow thinks the tour took its toll on Monk, for this was his last year as president.

Vice-president Morrow, stationed at Alexandra, where the mood was pro-tour, was deployed to Dunedin. He was aware some police did not wish to be involved for moral or ethical reasons. The police image was the big worry, he says. Without public support the police were lost, and they were not far from losing it. For the first time, the police came into conflict with decent, law-abiding citizens who had taken to the streets on a matter of principle and came smack up against the nice policeman who had drawn the raffle at the Country Women's Institute, now dressed in greatcoat and riot helmet with a PR24 long baton directed at them, telling them this far and no further.

Moodie worked mightily to bring the opposing parties together. Acting Prime Minister Duncan MacIntyre agreed to start discussion on an accord. In the process of talking to Halt All Racist Tours representatives and Race Relations conciliator Hiwi Tauroa, alternatives proposed were cancelling one test to give spectators a chance to stand for one minute's silence to show their opposition to apartheid. Nothing concrete came out of the meetings, but there was no trouble on the streets while the talking continued. Then Muldoon returned and the discussions ended.

Moodie asked Muldoon to increase police numbers by 150. He and his management committee were concerned

Commissioner Bob Walton presents a Springbok tour plaque to association president Keith Morrow. On his other side is a subdued Rob Moodie, the first person Walton contacted after the debacle of the Hamilton match which the commissioner cancelled. Moodie and Walton, Rob and Bob, were perhaps the most effective duet in the history of association/administration relations, and the tour was their most critical period of co-operation

that their members were not sufficiently trained to deal with riot conditions. He lobbied the commissioner against the appointment of unsworn temporaries or specials in whose untrained baton-wielding hands the police reputation would lie. As in 1951, the police managed to keep the vigilante brigade out of their ranks, which Muldoon did not agree to increase.

Moodie was the focus of hundreds of letters from the public fearful of police state behaviour, or the lack of it. Many, like Julie Pickard of Hamilton, begged Moodie to stop the protest. Moodie answered with his even-handed approach, saying the police did their best to maintain balance in a bitterly divided society. As in the overstayer issue, the police were the meat in the sandwich.

Butterworth offered a stout defence of members against the railings of a Christchurch lecturer. He reminded him that the police did not ask the tourists here, that they did not ask people to go to watch them or people to try to stop them being watched. Police were the only people required to be at games, to try to keep the peace. Many police were opposed to the tour, but had to suppress their feelings to attain balance. If there were some failures, bear in mind that these men were working 12-hour days for weeks on end. It was easy to see the police as 'expressionless zombies' and hate them as authority figures, 'making them the scapegoats for a failure in our political life'.

As the tour progressed, it was Moodie rather than any church, union or political figure, who came to be seen as the principal establishment opposition to Muldoon. In August the protest movement asked Moodie if the police could remain impartial defending an unpopular tour. Moodie said the administration policy had been one of minimum force, with the possible exception of the Molesworth Street clash. The police did not write the laws, but established a balance around them in a more violent and difficult situation that was a consequence of the tour, not of police partiality. 'Many people,' he thought, 'feel that the Prime Minister has in some sense given some encouragement to this tour.'

Moodie and Muldoon were interviewed on the television news at the end of August. Moodie warned against looking for communists among the protest movement leaders. Muldoon said Moodie had contributed little that was constructive. He did not think Moodie represented the view of the police 'in supporting the subversive element' and he wanted a policeman there alongside Moodie next time they met. He called Moodie volatile and spectacular. Resisting any such response, Moodie insisted that he was aiming to diffuse the situation in a bitterly divided society.

The members were publicly behind Moodie. Southland secretary Sergeant Brian Walkinshaw expressed dissatisfaction with the government doing nothing about

PRINCE CHARLES MAKING HIS FORMAL ADDRESS AT THE OPENING OF THE COLLEGE.

The Porirua Police College opens at last, the rotten meals, rough quarters and sub-standard facilities at Trentham consigned to history. The long-awaited college was the only good news for the police through most of 1981

compensation for overtime or requests for additional staff. Muldoon's solution was to suggest that the public show their support for the police by subscribing to an appeal for a police holiday home. He came to the association conference in October well pleased that $150,000 was subscribed, costing the government nothing. Telling the members that the public saw them at their strongest and that he and Moodie disagreed on methods but not on feelings about the police, he announced that Walton would have his term extended by two years.

The holiday home subscription was a sop. Another, an offer for 15 police and families to holiday in South Africa, was rejected by the management committee as 'quite inappropriate'. As well as lost overtime and disrupted family life, the members also had to cope with departmental investigations of allegations against members. Moodie was busy advising members of their rights and ensuring legal assistance; to a large extent the association was successful.

The association, aware that the public suspected a whitewash, initiated the idea of an independent police examiner so that the police were not perceived as judge and jury of their own cause. The situation was made worse when the Ombudsman lumped together 25 complaints against the police in his report to Parliament, and then there was public concern expressed at the fatal shooting of Paul Chase in his Petone home.

What eventually emerged was the Police Complaints Authority. The association was able to warn against the excesses of a police authority such as the Victorian version that had to be disbanded after the ombudsman was advertising his appearance in local pubs to hear complaints. They were also able to show that when anonymous complaints were allowed in New South Wales, they stymied promotion, for whenever there were applicants for a position, there would be anonymous complaints about the applicants. The association failed to get agreement to allow complaints against administrative practice.

In his last presidential report Monk suggested there was another Australian model in granting a general amnesty to overstayers. He suggested regularising the status of overstayers so that the police and immigration authorities could avoid having to hunt them down.

This liberal approach from association headquarters did not find favour with the government and some members, particularly in Auckland. Moodie had taken a management committee meeting to Christchurch, where he insisted that local members reverse their vote not to admit wives into discussion of housing. In September 1980 he took a management committee meeting to Auckland, where he clashed with the local national councillor Peter Hilt on the liberal overstayer line. Hilt said Auckland members were totally opposed to Moodie's line. Moodie countered that they did not want the association to be just a union—'we must have a social conscience'. When Ian Revell joined his Auckland colleague in claiming that overstayers were a local issue, he was reminded that Tokoroa had a large Polynesian population. The resentment had continued over the years at the police being blamed for doing the dirty work for Immigration. Only Nelson , however, supported Auckland's stand.

Moodie had shown, with the Auckland and Christchurch meetings, that he not only believed in communicating with members, but in confronting tricky issues directly. When Nelson in the December accused Moodie of 'abject capitulation' to the administration over civilianisation, he went directly to Nelson to face the criticism. He was not met at the airport or the police station, as was normal, and the meeting had begun when he arrived. When the chairman denounced him, Moodie tried to deflect the criticism away from personality to the issue. He reminded the meeting that the annual conference had accepted the commission-

The Queen visits, a welcome respite for the police from the rigours of controversial rugby tourists

er's assurance that he would negotiate at district and national level and the association could propose alternatives. When Moodie's protest was ignored, he walked out of the meeting.

Moodie's upfront manner provoked criticism throughout his nine years in the job. Even the management committee occasionally objected to being what Morrow called 'sheep rubber stamping everything, told after it happened'. Once Morrow was voted into the presidency and paid to do the job in Wellington, he appreciated Moodie's defence that there was no time to get approval when you were in the thick of negotiations.

Morrow also saw the unpleasant clashes Moodie had with the second tier of police administration. Moodie wanted Morrow in to deal with this level, which was where association and administration clashed head on over the implementation of the government's cost-cutting and sinking lid policies. The crisis blew up in mid-1982 over a Turangi staff application for the agreed condition of a standby allowance. 'All we wanted,' says Morrow, 'was an on-call allowance paid to staff at Turangi and ultimately throughout New Zealand, in recognition of being in a state of readiness throughout the night.'

The Turangi issue had been in contention since February 1981, with the administration failing to implement the agreed conditions of work. Moodie was concerned that Acting Commissioner Ken Thompson would not accept that the association's national council had resolved to make this a national issue and would not tolerate any further procrastination. On 18 June 1982 Moodie advised Thompson of the Turangi staff's resolution to exercise their right to refuse to receive telephone calls after 11 pm from Tuesday, 22 June next. With Walton away, Morrow believes Thompson was going to work with his senior staff 'to break the association once and for all'.

Moodie rejected Thompson's plan to extend shifts at Turangi to 3 am, just to accommodate one call after 11 pm once every three or four days. The standby allowance had been agreed to meet that contingency. The association set up a relay call so that when the Turangi staff stood down, there was no interruption of any service to the public.

On his return Walton met with Moodie and Thompson, and was not impressed with his deputy's plan. Thompson argued that the roster should be extended in line with the Picton one, an anachronism from the days of the 2 am ferry sailing. Moodie suggested Walton was receiving bad advice, he thought intentionally. The decision on Turangi had been made by the head of operations, who knew nothing of the standby allowance negotiations with the SSC. The decision should have been made by the head of administration or the industrial relations officer. Walton investigated the matter and agreed to the on-call and standby allowances.

Ken Thompson was Acting Commissioner when he clashed with Rob Moodie over police conditions of work at Turangi, the beginning of a less harmonious period for association relations with the administration

Behind the Turangi procrastination was the political pressure on the police administration to go along with other government departments and achieve a 3 per cent cut each year for three years. Moodie believed Ben Couch had confused matters by saying he would ask his colleagues if the police could be exempted from the cuts, but nothing happened. Finally the administration had planned to close 19 one-man stations, let staffing run down through no replacements of 110 to 120 officers, and axe the Wellington police rescue launch, *Lady Elizabeth II*.

Public protest saved the *Lady Elizabeth II* and Moodie made it clear to the Public Expenditure Committee that, while the association supported the effort to reduce public expenditure, it would not accept cuts for cuts' sake. The police had a responsibility to maintain public order.

The situation had twisted to the stage where it appeared that Moodie was the defender of the thin blue line, the police administrators part of the control department's cost-cutting philosophy. Moodie accused the administration of playing cat and mouse games with the association, refusing to discuss the rumoured closures. He wrote to the Minister of Police, but got no reply. He wrote to the Public Expenditure Committee asking them to reverse any decision on total closures and allow administration and association to find the 3 per cent savings required.

Moodie cranked up his campaign of informing members what was really going on through his extensive minutes of management committee meetings, distributed throughout the country. The administration had, he said, virtually abandoned members to public sources of information. He accused Thompson of spreading misinformation when he said any proposed closures would be discussed with the communities and police concerned, and that the closures represented rationalisation of resources and were not part of the cuts programme. Eastbourne in Wellington was one example where people were told the closure would be discussed, but were then told the decision had been made to close the station there. Thompson saying that officers were advised, when they had not been, was, Moodie said, seen by them as 'a lie'. Statements that closures were made where only eight hours duty was worked five days a week were 'highly misleading and denigratory'. Moodie said the administration's approach was unsympathetic to the human problem of police families.

The management committee of 21 July 1982 meeting passed a vote of censure against the commissioner and deputy commissioner for their mishandling of the 3 per cent cuts issue, specifically station closures, reflecting a lack of sensitivity to the needs of the public and police officers and their families. There was a demand that the closures decision be reversed. A further vote of censure was passed against Thompson over his 'denigratory' remarks about one-man stations.

These, Moodie said, were painful steps to take, but some nails had to be driven into 'the coffin of this civil service mentality'. He suggested that savings could be made through regionalisation of the CIB, lower pay to recruits and greater technological integration of emergency services.

National councillors confirmed the management committee position, agreeing that the administration showed negative thinking in trying to settle industrial disagreements quickly. The media rushed to report these divisions. TVNZ's *EyeWitness News* said that, despite the assurances of the commissioner and the deputy commissioner, memos advising officers of closures had not reached them. This programme and other media went further in suggesting personal conflicts and that the association was seeking to influence the government's choice of a successor to Walton. Moodie, feeling he had been defamed by this calling into question of his professional standing and his ability to negotiate for the association in the future, asked for, and got, a retraction.

While the administration was concentrating on computer statistics, the association was concerned with the effect closures had on people—the officers, their families and their communities. Moodie and Morrow toured stations under threat—Duntroon, St Andrews, Ahaura, Granity, Kimbolton, Eastbourne and Paekakariki. After talking to those affected, the association made submissions to the Minister of Police to present to Cabinet. As a result the decision to close stations was rescinded and the matter sent back to Walton for reconsideration.

Walton announced that all stations would stay open except perhaps for Mission Bay. He also said savings of $2.5 million had been made within the administration; the police had been spared the full 3 per cent cut. Suitable economies could be achieved without frontline services being seriously affected.

Moodie was firing on all cylinders. Not only had he piloted the police against the tide of public retrenchment, but he had turned around the fortunes of the association. The welfare fund, and particularly the credit union, had been on the brink of disaster. Now they were multimillion-dollar enterprises. Morrow reckons that if Moodie had been run over by a bus in 1983, his loss would have bankrupted the association.

With the social traumas of the commission and the tour behind them, Moodie told the management committee meeting of 28 April 1982 that he and Butterworth were 'psyched up now for early retirement'. He said the Springbok tour had had a big effect. One obvious signal was how many police were not up to frontline policing. The traditional 40-year public service career was no longer possible in the hectic world of contemporary policing.

Early retirement would be Moodie's crowning achievement. All he had to cope with were a few pesky civil servants and politicians. The Muldoon regime had given the police a few unnecessarily traumatic years. Now it would be their turn, and for them it would be terminal political trauma.

DR MOODIE'S MESSAGE

In this 1981 seasonal message I would like to express to you my sincere thanks and gratitude for the support you have given me as National Secretary of the Police Association. I record also my acknowledgement of the enthusiasm and dedication of members of my staff whom I sincerely thank for having ensured a year's smooth working in all th departments of our office.

The year has been one in which our negotiations on Departmental issues have at all levels been carried out with a sense of realism and progress.

To the Commissioner and his staff who, while they have not met all the Association's demands, have received patiently and with consideration matters which have been submitted to them, I also express my thanks. It is the steadfast aim of the Association to keep these negotiations at all times on the highest plane of cordiality.

Our vision of the future is not clear. In hindsight it has not surprised me that all of the difficulties of the past year should have left untrammelled the reputation of the New Zealand Police Force and its countenance unmarked. For this, in pride and humility, I congratulate members for their individual courage, discipline and patience in dealing with all of the situations, many of them new ones, imposed on them in the past year.

It is inexplicable and saddening to me that so many New Zealanders should have sought to transfer their feelings ar emotions on racist issues to the police because they happene to be there at the time. Many of those in conflict must have wondered afterwards at what really prompted their actions, while others, in performing a role of lawlessness took as a bonus the new auspices provided for them by a strange, self-justifying element in our society.

In time there will inevitably be fresh testing of the police in new ways and our adaptability will bring us to meet such challenges with an integrity and an ableness to stand fast on the issues as they arise.

For the Prime Minister recently to have publicly stated that we have "an efficient Force, publicly supported" was due in no small part to the leadership and direction of the Commissioner, Mr Walton himself along with that of his senior officers. The extension of his time of office was, for this reason I believe, not merely gratuitous, but a mark of the confidence shown in him by the Government and the New Zealand Public.

Seasons Greetings to you all, your families and friends.

Chapter Eighteen

The Lobbying for Early Retirement

Early retirement at 55 was something the association had been talking about since the early 1970s. Moodie spent over five years developing the package, after the department told him in 1978 that they had worked on the subject and concluded it was not justified. Moodie told them he was not negotiating with them because early retirement was not an industrial issue, like the Turangi standby allowance, it was justified on political grounds. The politicians had to make the decision.

The association appreciated the urgency of early retirement after the Springbok tour, when all hands had to be on the frontline and, in Morrow's words, 'we really produced the crocks'. The government and the department, he says, had not come to grips with the number of passengers the police were carrying, unproductive officers coasting towards retirement. The SSC and Treasury were not interested in this association initiative, a venture into the unknown that would be seen as pouring more money into what, to them, was an unproductive department anyway. The association cast around for precedents to bolster its argument.

A tired-looking Rob Moodie back on his advocacy track, announcing what was perhaps his greatest union achievement. It was a little premature; he still had to help bundle out the National Government

Moodie was offered an open ticket round the world to collect data. But he and Butterworth had had enough trips to Australia, attempting unsuccessfully to consolidate the Australia and New Zealand Police Federation to know that they had moved New Zealand ahead of any thinking over there. After making a few phone calls, Moodie soon discovered that there was nowhere he would find anything useful. Other police unions were way behind.

What had convinced him of the need for early retirement was the stress level. It was too high—police were not coping with the job, and he did not mean the criminals and the violence. As a detective he had faced violence and knew it got the adrenalin going. There were plenty of police volunteering for the Armed Offenders Squad. The stress was coming from working in a system that was not working properly.

'I looked at the police from the family position,' he says. 'They wanted promotion, but they wanted to keep the family together. The second factor was to insulate the family against the danger aspect of the job. Third was to get our health standards up. We had 20 per cent of the police who couldn't turn out if there was a major job on.'

When this became apparent in the Springbok tour, it gave an impetus to Moodie's argument. Yet he was finding that it was not just older police who were fit only for light duties. He remembered a 19-year-old Wellington constable who weighed 140 kilograms (22 stone). As he grew fatter, he became more an object of ridicule and his stress level rose, so he put on still more weight. Moodie knew of undercover cops in their early 20s who were stressed out by the job, sleeping with revolvers under their pillows.

'I wanted a situation where you didn't continue with your staff problems,' he says.

> You allowed these people to leave with a certain amount of dignity. We needed psychological services. Many thought they were a lot of crap, but I knew from the *Wahine* disaster what stress does to you. I was locking up my daughter in the house when I mowed the lawn. It was stupid. One day I woke up to what I was doing. It was all stress coming from the *Wahine* incident. I saw it with tough, hard-nosed policemen with a problem they could not cope with, ending up in tears in my office.

Moodie worked through the stages of police health, the insurance scheme, optional disengagement, which became

Perf or the Police Employees' Rehabilitation Fund, then early retirement, optional for a number of years, eventually to be compulsory at 55. The realisation in the service was that, apart from those in senior positions, most police aged between 55 and 60 were not coping very well.

The example that stuck in Moodie's mind was the policeman at Palmerston in the South Island who had been written up in the *Newsletter* as the oldest serving frontline officer in the country. Moodie visited him. 'It was sad,' he says. 'The man was a nervous wreck. He didn't realise it himself. He was hanging on there, *True Grit* stuff. He confirmed what I already knew. I had been pretty active in the police and was aware by age 30 I'd had enough. I was getting that message from everybody else.'

He had seen police officers attempt suicide because they did not know when to shed a tear, or how to. Big boys did not cry. It worried him that staff would sometimes go off the rails, committing assaults or burglaries. Senior officers were not responding to the warning signals. There was the example of an officer in charge of the Armed Offenders Squad in a small city who was psychologically disorientated. There were complaints from the public to the police administration, and all the administration did was defend the officer. Moodie says he was condemned for the association's repeated request that the administration take the pressure off the officer and get him under psychological supervision. The officer ended up on a serious assault charge. This, Moodie says, was entirely predictable and could have been avoided. He had seen this situation span the commissionerships of Walton and Thompson. He welcomed the Police Complaints Authority because he believed the police needed it as much as the public. However, his principal interest was in prevention rather than cure.

The Police Health Plan introduced on 1 April 1982 was the beginning of the process. Several years of research and negotiation revealed an urgent need to provide comprehensive medical insurance for police families beyond the existing benefits from the welfare fund. The association shopped around and got a good premium from New Zealand Medi-Care. The welfare fund owned the scheme, the credit union collected the premiums. By 1984 the scheme had proved itself, with over $250,000 paid out to 2000 members in reimbursed medical expenses.

Throughout the early 1980s Moodie reported regularly to the management committee his progress with 'Early Retirement/Optional Disengagement/Superannuation/Housing'. He decided that term disengagement was not on because, while it allowed an officer to decide whether he stayed in the job, it also gave the boss the same opportunity. 'We were trying to build security into the police, not insecurity. Term engagement might have delivered a handout, but it did nothing for those who wanted a career in the police. I knew people in the military who had similar problems building a second career, not knowing whether their first one was going on.'

Keith Morrow had seen the genesis of the problem often enough as an instructor at Trentham. Cadets came into the police straight from school, from one disciplined situation to another. They did well academically, but after 12 or 14 years in the police they got itchy feet. They had never done anything else, but some fancied themselves, perhaps based on good exam results, as entrepreneurs, and many resigned to try their luck. Months later they were seeking to rejoin. They had no other skills, no way to get started in another occupation. He says association thinking moved from term engagement to Perf—choosing to disengage, with the buffer of superannuation if things did not work out.

Agreement was reached with the administration that police would maintain a level of physical, mental and emotional health necessary to do the job. The agreement was framed so that if a person was not performing, a series of tests was applied to determine the cause. The Hickson Committee of police administration and the SSC had also identified such non-performers who ended up in sheltered, sedentary police jobs.

On 10 June 1981 Moodie told Walton that the association wanted early retirement implemented by the following April. He said a large number of police were forced into resignation before retirement age because they lacked the physical or emotional resilience to cope with the stress of modern policing. Others, for financial reasons, clung to jobs they could no longer perform, to the detriment of themselves and their families, as well as of the service and the public. For those who had to choose or wished to choose retirement before their government superannuation matured, Perf would give them enough of a payout to change to another career. The Perf initiative would be compulsory, with members contributing 7 per cent of their salary and the government about double their contribution. Although this was almost the way it was implemented, the implementation took some time and a good deal of stress for Moodie and the executive.

On 30 November 1982 Moodie reminded his minister,

The May 1985 *Newsletter* carried an update on the protective measures available to members to avoid contracting hepatitis B and other infectious diseases, including the new horror occupational hazard, AIDS (Acquired Immune Deficiency Syndrome)

Police Minister Ben Couch, one of the Muldoon ministers for whom Moodie and the association had least time

Ben Couch, that the government's Hickson Committee had confirmed the association position on early retirement, for which application had been made 17 months ago. The employment situation had deteriorated since then. Members required to leave the police for stress reasons and possessing no marketable skills needed the Perf financial cushion, and the Perf scheme could be fine-tuned as a liquid investment fund to provide home mortgage finance at favourable rates. In the interim the housing survey had shown a quarter of police without any housing security, some of whom would have to resign or retire without a roof over their heads.

The government stalled in committees such as the Review Committee on Government Superannuation. The SSC had agreed the terms of the Police Personnel Policy Committee for which Moodie was pushing, but by the middle of 1983 the SSC approval was stuck in the minister's office and Couch was overseas. Even Cliff Terry of Treasury had conceded that the police had special needs and was sympathetic to Perf, while the Personnel Policy Committee was studying Palmerston North as a middle range district example of why the police should be given something over and above everyone else. Butterworth was busy with the econometrician and the actuaries working out the fine figuring. And the association was getting restless.

At the 24 August 1983 management committee meeting Ian Revell repeated complaints he had made for several months that Auckland members demanded an early resolution of early retirement and were sick of procrastination. He could not have been as sick of it as Moodie, who had been working on the project since 1978. He had already told members it was ultimately a political decision.

At the meeting of the management committee on 21 September Moodie told members that this government was neither willing nor able to put anything in place for the police. It had had its fingers burned with Think Big energy projects, with broadcasting and with industrial relations generally. No longer listening, it was out of touch with the public. The national council had narrowly avoided a vote of no confidence in the government and the administration, so Moodie had begun lobbying other parties. Although he had no political ambitions, if he stood in Ben Couch's Wairarapa electorate at the next election 'it would simply be a statement of having no confidence in the Government'. That evening he and President Keith Morrow would be dining in the association office with the Deputy Leader of the Opposition and the Labour spokesperson on police. The die was cast when he had written to Muldoon about the serious concern in the police over public confidence in the service falling to just 55 per cent in the recent Heylen poll; Muldoon snapped that there was no basis for it. Moodie told the meeting Muldoon was 'either mad or blind'.

Moodie continued to put his submissions on record. On 27 September he submitted to the State Services Conditions of Employment Amendment Bill committee that only those with exceptional mental and physical resilience could expect to serve in the police into their late 50s. This year two out of about 16 chief superintendents were forced to retire through work-related psychological problems. Increasing numbers of police at all levels were experiencing such stress in the only 24-hour service in the country coping with offenders and victims. The police were described by the 1983 Report on the New Zealand Police as 'crime stoppers, law enforcers, social workers, conflict arbitrators, marriage counsellors, legal advisers and psychologists'. And that report, Moodie added, was at the recruit level!

Moodie called for a major change of direction to restore public confidence. Technology-based reactive policing brought in in the late 1960s had sundered the police from the community. Recruiting was down and there were several hundred police not fit for frontline duty, where the incidence of police suffering assaults had gone up from 17 per cent in 1976 to 29.88 per cent in 1982.

Career restructuring was the solution. Police could now serve only 10 or 15 years as opposed to the traditional 35 to 40 years in the job. These shortened career prospects required the means to establish themselves in civilian life through a lump sum instead of a pension, hence the push for Perf. It was a unique situation with no relativities to other occupations. Moodie argued that Parliament must acknowledge the need to create and maintain a fully fit and trained police service and to grant the authority for the police administration and the SSC to negotiate appropriate salaries and conditions of service to do this.

This was no more than Moodie had been saying for some years, but now he was saying it very publicly. Incredibly, on

25 June 1984 he was still getting from Kelly of the SSC the old line that the police were no different from any other group of public servants and he could see no justification for a special scheme. Kelly even said the government had never agreed to retirement at 55.

Ken Thompson was now commissioner, and it was at this meeting that he launched into accusations of misinformation and making a statement that was 'blatantly wrong'. Moodie rated it the best performance he had seen from a commissioner. He also observed that Ben Couch did not know what was going on.

State Services Minister David Thomson said the government could not commit the incoming administration to such costs, so nothing could be done about this police scheme that would cost about $7,500,000 until after the 16 July election. Two days later Thomson, as Minister of Defence, announced the purchase of aircraft worth $68,000,000.

Moodie invited Couch to the special conference on 5 July to announce government policy on the police. When Couch asked Moodie what was happening about early retirement and optional disengagement, Moodie replied that he was supposed to have seen the Prime Minister about them. The next Moodie heard was the Prime Minister on the election trail in Christchurch saying he would not be intimidated by the Police Association over the early retirement issue. He also made derogatory remarks about Moodie.

Moodie responded by getting management committee agreement to placing large advertisements in the three major main centre newspapers showing which matters were of concern to the police and encouraging public and police to consider where they were putting their votes. The ads cost $5,000. Revell, several elections later elected to Parliament as a National member, objected to running the ads because he believed they would be counter-productive. Moodie defended the ads as aimed not just at the 1984 election but at the association's ability to achieve benefits for its members. These would not eventuate unless politicians had to take the association into account. The SSC would always try to deal with the police as an ordinary industrial body, so the association had to play the politics of the issue, without political preference. Moodie could not reconcile his personal preferences with the best interests of the association; he was forced into this situation because the government had absolutely failed the police service over the last six years.

The message of the advertisements happened to be consistent with the Labour Party election message and what Moodie had been saying over the last five years. This was no accident. Butterworth recalls drafting the Labour Party police policy in the association office and delivering it over the telephone to Geoffrey Palmer.

Butterworth had been a key figure in winning Labour over to an election commitment to early retirement. It helped that Butterworth had worked with Margaret Shields when she was also working for the Consumers' Institute. She was his first choice as Minister of Police. She got on well with the police in her Kapiti electorate and, a factor Butterworth and Moodie judged important, she was a woman. They wanted to get away from the macho image in pushing their sensitive social early retirement changes for the police service.

Moodie had never hesitated to use the weapons available. He caught flak from members for running on the front of the *Newsletter* for September 1981 an address by Leader of the Opposition Bill Rowling denouncing the Springbok tour and promising more money for police to own their own homes and for more staff. Moodie's defence was that he went for policies, whichever party it was, and he had invited the other parties to contribute statements of policy in the run-up to the election. Only Social Credit's Bruce Beetham had responded.

Earlier in 1981 members had indicated that early retirement was a priority. Butterworth sees the Springbok tour as the final flowering of the reactive style of policing, which was no longer working. Butterworth and Moodie took the view that the police should work with the community to defuse problems, and from 1982 they had begun talking about community policing, with early retirement the means by which the service was modernised.

Butterworth says the association thought Couch would be more responsive to community policing. As it happened, his blimpish predecessor Air Commodore Frank Gill had proved more receptive both to that and to early retirement. Couch was a great disappointment, particularly when he

Geoffrey Palmer was the principal Opposition figure Moodie and Butterworth dealt with in the rapid run-up to Prime Minister Muldoon's snap election

told police to put the boot in; Moodie told him that if some young police took his advice literally, they would end up in court and perhaps in gaol.

When Couch told the eve-of-election conference in 1984 that National had no policy for the police and Muldoon was not going to make one, the association's National-leaning members, according to Butterworth, said they had had it. Moodie and Butterworth were asked to try and commit Labour, and if it involved attacking National, they should do so. Moodie notes that Labour have always been much better to the police than National, but the police do not see that. His members regarded him as a Labour man when in fact he was a member of the National Party. As usual, however, he was several steps ahead of his members in tapping into Labour early in 1984.

In March 1984 the *Evening Post* was welcoming the government promise to introduce early retirement and optional engagement because the police were suffering 'street fever' and should be properly compensated for it. That month Moodie and Butterworth began discussions with Geoffrey Palmer, Frank O'Flynn and Trevor Young. They knew what the government promise was worth. They met every Tuesday evening for five weeks. The snap election announcement was a surprise but not a disaster. Labour had not got to the stage of drafting their police policy, so Butterworth offered to do so, promising association backing if Margaret Shields would deliver the speech he wrote. Palmer agreed and Shields delivered the speech at Porirua. A policeman later told Butterworth that they knew he and Moodie were cooking something up so he and other police officers had gone to the meeting at Porirua and applauded the speech, then spread the word.

Butterworth had some difficulty getting the word spread through the television news, but he rang up and pressured his contacts. The story screened and was then picked up by the newspapers. The next stage was the *Newsletter* publishing the party political positions on the police. Butterworth wrote Labour's, checking it with Palmer. By now Margaret Shields was seen as too close to the police, so Butterworth and Moodie lobbied for Ann Hercus, and to have the portfolio stand alone.

The 17 July management committee meeting conducted a postmortem on the National Party defeat the previous day. Moodie said he knew now why the SSC and the government actuary had not been able to work on police early retirement—they were busy on Parliament's sweet super package, announced just before the election. Moodie spoke of the 'sheer bloodymindedness' of the Muldoon regime and of the ineffectual Couch trying to keep the association at arm's length. Morrow had spoken to two National MPs who said there were a lot of telephone calls between National Party people and the Prime Minister but that 'the decision not to grant us anything was in the hands solely of one man'.

The association allowed the new Labour Government its limbo period to open the books, before Moodie and Butterworth turned up to cash in. Palmer told them that early retirement was the sort of thing Labour would prefer to deal with later, in the second or third year, after the matter had been studied.

'Politicians love saleable words,' Butterworth grins. '"Minister", I said, "we are not talking here about just benefits to the police, but the rejuvenation of the New Zealand Police." Palmer repeated the word rejuvenation, wrote it down. After the meeting Rob said, "We've got him. He can't bear to let that word and concept go." Six years later people are still using it. We got our early retirement within nine months.'

The SSC tried to stop early retirement, but Hercus told the bureaucrats to go ahead. Still there was stalling, from Treasury objecting to the mortgage plan giving the police more than anybody else. Moodie told Hercus this was not acceptable, and she would face many angry police and major problems such as civilianisation if this package were not agreed to. On 19 February 1985 Moodie announced completion of the early retirement negotiations, including the 20 per cent of members' superannuation funds available for mortgages. It marked, he said, the end of the 'major part of our rebuilding of the Association and associated organisations'.

Now for the next stage. The service organisations would require 'managerial, administrative, technical expertise which far exceeds that currently possessed by myself and Mr Butterworth'. He called for a return of power to elected committees and councils of the association and the hiring of permanent executive and administrative staff. He suggested clearer definition of the job of the chief executive officer, who would be an administrative officer, with the president responsible for internal and political issues, and an advocate or negotiator who would be chief negotiator and political lobbyist for the service organisations.

Moodie had written himself out of a job, and specified the three people needed to take over. And that is the way it happened. He walked away, to farm goats.

The success of his dazzling nine years in the job was apparent in the black bottom lines of the annual accounts. The success of Perf was instant; in April 1985 the new secretary Gary Fulton announced that in the first week of operation 20 applications had been made for mortgages, averaging $37,000, totalling $750,000.

Why did the association's most brilliantly successful servant walk away? Moodie said he had done his job. Keith Morrow thinks he had run himself ragged. Butterworth feels that Moodie had got on a cycle of achievement that was hard to sustain, a rollercoaster ride with no stop button. Butterworth includes himself in the feeling that the drive for achievement was bringing them down. He also notes that Moodie had ended up where he began, handling some punishing personnel cases as rough as Constable Bob Fleming's. There was, for instance, Darby, the cop who lost a leg. It took a lot of lobbying to get him transferred to the Fraud Squad, where his disability would not stop him doing his job; the PCT or Physical Competence Test had not yet been distorted to the stage where if you cannot leap over a 2-metre wall you are considered unfit for the police.

It is perhaps appropriate to end an account of Moodie's

N.Z. Police Association, February 1986

Alan McWha

July 18, 1951 — December 13, 1985

An open letter from Alan's parents

Our Dear Friends,

It is with much sadness that we advise of the passing of our loved son, Alan.

He died on Friday, December 13 as the result of a self-inflicted gunshot wound about 24 hours previously.

As you will know, Alan had undergone extensive surgery in a id to halt a facial cancer. We believe that the growth had a continued and that he endured considerable pain over an extended period.

After his last operation, in 1982, he confided in friends that he would never undergo further surgery. It now seems that Alan knew that another operation was necessary — but would be a life-extending exercise which he didn't want to endure.

As the Rev Trevor Bennett commented in the funeral service attended by several hundred people in the Morrinsville Methodist Church on December 17, we should reflect with some comfort on the pleasure which Alan brought us during his short but active 34 years.

He was a kind, giving person and no couple could have wished for a better son.

Outstanding tributes were paid at his funeral service.

His days in the church's junior choir, sporting days at college — particularly on the hockey field — his love of animals, an interest in gardening and a liking for the outdoor adventures of hunting, fishing and diving were recalled.

Special and detailed mention was made of his association with teenagers generally known as "street kids" in the Glen Innes and Panmure suburbs of Auckland.

Barbara Te Kare, who is in charge of a halfway house (for youngsters who have fallen by the wayside in terms of obeying the law but who are now making an effort to mend their ways) at Glen Innes says Alan was a policeman in whom the teenagers trusted.

"Kids in trouble would sometimes ring me and say I'll only give myself up to Alan' because they knew he would treat them fairly," Mrs Te Kare said.

Alan didn't give idle or only verbal support. He was a man of action.

He had many of these youngsters often termed as 'undesirable', in his home. He trusted them — and earned their trust in return.

Alan was paid a rare tribute by the youngsters on his funeral day. Representatives of a group of teenagers, with whom he had had some association, removed their scarves — the valued article of clothing worn to shown an allegiance to their particular group — and draped them over the respected policeman's coffin.

"Why did you like him?" one member of the group was asked. "He used to come skating with us," the obviously sorrowful lad replied.

Alan was a man of action.

Constable Pauline Joblin, youth aid officer for the Auckland Police district, recalled many incidents in Alans 17 years of service where he had gone considerably further than was required of his duty.

Aware that a youngster was being hassled because he didn't have the correct footwear at school, Alan purchased shoes for the boy.

Another lad was able to buy a much-needed school back pack — with money from Alan's pocket.

He spent two weeks searching — eventually successfully — for a job for a young man knowing that steady employment was the boy's only hope of regaining a stable life style.

In his usual unselfish way he took into his care, some years ago, a young boy, Rodney Anderson. Alan has guided and provided for this now 17-year-old whose early tragic life prompted support from a man who lived by strong Christian principles.

Rodney has been provided for in Alan's will and we have accepted a request, made by Alan, to watch over him.

In this typical methodical way, Alan's death was meticulously planned. On the pretext that he would be spending some weeks at home in Morrinsville, he sold most of his loved cage birds. Rodney was instructed in how to care for the special ones retained.

His financial and property affairs were in order. Official papers were easily accessible, instructionss as to how various items were to be distributed were noted and heart-warming letters were left for those dearest to him.

His police uniforms were freshly cleaned and left hanging at the Glen Innes police station.

His final act, before uplifting a police issue pistol, was to write a report for his police colleagues.

Alan gained some notoriety by becoming the first officer in the New Zealand police force to win official approval to grow a beard. He didn't attempt to change the rules — he just wanted to cover the disfigurement which was the result of extensive cancer surgery.

Alan will be remembered by some as the bearded policeman. But those who had the pleasure of working with him will remember him for his more positive virtues.

He was a good man.

BERNICE and HUGH

Alan McWha was a poignant example of the beard issue Moodie spent five years campaigning to have approved by the commissioner. Moodie always fought for the individual against the system. McWha was a clear case of a beard being required on medical grounds, and so it was approved. But it was another five years before the administration could accept that any policeman could be as neatly bearded as Commissioner O'Donovan and his senior officers had been 70 years before magnificent contributions back where he began—concerned about helping an individual police officer overlooked by the system. Constable Fleming inspired his entire approach to the job. Almost a decade later Moodie ensured that Darby would not be dumped, and then promptly dumped himself. On his Feilding goat farm he shows no signs of regretting any of it. The only difference is that now he wears shirts and trousers most of the time. There is no need anymore to don a dress.

• Former Association President, Keith Morrow, receives his Life Members' certificate and badge from President, Steve Hinds.

Rob Moodie resigns to become a goat herder

Chapter Nineteen

The Unionisation of the Association

Graham Harding was chosen for the new association post of industrial advocate on 29 October 1985 and signalled his intentions in his first speech. 'It seems that in the United Kingdom and North America,' he said, 'social and economic tensions within the Police have led them increasingly into organising collectively in an effort to find self-reliance and industrial independence. Policemen and women are increasingly recognising the advantages of unionism, as is the case with most other white collar workers within New Zealand.'

The selection of this former secretary of the Canterbury Hotel, Hospital and Restaurant Workers Union by a committee of the management committee and national council members recognised the changing conditions being created by the Roger Douglas-driven restructuring of New Zealand, in particular the public service.

Graham Harding was chosen for the new association job of industrial advocate. Rob Moodie and most of the association executive decided that this solid union man was right for the job. His Labour Party connections, however, proved to be anything but useful as the association came on to a collision course with the second term Labour Government. *Evening Post*

'We were picking up the winds of change as part of the Labour Government strategy,' says Keith Morrow. 'Clear signals were being given to us to look seriously at going down a more industrial road.' The interim measure, Morrow says, was the creation of a triumvirate to run the association, consisting of his job as fulltime president, the new industrial advocate and a national secretary who was concerned only with administration. The three would be of equal standing, but the president would have the casting vote. Moodie had argued successfully that his job had become too all-embracing for one person. The many functions, the widening range of responsibilities, the rapidly expanding service organisations—doing all this would tear any individual apart.

The signal of the change was the appointment of the association's financial controller Gary Fulton as assistant national secretary on 12 July 1985. Internal office space problems had, back in November 1982, meant a move from 11 Manners Street to Princess Towers, 180 Molesworth Street. It was an immense relief for the cramped staff, which had jumped in one year from eight to 13. An attempt to spread over two floors of the association-owned Manners Street building was stymied by leasing commitments. The move uptown was regarded as convenient for its proximity to the administration, Parliament and the control departments the association so frequently met.

When talk began of Moodie's replacement, a solicitor was proposed. Moodie pooh-poohed this idea, saying his law degree was overrated and he did not use it. He suggested that the association concentrate instead on developing the administrative and computer side. They would make no more headway through the police administration and should look directly to the SSC in regard to industrial matters. That was where the power lay.

There were many applicants for the industrial advocate job. Butterworth was alone in preferring a bureaucrat who knew the way that Treasury and the SSC worked. Harding got the job, defined as being responsible for the public profile of the association, the *Newsletter* and all negotiations on behalf of members. With their eyes wide open, the association representatives chose a man who had been a fulltime trade unionist since 1972, dealing with members' complaints, negotiating for individual employees, an assessor on the national award conciliation council. Having lobbied for a woman minister, Moodie would have noted that most of Harding's recent clients were women.

When he was appointed Harding specified his interest in

Gary Fulton took over from Rob Moodie as secretary of the association, representing the first stage of restructuring Moodie's job. Fulton had been financial controller of the association before becoming assistant national secretary on 12 July 1985. For the following four years he was secretary, handling the financial management of the association, while Harding dealt with industrial matters

winning pregnancy leave provisions for policewomen. His primary goal he announced to be the introduction of a police industrial award. This would effectively be a members' Bill of Rights, defining their conditions of employment and their rights much more specifically than the 1980 Conditions of Work, which he thought inadequate because they were general and at best open to interpretation.

National secretary in all but name, Harding told Morrow he did not mind what title he was given, so long as he had the powers of national secretary. Although the titles were different, he was the third secretary of the association from Christchurch, after Lee and Thomas. In every other way he was from the other side of the tracks, the Moodie side, one of half a dozen children brought up by his mother after his army father left. His mother told him he should join the Labour Party at 16. He did. He tried the university, but it was not for him, so he worked at a local hotel, where the president of the union took young Graham under his wing. He paid his union dues by collecting them, 1s 3d a week from the tea ladies of Christchurch.

For such union activism he got the sack several times, but the union got him his job back. He says he became something of a militant, but he was militant within the Labour Party, moving up through its local structure to become president of the Canterbury region. Four of his electorates were represented by Ann Hercus, Geoffrey Palmer, David Caygill and Mike Moore. When Moore lost his Auckland seat of Eden, Harding employed him in Christchurch as a researcher for the Hotel Union. The traditional next step for a local president would be a local Labour seat. Instead, he had a family conference about the future, at which a life in politics was vetoed. They agreed on a change of place. The association job came up.

There was no question that Harding was in the job to promote industrial awareness in the police. His first speech to about 600 Auckland police was a shock. When he addressed them as brothers and sisters, a voice from the crowd yelled 'Commie bastard!' He picked up the El Pinko label, but he believes the success of the first salary round in which he was involved helped make him acceptable.

In his first media interview with the *Sunday News*, which had adopted much of the stroppy fair go stance for so long taken by *Truth*, Harding declared that the police had been industrial pussycats for too long and had thus paid the price of being ignored by politicians. It was no more than he had told the selection panel, and he had not expected to get the job when he saw on it the likes of true blue Peter Hilt, now a National MP.

For the crucial salary round Moodie offered to walk away or to act as Harding's mentor. They agreed over a few beers that Moodie would stay on. Harding noted that they were talking of coercing a pay rise out of government, so where was the industrial plan? There was none. It was not Moodie's style. In late 1984 he had pressed the commissioner to negotiate a salary claim directly on behalf of members, the way Barnett had worked in the 1950s. Thompson had agreed and was asking for 18 per cent.

The SSC had offered nil, and when the government offered 5 per cent, Thompson agreed. The association would not agree. Members had been waiting since 1979 for a review of salaries. They had forgone this in favour of early retirement, and then endured the wage freeze. Inflation had eroded their salaries at a time of increasing danger and stress. There was talk of industrial action, and Harding's appointment signalled this frame of mind.

After Thompson made the 5 per cent deal, national councillors voted to give him 14 days' notice of industrial action. This would include refusal to relieve traffic officers and civilian workers in the police, to staff the computer or to file reports. A budget of $20,000 was allocated for informing the public that the association was not reducing any law and order services.

Harding worked out the graduated list of industrial threats, a usual union tactic. He carried the letter of intent around with him for days, including his visit to see the commissioner. He was rather surprised when Butterworth burst in on the meeting, outraged that Harding had done something on his own initiative when knowing nothing of the delicate negotiations and likely to do untold damage. This was how Thomas had reacted to Moodie's arrival, to a changing of the guard. Butterworth resigned a few months later.

'We were within seconds of industrialisation,' says

Harding. 'Lange had gone public and said the police won't get a cent more than 8 per cent. We accepted that for constables, and bodgied up the rest, all the allowances and so on, and got 40 per cent. We delivered a dozen red roses to Ann Hercus in appreciation of her assistance.' Keith Morrow doubts if they would have got this settlement with any other minister. He remains an enthusiast for her performance then, despite being perceived as a key mover in bringing about her downfall a few years later.

There was an unprecedented level of discontent in the association, although Morrow regards the industrial action as pretty token. There was talk of the officers protecting the Prime Minister and VIPs withdrawing their services, of airport police refusing to work, which would have grounded all international flights.

After several meetings over the Christmas break, Ann Hercus was convinced by the police negotiators. Then she came out of a Cabinet committee meeting with the news that Treasury had rubbished the figures the negotiators gave her. She did not think Treasury made mistakes. Moodie, Harding and Brian Donnelly of the administration's Industrial Services checked that the figures were correct and took them back to Hercus next morning.

Hercus got the pay rise. It was the biggest pay rise in police history. On top of the 20 per cent general adjustment came the 18 to 20 per cent negotiated increase.

In classic Moodie style, the negotiators went straight on to a working party to create reforms in rating, rank and promotion structures and introduce a better appeal system. Most police never progressed beyond constable and the association wanted a senior constable designation to create a career structure. The guild, too, recognised that the police were overranked and favoured dropping the chief inspector level.

Once the rise was announced, the public perceived the police as having a cushy job. The *Dominion* cartoon of a lad going to school in his police Dad's Rolls Royce summed it up. Morrow remembers the phrase 'the insatiable Police Association'. Butterworth predicted that these increases would bring pressure for civilianising more police positions as a way the government could save money.

Harding geared up for the fray by announcing his new industrial team in May 1986. Greg Fleming, Tania Winkels and Geoff Terpstra, the *Newsletter* editor, would share with him the handling of a region each, Harding himself taking the most restive Auckland north. The new structure was also intended to improve communication between the office and members.

Where Moodie had relied on his oratory and its recording in extensive minutes, Harding changed tack to a livelier newsletter. The August 1986 *Newsletter* asked 'What is the Industrial Clout of the Association?' He answered that in the police there was an unfortunate misunderstanding that they had little industrial power. On the contrary, they were one of the few essential services, and more so than doctors, nurses and firefighters, whose withdrawal of labour had a huge impact on the public.

Police had traditionally seen themselves, Harding argued, as the forces of right upholding the law against industrial agitators. The Minister of Justice claimed the oath required police to be industrially responsible; this Harding regarded as the minister trying to impose his will on the police. The police had the same rights as other workers to represent their views on work matters.

The police had chosen not to promote their concerns in a traditional union manner because of their acute sense of social responsibility. This restraint should not be interpreted as a weakness, but rather 'as a great strength'. The authorities should not abuse this attitude of putting the concerns of the community first. That responsibility had a

The *Newsletter* for February 1986 carried this public appreciation by *Dominion* cartoonist Eric Heath of the most desirable job Moodie had made of policing

NEW ZEALAND POLICE ASSOCIATION (INC.)

newsletter

MAY 1986 ★ Vol. 14 No. 5 ★ Part Series "NZ Police Journal

New Direction For Industrial Section

Exciting changes are beginning to take place within the Association's Industrial Section. With Industrial Advocate, Graham Harding, having completed his first six months in the position, he is now implementing new ways in which to represent the aims, aspirations and views of Police members and to achieve a more equitable status for Police within our society.

A new team of Industrial Research staff have now been appointed. Geoff Terpstra (also the Editor of the Newsletter), Greg Fleming and most recent appointee, Tania Winkels, will in future assume responsibility for the majority of industrial activity within the Association.

To enable this to be achieved, the country has been segmented into four geographical areas for which one industrial person will be responsible.

Greg Fleming
Hamilton, New Plymouth, Rotorua, Gisborne, Napier.

Tania Winkels
Greymouth, Christchurch, Timaru, Dunedin, Invercargill.

overleaf

Graham Harding
Whangarei; City, Western and Southern Auckland.

Geoff Terpstra
Palmerston North, Wanganui, Wellington, Hutt, Porirua, Nelson.

Harding did his own restructuring of the association administration to achieve better communication with members value. Policing required a wider range of responsibility than ever before and if this was not recognised then the police 'will be left no alternative than to bite with whatever industrial teeth they can find'.

Harding decided to take his police advocacy direct to the public when members agreed that the government was not listening to their arguments for increased staffing. The Roper Report into violent crime had recommended community policing and youth aid, but the immediate problem of more frontline police was not addressed. The association called for 600 to 700 extra officers, the guild for 1000. The level of service to the public was stretched thin. National councillors were reporting large-scale burglaries filed without enquiries being done, little action on stolen vehicles, a recovery rate in other areas of 16 per cent of reported crime. The public itself was drawing up petitions and having street marches over violent murders involving child victims.

Harding made one more try to get a government commitment. This failed and the association launched its full-page newspaper advertisements. The newspapers were happy to have the cake and then bite it, sharing the view of Police Minister Hercus that this was politicising of the police in the run-up to a general election. Unamused by the tactics of her old Labour Party colleague, Hercus was reported as calling the police 'the National Party in uniform'.

Harding had acquired his tactics abroad. Moodie had felt that there was nothing to be learned from counterparts overseas, but Harding and Vice-President Jeff Taylor had visited Australia and the West Coast of the United States. Harding had brought out cops from the United States and Britain. Impressed with the hard-hitting campaign mounted by the police in the British press, he sought to emulate it here.

Harding received professional help from another of his new team, public relations consultant Richard Griffin, on the payroll as a lobbyist for the association in Parliament. Harding worked with Griffin on the newspaper ads that showed such graphic images as a snarling dog, a cricket bat and a padlock—'things you will need if the Government doesn't increase police numbers'. Another showed a hangman's noose above the line 'criminals should not be slipping away'. Readers were asked to clip out and send to Parliament the coupon saying 'I believe New Zealand needs 1000 more police now!' Such ads were in the same mould as the dancing Cossacks that had waltzed Muldoon into power a decade before.

Hercus never disclosed how many of the 12,000 coupons arrived, but it was a very public campaign. Harding admits they were over the top, even though they did talk about what was in fact happening, such as the woman with her face covered in sticking plaster as a result of violence and a wrecked home. Members had no quarrel with his message, but some were getting nervous at the stridency of his method. He canned the proposed television ads, which were too expensive anyway.

Harding's relationship with Hercus deteriorated from this time, which was hardly surprising. She held to the view that they had done a trade-off—the association would take the pay increase and not pursue increased staff numbers. Harding says he was a party to all the formal negotiations of the pay round in 1985-86 and never heard a whisper of such a deal. Yet whenever the association was in conflict with the government, they had this reminder and were accused of going back on their word and being untrustworthy. Harding points to Hercus being applauded at the October 1985 association conference for promising increased police staffing over the next three years. The figure of 600 extra staff was bandied about, and Harding could not help noticing that every delegate at the conference was worried about staff shortages and the negative effect it was having on police work.

Graham Harding believes that the Police Association had to develop into a more effective lobby group as the administration became 'less willing to defend the role of the

Civilianisation was the downside of improved police pay and conditions, and a constant worry to the association over the years

The Wellington police launch service has been under regular threat from cost-cutting politicians and administrators, but police and public agitation have piloted it through, especially after the *Lady Elizabeth II* was lost at sea in 1986

police and is seen more as a tool of Government'.

He also had problems with the commissioner, telling the management committee meeting of 16 July 1986 that he and Thompson had not been getting on for some time and that the situation was now somewhat confrontational. Thompson blamed Moodie and Butterworth for the association vote of no confidence in him, and Harding felt this attitude had rubbed off on to him. Harding objected to having to write and make appointments to see the commissioner. Thompson denied that he was blocking access; he simply felt it was appropriate that his senior officers should deal with straightforward administrative details. This was really a leaf out of Moodie's book, when he brought in Morrow to deal with the level below commissioner. It was suspected that Walton had agreed to Morrow coming in on police pay as president because he was a voice of moderation at a time when Moodie, in Morrow's words, was 'running absolutely rampant'. Moodie observed that Morrow was soon making statements off his own bat and because the association spoke with two voices its impact was split. Harding inherited this split, and those officers who moved up as Walton moved out, brought with them resentments towards the association developed in Moodie's time.

Harding credits the success of the association directly to their articulate advocacy, but the approach was becoming less effective when he became involved. It could not stand alone in the current government destructuring climate. He points to the association decision in 1988 to affiliate with the New Zealand Council of Trade Unions as having a significant effect on the government attitude. The first attempt at affiliation, with the non-aligned service organisations and unions outside the big umbrella and led by Tony Neary, had not worked because the government froze them out of the consultative process. It was only through affiliation with the CTU that Harding learned what was in the government pipeline, information critical in ascertaining planned superannuation scheme changes.

By now he was offside with those Cabinet ministers he had once been closest to. Attorney-General Geoffrey Palmer had declared that 'Police officers cannot and do not strike or take lesser industrial action'; such action was 'unlawful'. Now Hercus was putting Harding in the National Party camp, particularly after he accepted speaking engagements with the Coalition of Concerned Citizens, who attacked the Labour Government on a broad range of issues. At 40 Harding had been a member of the Labour Party most of his life, and had served to boost its path to power. He had even helped implement its policies when, as secretary of the Canterbury Hotel Workers Union, he delivered a block of vital votes that gave South Island conference approval of the GST policy. Like many a Labour stalwart, he was severely tested by the Labour Government.

Harding focused purely on police concerns, accepting publicity wherever it offered. Throughout 1987 he spoke out against many government policies affecting the police, such as the Police Complaints Authority Bill, which offered no safeguards and civilianisation, which was making inroads into job opportunities for members. He had a McNair survey done which showed that the public shared the police call for more staff.

Labour won the election but the wheels were starting to come off. Hercus had been the first puncture. Moodie had detected her Achilles heel, qualifying his praise for her by observing that 'she has to learn to listen to people other than officials'. He argued over her parroting the administration line about staff and resource shortages in Christchurch. He warned that although she was the best minister they would have for a very long time, she would get into trouble 'because she shoots from the lip'.

In October 1986 a Diplomatic Protection Squad file on the Prime Minister's security was found in a Wellington street and passed to the *Dominion* newspaper. Ann Hercus shot from the lip, saying that her faith in the police was

Moodie had rated Ann Hercus highly, but he had one reservation—that she shot from the lip. Not long after his departure, Hercus duly shot from the lip over her ill-advised check on police security on the Chathams and became the first wheel to fly off the speeding Labour machine

Harding differed from Moodie in raising the police profile to an all-time high, as opposed to his profile as police spokesman, by running these scaremongering ads in the run-up to the 1987 election. Although his members agreed with the message that the police needed more numbers, they eventually balked at such confrontational methods

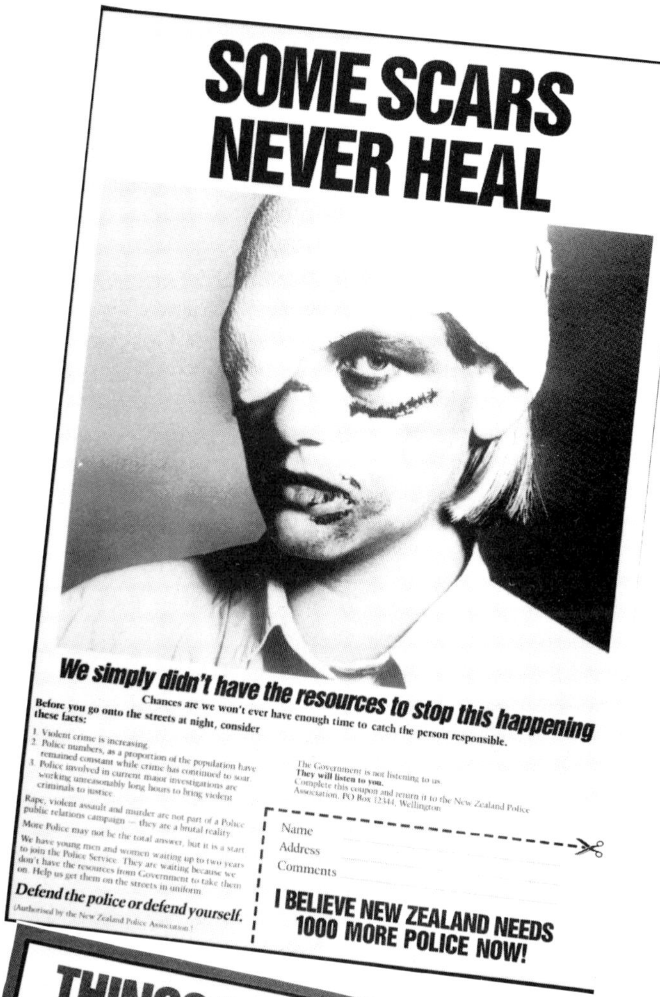
SOME SCARS NEVER HEAL
We simply didn't have the resources to stop this happening
Chances are we won't ever have enough time to catch the person responsible.
Before you go onto the streets at night, consider these facts:
1. Violent crime is increasing.
2. Police numbers, as a proportion of the population have remained constant while crime has continued to soar.
3. Police involved in current major investigations are working unreasonably long hours to bring violent criminals to justice.
Rape, violent assault and murder are not part of a Police public relations campaign — they are a brutal reality.
More Police may not be the total answer, but it is a start.
We have young men and women waiting up to two years to join the Police Service. They are waiting because we don't have the resources from Government to take them on. Help us get them on the streets in uniform.
Defend the police or defend yourself.
(Authorised by the New Zealand Police Association.)
The Government is not listening to us.
They will listen to you.
Complete this coupon and return it to the New Zealand Police Association, PO Box 12344, Wellington
Name
Address
Comments
I BELIEVE NEW ZEALAND NEEDS 1000 MORE POLICE NOW!

CRIMINALS SHOULD NOT BE SLIPPING AWAY
As the crime wave gathers momentum some people are calling for the death penalty to be considered
Harsher penalties may help, but unless Police have the resources to ensure criminals are caught, all the penalties in the world can have no effect.
That has become more difficult because —
1. Violent crime is increasing.
2. Police numbers, as a proportion of the population have remained constant while crime has continued to soar.
3. Police involved in current major investigations are working unreasonably long hours to bring violent criminals to justice.
Murder, rape and violent assault are not part of a Police public relations campaign — they are a brutal reality.
More Police may not be the total answer, but it is a start.
We have young men and women waiting up to two years to join the Police Service. They are waiting because we don't have the resources from Government to take them on. Help us get them on the streets in uniform.
Defend the police or defend yourself.
(Authorised by the New Zealand Police Association.)
The Government is not listening to us.
They will listen to you.
Complete this coupon and return it to the New Zealand Police Association, PO Box 12344, Wellington
Name
Address
Comments
I BELIEVE NEW ZEALAND NEEDS 1000 MORE POLICE NOW!

THINGS YOU WILL NEED IF THE GOVERNMENT DOESN'T INCREASE POLICE NUMBERS
A crash helmet is a useful form of protection on the streets
The sight of a cricket bat would be enough to make an attacker think twice
Security in the home is unfortunately now your problem. Police no longer have the resources to protect property
A trained German Shepherd would be more than a handful for an assailant
A black belt in Karate and a few hints on this page may help you, but a visible policeman is still the best deterrent.
Remember these facts:
1. Violent crime is increasing.
2. Police numbers, as a proportion of the population have remained constant while crime has continued to soar.
3. Police involved in current major investigations are working unreasonably long hours to bring violent criminals to justice.
Murder, rape and violent assault are not part of a Police public relations campaign — they are a brutal reality.
More Police may not be the total answer, but it is a start.
We have young men and women waiting up to two years to join the Police Service. They are waiting because we don't have the resources from Government to take them on. Help us get them on the streets in uniform.
Defend the police or defend yourself.
(Authorised by the New Zealand Police Association.)
The Government is not listening to us.
They will listen to you.
Complete this coupon and return it to the New Zealand Police Association, PO Box 12344, Wellington
Name
Address
Comments
I BELIEVE NEW ZEALAND NEEDS 1000 MORE POLICE NOW!

'somewhat shattered'. Morrow says this came at a time when the DPS was frustrated by the failure of the administration and politicians to co-operate in regularising their conditions of work. Muldoon had taken 'unholy delight in hiving off' and disrupting DPS arrangements. There had been several incidents of visiting VIPs going off on their own. There were also petty problems such as getting laundry bills and hotel accounts paid.

Early in April 1987 Hercus and her Cabinet colleague Richard Prebble were caught allegedly attempting to test the vigilance of the DPS guarding their plane on the Chathams. This, Morrow says, came at the end of a long line of DPS complaints, so he decided to complain to the Prime Minister, and ask him to issue instructions to his ministers, and through them to overseas guests, to comply with DPS requirements. He knew he could not get to see Lange through official channels, so he contacted Richard Griffin, who had been on the association payroll, but was now back with Radio New Zealand as political editor. Griffin got him a back-door appointment with Lange, but this was cancelled after Lange spoke to Hercus and she decided to handle the situation. The Prime Minister was not impressed, Morrow understands, but decided he should not be dealing with the matter.

Hercus put out a press release characterising the incident as a light-hearted check on police efficiency, a bet between her and Prebble as to whether the police would be asleep. Morrow says there had been worry for some time about the fine line between the role of the minister and that of the commissioner, and it was felt Hercus had stepped over that line by involving herself in police deployment. Morrow would not, however, have gone public on the Chathams incident if Hercus had not done so first. He believes the media blew the incident up and denies leaking anything.

The police administration investigated Morrow's behaviour after he contradicted a statement by Commissioner Mal Churches. He explained that he had seen Griffin as a consultant, not as a journalist. After this he could see that there was not much future for himself as a senior sergeant returning to duty, but he notes there was no further trouble for the DPS. Harding says that the arrangement had been between himself and Griffin; Morrow was not party to it.

By now the association was separating from the administration. At the October 1986 conference outgoing Commissioner Thompson warned the association that industrial action was incompatible with the oath of office. At the 1987 conference Commissioner Churches attacked both the method and the message of the association's staffing campaign. Morrow defended it; the days were long gone when everybody was polite at conferences. Harding wrote that the message had reached the public and the public supported it. He believed it ultimately helped National commit themselves to 900 extra police and immediately led to the Prime Minister choosing as Minister of Police Peter Tapsell, of whom the association approved and with whom it established a good working relationship.

The extent to which the association was now prepared publicly to debate its role was seen when the *Listener* of 5 September 1987 claimed that the New Zealand police were increasingly militant, were leaking politically sensitive information and that 'the Government considers the law is out of order'. Senior Sergeant Ian Revell of Otahuhu, a long-time management committee member, wrote a rebuttal of what he called an attack on the association's integrity with innuendo and half-truth. The service organisations were, he claimed, the only independent bodies able to tell the public the real needs of policing. Because the commissioner was not permitted to speak out against government policy, he and the minister did not reveal that when he had asked his 16 district commanders what was needed for full efficiency, they had replied over 900 extra staff.

The association made its industrial threats against the government and the administration, not against the public. There was every intention that police would do their sworn duty, but they would not be intimidated by the Attorney-General, and they would continue to inform the public on matters of public concern. However, as Otahuhu delegate Stu Mangnall said at the 1987 conference, the association did not appear now to have any short-term or immediate objectives.

In 1988 the initiatives remained with the administration and the government. Harding accepted a 7 per cent salary increase offer. The administration restructured into regions. The government got on with its plans for restructuring superannuation.

The Labour Relations Act of 1987 had abolished the Police Staff Tribunal, its functions taken over by the Arbitration Commission. The next stage was for the State Sector Bill to bring the police out of their special and unique position and from under the public service umbrella. The association and guild argued that the police were unique and that the obligations of their oath required retention of special conditions. The government agreed, but did not act as though it did.

Harding kept working to bridge the traditional gap between police and the workers. He spoke of association solidarity with PSA views in submissions on the State Sector Bill. The association argued successfully against members being used as an 'industrial tool' to bring the Rixon workers' sit-in at Levin to heel.

Morrow played a duet with Harding in achieving CTU affiliation. He had brought the idea back from Australia, where New South Wales police had been affiliated for 35 years. Having been briefed there on the need to affiliate to avoid being taken over by a big union, he saw this warning confirmed when the Caretakers and Cleaners Union complained about the association being allowed to affiliate. This union, which represented the security guards, the only workers who had commonality with the police, might well have been eyeing the big dollars in the Police Welfare Fund.

Harding acknowledges that the association was in a reactive role in 1987 and 1988, trying to cope with a stream of government initiatives. One was part-time policing, where an unpaid individual was to act at certain times as police representative. The concept, tried out in an Otago town, was quietly dropped; it was difficult to establish when a police officer is not a police officer and vice versa.

Morrow says the first the association knew of user pays was when the commissioner issued directions that the police would no longer attend burglar alarms. Morrow believed that this was contrary to the police oath, particularly as presented in the security company ad showing a police car driving past a burglar alarm and another suggesting that neighbours check the alarm before ringing the police. Morrow called it a widow-making policy; and, in an Auckland incident, it was the burglar who was shot dead.

A legislated list of what the police would charge for was eventually withdrawn, officially because it would not yield much money. The real reason, Morrow says, was because the association kicked up a fuss about police going to draw charity raffles, for instance, and then charging for their time. He thrashed the idea because he saw it as contrary to New Zealand ways, dreamed up by people who knew nothing of the police and who saw it being run as a business, not a service. He argued that if a sponsor was footing the bill for police protection at a U2 concert at Wellington's Athletic Park and the police arrested some of his friends, he would want them released. The police were there for the protection of the audience, not to be at the beck and call of a promoter. That was what the audience paid taxes for. Morrow's pitch prevailed. He was surprised to see that Derek Quigley and his Strategos consultancy were asked to have another look at this when reviewing police efficiency. Apparently they sidestepped it.

What did go ahead from this review was Operation Blueprint, as part of the restructuring treatment being undergone throughout the state sector. Hay Management Consultants were brought in to evaluate every job in the police. Morrow, included in the evaluation panels, thought them fairly done, but then the administration interfered. The commissioner changed the assessment of the liaison officer at Canberra as senior sergeant up to detective inspector, and the officer in charge of internal complaints from chief inspector to superintendent. Conversely, the officer in charge of media services went from inspector to senior sergeant. This was policing by commissioner's decree. Morrow objected that the whole exercise failed to make frontline policing more efficient.

The management committee decided, on 22 July 1988, to pull out of Operation Blueprint because members were

In 1989 the association used graphs and cartoons to drive home to members the government's failure to appreciate their problems

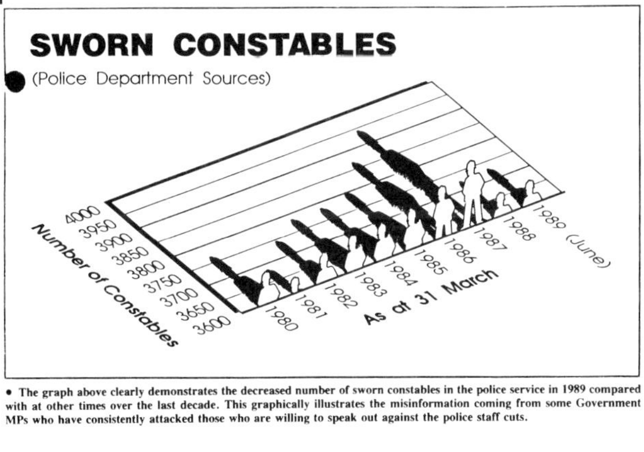

• The graph above clearly demonstrates the decreased number of sworn constables in the police service in 1989 compared with at other times over the last decade. This graphically illustrates the misinformation coming from some Government MPs who have consistently attacked those who are willing to speak out against the police staff cuts.

being displaced and the administration would not respond to association concerns about members being held in downgraded positions while the two responsible for administering Operation Blueprint were evaluated upwards. Harding wrote of the discontent through the districts and claims of 'jobs for the boys'.

The association had participated in the new approach because it believed nobody would be disadvantaged, particularly financially, and because it believed in the objectives. In practice, control room senior sergeants went up to inspectors, while regional dog co-ordinators, the computer instructor and the officer in charge of firearms training were downgraded from senior sergeant to sergeant. A stormy Wellington district agm was followed by a meeting of senior sergeants from Wellington and Christchurch with the commissioner. He would not act on their concerns. Furthermore, the much-touted devolution of decision-making to regions had not eventuated.

The association, reminded that, as part of the Operation Blueprint team, it could not attack it, pulled out, Harding describing the programme as a nonsense because it required officers to apply for jobs they were already doing. A lot of it was change for change's sake and he called for what the country generally wanted—to slow the pace of change, to devote more time to explaining the purpose of these new directives. Loyalty, that fragile but essential commodity, was being strained.

Commissioner Churches responded that the common management practice of applying for your own job affected only commissioned officers, and he had guild approval. He suggested that downgrading to sergeant was better than the redundancy practised elsewhere in the public service. What was clearly happening was a return to the Them and Us perception, but this time the Them was the commissioner and, increasingly, the guild.

In his annual report Morrow mentioned another area where the association was Us and the guild Them—the eight members facing criminal prosecution in the Gisborne courts over the Ruatoria arson investigation. 'It has been a great sadness,' he wrote, 'that not one senior police official took any administrative responsibility—these eight police officers stood alone.' The moment the investigation into their conduct began they were suspended without pay, relying on association and public subscriptions to keep them going financially. The association could only obtain a copy of the investigation through the Official Information Act.

This high conflict profile brought the association into public prominence. As exemplified in the comments of two of New Zealand's more thoughtful periodicals, the media was split for and against. The 5 April *National Business Review* editorial stated that the association was out of line with its 'hypocritical' staffing campaign, its objection to the Police Complaints Authority and in claiming back legal expenses after the eight Ruatoria officers were acquitted. It wanted the association to confine itself to purely industrial matters, to be more grateful to Ann Hercus for getting its members more than most unions received, to embrace the administration's 'realistic view of policing methods'.

Morrow wrote a lengthy rebuttal. The association believed itself justified in opposing sponsorship of the police, user pays and part-time rural police. The association was on record as praising Hercus as the most effective Police Minister of modern times. Other youngsters, such as tax consultants, earned more than police without the overtime and hazardous job conditions. The magazine had confused early retirement with optional disengagement, in which officers got back their contributions to superannuation plus their employer's contribution, the case in many other schemes. Morrow's understanding, as distinct from Harding's, was that the association traded the early retirement award for holding off its request for more staff for 18 months. It was not hypocritical to campaign for more staff some years later.

The publicity campaign he defended as the only avenue available, when the police could not strike against an intransigent employer. The association rejected the quiet administration policy because it had achieved nothing in five years; its objection to the Police Complaints Authority was that there was no balancing protection for police rights; seeking legal costs over Ruatoria was what any acquitted person was entitled to do.

The *National Business Review* appeared to be attacking the police because more selfless conduct was expected from them than was current in the community. The Catholic journal the *Tablet* took the opposite tack of condemning the police administration for not giving the leadership it should and affecting morale with the 'Ruatoria fiasco' and by requiring two Te Puke officers to receive counselling for attending a meeting with a local MP to discuss law and order concerns 'involving a disproportionate percentage of Maori'. The paper saw a farcical conflict between the top police brass promoting community policing and objecting to police who were trying to get close to their community. Was it time for a return to the 1950s solution of putting an outsider in the top police job?

Commissioner Churches replied that he was obliged to investigate a complaint, that the Ruatoria incident followed proper procedure of a prima facie case being made in the district court and going to the High Court, that the sergeant at Te Puke had exaggerated Maori offending figures. He also published in the August 1988 *Police Bulletin* a rejection of Harding's attack on Operation Blueprint and his communication with staff as 'negative, totally unproductive and often unsoundly based sniping'.

The association and the administration were back to the bad old early days of mutual suspicion. While they sniped, the government got on with its restructuring of superannuation.

In December members read that the government had appointed consultants to review the government superannuation scheme, and it was up to the consultants whether they consulted with the association and/or guild. Harding used words such as arrogance, total contempt, disgraceful, inexcusable and double standards to describe the seven minutes it had taken Parliamentarians on the eve of

Association office manager Tui Hunter worked behind the scenes organising the 1990 police march on Parliament. Here she is visiting Parliament in 1989 with one of the petitions opposing police cuts

Christmas to vote themselves a significantly enhanced superannuation package, which was now exempted from this review.

Throughout 1989 the association wound up its counter-attack. In March it renewed the call for more frontline staff. It lobbied Peter Tapsell successfully on the selection of Deputy Commissioner John Jamieson as the new commissioner, after the scare of seeing the minister take Assistant Commissioner Steve Rusbatch abroad with him, a traditional indication of who was being groomed for the job. Harding said Jamieson was an honest John who was trusted by the frontline cops as district commander in Christchurch. The objection to Rusbatch was that he was a headquarters man, allegedly out of touch with the troops.

In May a 5 per cent wage increase was granted and two hours off a week to maintain the fitness needed to pass the PCT. It made a welcome change from the administration stalling the previous year over the association application to the Arbitration Commission for a salary increase. That month, too, the *Newsletter* began a series on 'How to Retire Successfully', something Keith Morrow did not do, since he was off to a new job as general secretary of the Police Association of Tasmania. Harding was not surprised, for he rated Morrow a natural as a unionist.

In July the government ran its ad saying that it was increasing police numbers again as it announced planned government staff cuts. The *Newsletter* invoked George Orwell's *1984*, where the famous phrase 'doublethink' was coined for governments who promised one thing and did the opposite. Tapsell expressed his disappointment, while Opposition Deputy Leader Don McKinnon said that, when people were fearful to go out at night, it was time to put more emphasis on the police. The *Newsletter* devoted four pages to hammering the government for turning away from crime in order to balance the books.

The administration's preoccupation with balancing its budget saw increasing civilianisation of such jobs as document examiners, physical training instructors and fingerprint officers. The August 1989 *Newsletter* expressed its bewilderment at the strictures on a police budget that absorbed 1.89 per cent of the government take, a mere $473,000,000, something the Department of Social Welfare chewed through in 21 days.

Next month came the news that Roger Douglas, the man behind the entire restructuring programme, was their minister. With him came more unwelcome news—the State Sector Restructuring Bill would deny the police any right to strike or take any industrial action and require them to accept a final offer from the Arbitration Commission. Under the new act they would have to accept remand prisoners in overcrowded cells; it would be illegal to strike on health and safety issues; the commissioner would replace a Promotion Board, deciding at his own discretion who was best suited to any position. The Police Appeal Board would be replaced with a personal grievances committee and ultimately the Labour Court. Dismissal grounds would be extended to include incompetence, which applied to 'inoperational effectiveness', bureaubabble for the boss knowing best whom he wanted.

The draconian changes made civilians non-sworn members of the police, but not represented by the association. The association's negotiating framework was so narrowed that Harding described the environment as 'industrial

Roger Douglas had provided the police with any amount of protest fodder when he was Minister of Finance. Just when they might have thought there were no more surprises possible, Roger Douglas was back as Police Minister in 1989

Russian Roulette'. He called the changes cowardly and underhand, an attempt to drag the association back to pre-association days.

Senior Sergeant Steve Hinds beat out three others in October 1989 for the top job in these straitened times. This former Wellington rugby rep was soon up to his considerable lock's neck in the superannuation struggle. It was an uneven contest packing down with Graham Harding against the Parliamentary Select Committee on 7 March, opposite the likes of Roger Douglas, Trevor de Cleene, Ruth Richardson and Wyatt Creech, with Douglas hit man Richard Prebble now Minister of Police. Committee chairman Bill Sutton asked Harding if the association would accept a scheme comparable with the private sector. Harding said they preferred the scheme they had.

Harding saw their submissions ignored, which was par for the course of the last two years. The government had, in his phrase, knee-capped the police by forcing them into the mainstream employer/employee relationship, but forbidden them to take industrial action. The association fell back on lobbying Commissioner Jamieson, whom it felt did not wish to impose his will on them.

As Minister of Police, Douglas had acknowledged that the government was introducing reduction of superannuation in a very offensive way, given that the police, unlike other state servants, were compelled to be in the fund. Harding felt justified in describing the government behaviour as cowardly, for the superannuation legislation was brought in on 17 December, just before the holiday break. The New Year was initially given over to police commitments to the Commonwealth Games and the Royal Tour. What shattered the association and the guild was that the clawback on superannuation was expected to be 25 per cent, but it was 40 per cent.

Harding and Hinds hit the road in late February 1990. It took little persuasion to get the members incensed. The suggestions were much more extreme than merely striking. There was talk of blue flu, practised some eight or so years before by New York cops, involving whole precincts calling in sick; within two days Mayor Koch had capitulated rather than see whole areas of his city unpoliced.

Harding and Hinds diverted the anger over superannuation into what they saw as a more productive arena, a march on Parliament on 30 March. The politicians sneered at this anticipated fizzer, suggesting they would be lucky to get 200 participants. The march attracted 1173 officers from Invercargill to Whangarei, the guild secretary and acting president marching either side of Hinds at the head of this unprecedented blue-uniformed procession. Prebble had tried to stop the wearing of uniforms, but the

Association president Steve Hinds re-establishes contact with overseas police groups, here addressing the Peace Officers Research Association of California conference in 1989

They don't want to do it but marching to Parliament is an act of desperation for our police officers

WHY?

Radical change to Police superannuation is just the latest in a string of attacks on Policing in New Zealand over many years.
As crime in our community has risen, so Police resources and conditions have been eroded.
Now Policing in New Zealand faces a real crisis of confidence.

How would you react if you faced these frustrations?

- Ever-increasing stress levels due to work pressures from lack of staffing, longer hours and increasing violence, both in society and against police.
- One person patrols in violent areas or dangerous situations.
- The removal of the right to any form of industrial action and final offer arbitration only on a limited range of conditions.
- Spiralling increases in crime and offending.
- Operation Blueprint – a major restructuring in Police duties, ranks and subsequently salaries.
- Cancellation of recruiting.
- Strategos Review.
- Increased workloads resulting from Children and Young Persons Act.
- Axing of six-week rosters.
- Civilianisation of key Police responsibilities and duties.
- Demands to hold Justice Department prisoners in Police cells.
- Proposed introduction of voluntary Police simply to save money.
- Drastic reductions in superannuation.
- Police house rental increases.
- Closure of rural stations.
- The impact of regionalisation and the resulting "splitting up" of Policing.
- Rejection of initiatives to improve working and safety conditions essential for rural stations.
- Lack of Government commitment to real community Policing rather than pseudo community Policing.

These frustrations, and more, mean that now Policing has reached a crisis of confidence.
Police cannot provide the service and protection the community expects.
The community knows that and Police officers know that too.
But the Government ignores these facts.

Police officers have to march to make the Government realise the crisis this nation faces.

The pamphlet presenting the reasons why the police came as close as they ever have to direct industrial action

commissioner would not agree. Prebble warned them that if they took industrial action he would take them on. Almost every cop who was not committed to duty took part. It was a proud day for the police.

The government announced, on the eve of the march, that the police superannuation take would be reduced from 40 to 30 per cent. The march went ahead. Harding says it was a great fillip for the service organisations. It symbolised, he believes, how members could change things if they were determined to do so. 'It came at a time when the members had been bashed by politicians, demoralised by Hercus, Douglas, Prebble. I think the march acted as a catalyst that allowed the cops to reform and fight back. It was the beginning of a new era.'

Hinds was a symbol of a rejuvenated association. At only 33 symptomatic of the younger balance in the service, he was born in Wainuiomata, and attended St Patricks College in the city, a favourite recruiting ground for the police. His year was no exception; half a dozen signed up. The peer group inspired him to join, but not before he had done two years of a law degree. A Marist St Pats rugby trip abroad annihilated both his academic year and his wallet, so Hinds signed on with the police. He started on data files, then went to Police College as Number 5660. He was the first of his intake to make sergeant, then senior sergeant, by which time, after 10 years in the police, he had done team policing,

New association President Steve Hinds marches shoulder to shoulder with guild executives and 1200 frontline police in the first demo the police did not oversee but participated in

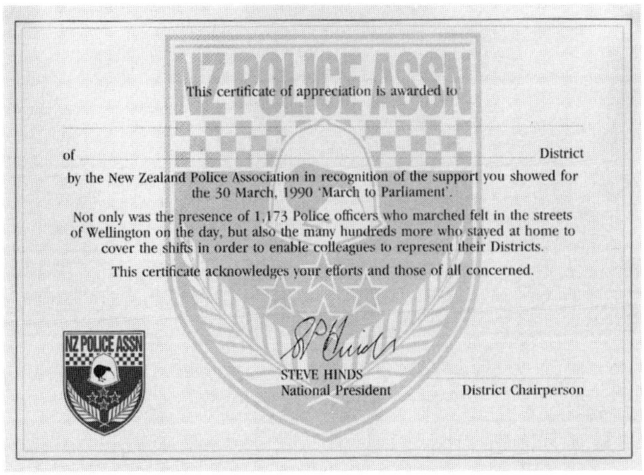
NZ POLICE ASSN

This certificate of appreciation is awarded to

of .... District

by the New Zealand Police Association in recognition of the support you showed for the 30 March, 1990 'March to Parliament'.

Not only was the presence of 1,173 Police officers who marched felt in the streets of Wellington on the day, but also the many hundreds more who stayed at home to cover the shifts in order to enable colleagues to represent their Districts.

This certificate acknowledges your efforts and those of all concerned.

STEVE HINDS
National President

District Chairperson

The association now perceived the administration as part of the bureaucratic and political opposition, as its history came full circle to the early days of battling the bosses. The difference, in 1990, was that the association confidently confronted its employers

joined the CIB and been an instructor at the college.

His older sister Pauline was registrar of the State Services Industrial Tribunal and they spent hours talking industrial matters. The association work caught his interest. He noticed that most association executives were senior serving police and their abiding interest, when he became involved in the early to mid-1980s, was early retirement. Hinds recalls how dominating Moodie was. If there was any objection, Moodie would threaten to resign and leave them without early retirement.

Hinds says it was clear that the employment environment was getting tougher and a more unionist approach was required. Enter Harding, who soon assembled a young office team. Harding says this democratising of the association worked only too well. They were run off their feet, with Terpstra also handling the dog section, Fleming trying to keep the lid on civilianised members, Tania Winkels handling women police issues. Harding was also trying to keep in touch with the overseas developments brought back by travelling politicians and administrators. He was relieved that New Zealand tried community policing as opposed to using auxiliary police, the weekend warriors who were unable to prevent the Hillsborough football stadium tragedy. The result, however, of coping with all these initiatives and changes was, says Harding, that by the late 1980s the association was punch-drunk and reeling. The 1990 march revived it.

Hinds credits Harding with bringing a trade union assertion of workers' rights into an old service organisation that implicitly trusted the commissioner. When he said jump, they asked how high. His peer group in the 1960s was gradually ending all that with its more inquiring approach. His era was less inclined to take things on face value, more inclined to greater militancy.

The commissioner's role was changing in the same period, Hinds observed. Instead of heading a team he would never rat on, the commissioner now qualified any commitment with comment about his responsibility to government, to saving money, to being efficient and effective; his contract made him accountable. According to Hinds, this might be fair enough for the taxpayer, but not for the frontline cop who used to believe he could concentrate on his job because the commissioner was watching his back. When the administration countered the appointment of Harding with an industrial officer, Hinds says they ceased to be the same team and became Them and Us. The police were no longer special, but part of the public service system. Any pay gains were matched by a clawback, such as an increase to 12 hours a fortnight in the period eligible for time off in lieu.

As early retirement and perfing had become established over the last five years, the average age of the service had decreased. This brought back into focus the part of the original package Moodie had rejected, the term engagement. Hinds says perfing ran up against the macho cop image that big men did not cry. Harding notes that most cops reaching 40 are still constables, but they are having to foot it with younger officers, out on the street arresting youthful offenders, and becoming less capable of cutting it. The trade-off in getting early retirement had been acceptance of increased civilianisation. This had got rid of the back-room boys, and removed that refuge where ageing cops used to find some degree of safety and security. In the late 1980s term engagement became the popular topic in the association.

'Under perfing,' says Harding, 'officers have to fake madness or illness or physical incapacity. It's not satisfactory as an exiting mechanism. We want them to sign on for, say, 15 years and then, if they are not performing, they can leave with a nest egg to start a new career. It doesn't have the perf stigma of establishing something that may not be totally honest.'

While the association spent most of 1990 objecting to Labour's super scheme, the politicians wooed the police. Opposition police spokesman John Banks promised 900 more staff; Prebble began opening police stations around the country. Hinds called these Hollywood sets. Marewa in Napier was a good example. The police officer there was brought off the night shift to be photographed with the minister, who then returned to Wellington while he returned to his night beat and a sign went up on the door telling citizens what number to call for help.

It was a stormy year, but the association was back on the offensive. The deswearing of members into civilian jobs was objected to because it reduced sworn police numbers and financially disadvantaged those affected. The association voted to accept civilians, however, and this would lead to hundreds preferring the association to PSA representation.

Negotiations with the administration were getting worse, as the administration negotiator Harry Baynes objected to the association representative being present at PSA non-sworn salary negotiations. Yet in his presidential address to the October conference Hinds presented a fighting spirit, saying they were locked in mortal combat with the administration, who were adopting the 'aggressive and traditional employer-class attitude' that would lead to more acrimony, while the pay cuts sought were based on 'a demonstrably inaccurate survey'. He welcomed the haemorrhaging in the

NZ POLICE ASSN

NEW ZEALAND POLICE ASSOCIATION (INC.)

newsletter

MAY 1990 ★ Vol. 23. No. 5 PART SERIES "NZ Police Journal" ★ ISSN 01128019

Regulation 24 members to be desworn 1 July

The police administration, in a unilateral move, has decided to deswear Regulation 24 members as of 1 July.

Commissioner John Jamieson, in announcing this decision recently, said that all Regulation 24 members would be desworn as of this date, with the possible exception of TSU members, whose case was "being looked at very closely because they are involved in law inforcement."

The decision is another slap in the face for Reg 24 staff, who have been 'left in Limbo' regarding their future with the police. This has created considerable stress and resentment amongst Reg 24 members over the handling of the issue.

During his address to delegates to the Association's Special Conference of 18 and 19 April, Commissioner Jamieson said that he was "very keen on this change" (to deswear Reg 24s). He said that he viewed many of the Reg staff as retaining outdated positions. "They are now in the wrong category ... and the Acts have no relevance to their positions anymore. Their tasks simply to do not relate to sworn police work anymore," he told Conference.

Reg 24 concerns

When quizzed about delays in allaying fears held by many Reg 24s over them being significantly disadvantaged due to being desworn, Commissioner Jamieson said that the administration viewed it as "an important issue and we are not trying to shy away from it." He said the administration was preparing a document which he hoped would allay those fears.

"I intend to have these issues resolved well before the first of July," Commissioner Jamieson assured delegates.

The document to which Commissioner Jamieson referred was presented to Reg 24 staff on 23 April but many have since told the Association that it fell a long way short of resolving the fundamental issues facing them. Many said that it was "contradictory" in its content, in that it said that subsidised insurance and sick leave bank benefits would be retained whilst later in the letter it stated that "arrangements are being developed to facilitate the retention of current levels of insurance and the sick leave bank benefits."

Reg 24 members are set to lose benefits in respect of their pay rates, superannuation, mortgage entitlements, sick leave, insurance, access to holiday homes and legal aid, which come in tandem with their sworn status. Many of these benefits, particularly those relating to welfare-oriented issues, cannot be resolved by the administration as they are a result of Police Association membership. Reg 24 staff will be legally barred from retaining that membership due to being desworn.

Delegates told the Commissioner that the amendments to the Police Act (1959), which were part of the State Sector Restructuring Bill, meant that the Police Department was now "disenfranchising" some of its own members and many sworn police officers felt that the administration was displaying a cavalier attitude to staff who had given many years loyal service.

150 affected

It is thought that the deswearing will affect about 150 members. Reg 24 members have made it plain that they are unhappy about losing Police Association membership and being forced to come under the jurisdiction of the PSA.

It was suggested to Mr Jamieson, during a question and answer phase of his address, that the more simple solution was to wait for natural attrition to rectify the situation and that new people coming into the job would not be given sworn status in future.

In reply, Mr Jamieson said that the administration "could not sit around for 30

continued on next page

In this issue

Police Minister Richard Prebble stands alone at an association agm, a position not unfamiliar to members

government which ensured that the ill-conceived Strategos review, aimed at reducing police numbers and state responsibility for policing, slipped quietly away.

After this barrage directed at the commissioner, Hinds turned to Prebble, belting him back for his 'volatile and vitriolic' attacks on the association as 'greedy, ungrateful louts' for making a noise 'when the Government was stealing away the superannuation entitlements of our members and their families'. He reminded Prebble that community policing was resource intensive.

Hinds ended by saying that if he represented the commissioned officers with their fancy cars and overseas trips he might be in a better frame of mind. But he represented cops who had had a gutsful, these loyal and dedicated officers about to perf or hang on for term engagement, 'so they can get out of this nightmare with some degree of dignity and financial recognition for all they have given'. The bearer of bad news put his message across in a vigorous, chipper, upbeat fashion. He got a standing ovation.

A month later a new government was promising that the police would soon get their extra 900 staff; the first 300 were on the way. The first crisis for the new minister, John Banks, was the fatal shooting at Aramoana of Sergeant Stewart Graeme Guthrie, aged 41, and several civilians. Guthrie was the second officer to die in 1990; Senior Constable Peter Umbers had been bludgeoned to death at Ranfurly in May. Guthrie was the 20th officer slain in the line of duty since 1886, a grave reminder of the special nature of police work.

The job was getting grimmer, but the association had 5000 members dedicated to ensuring there would not be a return to the 1890s, that the right Peter Fraser gave them to assemble to seek better conditions and a more effective service was a right they were in good mind to exercise for another half-century and beyond. After 50 years of trying to be a union, the association was being led by Harding and Hinds to unionised status at a time when the union movement was collapsing around them. Achieving that status had taken a long time, and it had been forged by determined men battling a stern system. One of its best battlers, Dave Lee, also died in 1990. The association has worked successfully to ensure that, like Lee, almost all its members go to their final rest in peace.

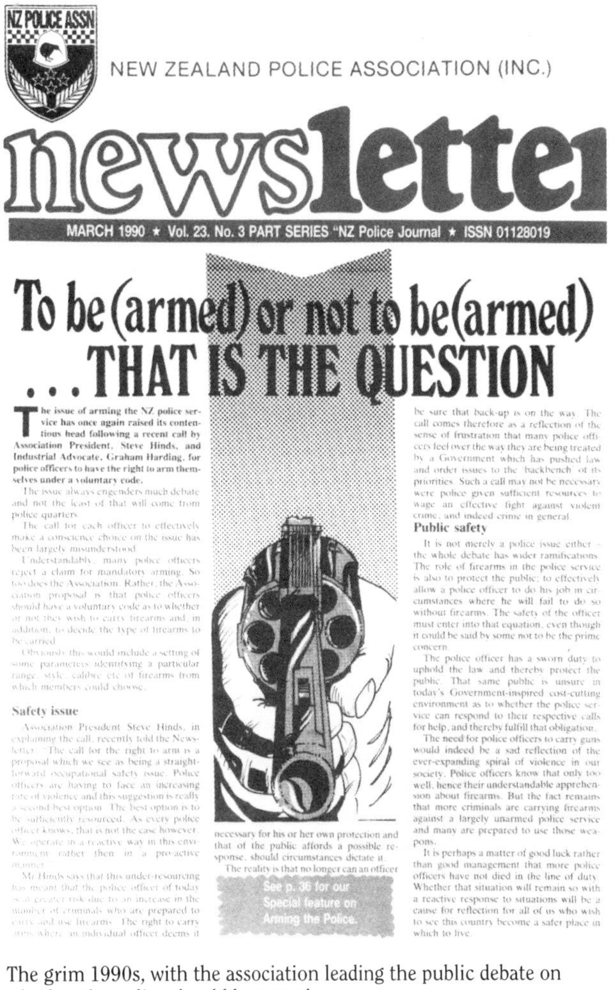
NZ POLICE ASSN

NEW ZEALAND POLICE ASSOCIATION (INC.)

newsletter

MARCH 1990 ★ Vol. 23, No. 3 PART SERIES "NZ Police Journal ★ ISSN 01128019

To be (armed) or not to be (armed) ...THAT IS THE QUESTION

The issue of arming the NZ police service has once again raised its contentious head following a recent call by Association President, Steve Hinds, and Industrial Advocate, Graham Harding, for police officers to have the right to arm themselves under a voluntary code.

The issue always engenders much debate and not the least of that will come from police quarters.

The call for each officer to effectively make a conscience choice on the issue has been largely misunderstood.

Understandably, many police officers reject a claim for mandatory arming. So too does the Association. Rather, the Association proposal is that police officers should have a voluntary code as to whether or not they wish to carry firearms and, in addition, to decide the type of firearms to be carried.

Obviously this would include a setting of some parameters identifying a particular range, style, calibre etc of firearms from which members could choose.

Safety issue

Association President Steve Hinds, in explaining the call, recently told the Newsletter: "The call for the right to arm is a proposal which we see as being a straightforward occupational safety issue. Police officers are having to face an increasing rate of violence and this suggestion is really a second-best option. The best option is to be sufficiently resourced. As every police officer knows, that is not the case however. We operate in a reactive way in this environment rather then in a pro-active manner."

Mr Hinds says that this under-resourcing has meant that the police officer of today is at greater risk due to an increase in the number of criminals who are prepared to carry and use firearms. The right to carry arms when an individual officer deems it necessary for his or her own protection and that of the public affords a possible response, should circumstances dictate it.

The reality is that no longer can an officer be sure that back-up is on the way. The call comes therefore as a reflection of the sense of frustration that many police officers feel over the way they are being treated by a Government which has pushed law and order issues to the 'backbench' of its priorities. Such a call may not be necessary were police given sufficient resources to wage an effective fight against violent crime, and indeed crime in general.

See p. 36 for our Special feature on Arming the Police.

Public safety

It is not merely a police issue either – the whole debate has wider ramifications. The role of firearms in the police service is also to protect the public; to effectively allow a police officer to do his job in circumstances where he will fail to do so without firearms. The safety of the officer must enter into that equation, even though it could be said by some not to be the prime concern.

The police officer has a sworn duty to uphold the law and thereby protect the public. That same public is unsure in today's Government-inspired cost-cutting environment as to whether the police service can respond to their respective calls for help, and thereby fulfill that obligation.

The need for police officers to carry guns would indeed be a sad reflection of the ever-expanding spiral of violence in our society. Police officers know that only too well, hence their understandable apprehension about firearms. But the fact remains that more criminals are carrying firearms against a largely unarmed police service and many are prepared to use those weapons.

It is perhaps a matter of good luck rather than good management that more police officers have not died in the line of duty. Whether that situation will remain so with a reactive response to situations will be a cause for reflection for all of us who wish to see this country become a safer place in which to live.

The grim 1990s, with the association leading the public debate on whether the police should be armed

This association history comes to an end with a bullish new president and three former active association members elected as parliamentary representatives of the new landslide National Government

Chapter Twenty

The Growth of the Guild

On 11 January 1955 commissioned police officers were called to their first administrative conference in three years. When Commissioner Compton arrived, Superintendent John Edwards presented the motion that Police Commission member Peter Munro be chairman because the officers present had no confidence in Compton. They went well beyond the Kennedy investigation in saying effectively that Compton was not fit for the job.

Compton overruled the motion on the grounds that he had been appointed by the government to chair the new three-man Police Commission. A point of order argued that this was a meeting of senior police officers, not a conference between them and the commission. Compton declined to accept the point of order. An attempt was made to pass a motion to give the conference the right to appoint its own chairman. Compton overruled this. When he attempted to shake the hands of all present, at least four declined.

When Compton left the conference room at the luncheon adjournment, the vote of no confidence in him was passed by 22 of the 24 officers, with one absent and one abstaining. The vote specified the public findings against Compton. He had assured the Prime Minister by radio telephone from Australia that he had not tapped telephones when he had. He had improperly used police labour and materials. He had illegally promoted three specialist police

Superintendent J. Edwards, centre, upon his retirement in late January 1956, months after he and his brother, Frederick Walter Edwards, left, worked to form the New Zealand Police Officers' Guild. On his right G.B. Edwards, a third brother in the force, retiring in 1946 as officer in charge of the Wellington district. A fourth policeman brother was killed in World War One

Eric Compton, the commissioner who provoked protest in his officer ranks, leading to the formation of the guild

sergeants. Superintendent Edwards had already told Compton to his face that he objected to the non-promotion of himself, his brother and three others entitled to it. Now informed of this vote, Compton overruled it.

The next day the Prime Minister Sid Holland and his assistant Eric Halstead arrived at the conference. The vote of no confidence in Compton was passed to Holland by Superintendent G.H.L. Holt. Holland told them that, under the constitution of the conference, only the government-appointed chairman was acceptable. He was asked if the commission had any legal existence; the Police Force Act 1947 made no allowance for such a body. Holland said validating legislation would be brought down, as was frequently the case; an example was the legislation to allow the pre-Christmas social security benefit increases.

Holland told them it was high time the officers kept their troubles to themselves. He would welcome the formation of a police officers' guild 'to promote welfare and efficiency within the Force'. Any complaints about police organisation should be made through this organisation, not through the press.

And so another Prime Minister could take credit for bringing another police service organisation into existence, even if his reasons were rather different from Fraser's. Indeed, Holland was up against a wall largely of his own making. The meeting told him bluntly that promotion other than by seniority was unacceptable. Holland told them this view was unacceptable to the government. He did say promotion out of order would be considered 'with the greatest care before it was made'.

Holland then told the press that he would be discussing with Scotland Yard an exchange scheme for police officers, and took off for London, leaving this legislative limbo behind him. Only the stable, she'll be right New Zealand of the 1950s could have sustained this hiatus in the ordering of the law.

While the cat was away the press played, already tipped off about the conference crisis. As usual *Truth* led the charge with full coverage of the juicy details in its 19 January edition. The only press opposition came from the National Party magazine, *Freedom*. On 26 January it demanded to know who the officer was who ratted to *Truth*, accusing him of 'arrant disloyalty and wilful unreliability'. When *Freedom* accused *Truth* of having no scruple about undermining police morale, the paper robustly replied that the government had set up the commission of inquiry, which was 'generally regarded as inadequate'. Replacing the commissioner with a three-man commission gave 'no plainer indication of no confidence in a departmental head, short of his dismissal or a call for his resignation'. And so the press circus continued until Compton, a general without the support of his officer corps, handed in his notice.

On 1 June 1955 Sub-Inspector Frederick Walter Edwards incorporated the New Zealand Police Officers' Guild. In August the *Police Journal* congratulated the officers 'on at last obtaining some form of organisation'. Meltzer pledged the association ready at all times to co-operate with the guild to mutual advantage.

The New Zealand Police Officers' Guild is a singular structure in that it came into being to topple its leader. Those who formed the guild were mostly those he had leapfrogged over to get his job. The unprecedented action of the new National Government of the 1950s in ignoring the old seniority route to the top of the police proved a disaster more in choice than in principle, but it slowed the introduction of merit promotion and provoked the formation of a gentlemen's union among the previously unrepresented commissioned officers.

It had concerned Jack Meltzer for some time that upon promotion to commissioned rank an officer must resign from the association and lose its privileges. That had been Peter Fraser's decision, a concession in 1936 to anxieties about a collapse in discipline or a conflict of role if the bosses were in the union. Given the traditional separation that existed then, it was understandable, at least until that generation of bosses went through to retirement.

A decade later a new generation of commissioned officers emerging from the association sparked discussion at the 1944 association conference to allow commissioned officers honorary membership, the death benefit and the *Police Journal*, at the price of 10s a year. Meltzer had already circularised 70 staff who still were or had been members of the association. He received four replies favouring a separate organisation, four with no opinion,

MINISTER ATTACKS "TRUTH'S"
OF SENIOR POLICE MEETING

THE acting Minister of Police, Mr. Halstead, has supplied a statement to "Truth" claiming that the recent "Off Cuff" comment by this newspaper on the recent conference of commissioned police officers in Wellington was "off the beam." "Truth" leaves its readers and the police officers who attended the meeting to judge whether this is so or not, but in fairness to Mr. Halstead it gives his comments. They are as follow:

"MR. HOLLAND'S statement on his meeting with the Police Commission and senior police officers was the Prime Minister's own statement, which surely he was entitled to make, rather than a report of the meeting.

"The statement was published while the conference was sitting and was not disputed by it," says Mr. Halstead.

"'Truth' says that the statement purported to show that the conference had carried a motion of confidence in the Police Commission. This is not a matter of purport but of fact and the fact is that the conference did carry a motion pledging loyalty and assistance to the commission as constituted and for the duration of its term. This motion was spontaneous and was carried unanimously," Mr. Halstead says.

"Mr. Holland made no statement that he 'wanted the police force to keep its troubles to itself and not to go to the Press with them.' What he did do was to urge members of the force to settle matters of organisation and administration through the channels set up to deal with them.

"The Prime Minister did not 'devote a good deal of time to talking the conference out of a resolution,' concerning the chairmanship of Mr. Compton. After he had been handed a letter containing this resolution Mr Holland read it and gave an immediate answer that Mr. Compton, as the Government-appointed chairman of the Police Commission, was the only conceivable chairman of what was essentially a meeting between the commission and senior police officers.

"Mr. Holland did not refer to the resolution again and devoted his address to a survey of police matters and the Government's plans for making improvements in organisation and conditions," says Mr. Halstead.

"Several of the officers who spoke after Mr. Holland had finished his address said that the conference would have followed a very different course if it had had the opportunity of hearing Mr. Holland earlier.

"Whatever 'Truth's' informants may say, I came away from the conference under the impression that Superintendent L. G. H. Holt, who had handed the resolution concerning Mr. Compton to the Prime Minister, asked him in subsequent conversation to ignore it.

"This was certainly in keeping with the resolution of loyalty and assistance to the Police Commission and the opinions expressed by several police officers that the information given by the Prime Minister had opened up a happier prospect for the force.

"These speakers had assured Mr. Holland that they would convey this feeling to officers and other ranks in their districts," Mr. Halstead goes on.

"It is not correct that the Police Commission is 'virtually impotent.' Besides dealing with purely organisational and administrative matters the Commission has met me and made a number of recommendations concerning major matters which need attention between now and the time that the Prime Minister will return from the United Kingdom.

"I do not propose to go into detail on the case of the Christchurch constable whom 'Truth' mentions, but I am informed by the Police Commission that his offence has been considered by it and as a result he has been dismissed from the force. It is quite true that the Commission still requires validating legislation. The Government often has to act in advance of legislation, as for example, was the case in the payment of increases to age beneficiaries.

"Validating legislation for the Police Commission will be brought down at the first opportunity but in the meantime it is functioning with support from the Government, the Police Association, and the senior officers," he concludes.

"Truth" makes these comments in reply:

There is no difference that this newspaper can perceive between an official "hand-out" or supplied official statement and a statement made by a Minister (in this case, Mr. Holland) and supplied directly to the Press. There was no independent reporting of the meeting.

It is a fact that the conference did pass a motion of confidence in the police commission at the end of its deliberations. It is also a fact that earlier it passed a motion of no confidence in Mr. E. H. Compton as chairman of the conference and that no mention of this was made in the report supplied to the daily Press by the Prime Minister.

Supt. L. H. G. Holt

When this newspaper and others published the fact, it was contended by Mr. Halstead that the motion of no confidence had been withdrawn. Police officers who were present at the meeting say they have no knowledge of this and that if it was done it was done without conference authority.

An objective report of the meeting would have mentioned the motion of no confidence, not withheld mention of it altogether.

Mr. Halstead denies that Mr. Holland said that he wanted the police to keep their troubles to themselves and not go to the Press with them, but says that the Prime Minister "urged members of the force to settle matters of administration and organisation through the channels set up to deal with them." This is saying the same thing in more official and therefore more indirect words. "Truth's" information is that Mr Holland was, in fact, quite blunt in what he said. This newspaper does not contest his argument except to point out that experience has shown that unless certain official grievances are ventilated in the Press they receive very little official attention.

If all grievances could be kept out of newspapers, it might suit the official book very well, but nothing would be done about the grievances.

In this case the conference expressed its opinion of Mr. Compton. That would not have mattered, apparently, if the fact had not been published. Now it has been published it becomes a matter for Ministerial concern.

Mr. Halstead denies that the Prime Minister spent a good deal of time talking the conference out of the resolution of no confidence. Mr. Holland's address on his own estimate occupied 90 minutes. There ... obv... be some explanat... the meeting after pass...

of no confidence
finally carried wh
describes as a "sp
of confidence in th
commission of whic
chairman.

Presumably that
only be found i
address. To clarif
commissioned offic
force could possibly
a similar motion of
Compton as chairm
mission. The mot
finally passed was
of three, not in M

Mr Halstead sa
correct that the t
sion is "virtually i
it has no legal sa
is quite true that t
requires validating
distinction withou
What would be the
ment rejected or
posed validating
only deduction to
the Government is
it, whether it is r
Parliamentary ma
but the public can
clusions.

**At the same
Halstead issued
ment to "Trut
National Party
published a fr
headed "This
Should Get Out-
Police?" It also
ing article on t**

The front-page
officer who it assu
formation about
motion on Mr. Co
and disloyalty a
resignation from
strongly attacked
that it was conc
vendetta against t
Police, and made
to members of its
directors who gav
Police Commission

REITE

The leading arti
of these charges
added: "The charg
police inquiry) we
the Government
gated lengthily a
Royal Commissio
Robert Kennedy
analysis, painstak
capable cross-e
charges fell down
stantiation. All
managed to prove
footling trifl of t
tions and these s
from malicious
usually associate
wenches and back

**The public kn
from the inqu
"Truth" is very
has formed its
opinions which p
well ascertain if
touch at all with
have not all app
register for the
replaced the C
Police by a temp
commission and
action and reor
Mr. Holland has
advice.**

There could be
tion of no confid
mental head, short
a call for his resig

Mr. Holland is also in
whatever about the
police force or
inquiry is
adequat
fac

FREEDOM

FIRST PUBLISHED 1943

Box 1240, Wellington. Tel. 46-520 (2 lines).
Registered for Posting as a Newspaper.

THIS POLICE OFFICER SHOULD GET OUT

Freedom 26/1/55

Who 'Ratted' On Police?

(Parliamentary Representative)

SOMEONE in the hierarchy of the New Zealand Police Force is guilty of arrant disloyalty and wilful unreliability. This conclusion is inescapable when events, following the recent conference in Wellington of more than 20 superintendents and inspectors, are reviewed.

Someone who attended that conference by virtue of his senior position in the Police Force, and therefore his reliability, integrity and responsibility as a police officer, did not hesitate to "rat" on his fellow officers and go running off to a couple of weekly newspapers to give them his account of part of what ensued at the conference, an official gathering not open to the Press.

WHOEVER THAT OFFICER IS HE SHOULD HAVE MANHOOD EITHER TO RESIGN THE FORCE OR TENDER HIS NAME TO THOSE OF HIS NEWSPAPER FRIENDS INTERESTED IN DREDGING THE LATRINE-RUMOUR MARKET.

THE outcome of the recent conference of senior police officers, presided over by the chairman of the new Police Commission, Mr. E. H. Compton, and addressed for an hour and a half by the Prime Minister, Mr. Holland, was a unanimous resolution of loyalty to the Police Commission as constituted and for the duration of its term.

But while that goes in general for the officers who attended, it appears unfortunately only too true that one, or some, officers are not prepared to play fair under the new dispensation—or to respect the Prime Minister's wish for a fresh start, "forgetting the past and working for the future."

From the kind of stuff they have published it is clear that nothing was further from their minds. Indeed, what they have published would tend to accentuate discontent and uncertainty.

Unjustifiable

FOR a member of the Police Force to take secrets to any section of the Press, either because he thinks he has been unjustly treated through an officer's promotion over him, or harbours a grudge, is unjustifiable. It is disloyalty of the first magnitude, and would be so regarded in any disciplined organisation.

Under the system that the Prime Minister has provided the Police Force there is not the slightest excuse (let alone any question of justification) for a member to make himself a servitor of the Press to get his revenge.

Such conduct shows a wilful disregard and utter contempt for the oath that every member of the Force must make on entry.

It is obviously impossible for admitted points of dissatisfaction in the Force to be rectified if petty-minded, vindictive individuals are going to agree in the conference room and then snipe at their own decisions outside it.

The simple fact of the matter

Freedom and *New Zealand Truth* took opposing views of the police crisis, but both recognised the key role played by commissioned officers eight senior sergeants wishing to remain members, nine thinking it impracticable for officers to remain association members. The silence of 43 was evidence enough of indifference.

The association delegates expressed misgivings about senior men in the association damping down the juniors, who would be unwilling to speak against those who controlled their livelihoods. One delegate favoured an officers' guild within the association, given that Britain's Police Guild had three sections for officers, non-commissioned officers and men. Meltzer noted it would require ministerial intervention to change the rules. Nothing was decided.

Over the next decade the matter periodically came up for discussion. Meltzer kept it alive with such reminders as a June 1947 editorial asking if it was in the best interests of the police for men who had been promoted to be debarred membership. He confessed, however, that those commissioned officers to whom he had spoken preferred to leave it to the department to decide. And that is how the matter might have stayed, if not for the Compton crisis.

Once that crisis was passed the guild reverted to dormant status. A Wellington monopoly in terms of its executive committee, it scarcely rated as a national organisation. No minutes were kept. It was safer not to have anything on paper, particularly if you were climbing the promotion ladder in those hierarchical, disciplined times. The boldness of its beginning was not to be repeated.

The mood that soon resurfaced was evident in a letter written to Holland by guild representative Superintendent William Carran, thanking him for 'unprecedented progress' under his control. 'You at the helm of our ship,' wrote Carran, 'have steered us out of rough into smoother waters, and you, too, have been responsible for the restoration of morale and confidence.' That sycophantically said, the guild took a long sabbatical.

In 1965 the guild came briefly out of its gentlemen's club torpor. By 1964 all the executive committee had retired except for Superintendent Roy Trask. In early 1965 he got Wellington members together to revive the guild. The 92 commissioned officers were approached and divided into six areas with one representative from each, so that a national organisation could be seen to be operating. The first annual conference of the guild was held on 28 and 29 July 1965 at 10 Brandon Street, Wellington.

Police Station,
Wellington.

2nd May 1955.

Rt. Hon. S.G. Holland, P.C.,
Minister of Police,
Parliament Buildings,
WELLINGTON.

Dear Mr. Holland,

Since the introduction of the Police Force Amendment Bill on the 29th April last, the Commissioned Officers of the Force have considered the matters contained in the Bill.

While the Police Officers' Guild recognises the right of the Government to appoint any person or persons it wishes to control and direct the Force, it considers that the Force and the country as a whole would b e best served by a return to control by a Commissioner. Such Commissioner to be chosen from the New Zealand Police Force.

The Guild tenders this expression of opinion with a view to assisting you, as Minister of Police, and the Government in restoring the morale of the Police Force.

I am further instructed to convey to you an assurance of the loyalty of the members of the Guild at all times.

Yours faithfully,

(Signed) F.W. EDWARDS

Secretary.

The formation of the Officers' Guild boosted officer morale. Now the officers wanted to do something about force morale

Senior police officers' course from 11 to 15 June 1956 at the Majestic Hotel, Paraparaumu. Front, left to right: Superintendent Frank Aplin, Assistant Commissioner Peter Munro and Superintendent Bill Carran. Directly to Carran's right, in the second row, Superintendent Denis Sugrue. Fourth row back, on left: Inspector E. J. C. Hay, and on his right, CIB's Inspector Frank Brady. Behind Hay, second from left: Sub-Inspector Les Spencer, and to his right Deputy-Controller Peter Nalder. Back row, left to right: Brigadier L. G. Goss, Commandant of the Training School, Controller-General Sam Barnett and his successor Superintendent Willis Brown and Assistant Commissioner (Administration) Ned Dobbs

'As you know, gentlemen,' Provisional Honorary Secretary Trask told them, 'the Guild came into being late in 1954, incorporated 1955.' He was probably referring to brothers Superintendent John Edwards and Sub-Inspector Fred Edwards, believed to have been active in discussing the formation of the guild some months before it became a reality.

Present at the first agm were W.J. Robertson, Auckland; T. Jones, Hamilton; C. McKenzie, Christchurch; J.G. Williams, Dunedin; A.I. Knapp, Wellington District and G.A. Dallow, Wellington Headquarters. The geographical spread would be the key to the guild's survival.

Commissioner Spencer addressed the first conference, reminding them that he was in the guild at the beginning, when 'officers tended to be individualists and the interest of the individual was paramount'. He hoped this marked the beginning of teamwork among officers, who would help him break down the dividing line between headquarters and the rest of the country.

Detective Superintendent Knapp was elected president. The first item of business was whether to amalgamate with the association. Meltzer and Butler were present, Meltzer expressing himself happy with the idea of amalgamation. There was also agreement that an outside secretary would be better because he would not be intimidated by the commissioner. Meltzer offered to do the job part-time.

The problem was that 60 paid-up members did not generate enough money to pay anybody. Worries were expressed about losing the death benefit and legal aid when officers left the association. Affiliation was suggested, but deferred for consideration. It was determined to ask the commissioner to provide better quality white shirts that would not fray after a few washes and mess jackets, because of closer ties with the armed forces and public relations requirements. There had been occasions when officers were seen at functions, some in mess jackets, some in uniforms, some in dinner suits.

Concern was expressed at junior and inexperienced headquarters personnel signing, in the commissioner's name, a denial of replacement gas grenades for the Armed Offenders Squad. The remit was amended to expressing concern where a matter involved safety of personnel. Full consideration was to be given to an administrative course along the lines of other government departments.

There was an agreement to negotiate with the department for increases in pay. Meantime the guild would link up with the association. The problem was recognised that flat rate increases left commissioned officers with a restricted increase; the gaps between the ranks were closing and these needed adjusting.

It would be a decade before they were adjusted, by former commissioned officer Rob Moodie. This conference was a tentative exercise in remaining tied to the association coat-tails. Meltzer and Lee had already, on 30 June, signed an application for the association and guild to the Police Staff Tribunal, which at the top sought an increase for superintendents after one year from £2,320 to £2,360 per annum.

Dunedin delegate Williams expressed the restrained nature of the conference when he said 'we are not desperate for a rise in pay'. He felt the pay structure was out of proportion a constable starting off was paid too much, when he was no use to the force for four or five years. Williams proposed starting the constable lower and giving him a £200 rise when he was worth it.

Knapp told Meltzer and Butler the guild was in its infancy and its resources limited. Meltzer argued for them not rocking the boat with any demands for a committee of inquiry. The police had slipped through the public service negotiating net with the tribunal and any comment might draw attention to this. His game plan, he explained, was to emphasise to the tribunal the special conditions applicable to the police and he wanted guild support to push this view through Cabinet. Meltzer feared linkage with the rest of the public service.

With the sub set at £1, the guild adjourned its first conference. A management committee was set up, its first meeting held at lunchtime on 24 August in Room 27 on the second floor of Police Headquarters in Waring Taylor Street, Wellington. Knapp was in the chair, and present were Chief Superintendent G. Claridge, Trask as secretary, Inspectors J.W. Overton, J.R. Harman, who would be long-term treasurer, and G.A. Dallow, with apologies from Inspector Kyle, who was attending court and arrived late. The meeting discussed working with the association before the tribunal and relations generally with the association. On 31 August the keen committee met again—same time, same place—to discuss remits.

On 27 October the meeting discussed how to protect its members from the proposed increase in state house rentals. This was the first specifically guild problem considered by the guild, for the rent increases applied only above a certain salary, which excluded association members. The meeting considered going to the commissioner or direct to the press. The decision was not to go to the press, but to think about it.

Superintendent Gideon Tait came in for Kyle at the next meeting on 5 November and promptly moved that the guild president and secretary meet their association counterparts to discuss the threatened increased house rentals. The guild lobbied the commissioner throughout November that, as Trask wrote, 'advancement should not carry an in-built penalty, thereby placing a premium on mediocrity'. Many commissioned officers had to sell homes they had purchased because of transfers, which occurred, on average, every 26 months and could not, under regulations be declined.

Trask argued that the police were a special case because they could not buy state houses and if a policeman died in the service, the widow must vacate the house. The proposed salary loading of 12.5 per cent per £100 over £1,500 salary was 'a direct attack on the officer's ability to plan for his home on retirement, and it is no encouragement to advancement'.

The proposed loadings had caught most officers unready to buy. They had sacrificed home ownership to indulge the department, and their reward was that a superintendent could end up living in an inferior house alongside a sergeant, yet paying double the rent! Furthermore, the senior sergeant level had £238 a year overtime, commissioned officers none. It was the opposite situation from Britain where a chief superintendent was paid £375 rent allowance on top of a salary up to £2,790, whereas here the salary was £2,550, and £380 was taken in rental on a house worth £5,000. The present rental system was, Trask concluded, outdated and a revision of rents should include assistance to officers leaving departmental houses to buy their own. It was a good case, but it would take over a decade and much more aggressive advocacy to resolve.

In 1966 the guild got its mess jackets and an extra shirt from the commissioner, along with the promise that no more juniors would be signing on his behalf. By now the guild was also aware that the much-touted tribunal could increase salaries only up to what the government approved in an order in council. Superintendents and chief superintendents were excluded from the tribunal findings, and most of the applications were for association members.

The guild could not afford even a part-time secretary. Trask tried to do guild research by writing to detectives to see what they spent cultivating informants and paying them. Trask filed an application for a CIB allowance and sought to have the tribunal look at salary margins between ranks.

The November 1966 conference considered capital punishment for the murder of a police officer, requested lightweight summer uniforms for commissioned officers and decided against amalgamation with the association because the guild aimed to preserve margins.

At a special conference on 1 May 1967 regarding a pay claim, Dave Lee told them the government was keen to fit the police into the public service, as Meltzer had feared. Lee seemed to argue in favour of this by saying that his overtime claim was successful for the association because he based it on the *Public Service Manual*. The police would have to prove special conditions. They had failed to prove their cars suffered more wear and tear than those of other government departments, so they did not get a special mileage increase. The Treasury and SSC examined the claims on behalf of the government, and the government told the commissioner what to do. Only then, if the commissioner's offer was rejected, did the claim go to the tribunal.

Dave Lee advised the guild to do what he did with the

association—a survey based on personnel files as to marital status, family numbers, all the things that could disrupt family life. Knapp said the guild would do this through the department. With no resources for such a survey, they had little other option.

Harman had managed some number crunching for the guild. Margins had declined from a high in 1948 of 15 per cent between senior sergeant and first-year inspector to the present 5.4 per cent. The differential between inspector and chief inspector was 6 per cent, between chief inspector and superintendent 4.9 per cent. To preserve this the guild sought £157 for inspector to £1,997, £176 for chief inspector to £2,221 and £194 for superintendent in the first year to £2,444. They settled for the offered £150, £130 and £80, since it was more than they expected.

Having revived the guild, Trask resigned in April 1967. Jim Nancarrow was appointed secretary. Tait resigned on his promotion to Dunedin, his position as service organisations' representative on the Government Superannuation Board taken, through rotation, by the association's Senior Sergeant Butler.

In August 1967 the guild sought affiliation with the association, but the association was not interested. The guild also sought a joint application with the association to the tribunal, the right of appeal on non-promotion up to chief superintendent, the restoration of margins, public service salary adjustments, summer uniforms and the department paying for mess jacket tailoring and telephone rentals.

The 1968 conference was told by President P.J. McKenzie that they had 100 members, all fully committed to the department, with no offbeat types likely to rise to their ranks. McKenzie said the guild placed its faith in the commissioner and the minister; the job of the guild presented 'few problems'. 'It is not our function,' he told delegates, 'to prove irksome or awkward. Fair play is possibly the basis on which we aim to function.' Dave Lee represented them ably. Such complacency was not going to win any improvements.

New delegate Detective Superintendent Mal Churches, representing Christchurch, Timaru, Greymouth and Nelson, suggested that members keep an eye on early retirement and look 10 or 15 years ahead with superannuation and insurance policies. Most delegates, however, appeared to prefer to relax like McKenzie and settle for discussing badges of rank appearing on epaulettes, the need for summer allowances and allowances to cover such costs as $80 a year to belong to Rotary. They agreed they needed evidence of such costs, 'otherwise Treasury would laugh at us'. After all, Treasury had said they were well done by, even though there had been no increase in the plain-clothes allowance for 22 years.

While not being prepared to do anything, guild members moaned about not getting the same benefits as the association. Those in the association did not have to pay as much as guild members for uniforms, such as $158 for suit, shirts, hats, ties, cardigan, top coat and raincoat and $84 upkeep, compared with a constable paying $120 and upkeep of $20. The meeting did decide it was 75 per cent in agreement with the association, but would not amalgamate until it was 100 per cent.

Minister Allen told the 1969 conference they were all men of sufficiently high ability to make a substantial contribution to police administration 'to the everlasting benefit of your country'. President McKenzie basked in the improvements seen from the days when they were regarded as agitators if they sought betterment of conditions. Now they enjoyed a reduction in weekly hours of duty, better stations and barracks, improvements in pay and conditions. Amalgamation with the association would lose them their separate representation to the tribunal. Pop concerts by P.J. Proby of pants-splitting fame and the mop-top Beatles provided entertainment 'for some classes', and thus deserved police protection—but only in and out of the hall, and the police would resist being used for publicity purposes. The drinking of liquor had to be stopped in public places, unless those involved were young married couples.

Minister Thomson gave the 1970 conference a jolt, telling them they had been largely inactive for 11 years. He exhorted them to seek administrative progress and operational efficiency. President Saunders concurred, regretting 'a lack of interest by members in the functioning of the Guild'.

Assistant Commissioner Ken Burnside rocketed the 1971 conference by saying the guild was 'a moribund body' whose continued existence was of questionable value. There were 127 officers contributing their thoughts to a 'Busbyish' organisation achieving little. He suggested the guild pursue the matter of the ratio of officers to other ranks in comparison with police overseas, and consider relativity of pay with equivalents in other state services and retention of proper margins.

The members duly beat their breasts over their paltry numbers, lack of money and an independent spokesman. Amalgamation with the association was a suggested solution, but the vote was lost. Instead the guild approved a remit on the colour of caps and passed again the request for right of appeal against promotion. They did not like this demotion idea and wanted the department to do a survey about using police in direct employment, a watering down of the remit against civilianisation. Guild protest had the punch of a day-old kitten.

In 1972 the management committee pushed for braid to be worn on mess dress only. An Inspector Moodie spoke to the management committee about compensation for police, and it was agreed they would get back to him as the situation developed.

On 9 May 1973 the Auckland district of the guild went out to bat on its own, taking Prime Minister Kirk to task for implying a lack of confidence in the ability of the police to control a Springbok tour. This protest was no more than a bleat. Normality was restored on 13 June when Hamish Thomas told the management committee that he would urge the commissioner, on their behalf, not to go ahead with all this civilianising.

It was about this time that there were stirrings in the

guild, with Detective Chief Inspector Wally Baker as acting president and Earle Cooper as secretary. Joint meetings began with the association, the guild agreeing to support the association on unfair leave provisions preventing holidays with families and the need for more staff. The association agreed to help the guild on margins and objections to a civilian public relations officer being ranked an inspector. The two organisations stated that there was no need for a disciplinary hearing if a member pleaded guilty and agreed that police vehicles needed better maintenance. The guild would hold its agm on the last few days of the association conference.

The Arthur Allan Thomas case jerked the guild wide awake. On 18 September the management committee met Minister Connelly to discuss the Prime Minister's displeasure with police handling of the case. Connelly claimed Kirk had been misquoted; the police had to learn to live with criticism, as politicians did. The committee agreed it had to live with criticism, but did not expect it from the government. The minister was warned that if he did not quieten the government, the guild would 'be compelled to make the facts known to the public', even if that meant criticising MPs and the government in general. The guild felt Kirk had attacked police integrity. The commissioner supported the guild action.

The next month the guild wrote to former guild member Bruce Hutton in Australia. On 30 October Hutton attended a management meeting, thanking them for their support. The Hamilton Retrial Committee had, he claimed, distorted the truth. Dr Jim Sprott was well known for presenting last-minute evidence in court without telling the police. Hutton told them Sprott was a freelance chemist with expertise in oil contamination and metallurgy, but not in ballistics. He claimed sensationalism by articles in the press and by television. E.M. Timms expressed himself glad that there was not a news media at the time of the Last Supper. The meeting discussed tactics and the best lawyers to defend Hutton; Paul Temm was favoured despite being from the other side and Lloyd Brown also won approval.

This was the first year of simultaneous conferences with the association. President Baker spoke of both organisations being increasingly aware of matters of common interest. The conference called for greater powers to deal with gangs and other antisocial elements, for an end to the antiquated system of taking down all the evidence in disciplinary hearings, for the department to pay for legal assistance and redesigned uniforms. There was a call to build a more professional image, with somebody employed to review commissioned officers' salaries, now that margins had narrowed under the tribunal. The joint submissions with the association to the Royal Commission on Licensing Laws demonstrated closer ties with the association and more involvement by the guild.

Professionalising of the guild began with the hiring in 1974 of management consultants John P. Young and Associates to do a feasibility study into a salary survey. The consultants estimated it would cost $4,000, the guild had assets of $4,947, so the consultants were given the go ahead. A questionnaire was sent out to members on their educational qualifications, their reponsibilities and hours worked.

When Kirk met guild representatives in June he supported early retirement and said he was no critic of police procedures. The department, however, said early retirement was not possible because of the cost and the impossibility of replacing lost manpower.

The next year the guild was disappointed by receiving opinions from the consultants, rather than hard information they could use to argue for true relativity. President Baker joined the association in the meeting with new Prime Minister Rowling and found him more difficult than Kirk. Rowling was warned against legislative changes based on minority group approaches. There was also continued concern at Martyn Finlay's habit of criticising the police, going back through the Arthur Allan Thomas case to call police handling of security in the days before the SIS the work of 'bumbling amateurs'.

Despite disappointment at the Young report, the guild was not about to fade away once more. It was demonstrable, the 1975 conference asserted, that since 1958 commissioned officers had worked much more unpaid overtime. They called for the commissioner to change the pay scale or compensate for overtime.

Their general requests were stronger too. They wanted the department to ease stress on senior officers. They expressed concern at civilians supervising police and issuing orders, an example being the civilian in charge of police transport. They wanted the department to appoint its own architect so that buildings would be designed to police requirements; the department should pay for carpets; there should be fleecy-lined gloves for southern sector police; transferees should be eligible for Housing Corporation loans up to 80 per cent. They also called for a redesign of uniforms, new headquarters and Wellington station, the commissioner's memoranda to be made obsolete after one year, a repeal of the commissioner's right to any extension of his term, out of pocket allowances for plain-clothes police. There were 15 new remits, the correspondence files deepened. The guild was setting itself up for a professional posture.

The guild became more vocal. Submissions were made to parliamentary select committees on the Criminal Justice Act, the Police Offences Act, the Wanganui Computer Centre Bill, the Listening Devices Bill, the Privacy Commissioner Bill. Representations were made to the administration against the Ombudsman investigating complaints against the police. The guild warned that, in future it would publicly refute any 'unwarranted' criticisms of the police by government MPs. There was talk of starting a newsletter.

Senior Sergeant Ray Cook of Christchurch wrote to guild secretary Earle Cooper on 15 September 1975 a letter that mapped out the way they must go. Having followed departmental advice to get some tertiary education, he had been studying with Dr Weir in the Mathematics Department at Massey University. He concluded that the anomaly in pay rates could have been rectified in 1972 before the

Stabilisation Regulations came in the following year. He said so at the association annual conference, but Hamish Thomas disagreed. Cook took legal advice from Dr Rob Moodie at Victoria University of Wellington, who supported his view that Thomas's approach was 'defective'.

Cook had worked out, with Dr Weir's formula, that 2 or 3 per cent was needed between increments and a 5 per cent margin between ranks to establish a self-correcting formula. His research showed that a constable's salary had gone up 327.7 per cent since 1956, an inspector's 295.5 per cent. In 1937 the margin between senior sergeant and inspector had been 12.3 per cent, in 1975 it was 6.33 per cent. Asking for 4.9 per cent was a further decline.

Based on his research, Cook had made submissions to the Secretary of Labour in the hope that he might get bureaucrats to see the light and stall a few police resignations. The police administration had, he claimed, failed to comply with the 1968 Royal Commission into State Salary Fixing Procedures. Cook favoured a move to a percentage adjustment instead of the flat rate adjustment of salary. Such mathematical lobbying would have to await somebody who could do it, namely Graham Butterworth, and somebody who would promote such figuring, namely Rob Moodie.

Meantime Commissioner Burnside could now see that the guild was active. Baker assured him at the 1975 conference that the guild was not a pressure group, then proceeded to demonstrate that it was by saying the rewards were not keeping pace with the stresses; as a result officers were leaving for outside employment. Baker expressed concern again at the lack of overtime pay and called for research on early retirement, pay and conditions.

Ex-inspector Rob Moodie moved into the association driving seat, and the guild was picked up as passenger. Moodie told the guild it should retain its separate identity, but act with one voice on pay and conditions affecting both organisations. Moodie was to be that one voice in his de facto amalgamation of association and guild. He nudged the guild into contributing to the cost of a researcher on pay and conditions, telling them that $20 per member would be satisfactory, so they made up $1,000 of the $10,000 researcher fee.

The guild agreed to Moodie's initiatives, although it, too, had trouble keeping up with them. Moodie was moving faster than the guild could manage. He advised members that the death benefit cover would be increased and subsidised or underwritten by the department. He told them about the salary margins review, career restructuring,

Auckland Assistant Commissioner Fergie Scott, right, a former association president, invited three association members to a meeting to discuss problems. In the back row, right to left: Eddie Edwardson, Auckland District Secretary, District Chairman Ron Halpin, then Auckland delegate Brian Middleton. Front row, right to left: Detective Superintendent Mal Ross, Superintendent Cromwell, Superintendent 'Chook' Taylor, Superintendent Tommy Jones, Superintendent Ken Sykes. Seated front left with back to camera: Frank Diggle, past member of the Auckland District Committee. Back row far left: Staff Welfare Officer Frank McKenna, next to him Ken Thompson, a future commissioner, and Norm Hardy extended insurance cover. They went along with what he had done. By 1978 they had accepted his advice to cut back on remits and let their management committee deal with problems as they arose.

Moodie had to remind the guild that he ran the cutter. They must prevent Auckland branch chairman Inspector Bruce Scott putting out press releases to the *New Zealand Herald* which 'neutralised' Moodie's case to the Minister of State Services for a higher departmental grading because of the loss of young officers. Scott had suggested that the resignations were for personal reasons and little could be done about them.

Bryan Rowe had been active in the association, and when he moved up to inspector he stayed active in an association case. Association members objected to this guild member's involvement, but Moodie was having none of that. He declared such thinking 'contrary to the whole philosophy' of finding common ground. Promoting differences was a union tactic 'to help feed the ego of union executives'. Moodie sought actively to tie the guild and association knot, writing overseas to get advice on federation from other police organisations.

Moodie and Butterworth addressed guild conferences regularly. Detective Superintendent Stu McEwen, as guild president, thanked Butterworth for his papers on pay, allowances and margins, the efforts made to raise the salaries of the commissioner and deputy commissioner in order to provide the proper salary margin review. McEwen observed that the increased work of the guild management committee indicated awareness by members of the value of their organisation.

Typical of Butterworth's research value to the guild was a letter he wrote to its secretary, Brian Hartley, on 18 December 1978, saying that he had begun processing the financial section of term engagement and a disturbing picture was emerging of 'too many officers homeless' who 'appear to have made no provision to meet the eventual need to buy a house'. Typical was a senior officer aged 50 to 54, married with one child, with no property and debts of $500, his one asset a $12,000 insurance policy. Butterworth said there was a need to discuss this and to counsel younger members.

Butterworth told the guild conference in 1980 that their department now had Grade One status and a margins formula had been found. The commissioner's salary had moved from $21,000 in 1976, when Moodie arrived, to $51,500. With the average New Zealand wage at $8,500, Butterworth warned the officers to be careful not to ask for too much, but now the formula was in place that would allow a salary flow from deputy assistant commissioner to superintendent to chief inspector.

The guild had indulged its independence during these

Detective Chief Inspector Wally Baker, centre, did much to revitalise the guild when he came in as president in 1973. A few years later he was able to point the pen at Rob Moodie, to his right, the man who carried the guild along with his association triumphs, and in 1989 became executive director of the guild, its first professional advocate. Far right Assistant Head of Administration Dave Mabbett. On the left Deputy Commissioner Walton, at far left Assistant Commissioner Ken Thompson delicate negotiations. Moodie was furious, Butterworth recalls, when guild members held up the margins claim in 1979. The negotiations were more for the guild than the association, but Moodie says valuable hours of negotiating time were lost trying to persuade guild members to agree to a counter-offer to the government's interim offer, rather than simply accepting it. He says some officers thus sabotaged the counter-offer when they had neither the expertise nor the knowledge to judge and were motivated more by 'the rank that was sitting on their shoulders than by the knowledge and understanding that was in their minds'. He credits Bruce Scott with bringing the guild together on the issue, but too late.

Moodie had to cope at the same time with letters written by the guild to the Prime Minister, the Leader of the Opposition and the commissioner objecting to 'my comments and my mode of dress'. Guild members were among the stuffiest when it came to Moodie's flamboyant appearance.

In regard to the margins claim, Butterworth suspected that the commissioner may have been pressuring the guild, which always has one foot in the management or administration camp. He says Moodie considered ringing every guild member and asking to be his personal negotiator, a prescient proposal as things turned out. Back then, however, Moodie always worked as if he had a united association and guild team behind him, and used guild members out of proportion to their numbers. This was particularly true on the welfare fund board. Moodie's policy was simply to use the best person available for the job.

Detective Superintendent Bruce Scott as president told the 1980 conference how much the guild leaned on the association, but they did pay for it with $7,040, one-third of the research officer's salary from its 200 members compared with the 4000 in the association. There was, of course, the quid pro quo of the association pitching in for most of the legal assistance fees in the Thomas commission challenges.

Butterworth tended to be the one who dealt mostly with the guild. He told the 1980 conference that he and Moodie were impressed at the guild's professional handling of the Thomas commission. He thought it a pity that the public had not been told earlier of police procedures in such cases.

The long agony of the Thomas commission problem drew the guild and association closer together, with Moodie calling the positional play. On 3 July 1980 he led the joint delegation to Commissioner Walton to tell him that the police counsel really represented the minister and was under political control. Moodie charged that the commission was excluding police presentation of facts but 'allowing any oddball evidence, even down to the point of [journalist Pat] Booth giving scientific evidence'. It was, he said 'absolutely disgraceful and intolerable'.

When Walton disputed this, saying he chose counsel and had not met with the minister, Moodie exploded that the police were in there 'as the chicken for frying'. He accepted the commission's implication of some irregularities concerning the police case, but the commission had not revealed its grounds for saying that two policemen had planted evidence. The association and the guild challenged this and questioned the bias of commission members.

There were areas in the early 1980s where the guild did stand alone, and came into conflict with the association. In 1981 the guild was upset at the extension of the commissioner's term. Moodie had no objections to his excellent working relationship with Walton, but the guild had been campaigning for 15 years to have any extension of the commissioner's term repealed. The guild accepted that Ken Thompson, at 49, was young for the top job, but his administrative ability was well known, coming to the fore in his organisation of the Springbok tour police dispositions.

When the Turangi incident flared in 1982, Bruce Scott publicly deplored the association going over the commissioner to the minister. Scott then did the same thing, going to see Ben Couch about the association 'seeming to discriminate against a senior police officer whose integrity and ability have never been in doubt'.

Behind the clash was the philosophical disagreement between the association favouring what it had most of, manpower, over the administration, and at least a good number of the guild having a preference for high-tech solutions. Moodie insisted that these differences were professional and not personal, yet it was his outsize personality which dominated proceedings.

Moodie expressed reservations about many commissioned officers as part of his argument for early retirement. On 2 September 1981 he wrote that the Springbok tour 'has shown up one serious weakness in the police service and that is the calibre of its officers. Some of them have proven useless. It is the frontline NCOs and constables who are holding the show together.' He was 'absolutely appalled with the conduct of some of them, their lack of initiative and their simple inability to come to grips with what is required in a fluid situation'. To his mind there was 'too much pontificating and airing of opinions on the part of the Guild' and 'not enough resort to analysis, reasoning and getting on with the job of providing up front leadership and standards in the police service'. Such people, he concluded, were unable to do the job but criticised anybody who could, including their commissioner. He vowed that once the tour was over he would raise his reservations with the commissioner.

The reservations were present within the guild too. In 1981 a split was threatening in the guild, with the non-executive lesser three ranks of commissioned officers considering moving to association membership. Nothing came of it, apart from conference discussion.

Moodie was as good as his word about raising the matter of non-performing commissioned officers, except that he raised the question not just with the commissioner. He won the Labour Opposition over to his programme for early retirement, and they fulfilled their promise once in power.

'We managed to lop off a lot of elderly commissioned officers in 1985,' Butterworth says. 'A lot of guild people came through very quickly. For the first time they started

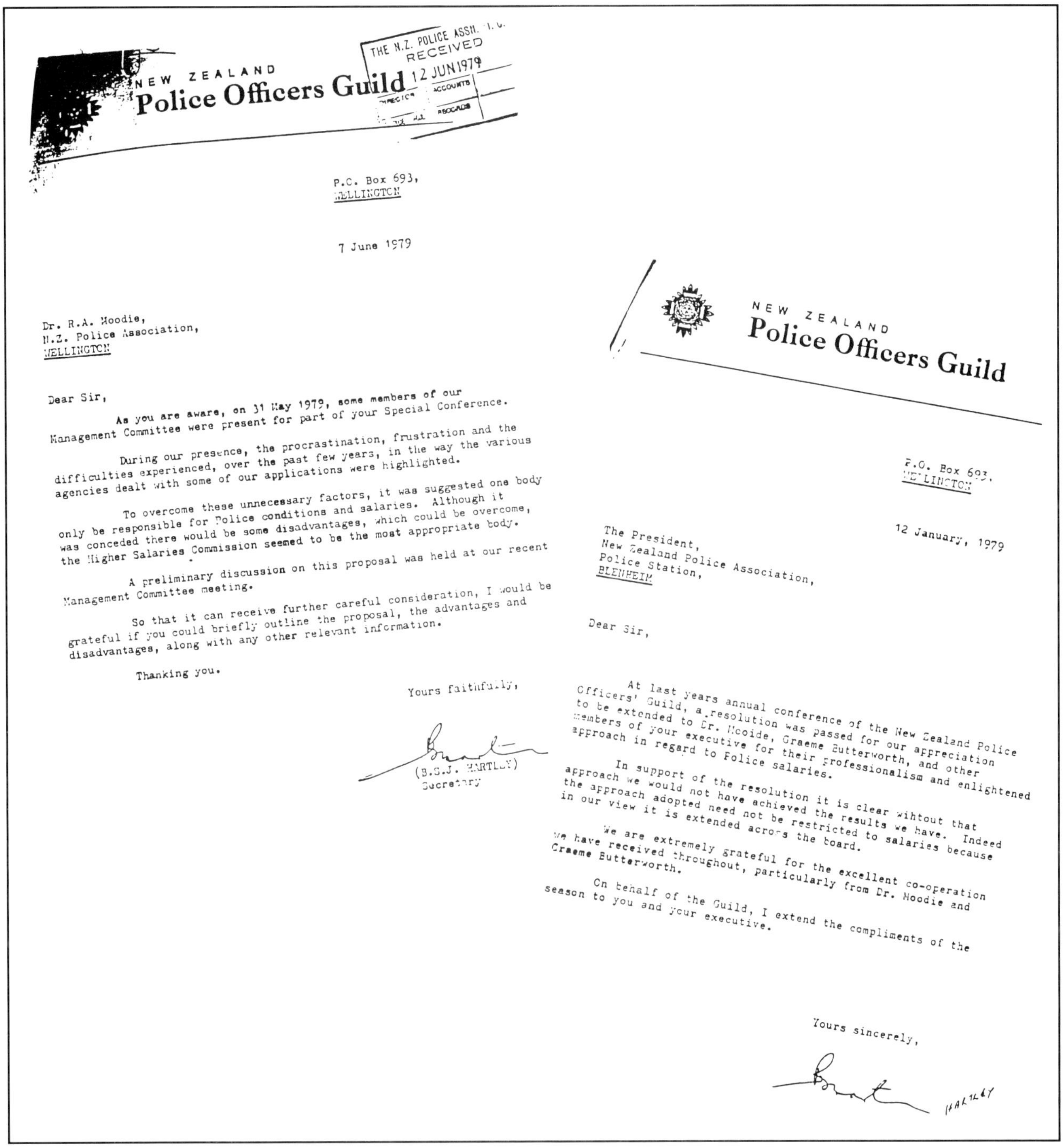

NEW ZEALAND
Police Officers Guild

THE N.Z. POLICE ASSN. I.U.
RECEIVED
12 JUN 1979

P.O. Box 693,
WELLINGTON

7 June 1979

Dr. R.A. Moodie,
N.Z. Police Association,
WELLINGTON

Dear Sir,

As you are aware, on 31 May 1979, some members of our Management Committee were present for part of your Special Conference.

During our presence, the procrastination, frustration and the difficulties experienced, over the past few years, in the way the various agencies dealt with some of our applications were highlighted.

To overcome these unnecessary factors, it was suggested one body only be responsible for Police conditions and salaries. Although it was conceded there would be some disadvantages, which could be overcome, the Higher Salaries Commission seemed to be the most appropriate body.

A preliminary discussion on this proposal was held at our recent Management Committee meeting.

So that it can receive further careful consideration, I would be grateful if you could briefly outline the proposal, the advantages and disadvantages, along with any other relevant information.

Thanking you.

Yours faithfully,

(B.S.J. HARTLEY)
Secretary

NEW ZEALAND
Police Officers Guild

P.O. Box 693,
WELLINGTON

12 January, 1979

The President,
New Zealand Police Association,
Police Station,
BLENHEIM

Dear Sir,

At last years annual conference of the New Zealand Police Officers' Guild, a resolution was passed for our appreciation to be extended to Dr. Mcoide, Graeme Butterworth, and other members of your executive for their professionalism and enlightened approach in regard to Police salaries.

In support of the resolution it is clear wihtout that approach we would not have achieved the results we have. Indeed the approach adopted need not be restricted to salaries because in our view it is extended across the board.

We are extremely grateful for the excellent co-operation we have received throughout, particularly from Dr. Moodie and Graeme Butterworth.

On behalf of the Guild, I extend the compliments of the season to you and your executive.

Yours sincerely,

HARTLEY

Moodie and Butterworth worked as well for the guild as the association, as these letters suggest

to get a lot more educated, thoughtful people. They began to resemble the armed forces officer corps. We had pushed very hard for training and the nature of police work became more complex. There was a qualitative change in the commissioned officers.'

Butterworth had thought up the phrase 'rejuvenation of the service', and he promoted it vigorously. On 7 November 1985 he reported on his 10 days in Australia, where he observed the worldwide trend to performance pay. This had just surfaced here in the salaries of deputy commissioner, assistant commissioner and superintendent. The lesson he had learned was that the connection between rank and salary was disappearing, replaced by positional payments, or payment for what you proved you could do. Under this theory a constable could apply for a superintendent's job. Butterworth urged the guild to go with the change and put in what they wanted, rather than resisting and having the SSC force change on them. He suggested accepting the Hay management system in place in Australia's police services, where it had proved fair. He warned how fast the change would be.

At the 1985 guild annual conference Butterworth repeated his message. He told delegates that Sam Barnett had shaken the police into the 1950s, Burnside and Thompson had brought the police organisation into the reactive policing from the 1970s, and now, in the 1980s, management systems were coming fast. Australia had them, while here the organisation did not even know how many people, as an average, were away on sick leave. Salary reviews and special circumstances claims showed some appreciation that a police officer who had coped with 38 offences in 1970 now coped with 69 in 1984. Extra pressure meant a case for extra pay. It was up to the association and guild to agree about the need for change, then take their common case to the SSC and the administration.

Butterworth suggested staking out positions on career development, rank structure and review and appeal. He saw the change beginning in the guild's operational ranks. He suggested creating problems by getting paid overtime in the inspector rank, which could lead to refusing promotion to chief inspector unless there was an attractive margin. This would jostle the margin case up to superintendent and chief superintendent before the Higher Salaries Commission. Creating such rank problems would force review.

He told the guild that association members were now 'more docile, a larger, younger group' who would take direction. The guild was 'the professional elite of the Police and moves much more by consensus'. With guild members addressing and informing a wider group, it would not take long for the broad principles to be established.

In this guild display the uniforms depicted alongside Commissioner Brown are all mess jackets. Top left is the mess jacket worn by C.L. Spencer, commissioner from 1961 to 1967. Below left is the jacket worn by D.J. Cummings, commissioner from 1936 to 1944, the oldest known mess jacket of any police officer. Middle top jacket was worn by R.J. Walton, commissioner from 1978 to 1983. Below centre is the mess jacket of guild vice-president Chief Inspector Jean Dougall. The first female police officer was Inspector E.M. Bennett, promoted in 1966

Former Commissioner of Police Willis Spencer Brown (left) is being welcomed by guild president Detective Superintendent Colin Wilson to the guild's display opening at the Police Museum, Porirua, on 11 November 1986. Between them is Commissioner Ken Thompson. Directly behind Brown is his facsimile. Brown was the only commissioner to retain membership of the guild during his term as commissioner. In 1968 the guild changed its rules to allow membership only to officers below commissioner rank

Two of the newer, younger members of the guild, Alec Waugh and Lindsay Hunter, moved and seconded the motion that 'the combination of early retirement, social environment and the emerging principle of performance measurement in management have resulted in a need for substantial changes in the police career, ranks and salary structure'. An urgent working party of guild, association and administration should establish principles for change. The motion was carried.

New president Colin Wilson welcomed Butterworth, Moodie and administration negotiator Peter Mairs to 'this particularly important conference' and offered them 'maximum flexibility' in negotiations. He saw this as 'a watershed in the police rank structure'; he and his two vice-presidents, secretary and treasurer were the working party ready to consult on change.

Moodie told the conference they had come out of 'probably one of the most successful negotiations of the New Zealand Police—the Early Retirement/Optional Disengagement package'. He commended the motion passed, telling them they had to convince the Higher Salaries Commission, the SSC and the government that 'what we have had for the last 100 years does not work now. There has to be a major restructure of the Police service to cope with the demands of the present and the demands of the future. New scales, new rank structure, broadbanding.' The changes of the last nine years meant guild members now had much more management work to do.

Immediate past president Jim Glynn said Moodie probably achieved more for the guild even than for the association and had been an inspiration to everyone. He hoped Moodie would consider working for the guild as a consultant.

Moodie replied that he knew some police officers would get a bit anxious 'if a man in a dress said he loved the people he was working with' but 'that is the reality'. He said he had a functional appreciation of frontline work. Recently he had seen a sergeant running from a patrol car to some domestic incident and remembered an incident in Lower Hutt where the police went back in the mortuary van. He hoped guild members would look at their staff in a better light than the administration had.

With that, the compassionate and creative secretary of the Police Association took his farewell, significantly more emotional with the guild than with the association. He praised Butterworth, Mairs and Rana Waitai of the administration as the brilliant research team that he had led for nine years. 'I have the logic,' he said, 'but they do the work.' He said he was off to be a goat herder. 'It has been,' he concluded, 'a privilege to work with you.'

Over the next few years the guild worked without Moodie, reaching its own accommodation with the association, the administration and the government, during a period of bureaucratic revolution. In 1986 the police celebrated 100 years, but the guild, dramatically changed, was looking to the next 100.

Jim Glynn was not only guild president in the mid-1980s and chairman of the welfare fund, but also author of *The New Zealand Policeman*. In 1987 he was made an honorary life member of the guild

Chapter Twenty-one

The Rejuvenation of the Guild

Chief Inspector Sherwood Young has seen the scope of the guild change. Having come on to the management committee in 1976, he is its longest-serving member. He was one of the first wave of more educated commissioned officers, passing his commissioned officer exam in 1968, soon after paid study leave got under way. In 1969 he started part-time at Canterbury University, graduating with an MA in history, with first class honours.

In his early days the guild was directed by its superiors. When Young shifted to Wellington from Christchurch, Christchurch District Commander George Twentyman asked him to be their guild rep. The guild management was made up then of Wellington-based officers who represented the regions they came from. When he joined the management committee in 1976 the sub was $1 as compared with $18 per pay now.

What has not changed is that the junior members of the guild were restive, considering starting their own association separate from association and guild. Young has seen this tension all the way through. Some inspectors who are the guild junior members have, from time to time, considered joining the association. There have been periodic calls for the senior members at assistant commissioner level, the top 10 of the guild, to pull out. The strains at both ends will probably remain while the guild is so structured.

Young's father was an accountant, which might have helped him take the job of guild treasurer in 1981 and work for a decade to expand its capital base. He increased the sub from $2 to $3, then to $5.50, to $8.80, to $13.92, at last the same as the association, and finally above the association level to its present $18. One argument he used to get the sub up was that members were defaulting on payments for the association *Newsletter*, but with the increased sub the guild got the *Newsletter* for members. As Young made the

In 1989 Moodie was the guild's first professional employee. He is seen here, second from left in the front row, at the end of his two-year stint as executive director. On his left is Vice-President Bryan Rowe, to the right President Brian Hartley, Vice-President John Coomber, Vice-President Lindsay Hunter. Back row, left to right: K.B. Taylor, Region 3, J.D. White, College, G.J. Gilpin, Region 4, J.P. Schouten, Region 5, Sherwood Young, treasurer, J. Mathews, Region 6, and Alec Waugh, secretary. Waugh and Hunter were key figures in persuading Rob Moodie to return to police advocacy, this time for the benefit of middle management guild more financial, Lindsay Hunter began the guild's own newsletter to improve communication between members.

The guild needed enough money to get out from under the association umbrella. In the mid-1980s it was paying the association $12,000 for research, $50 per guild member. Guild and association needs were, however, changing as a result of the early retirement package and government sector reforms reducing the number of ranks and improving training. The higher ranked guild members were moving on to contracts and these needed to be negotiated. A negotiator cost money.

The substantial contracts negotiated offered every incentive for assistant commissioners to stay in the job until 60, as they were entitled to do. This held up the advancement of other guild members and created a new problem.

There was also the problem of PCT, which was losing its original intention of being one factor in assessing fitness for duty. The fitness test was never intended to be a stand-alone means of leaving the police, and certainly not a way of dismissing an officer who was doing a good job. The guild wants the PCT abolished, or used simply to keep staff fitter. The association has a ruling granting two hours a week for PCT and is committed to it. The guild and association have the matter before the courts, seeking a legal judgement as to PCT's intent.

Young identifies 1988 as the period when the guild really made its presence felt. By then it had evaluated the approach Graham Harding was pushing. As the association began to talk term engagement again, the guild reacted against it, seeing it as a limited service compared with security of tenure. Guild members, who tend to be those who have made a long-term career of the police, felt that term engagement would give the employer too much power to remove unwanted employees. The guild also disapproved of non-sworn members coming into its ranks and objected to the association voting in 1988 to change the Welfare Fund Board to include overwhelming association representation.

From his Feilding goat farm Moodie saw much of what he had achieved falling apart. He could not see the guild and association coming together under the present leadership which, in the association, did not impress him. He saw the guild as a group of well-educated, thinking, middle management officers, a good group to work with. He accepted the offer from Colin Wilson and Alec Waugh to become their negotiator.

Waugh, whom Young characterises as 'the personification of the rejuvenation of the guild', briskly dismisses the idea of rejuvenation reaching the top levels of the police. He thinks it was a mistake, in the 1985 settlement, to allow senior officers such a generous transition period to early retirement. With the huge pay hikes Moodie won them in 1989-90, as much as $30,000 for the regional commander in Auckland, the incentive was to stay.

Promoted to inspector in 1984, Waugh had initially steered clear of the guild, which he thought too small and basically a gentlemen's club. Getting bored with police routine, he attended a guild agm. He thought it a disgrace. It was held at Police Headquarters, the meal was awful, members were criticising the guild for being ineffective but not doing anything about it.

Waugh did something. The job of secretary was there for anybody who wanted it, so he took it and, with new President Colin Wilson, set about changing the guild image. Conferences from now on were held outside headquarters at conference centres, they were formal, guests were invited. The newsletters and minutes became professional. The response was the same as when he had run *Watchdog*. People with ability now needed little convincing about becoming involved; the likes of Lindsay Hunter and Brian Hartley came to the professional party.

Wilson made it clear to Moodie, in a letter dated 16 January 1986, that the guild would not support the association in industrial action, but would side with the administration and the commissioner. He commended Moodie for defusing association hotheads and for his commitment to a 'patient and dignified profile in these complex negotiations'. On the same day Wilson wrote to Deputy Commissioner Churches seeking general advertising of all vacancies to deputy commissioner rank, to ease the anxieties and frustrations that had emerged. The guild was becoming more active in several directions.

A special guild conference was called on 23 January 1986 to explain to administration negotiator Peter Mairs that the revised 5 per cent salary offer was unacceptable. Harding suggested that a unified view would help because the government might see the association as a union but the guild as 'an officers' club', for which it might have some respect. The guild took a narrow middle line of refusing to take part in industrial action but not saying anything against association action, and of supporting the negotiating position of 11 per cent for the association and 8 per cent for the guild. The guild agreed to pay its share of newspaper advertisements. It was useful for the guild to stay neutral while Moodie and Butterworth negotiated to the brink. The guild tactic was to be available if required as a negotiator between the association and the commissioner and government.

At the 1986 annual guild conference Ann Hercus reminded delegates that the police vote had doubled in her two years in the job. She quoted Jim Glynn's book *The New Zealand Policeman* concerning police not preventing crime as an argument against a simple increase in police numbers solving the the crime rate.

Lindsay Hunter published the new guild involvement in the *Paper Tiger*. Its third issue noted the need to address margins, opposition to civilianisation and promotion for those over 55, pursuit of appeal rights up to assistant commissioner level; it was reported that former treasurer John Harman and former president Wally Baker had been made the first life members of the guild at the 1986 agm.

Over the next two years the *Paper Tiger* and President Wilson signalled guild adjustments to the winds of change. The guild co-operated with the administration on Operation Blueprint, setting up performance appraisal. The guild was as shocked as the association at the proposed superannuation changes, and even more shocked by the government stopping any payment of union salaries, expenses or leave. Wilson called it an effort 'to deliberately blunt and restrict the capacity of service organisations'. While the association could afford to pay its staff, the 240-member guild lacked any professional input.

Waugh attacked the problem by calling for a monetary balance 'to defend the status quo to the extreme on the superannuation conditions and service and salary claims'. The 15 February 1989 management committee meeting agreed to negotiate to hire Dr Moodie to fulfil the need for professional input at all levels, including the restructuring of the inspector/chief inspector level and superannuation. Commissioned officers could not, Waugh noted, speak well on their own behalf because of the constraints on them. Moodie had worked for association and guild, introducing the health plan, holiday homes, insurance and mortgage packages and early retirement, and had moved police pay from the bottom to the top of the public service heap. Since he had left the whole structure he had introduced had been chipped away, partly because the association did not understand these structures and how to maintain them. 'We wanted Moodie,' Waugh says, 'as someone who would negotiate personal contracts and as someone with a vision about what policing was.'

Moodie was happy to accept a year's contract as an employment consultant, but could see that the commissioner would be unhappy. He insisted on being identified as the executive director of the guild, so that the commissioner would accept his negotiating status.

Initially he struck hostility from both administration and association. He thought the association wrong to withdraw from the restructuring negotiations, since it deprived itself of the benefits available to all those in the public and private sectors who gave value. He did not think the personal performance contract a threat. The commissioner might say it was the end of collective bargaining, but that could not be so if the union refused to accept it. Under individual contracts people were not only better off, but not as easily sacked as under the old system whereby the commissioner could dismiss anybody so long as he went through the right procedures. Moodie negotiated guild members into more secure jobs.

On 7 April 1989 he wrote to the commissioner stating that he did not accept the Attorney-General's opinion that the police could not now strike under the restructuring provisions. Another lawyer could give a different opinion, but his approach was to avoid the conditions that could give rise to a strike. He had in the past made threats of strike, but had not come near the reality. Now he was hearing the language of industrialisation in the police and he did not like it. He did not accept the claims of the control departments that he had rolled them in 1986. His belief then was that experienced constables deserved up to $50,000 for the responsibilities, dangers and psychological damage the job entailed. Now he believed that the commissioned officers he represented deserved increased remuneration for the extra management responsibilities.

Wilson gave his last presidential address in 1989, praising Moodie's contribution to a productive year for the guild in restructuring, salary and contracts. In the 4 December 1989 edition of the newsletter he had taken over from Hunter, Moodie warned members of the way the SSC and administration were using the contracts as 'secret management'. He advised them all to seek his advice about their personal contracts.

Moodie's professional advice was also important because it was independent of the job. Lindsay Hunter admitted that he found it hard to separate his guild function as an observer from his administrative job of implementing Operation Blueprint.

Once again Moodie was firing on all cylinders. He instigated an attack on PCT, calling its reputed costs of $12 to $14 million 'a grotesque waste of money' in these tough economic times. PCT was a joke when a member with an honours award for outstanding work was being pressured over his failure to complete the PCT. He identified the government as wanting in the race relations area by first generating unrealisable Maori expectations over the Treaty of Waitangi, with a corresponding fear and anger in European minds, and then doing an about face on the issue. He sought a report on superannuation implications from Eddie Jones Ltd, who had produced the critical actuarial figures that Ann Hercus used to topple Treasury opposition. When the government decision was announced, Moodie denounced its 'incomprehensible stupidity' that could cause industrial chaos and seriously endanger public safety.

Rowe as acting president and Waugh as secretary stepped out on either side of association President Hinds through Wellington to Parliament on the March 1990 police demonstration. It was a visible expression of the coalition pact the association and guild made in January to act in concert on matters of mutual agreement. Waugh saw the demo as 'a dignified march of principle, not industrial action'.

Moodie meantime was busy telling guild members that the secrecy of salary contracts had to go lest the power of the employer become absolute. The guild had to know what was going on if it was to bargain satisfactorily. At present he only had half the officers informing him of what they were offered. He was appalled at how much ground they had lost in comparison with other executive salaries, and this was because the administration was keeping the salaries secret, reducing individual officers to bended knee status and leaving them largely in the dark about what they should be getting.

At the December 1990 conference President Brian Hartley also emphasised the role of the guild as a watchdog to ensure that contractees received remuneration justice. He thought the informal coalition between guild and association had quickly recognised the need 'to reestablish the ability to influence the Commissioner, the Government, and society on police strategies'.

Waugh had stated at the special June conference his consistent stance that the two service organisations should amalgamate. The guild was too small to be effective and the police must speak with one voice. Australian evidence, he claimed, showed that split representation in some states had proved detrimental compared with those who had one police organisation. He memorably described the 1980s as 'the decade of service organisations' when they had been 'the movers and shakers' and 'without that quality input policing would be in a sorry state'. Time, though, had passed the guild by and it could not afford professional services.

Brian Hartley voiced the majority view in arguing against him on the grounds that the guild had singular interests, such as the elimination of the deputy assistant commissioner rank, margins, representation on the Police Appeal Board, promotions over 55. He favoured the loose arrangement with the association and, when it came to the vote, this proved to be the majority view, as has always been the case.

Waugh had lost again, as he had, when standing for president of the association, to the 'comfortable manner' of Morrow and now Steve Hinds. Waugh confesses to being abrasive and a promoter of unpopular causes such as asking the commissioner every year from 1987 to 1990 whether he would consider a golden handshake for senior commissioned officers, as every other government department did. This would bring in new blood at the top, and give the service true rejuvenation. The standard reply was that there was no need for severance pay for any commanders. Waugh says the result is that some assistant commissioners are aged 55 and older. With fewer than expected taking early retirement, 120 instead of 150 in 1987, the rejuvenation has not been as swift as was anticipated.

Waugh was the winner in getting Moodie on board, but personally has lost from this move. He was warned not to mention Moodie when he went for promotion interviews, since too many of those senior police dislike Moodie's methods, manner and mode of dress. Waugh thinks they are the ones who have killed Moodie's dream of innovative flexibility in the police service. The only solution, in Waugh's view, is to stop appointing as commissioners men with limited management or political skills. He advocates a return to the Barnett solution of a proven manager from outside the police service.

Moodie and Waugh both left—Moodie's contract expiring, Waugh resigning as secretary—but, from the 17 applicants for guild executive director, Butterworth was chosen at the end of 1990. He looked forward to coming into the guild alongside the generation of men with whom he had worked in the association and who had now been promoted. He saw his job as entrenching Moodie's initiatives, as the guild veers away from the association's more industrial path, perhaps looking to link with some other peer group. In Australia, he notes, some officer groups fed up with this industrial path have set up an Institute of Management. Butterworth believes that a less confrontational relationship between association and government could have seen the superannuation crisis resolved by negotiation, perhaps with the superannuation clawback taken down to the 24 per cent tax rate.

Waugh has gone off to study for a master of public policy degree at university, encouraged that he has increasing support in the police for an outsider running them. He has little faith in the possibility of getting a good negotiated deal out of term engagement, believing that this initiative will not meet member expectations and will further muddy relationships.

Waugh has been asked if he wants the job of president of the guild. He does not, because he does not believe in it. What Waugh does believe in is one police organisation, with maybe a niche in it for commissioned officers.

This could perhaps be the dream for the 1990s, a Moodie figure negotiating for all police with a skilled Barnett-style public service manager. Then the likes of Waugh, who describes himself as proud to be a police officer, can get on with highly educated policing in a department that is competently run.

Chapter Twenty-two

The Rags to Riches Welfare Fund

The £25 Death Benefit Fund was an early association initiative. Over half a century it has evolved into a multimillion-dollar dispenser of first and second mortgages, lump sum medical disengagement of $82,000, cheap holiday homes throughout New Zealand, insurance cover on everything from a serving officer's life to a boat and trailer, from a burn cream prescription to open-heart surgery. The New Zealand Police Staff Benevolent and Welfare Fund offers an all-embracing security blanket for a group that had, until recent times, never known such protection. And these service organisations flourished just in time to free the police from personal and family anxieties as policing became increasingly complex, dangerous and stressful.

Moodie's and Butterworth's philosophical commitment to a better deal for the average police officer set the scene for late 1970s change. Their key achievement was getting the government to accept the need for a government-subsidised insurance scheme that would handle medical insurance. This took from December 1977 to May 1979, and Butterworth says only the battle for early retirement was more arduous. Then, it was their good fortune and nous in hiring a recently retired insurance man, with all the commercial skills and the commitment to go with them, that accelerated the dramatic welfare improvements of the 1980s. The story of the welfare fund is dominated by the initiatives of Moodie and Butterworth and the know-how of Tom Robbie, turning a modest insurance scheme into a hugely successful enterprise. First, though, there were four decades of slowly improving self-help.

Members always knew what they wanted, even if their representatives did not know how to get it for them. General Secretary Ian Campbell proposed a group assurance scheme to the management committee in September

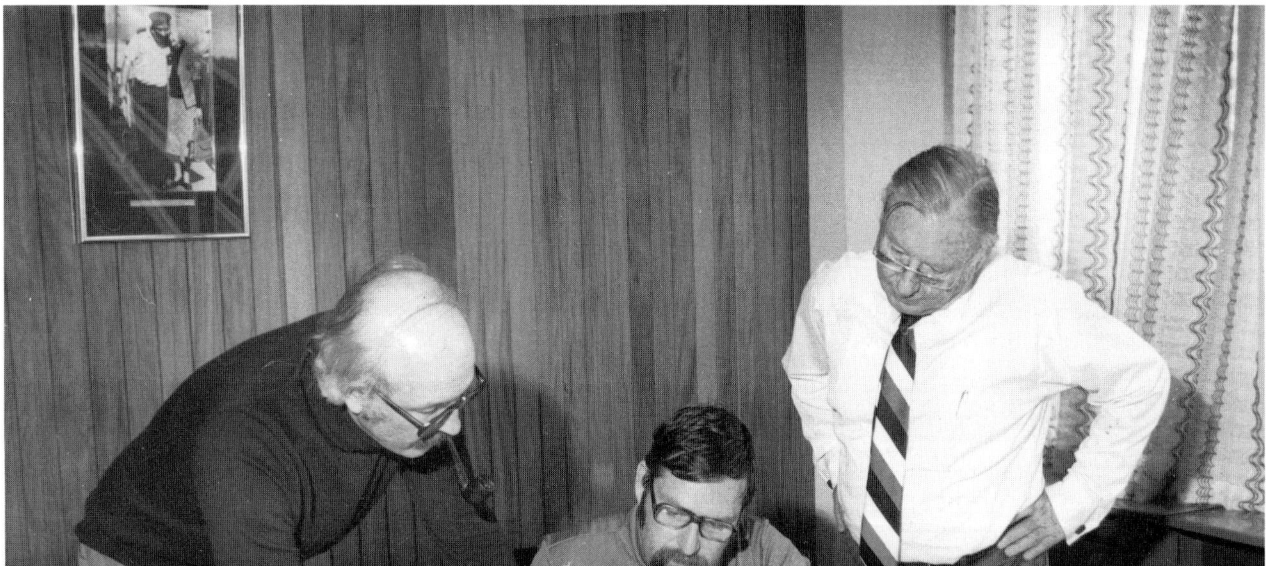

Tom Robbie, on the right, was the retired insurance man Moodie and Butterworth hired to run the health plan. Robbie helped to make the entire welfare fund and credit union operations a goldmine of security and success for the association and guild

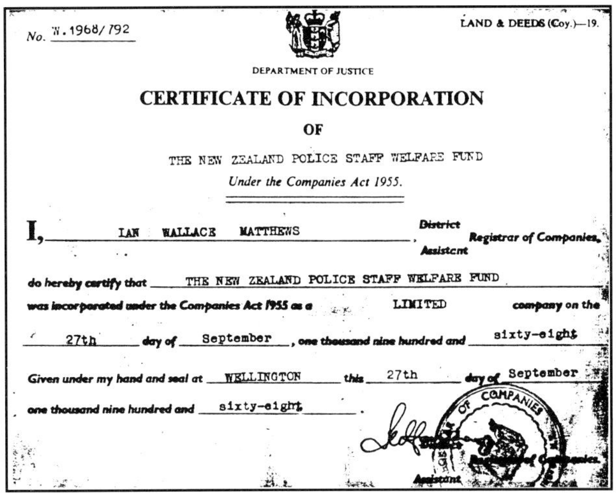

No. W.1968/792

LAND & DEEDS (Coy.)—19.

DEPARTMENT OF JUSTICE

CERTIFICATE OF INCORPORATION

OF

THE NEW ZEALAND POLICE STAFF WELFARE FUND

Under the Companies Act 1955.

I, IAN WALLACE MATTHEWS, District / Assistant Registrar of Companies,

do hereby certify that THE NEW ZEALAND POLICE STAFF WELFARE FUND

was incorporated under the Companies Act 1955 as a LIMITED company on the

27th day of September, one thousand nine hundred and sixty-eight

Given under my hand and seal at WELLINGTON this 27th day of September

one thousand nine hundred and sixty-eight.

Assistant Registrar of Companies.

The welfare fund certificate of incorporation, the start of what would be the making of the service organisations

1937, but no action was taken. The 1937 conference directed the management committee to report on a possible death benefit scheme, even though the management committee was against it 'in view of the coming Social Security legislation'.

By the 1938 conference a number of policemen had proposed schemes. H.J. Joyce suggested £100 payment on death. J.H. Ward added that members leaving the association through promotion or retirement should have the option of continuing to contribute to the scheme. A.B. Meiklejohn favoured a £25 benefit, with members paying 2s 6d a year, and an extra levy of 1s if more than six members died in one year.

Detective H.C. Murch of Auckland proposed a Mortuary Benefit Scheme paying out £100 and members paying in £1 per annum. He reasoned that, although some members were insured, the insurance policy may have been borrowed against or otherwise mortgaged. When some members died a local or national subscription list was circulated, but this provided a pittance, and there were many members who did not attract a subscription.

Murch wanted his scheme open to all police, including commissioned officers. He wanted it voluntary, co-operative and not exclusive of age or health conditions. To demonstrate his proposal, Murch prepared a table showing how the fund would have operated from 1921. Deaths over the period to 1936 averaged over five a year, payouts would have totalled £8,900 and income would have been £17,600. He allowed for £1,058 return of one-quarter of contributions to those leaving the scheme.

Remits at the 1938 conference from Christchurch, Timaru, Whangarei and Palmerston North generally favoured the £25 death benefit. It would be partly charitable, partly self-interested, in the words of the general secretary, 'to assist the widow and dependants of a member who had not left them in comfortable circumstances'. It would also be a useful channel for savings. Members took another year to agree to this Death Benefit Fund.

Payments began in 1939, £100 in the first year. By 1945 £925 had been paid out, and there was a move to extend the scheme to a benevolent or sickness benefit fund. Constable J.R. Williamson told his fellows that he looked upon the association 'as a society of men fighting for the same goal, that is, the betterment of all'. He hoped the association debate on a sickness fund would soon lead to its establishment, for the 1931 earthquake at Napier had involved constables there in considerable expenditure on furniture and personal effects. Members had contributed £741 to the Hawke's Bay Relief Fund, but if there was an established fund it 'could relieve comrades in stricken areas'. A questionnaire of members showed that 1024 agreed, 93 did not and 460 had no views.

Auckland had an existing model benevolent fund, largely as a result of the encouragement of then Superintendent James Cummings, soon to be commissioner. From figures supplied by the Police Department in 1944 the annual conference set about establishing a fund that would pay members half-pay sick leave for a sub of 7s per annum. Payments began on 1 February 1946, the payout established at 6s a day, the limit 12 weeks. That year 1259 joined, £435 1s was paid in and £231 12s was paid out to 24 members. By 30 September 1952 the total benefit payout was £1,527, and the total subs amounted to £3,439 17s 4d. The surplus had been invested in government stock to a value of £995, the remainder held in the current account.

From the beginning of 1953 subs were raised to 10s and benefits doubled to 12s a day, with no restriction on the period spent on the benefit. Meltzer observed drily that, by careful management and good luck in 'keeping the amount of sickness within due bounds', the fund had been able to consolidate and could meet future claims with confidence. The sickness benefit 'is one of, if not the greatest achievement of the New Zealand Police Association'. Most members belonged. In 1962 47 commissioned officers accepted the offer to join, boosting membership to 2420 in a year when subs were £1,281 13s 4d, payments £981 6s to 35 members.

President W.A.P. Back told the 1964 conference that the 1953 10s rise had been the only one in 19 years. By now £10,449 had been distributed and death benefit payouts were £5,575. He attributed the satisfactory reserve to 'a reasonably good standard of health amongst our members'. He thought the scheme showed 'we are not deficient in the art of do-it-yourself'. The next conference increased the death benefit to £50 and then Christchurch delegate Tommy Thomson argued for extending it to £100. This was agreed, in time for his widow to receive the first £100 payout.

It took several conferences of debate before delegates agreed to have the death benefit underwritten by the Royal Insurance Company, for $500. Meltzer had urged caution on the grounds that the insurer would take almost half the contributions as his profit. The requirement of compulsion was unpopular, with the recent compulsory contribution to the Council of Sport still rankling. Treasury Regulation H 62 held up the possibility of compulsory deductions.

The changes came in 1967 after a questionnaire showed 1042 in favour of a new welfare fund, with 76 opposed. Peter Matheson of Nelson had promoted the group insurance plan, and this was to be basis of the new scheme. On 27 September 1968 the New Zealand Police Staff Welfare Fund came into being, a company limited by the guarantee of its members. The management committee elected the first board—chairman Rob Butler, executive director Dave Lee, members Dan Ingram, J.S. Kuzmich, I.L. Mills, J.F. Quirke and B.A. Toomey. The board framed the mandatory and discretionary rules and took over the assets of the Sickness Benefit Fund. Retiring members could stay in if they paid the $3.60 sub.

The welfare fund paid out a $2,000 death benefit. The *Police Journal* warned members not to rely on this, plus the Government Superannuation Fund and some additional life insurance cover. There might be a payout of $20,000, but this would not provide a debt-free home, maintain it and the living standards of dependants, including education and holidays. All were urged to join, and most did; the membership was 2871, with only 21 police not in the scheme.

There were also suggestions about establishing a credit union and holiday homes, but the first matter addressed was that the welfare fund was not covering all medical expenses. In 1969 the board authorised a voluntary scheme with the Southern Cross Medical Society, with a 10 per cent discount. This began on 1 August 1969, and 350 joined. By 1971 there were 555 in the scheme, with payments of $3,683 representing 80 per cent of the costs on 38 claims, mostly for operations on wives and children of members. The family sub was $26.46.

In March 1974 the fund increased its death and disablement benefit to $5,000, doubling the payout to $400 for the death of a member's spouse or a retired member, $200 for a dependant's death, $50 for home aid, $4 a day sickness benefit. The sub was increased from 42 to 76 cents a fortnight. In 1975 a Benevolent Fund was proposed, the death benefit was increased to $8,000, discretionary grants were allowed following the death of a member.

At his last meeting in October 1976 Hamish Thomas reported the death benefit trebled to $15,000, after considerable research and negotiation with the Guardian Royal Exchange Insurance Group. Premiums were up $1.20 to $2.08 per fortnightly pay. A Benevolent Fund prospectus was being drafted by Bell, Gully & Co., and Thomas had hoped it would be ready for his last meeting. Although the board voted Thomas thanks for his 'untiring efforts and accomplishments', it was as well the Benevolent Fund was not ready.

Rob Moodie arrived and promptly declared the Welfare

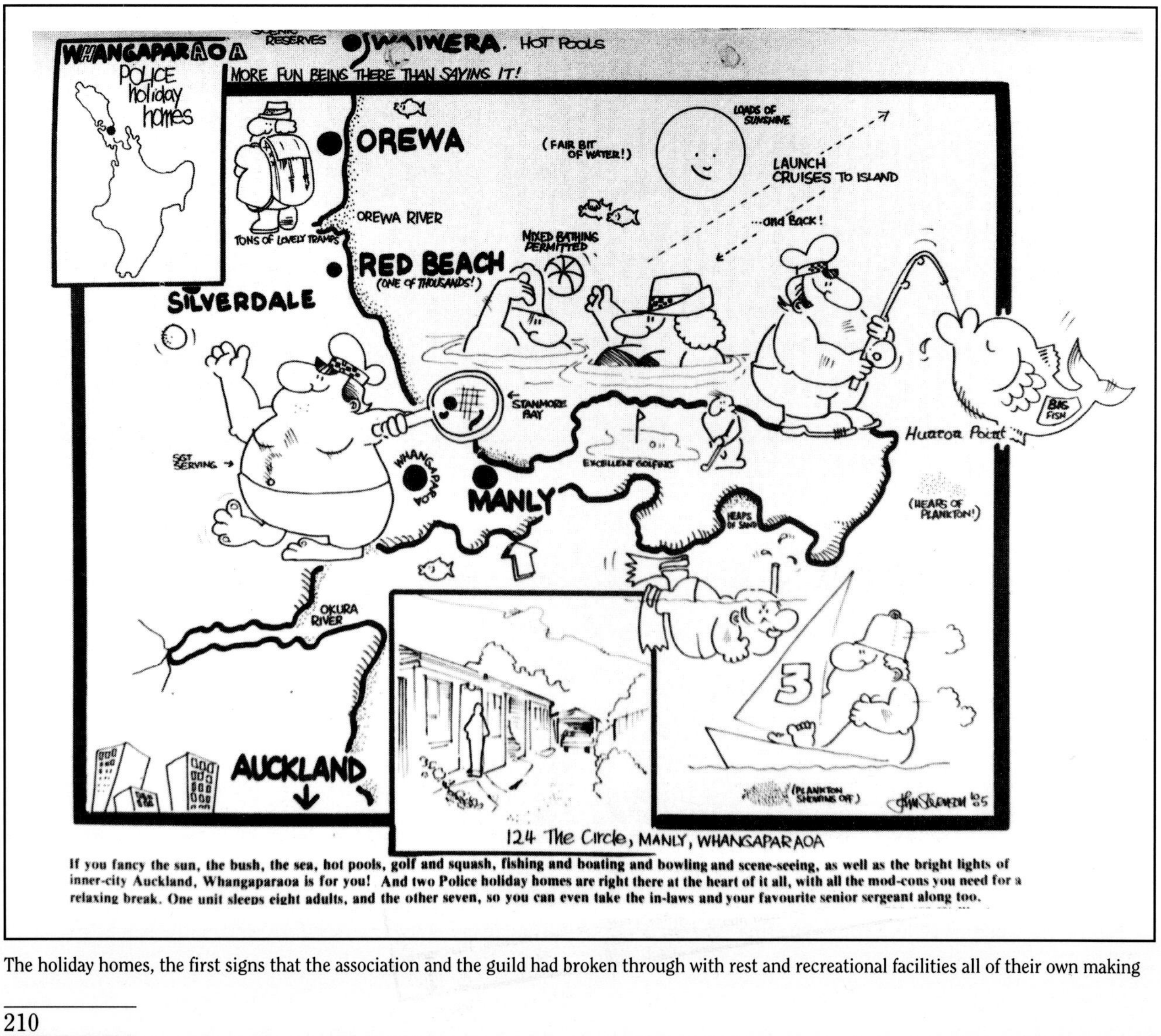

The holiday homes, the first signs that the association and the guild had broken through with rest and recreational facilities all of their own making

January 1982, NZ Police Association Newsletter *Page 7*

N.Z. Police Staff Benevolent and Welfare Fund

HOLIDAY HOMES

May School Holidays

The following are the rental periods set aside for ballots of the Police Holiday Homes.

Ballot 1, 12 noon May 8, 1982 to 10 a.m. May 15, 1982

Ballot 2, 12 noon May 15, 1982 to 10 a.m. May 22, 1982

APPLICATIONS FOR BALLOTS CLOSE AT 4.30 p.m. ON MONDAY MARCH 15, 1982.

The N.Z. Police Staff Benevolent and Welfare Fund now has nine holiday homes. They are situate at:—

1. Lake Tekapo
2. McKee Avenue, Rotorua
3. Ranolf Street, Rotorua
4. Lake Taupo
5. Lake Wanaka
6. Lake Te Anau
7. Napier
8. Raumati
9. Nelson

The present charges for each holida ... night with a maximum of $60 per week. A deposit of $10 is required no later than 14 ... booking, and the balance is to be paid on receipt of the final accoun ... month before the date of occupancy of any particula ... month) a deposit is liable to be f ... occupancy, the member is liable ...

Could all members please note th ... the National Office. You are quit ... not be made collect.

IMPORTANT: Long weekend ... than two advar ... continuing hc ...

HOLIDAY HOME AVAILABILITY

	MAY	JUNE	JULY	AUG	SEPT	OCT
CHRISTCHURCH 1	N	Y	Y	Y	Y	Y
CHRISTCHURCH 2	N	Y	Y	Y	Y	Y
TAUPO 1	Y	Y	Y	Y	Y	Y
TAUPO 2	Y	Y	N	Y	Y	Y
TAUPO 3	Y	Y	Y	Y	Y	Y
ROTORUA 4	Y	Y	Y	Y	Y	Y
ROTORUA 5	Y	Y	Y	Y	Y	Y
ROTORUA 6	Y	Y	Y	Y	Y	Y
NAPIER 1	Y	Y	Y	Y	Y	Y
NAPIER	Y	Y	Y	Y	Y	Y
TURANGI 1	Y	B	B	B	Y	Y
TURANGI 2	Y	B	B	B	Y	Y
NELSON 1	N	N	Y	Y	Y	Y
NELSON 2	N	Y	Y	Y	Y	Y
PARAPARAUMU	N	Y	Y	Y	Y	Y
TE ANAU	N	Y	Y	Y	Y	Y
WANAKA	N	B	B	B	Y	Y
TEKAPO	N	B	B	B	Y	Y
LIMESTONE DOWNS 1	Y	Y	Y	Y	Y	Y
LIMESTONE DOWNS 2	Y	Y	Y	Y	Y	Y

B: = Ballot
Y: = Available
N: = Booked

All the above are correct at the time of print. Any further queries please contact Hugh Johnson at the National Office (04) 720-198.

Please note NEW home at Limestone Downs, great for fishing or sheer relaxation. 15km approx south of Port Waikato. Caretaker Mrs. J. Taylor ph. 866.

May 1990

Fund a disaster. There was no money in it, there were no holiday homes, the subs had been used to run the office. 'It needed,' he said, 'leadership to think things through. We dumped virtually the whole executive.'

Moodie's first meeting with the board of directors was on 3 February 1977. Those present were chairman K.J. Holland, H.E. Bos, L. Maher, A.K. Waugh, A.J. Joyce, L.E. Cooper, T.W. Morley, Moodie and Revington, with apologies from Dan Ingram and Peter Matheson. Revington, as outgoing secretary, announced that the anticipated formality of appointing the benevolent fund trustees would not proceed 'following discussions with Dr Moodie'. Moodie explained to the board that he did not like two separate groups handling the same matters, two funds with two administrations, and could see no point in having Benevolent Fund trustees appointed by the commissioner, the association, the guild and the Welfare Fund. It would be administratively inconvenient. He proposed, instead, a merger of the two so that those concerned 'would be able to devote all their energies to the helping of policemen and their families'.

After general discussion, Monk moved and Joyce seconded the investigation of amalgamation. Before they dispersed Moodie suggested they look at the Welfare Fund itself underwriting the death benefit. Monk and Waugh put this and the board carried the motion. In May the amalgamation was recognised in the official name change to the New Zealand Police Staff Benevolent and Welfare Fund.

The minutes had soon trebled in size, indicative of Moodie's impact. He drove through death benefit cover of $35,000, with the government to pay three-quarters of it. The premium was renegotiated with Guardian Royal Exchange down to $1.40 a fortnight, the $53,000 saved to be used to raise the spouse death benefit to $2,500. Sick leave was increased to $5 a day and $16 a week when half-pay ceased. The specialist benefit was raised to 50 per cent of the fee charged, home aid was increased to $75, and a new 'benevolent benefit' up to $300 was paid where a member suffered serious injury on or off duty. Other new benefits were $15 per birth (with 300 births anticipated), $25 for an eye test, 50 per cent of the cost of a hearing aid.

Moodie brought immediate improvements, but the structure did not change. He was automatically secretary and a director of the welfare fund. His new board appointed in the December by the management committee of the association was Chief Inspector M.D. Cummings, Senior Sergeant N.B. Trendle, Sergeant W.T. McNeil, Sergeant H.E. Bos, Constable G. Dynes, Dan Ingram, Senior Sergeant R.S.F. Halpin and Sergeant A.J. Monk.

Holiday homes were a matter Moodie decided would no longer be pending. On 3 November 1977 he reported that Whangarei had recently circulated to all district committees a proposal to have sites owned by the department evaluated for possible holiday homes. Christchurch and Timaru indicated that they were keen, the latter negotiating to purchase a section at Lake Tekapo. The research officer of the association was directed to find out all the properties owned by the department. At the December meeting Butterworth reported back that the department's works officer had raised legal objections, so it was decided to take the matter up with the commissioner. Butterworth says it was Moodie forcing Guardian Royal Exchange to share profits on members' life insurance which financed the first holiday home.

Moodie got the commissioner's support for the homes. Sections at Paraparaumu and Lake Tekapo were assessed as suitable and a three-year-old three-bedroom home at Lake Wanaka was being considered at a price of $28,000. Moodie told the January 1978 meeting that the desired type of holiday home had not yet been established, but a suburban two-bedroom Lockwood he had inspected looked attractive for $22,000.

Monk and Moodie visited the Wanaka and Tekapo sites, which were approved for purchase as a joint venture of the welfare fund and the association.The rental would be $30 to $35 a week and another purchase at Te Anau would allow a cheap holiday circuit of the South Island lakes. Moodie and Monk also visited Taupo and Rotorua sites, Butterworth followed up with visits to Paraparaumu, Taupo and Russell, and Moodie negotiated with the department and government over these sites. He took the lowest quote for a McRae A-frame at Tekapo of $23,689.

By January 1979 members were being offered holiday homes at Tekapo and Te Anau for the May holidays, at a maximum rental of $35 a week. The *Newsletter* suggested that the homes were an opportunity 'for promoting a spirit of fellowship in the police'. At the October 1979 conference of the welfare fund Moodie announced that the holiday homes were going well and that the fund would take them over. This way the capital assets of the fund could be better invested in welfare securities.

Subs were increased because of the increased demand on the fund, after a two-year campaign through the *Newsletter* and posters to publicise benefits to members. Moodie was a champion for the fund. When Commissioner Walton questioned whether there was a legal obligation to collect subs from resigning or retiring members, Moodie told him that the issue was to identify and respond to obligations to all members, particularly retired ones, in relation to their entitlement to the group insurance scheme.

Typical of Moodie's approach was a case that came up at the 22 June 1979 fund board meeting. A constable had died suddenly at 51, and eight years later his widow was in trouble with expenses she could not recover. After paying her state house rent, she had only $45 a week to live on. Her husband had been a member of the Government Superannuation Fund, but that yielded only $3,000. The costs of travel and accommodation to receive osteoarthritic treatment had required her to get an overdraft from her bank. The welfare officer had told Moodie there were no other grants available to her.

Rick Bos moved and Neville Trendle seconded that the fund pay her $419, the welfare officer apply for a benefit for her and the Health Department pay travel and accommodation costs in future. Wayne McNeil spoke against the motion, asking what her several children were doing for her; he wanted more facts. Ron Halpin was inclined McNeil's way. George Dynes thought the situation should be looked at. Trendle, worried about the interest on her overdraft, wanted to amend the motion to pay $200 towards this. Bos was simply worried that she had had no help for eight years, and had come to the fund. She had mortgaged half of her investment, so he would not support Trendle's amendment.

Moodie cut short these ramblings. He would, he said, be disappointed if the board put obstacles in the path of people who sought assistance. That was something the government did. The woman already had trouble with her overdraft because she had not kept receipts. Yet her husband had paid into the fund all his life, on the agreement that his dependants would receive assistance. The motion was put and carried.

That year almost $36,000 was paid out on such benefits as one death, one wife's death, six x-rays, three chiropractic, four physiotherapist and eight specialist treatments, 31 eye tests, one hearing aid, three sickness benefits and 18 births. Total deposits were $46,000, including $404 holiday home rentals mostly from Taupo and Tekapo; Te Anau and Wanaka were less popular.

At the 13 September 1979 board meeting Moodie mapped the path ahead. The association had authorised a committee of financial and legal experts to look into the establishment of a viable long-term loan facility for house mortgage finance. The association was recommending that the police cancel their existing insurance policies because they lacked any savings element or equity built up with a lending institution. Moodie said they could do the savings job themselves, and relend money to members in conjunction with the credit union.

Butterworth added that when they had a computer paid for by the fund, the credit union and the association, they would record memberships, benefits, contributions, holiday home bookings and credit union work. Moodie said they were estimating $30,000 to $50,000 for a second-hand computer, and were not going to be sidetracked by computer world propaganda. Trendle wondered if they needed a consultant; Butterworth said they knew what they wanted. They could, Moodie pointed out, go round in circles and not get anywhere.

Alas, they got the runaround from computer salespeople. The first computer purchases were disasters. Moodie threatened legal action and three years later Philips accepted liability for the failure, agreeing to pay the difference between the original contract price and the large new computer Moodie had ordered from Wang. Moodie cited $180,000 as the Philips contribution.

Some in the association became thoroughly alarmed at these large figures. Revell objected to $120,000 of association funds being involved, but Walkinshaw pointed out that it was a three-way split between association, fund and credit union. Moodie said there was no alternative to the Wang system, there being no other computer at that level in the market. Revell made the traditional objection that the management committee was just a rubber stamp, while Waugh described it as an 'horrific exercise'. Moodie told them that if he had waited a month for them all to discuss the matter, they would have missed the bus. One of the reasons the association was so successful was that he and Butterworth felt confident to act when the occasion presented itself. Butterworth added that the most successful management committee meetings were when only half of the members made it to Wellington, and spent the day being briefed on what had been done. Revell wondered if they might come in the night before, but Waugh dismissed this as in danger of reverting to the old think tanks.

Revell and fellow Aucklander Hilt had not been happy about what looked to them like Moodie dictating progress. On 1 December 1981 the Invercargill district committee wrote to Moodie about the structure and election of the welfare fund board by the management committee was 'unconstitutional and undemocratic'. Invercargill wanted an elected board and a look at who decided where holiday homes were purchased, such as the one at Ohakune. Moodie tended to meet such criticisms with a suggestion that members look at the results; if they were not happy, he would step down.

In 1984 he was again being questioned, this time about office staff being involved in investment with regard to the Manners Street property being sold. The welfare fund had by now burgeoned to the extent of having $306,000 equity in the property, the association $92,000. Revell asked whether this imbalance in what had been half-shares in the building took into account loans repaid. Moodie confirmed that it did—the $107,000 the association owed the fund. Revell thought such sales money should go into another investment, but Moodie replied that the management committee of the association and the welfare fund had to look at a proper form of investment. He did not want to see them going into commercial property again—'that was a nonsense investment'.

Alan Monk, the man who bought the building at auction, told the meeting that the building had cost $190,000 and was being sold for $500,000; it had been a reasonable investment. He moved, and Halpin seconded, that the Manners Street property sale be ratified. It was.

When Boyd repeated reservations about staff being involved in investment, Moodie said that the welfare fund was at its present state because the staff had invested. In the past three years $1,000,000 had been invested in real estate, and money from those investments provided benefits for members. He advocated continuing the policy and avoiding the difficulties of the PSIS and some Australian credit unions. There was plenty of money around; he suggested going into motel complexes. The Police Centennial Trust would do just that at Whangaparaoa in 1986, but it managed to finish the job in 1988 only because the welfare fund bailed out the fancy chalet project with a cash injection of $100,000 and a loan of $300,000.

That the welfare fund became a big earner and a big spender in the 1980s hinged on the involvement of retired insurance expert Tom Robbie who, in 1984, began to run the fledgling Police Health Plan introduced in 1982.

Planning for this had begun in 1979, when a survey demonstrated that, despite some police being covered privately, there was an urgent need to provide comprehensive medical insurance for police families. National councillors and welfare fund directors were adamant that the scheme must be owned and controlled by members, so they could stipulate the benefits required, establish a premium and write their own contract. It was still believed that the established health industry would have the expertise to administer it. The existing benefits provided by the welfare fund would be taken over and extended by the health plan, providing a greater range of specialist treatment. Profit sharing would ensure that the bulk of any surplus was not lost to members. The credit union would collect the premiums and civilian employees could join. New Zealand Medi-Care won the contract.

The health plan was an instant success. Welfare fund chairman Peter Mairs, administration representative on the new-look board Moodie had deployed, reported that in the 17 months to June 1983 the plan had paid out $416,986 in benefits, compared with $18,877 the previous year. There were 5094 members and a further 3438 retired members and families paying into the plan through the credit union.

Mairs told the fund agm on 13 October 1983 that, as the department's personnel director, he was implementing the new employment structure for the police, based on earlier retirement and a system of fitness standards for 'alternative employment or compensation for staff who fail to meet those standards and who are medically retired'. The welfare fund was subsequently closely involved in developing the standards of physical, medical and psychological help, in the government-subsidised life insurance and administration of the 1985 mortgage fund.

The introduction of these standards and the lowering of the normal retiring age to 55 meant police had to face up to 'a foreshortened Police career'. Members therefore had to manage their assets so that, if they did not meet the standards, 'the family will not be catastrophically affected'. The police welfare officers, the welfare fund and the credit union had to work together to ensure the health and financial stability of police families. They already had a high level of protection at reasonable cost through the health plan, the group life insurance, the sick leave bank and Staffguard. With significant numbers of police retiring or disengaging, the welfare fund must ensure that they enjoyed reasonable cover.

Mairs was the key man to co-ordinate administration and welfare fund initiatives. Butterworth rates Mairs highly for his intelligence, warmth, humour and receptiveness to the unorthodox proposals coming from the welfare fund and association. Butterworth says the appointment of Mairs as chairman of the welfare fund was symbolic of the way the administration co-operated with Moodie and himself. Mairs also told the 13 October 1983 meeting that the fund had provided a marriage guidance and family counselling benefit and a podiatry benefit for those who chose jogging as their way to maintain physical fitness. The fund's insurers, New Zealand Insurance Life, later donated $500 towards the $2,500 costs of the gymnasium provided in the Princess Towers association office. Most important of all, perhaps, was the administration recommendation to the government in 1985 that the welfare fund should be the agency responsible for managing mortgage monies coming from the Government Superannuation Fund. There was no perhaps about it. The mortgage monies were the key to the big welfare fund expansion, but the government had to be convinced that the fund directors could do the job.

Alec Waugh played a key role as the association and guild representative on the Government Superannuation Board in the early 1980s, when the push was on to get some of the police contributions to government superannuation back in police hands. This would resolve the oldest problem for the police—how to afford their own housing.

The problem arose because the police had to maintain a presence throughout the country. To do this individual police usually had to accept at least three shifts in their career, those seeking promotion as many as six or more. The obvious disadvantage was that the officer and family had to accept a station house or other rental accommodation—about 900 still did in the early 1980s—which trapped them in the police housing structure. Even those who owned their own houses were disadvantaged by transfers. They had no time to build up a large equity in a house and the need to refinance new mortgages meant higher interest rates and shorter repayment periods.

Some police ended up in desperate straits. One had five mortgages piled on top of each other, each new one taken out to cope with the previous one. The officer collapsed under the strain. It was Tom Robbie who negotiated the five mortgages back to just one and saved the officer's career and sanity.

The 1981 census showed that 26.8 per cent of New Zealanders owned their own houses, 5.2 per cent of police. With the introduction of early retirement/optional disengagement, more police would be leaving, some because they were required to do so. The housing problem would be critical. The solution, said Mairs, was long-term transferable mortgages.

Alec Waugh had the job of getting this across to control department negotiators and others on the Government Superannuation Board. They did not, he says, see the police as a special case and were 'very conscious of Moodie, very worried about his dress and comments'. Waugh, the available butt of this anxiety, endured unpleasant remarks, once being called 'a wanker'. 'We bashed and bashed at the brick wall,' he says. 'One day Treasury said yes.'

Butterworth credits Dave Swallow of State Services as the key figure in allowing the welfare fund to run the scheme because he 'considered that we would run it fairly'. Experience suggested that if a department was in control, it could not resist using the scheme to retire difficult personnel. Another problem for the control departments, according to Waugh, was that Moodie was articulating concepts no other private or public sector union had thought of, let alone put on the table for negotiation.

Waugh believes there was jealousy and resentment, particularly from the PSA and the Post Office Union after the police won 20 per cent of their savings back from the superannuation fund. Other public service departments eventually got modified forms of access to their super, but the police received a huge cash injection of $14,000,000 over five years. And they got to keep and use it, adding to the rolling fund with interest and capital payments from borrowers, swelling the fund to huge proportions.

The Government Superannuation Fund Police Mortgage Scheme came on stream on 5 August 1985. Secretary Gary Fulton told the 1986 welfare fund agm that 369 applications had been received totalling $13,000,000, and so far 292 had been approved. A crying need had been met. The stream was soon a flood, and Fulton anticipated that, in 10 years' time, there would be $50,000,000 in the fund.

When Revell questioned whether the interest rates were too high, Fulton replied that it was not their scheme but that of the Government Superannuation Fund. They had proved their point in the early retirement negotiations—recognition that the police were often on the move and faced the shock of retirement with no home. The negotiated situation was that the government dictated the terms, and nothing could be done about that.

A lot could be done, though, to renegotiate better terms in private insurance schemes run by the welfare fund. Butterworth and Moodie had known the man for the job. They had dealt with Tom Robbie when he was managing Southern Cross medical insurance for them, and Butterworth had worked closely with him as a director of New Zealand Medi-Care. The company decided that Robbie should retire, but he had plenty of energy left in him and 18 years' experience in the medical insurance field. He was hired to run the Police Health Plan.

'There was a lot of dissatisfaction with the way it was run,' says Robbie. 'I was employed I think because I was confident we could by self-funding of health insurance give infinitely better value than an outside underwriter.' Moodie had always wanted that. The old theory of setting an insurance man to catch insurance profits was put to the test. Butterworth says Robbie added salesmanship and good business administration 'to breathe life into the credit union and the voluntary aspects'.

'When I arrived,' says Robbie, 'there was nothing. They had fire and general insurance, welfare benefits that were fairly restrictive in use, outside health insurers, about 10 holiday homes. Small potatoes.'

The first saving was himself; he would sell the new plan. In 1984, along with association president Keith Morrow, he took the 'Health Plan circus' on the road, addressing recruits, in-service training and retirement groups, visited every police station in the land. It was a six-week journey from North Cape to Bluff. Morrow would explain the early retirement and optional disengagement benefits to members, then Robbie would tell them how good the welfare fund was, what it cost, what the benefits were, why they should use their credit union. They held three seminars a day, 40 minutes each, such as Auckland Central in the morning, Otahuhu in the afternoon and Takapuna at night. Robbie says it almost killed him.

Robbie has the bounce and bravura to prove that insurance can be fun. Far from killing him, working for the police gave him a new lease of life, and he repaid his clients in megabucks, proving an irresistible salesman. Unlike the computer pedlars Butterworth and Moodie had to contend with, he offered real advantages. And the members could see it, from the word go in Invercargill, where 100 automatic payments into the credit union catchment were authorised on the spot.

The first objective was achieved, a good cash flow. Robbie had the flexibility to decide premiums and payouts on the spot, a phone call to a director or two and the matter was approved. There were none of the brochures with which insurance companies touted for business. There was no waiting a year to get a premium reassessed by an insurance company board. The assessment of the premium was a piece of cake, predictable within 1 per cent from knowing the incidence of claims and the rate of inflation, divided by 52 weeks. Robbie could offer greater benefits for the same premium.

In the first nine months Robbie and association historian Dave Paterson handled 4000 claims worth $360,000 and a yearly income of $500,000. Robbie had inherited a health insurance file of complaints by claimants as thick as a breeze block. In his first year there were three complaints, not enough to wrap the breeze block in. The complaints were settled there and then on the phone.

The police have a flourishing grapevine. It took no time for the message to spread that the insurance joker was performing. Robbie would get welfare officers ringing from all over the country. Some officer needed a break from work. Robbie would get him a holiday home. If he was broke, without a car, Robbie would telegraph $200 cash and set him up with a rental car. There was no waiting until the next board meeting chewed their collective cuds over the problem, as they had with the widow for whom Moodie had pleaded.

Robbie guesses that 75 per cent of police problems are overcome by the welfare fund, the remainder by the department. With him the problems were solved immediately; with the department a problem goes through a hierarchy of strict rules and lengthy delays.

The mortgage fund brought a big slice of money into the welfare fund, and Robbie made sure that money made money. Already he had swelled the coffers by persuading the board to appoint brokers Bain Clarkson Ltd, who provided specialist insurance expertise. Robbie brokered the brokers, making deals for a share of what was left after premiums and administration costs. The split, he says gleefully, was an even one, 80 per cent to us, 20 to them.

In the first 12 months Robbie sorted out the health plan. Robbie turned next to fire and general, getting the statistics from the underwriters and analysing them. The loss on household goods, mostly lost or stolen items, was very high. When Robbie dissected claims into geographical areas, he discovered that one member would lose a watch and then there would be a rash of lost watch claims from this area. In another area there would be a run of lost engagement rings, in another lost earrings. The underwriters protested that the police did their own investigations of burglaries and losses, whereas the general public had to get the police to establish a burglary or loss. The police had a loss ratio on household goods of 110 per cent, which meant that, for every dollar premium paid, the insurance company paid out $1.10. The national average was 72 cents on the dollar. The police were put into a separate file as the worst insurance risk group, and consequently their premiums were that much higher.

When Robbie reported his findings, the board authorised him to tell several members to go down the road. He wrote to another 20 members telling them that they had 12 months in which to improve their performance. He says the police grapevine did the rest.

Once this petty corruption was sorted out, Robbie could get the claims handled by the brokers and start making a commercial operation out of it. One of his problems was that very few police officers on the various boards were commercially trained, though they were expert on welfare matters. The task was to strike a balance between welfare functions and commercial viability. Profit was totally unknown. At each agm, he says, Moodie would announce what figure they were down, say $100,000, and then announce that they would only have to increase subs 50 cents to bring things right.

Robbie negotiated the fire and insurance collection fee from 1 to 5 per cent, half to the credit union for doing the collecting and half to the welfare fund. The cost was to the underwriters, not the members. The underwriters were not objecting because they were getting a cash flow of $2,500,000 annually from police fire and general insurance, guaranteed fortnightly. They were prepared to pay for that.

Then Robbie changed the name of the fire and general insurance to Staffpac, allowing the police to change underwriter without having to change their promotional literature. Guardian Royal Exchange was running it when he arrived, but each year it went out to tender.

In his third year Robbie announced a $250,000 surplus of income over claims, from health insurance alone. After putting some away for claims, most went into the welfare fund. Benefits were increased, new benefits added, premiums stayed the same. There was plenty of money.

Robbie turned his attention to spending the surplus on holiday homes, which he had doubled to 28 by the time he retired in 1990. Moodie favoured big homes with carpets and mahogany furniture, to give the cops some luxury they would not normally have, but Robbie soon discovered that the average cop preferred smaller homes that were easier to look after. The first two he bought were Lockwoods at Turangi, with brown tweedy carpets and formica tables. He sold the big Napier and Nelson homes far from the beach and bought small seaside places and had two more Lockwoods built in Christchurch, one in conjunction with the International Police Association. He paid cash, negotiated good deals with builders, bought the furniture—everything from light fittings to carpets—wholesale. He was having a ball, a late developer in the can-do tradition.

Robbie was not happy with 44 per cent occupancy rate for holiday homes, which was too low to make money. He wrote holiday home brochures, publicised the homes in every *Newsletter*, printed charts to show when they were available. Occupancy went up to 78 per cent, income to $130,000. Putting aside $35,000 for neglected repairs, he went round the homes himself to replace worn carpet and furniture.

When Robbie arrived the welfare fund board was dealing with relatively small grants of the order of $5,000. 'That changed,' says Robbie, 'when we got into managing a large fund. You couldn't sit and go through every claim. We were handling 200 a week.' So Robbie processed claims as he went.

The death and disablement insurance was another mess, because there was no written policy. Robbie, Bain Clarkson and the underwriters wrote one defining eligibility to claim, approving a claims panel, and setting the mechanism for claiming. Before this the policy solicitors were forever coming to Robbie with entitlement claims on behalf of members.

Death insurance was negotiated up to $120,000 for a member, half that for a spouse. Butterworth remembers this as his last negotiating session where he stuck to the objective even when the insurance company suspended cover for a week. He believes this shocked the administration to such an extent that they got the subsidy level they wanted. Robbie introduced more flexibility into the initial arrangements. The welfare fund sent a cheque for $1,500 to the widow immediately for funeral bills and to keep the house going where many had had only the fortnightly pay coming in. If the welfare officer suggested more, perhaps $5,000, Robbie dispensed it, deducting it from the insurance cheque.

Robbie was supposed to consider only specialists' reports, but he knew from years in insurance that specialists always write a report that favours the individual over the insurance company. He was punctilious about investigating claimants' medical background. He had to be when, as well as the 7.5 per cent contribution from members, there was the 15 per cent government contribution.

The grin disappears when Robbie considers the media suspicion that perfing was a golden handshake. In 1987 there was bad publicity about the 125 officers who had disengaged on medical grounds or perfed, along with 277 retiring early and 24 medically retired in the first two years of the scheme. The media had located the doubtful cases, such as a Christchurch detective sergeant acquitted of stereo theft while doing undercover work and disengaged. Robbie objects that no investigation was made of the conditions the member had endured in this most stressful and dangerous of police jobs. Another detective involved in a fatal shooting and disengaged, was reported by the media working as a real estate agent. Robbie is indignant. The policeman shot recovered physically, but not psychologically, and so received his $82,000.

What is Staffpac?

Staffpac is a special insurance scheme that your Police Association has arranged under which you can cover your home, contents and personal effects, cars, caravans, trailers and your pleasurecraft.

Benefits

- Plain English Wordings that are easy to understand.
- First Class Claims Service from any NZI INSURANCE BRANCH.
- All insurances under one Package for easy reference.
- Premiums paid monthly by your Credit Union to ease your finances.
- Wide choice of policies with competitive premiums.

What is Covered?

1. **YOUR HOME** — You can choose from our **PEACE OF MIND — TOTAL REPLACEMENT POLICY** which covers all accidental damage which is not otherwise excluded up to the **TOTAL REPLACEMENT COST** of your home. (A standard $25 excess applies on your home) **OR HOUSEOWNERS POLICY** which offers you protection from Fire, Storm, Flood, Burglary and several other events.
2. **YOUR CONTENTS** — You can choose from the **SUPERSURANCE POLICY** which offers cover for all accidental damage which is not otherwise excluded. Claims for Furniture, Fittings, and Home Appliances and Carpets up to 10 years old are paid on REPLACEMENT COST. Other items are on present value. **OR** you may select our **HOUSEHOLDERS POLICY** which covers you for catastrophes as well as water damage, burglary and some accidental damage. Claims are based on the value of your contents at the time of loss. (A standard $100 excess applies on your contents.)
3. Jewellery, Watches, Cameras and their Accessories are included in your Contents Policy up to $2000 any one item. If you require cover for more than this amount, simply specify the item and show us a valuation for it.
4. **YOUR CARS**, Caravans, Trailers that you use only for private use are insured either for **FULL COVER, THIRD PARTY ONLY** or **THIRD PARTY, FIRE AND THEFT COVER.** The vehicle is covered up to its market value at the time of its loss. (A Standard Excess of $250 applies. Also drivers under 25 will have an additional excess applying). Extensions include Windscreen Cover (no excess), Named Driver Discount, and Alcohol Abstinence Discount. New AUTOSURANCE also offers a number of new and exclusive covers. Ask at your local NZI INSURANCE office.
5. **YOUR BOAT OR YACHT** is covered for the usual risks insured under a pleasurecraft policy, including the transit risk for trailered craft. There is no extra Premium for racing your yacht.
6. **BUSINESSES** can also be insured under a NZPA Businessurance policy. You should discuss this specialist cover with NZI INSURANCE, or our consulting brokers, Bain Clarkson (NZ) Ltd, or simply ring our TOLL FREE Number 0800 809 809.

IMPORTANT

This is only a brief outline of the covers that your STAFFPAC POLICY provides. If you are interested in obtaining STAFFPAC or knowing more about it, contact the N.Z. POLICE ASSOCIATION or any branch or office of NZI INSURANCE.

SPECIAL FEATURES THAT CAN SAVE YOU MONEY

- **Voluntary Excess Option.** Generous discounts on your house, contents and car premiums apply if you elect to take a Voluntary Excess Option, instead of the Standard Excess.
- **Unique Package/No Claim Discount.** Special discounts apply if you provide us with proof of no claims for the last 3 years. This discount is available for both existing and new members.
- **Retired Members Discount.** If you are retired from the force and not working, but still a member of the Association and Credit Union, you will be eligible for special discounts.
- **Inquire** at any NZI Insurance Branch or Office or alternatively ring our Toll Free Number 0800 809 809 (Auckland 309 7309).

Staffpac, one of the successful police insurance initiatives of ex-insurance man Tom Robbie

John Turner is the present secretary of the welfare fund

MP Ian Revell made the headlines for getting medical disengagement. As a detective senior sergeant, he had received a serious back injury in the course of his duty. He was no longer fit to be a police officer, his bad back making arrest impossible, but his being medically disengaged did not mean he was not fit for anything else. There was even a woman of about 20 who was medically disengaged, having hurt her back in the police gym. Police are required by their terms of employment to maintain fitness.

Robbie's recommendations on such claims went to a panel made up of a broker, an underwriter and a nominee of the welfare fund. The payout, he says, is equivalent to two years of a senior constable's salary, intended for their rehabilitation into the community. Robbie favours a pension since few receive this lump sum. More would be advantaged by a pension, for it would continue to be paid to dependants.

In April 1990 Robbie retired. When he came in there was one staff member working for the fund; when he left there were four. 'I left,' he says proudly, 'every police officer covered by the health plan, and most police families, almost half in Staffpac, those who had applied had mortgages, all but two were in death and disablement insurance. Every fund was viable.'

With Robbie's departure and that of Fulton, and a new association president, the opportunity was taken to amalgamate further the association and welfare boards. The guild was not happy to have its unofficial representation on the welfare fund reduced. Butterworth particularly regretted this move that got rid of a useful area for talking through issues with the administration and the other service organisation. He recognises, however, that Commissioner Thompson began the process when he took his representative off the fund, objecting to this capturing of his people. He was talking about Peter Mairs, whom Butterworth reckons influenced them as much as they influenced him.

The welfare fund board is now more democratic on paper, with one guild representative. Its 1989 agm debated the reducing pot of gold and the high administration costs, but a motion that its costs not exceed the previous year was lost. Confidence in the welfare fund remained high.

In Robbie's last month in the job 1000 claims totalled $180,000; the health plan income for the year was $2,400,000. New welfare fund secretary John Turner announced in October 1990 that, since April, 150 mortgages had been approved worth $9,300,000.

The welfare fund was entering the 1990s with a range of benefits the police had provided for themselves. They had fulfilled the dreams of their founders that one day they would be able to do their job with dignity, secure in the knowledge that their families were well cared for, whatever happened to them in this dangerous and draining occupation.

Chapter Twenty-three

The Construction of Credit

Hamilton delegate Harry McCombe delivered a stirring speech to the 1967 association annual conference on the desirability of forming a police credit union. Much of his speech was delivered in the capital letters and exclamation marks of someone who had seen the light, like a born-again Christian or one of the then fashionable Moral Rearmers or Social Crediters. Where McCombe hit home, however, was in the examples he gave towards the end of his speech.

> One young policeman applied to an organisation which claims to serve him to the best of its ability, for a loan of $600 for a house he intended to build when transferred to Hamilton. He arrived in Hamilton in February 1967. In mid-February he was told his application had been declined. No good reason for declining the application was given. The money was needed for a second mortgage. He applied to the Credit Union in May 1967 for the same amount, and within 24 hours of application he was advised that the loan was approved. He received his money, completed his home and was happy.

Without the credit union of which McCombe was a director, it would not have been a happy ending. Many police had gone through what this young man had experienced, waiting for three months to hear if a loan was approved and then finding that it was not. And that was where the unhappy story usually ended, with no other recourse for the frustrated police applicant but to accept rental accommodation. 'The credit union philosophy,' McCombe declared, 'ensured that he should be served and that he should not go hat in hand to private money lenders to better establish his family in a decent home.'

McCombe asked the conference how many young policemen had had a similar experience. How many were lost from the police because of money troubles? His audience knew the answer—too many. There was not and never had been a problem more pressing than decent homes for police families.

The answer, in McCombe's view, was to join the 30,000,000 people in 25,000 credit unions in 70 countries, united in the single common bond of pooling their savings as loans to each other ... 'Not for Charity, not for Profit, BUT FOR SERVICE'.

His St Mary's credit union was of a similar size to what the police could expect. In 15 years it had built up assets of $309,705, savings of $299,889, membership of 1715, made loans to members of $235,531, and the dividend to members this year was 4 per cent. The directors did not get paid; the office staff, including a manager and treasurer/secretary, did. As with all other credit unions, members paid 1 per cent interest per month on the original capital, the next month the interest on what was the declined capital. Interest was paid only on the capital. This saved two-thirds of what a finance company charged. Legally loans were restricted to 100, but the credit unions were agitating for legislative liberalisation. Credit unions developed their own insurance on homes, vehicles and anything else desired. The scheme was unbeatable!

Mr. H. E. McCombe the new President who was elected at the 34th Annual Conference.

Mr. H. E. McCombe our new President joined the service in mid-1950 and was promoted to his present rank of Detective Sergeant at the end of 1957. Most of his service has been with the C.I.B. having served five years in Dunedin, six years in Auckland, six years in Hamilton before coming to Wellington. He was on the District Association Committee in Dunedin, Auckland and Hamilton and at the latter both Chairman and Delegate to the Conference in 1966, 1967 and 1968 and was made Junior Vice President of the Association on the 6th, June 1969. He is at present the Director of the Crime Prevention Section at Police Headquarters, Wellington, having taken over earlier this year from Mr. R. L. Butler the retiring President.

Mr. McCombe is a married man with five children and four grandchildren and during his life has played most sport but as he says, "never successfully in any". In 1939 he joined the Territorial Army being called up in 1940 in the Artillery. After this he became a physical training instructor then transferred to the R.N.Z.A.F. where he continued for a short time as a P.T.I. and then became a Sergeant Station Warrant Officer at Weedons outside Christchurch.

Harry McCombe first made his association mark by promoting the idea of a police credit union at the 1967 conference. He became president of the association for 1969-71, but he was still ahead of his members in his credit union ideas

McCombe got a round of applause. He answered questions, acknowledging that the PSIS had some of the advantages of a credit union, but could not match members' own credit union for fastest service, best terms and best advice. His address was printed in the *Police Journal* and enthusiasm was high. As he admitted, however, the association was committed at present to developing the welfare fund.

With the fund established, the April 1970 *Newsletter* carried a rendered down version of McCombe's address, asking whether consideration could be given to establishing a credit union. Hamish Thomas and the board were invited to discuss the subject with the PSIS. In the July 1971 *Newsletter* Thomas finally reported back. 'There was a threat made,' he wrote, 'that if a credit union is set up then the PSIS will consider whether or not policemen as a group should retain their eligibility to be members of the Society.' The management committee set up a sub-committee to look into the matter. McCombe was now association president, but failed to push his members past the PSIS threat to remove benefits from members.

'There it lay until late December 1973,' says Alan Monk.

> I was approached by several people and asked why not establish a credit union. There was so much support I had a meeting of eight people at my place in the Wellington suburb of Hataitai, including association treasurer Peter Isaacs. We looked at ways round the PSIS objection. Only groups were affected, individuals were separate from the association. The Police and Families Credit Union was founded then with $10 each, which we loaned back to ourselves to establish the credit union. We had regular monthly meetings to set new targets, increase members, and built up the share capital to about $60,000. The volume was exceeding the ability of volunteers to handle. I had to leave the board when I transferred to Blenheim in 1975. Later I became aware it had fallen into disrepair and was in effect in default.'

Alan Monk has put two decades into the association, a quarter of them as president. Perhaps his most important contribution was to establish the Police and Families Credit Union in his own house in late 1973. He has been a key figure in running the credit union ever since

There were 500 members, their savings too big for informal bookkeeping, too small for fulltime management.

Alec Waugh was the next mover and shaker. 'It was suggested I look at this village credit union Alan Monk and others had set up. I was interested in financial things, I had met a lot of Australians who had talked credit union banks. This one seemed incestuous; most of the directors had loans from it. One had 13 small loans.'

Waugh spoke to one director, warning her that he planned a bloodless coup, and the word soon spread. Joining the board, he identified 'unusual practices' that could lead to an inquiry into fraudulent practice. The implied threat was enough. Most of the board were absent when a new one was elected. The former secretary, who was in England, had left behind instructions not to hand over any of the credit union books. Waugh discovered that there were virtually no records anyway.

The 1977 New Zealand Police and Families Credit Union agm was held in a car at the Waring Taylor Street police headquarters in downtown Wellington. Present were Waugh, Brian Walkinshaw and two other policemen who subsequently left the service. Waugh told them this was to be a new credit union; they would talk to Moodie and Butterworth and see if they could collectively make the union what it should be.

'The issue from then on,' he says,

> was whether it should be a credit union bank worth $60 or $70 million like the Australian police credit unions, or a credit union with about $8,000,000 assets. Walkinshaw and myself advocated the big organisation serving all the requirements of police officers, including first mortgages. Moodie and co. argued against it in the New Zealand climate on safety grounds and as not necessary. That opportunity was gone by the early 1980s as building societies became big. Not that it matters now we have access to first mortgage funds through the superannuation scheme.

In the early 1980s Waugh and his successors Bull and Walkinshaw, as guild and association representative on the Government Superannuation Board, got the mortgage money scheme through, so effectively that they achieved what they had planned for in their 1977 car agm.

Getting the credit union relaunched ran into what Waugh calls the long-term anti-credit union departmental stance. The senior officers, he says, saw the PSIS as fulfilling that function. 'Finance,' he adds, 'was something police officers are damned scared of.'

The breakthrough against such opposition was

Alec Waugh, association vice-president, revitalised the credit union in the late 1970s. As chairman of the credit union in mid-1979 he hands a cheque for his surrendered insurance policy to Lucy Rangitonga, for depositing in his credit union account

Brian Walkinshaw has been alongside Waugh as a long-serving credit union board member and key figure in its development

Assistant Commissioner Bryan Gibson agreeing to join the revived credit union board for three years. Waugh knows that Gibson caught flak from headquarters for taking days off to take part in something they were against. Gibson brought credibility to the credit union.

At a special union meeting, this time inside the Waring Taylor police headquarters on the evening of 1 May 1978, Alec Waugh briefed those present: Brian Walkinshaw, Alan Monk, G. Gibbs, B. Johnson, L. Rampton, M. Gibbins, J. Webber and Charlie Hohaia, the man who had nudged Waugh into the job.

Same place same time the following week, Waugh announced that Moodie was appointed manager of the credit union. The new board of directors had Senior Sergeant Waugh as chairman and trustee along with Senior Sergeant R. Brown and Sergeant Walkinshaw. The last-named was also on the board with Monk, Constable Hamish Beckett, Constable G. Dynes, Superintendent J.W. McGuire, Detective Superintendent Jack Stevenson, Bryan Gibson and Sergeant Basil Johnson. Supervisors were Hohaia, Constable B.G. Mullane and Constable J.A.G. Webber. One or other of Waugh, Walkinshaw and Monk has been in the driving seat almost ever since.

There was no question about who was steering. 'When I arrived,' says Moodie, 'the credit union was actually bankrupt. People had grabbed and used the fund. The directors were making loans to themselves to pay off loans. It was a hell of a job getting it off them. I threatened to bring in the Fraud Squad if they didn't. It was that bad. It took about a year for that. I trod very cautiously because I didn't want it.'

'My first job,' Butterworth recalls, 'was writing to everybody who had a loan and reminding them gently it was an offence under Police Regulations to have a debt.' Moodie collected the credit union records, had them examined by an accountant and then declared the union suspended. The records were so poorly kept that the only course of action was to call in all passbooks and reconcile them with the ledgers. Once this was done, a new system would be introduced based on payments through the Treasury computer.

Moodie placed an ad in the June *Newsletter* explaining what passbook holders must do. The prime problem, he told readers, was lack of professional management, but the field officer of the New Zealand Credit Union League indicated that they were capable of being one of the strongest credit unions in the country. Australian police credit unions had proved this was possible, with over $100,000,000 assets on loan for all members, for second mortgages and even first mortgages. Waugh, Butterworth and himself had arranged a meeting with three Australian police credit unions. Within three years the aim was $1,000,000 available for loans. The unpaid pipe-smoking manager declared that this was no pipe dream. By 31 December 1978 there were $84,000 shares and 1100 members. Butterworth projected from this six-month growth pattern that the million would soon be realised. Operation One Million was launched.

The first glitch was the control departments blocking fortnightly deductions. Bryan Gibson was the administration chairman at what he recalled as one of the stormiest meetings he could remember. Moodie chased Treasury, and was told that access to their computer would open the way for 'fly-by-night operations'. Incensed at the implication, Moodie told them he would not take no for an answer. He reapplied for access, threatening, if unsuccessful, to make the denial public.

The 7 February 1979 meeting of the credit union board was full of dark suggestions that Treasury was protecting the ailing PSIS and that their credit union was being discriminated against, given that hospital employees had savings deducted from salaries. Butterworth suggested that the Police Department get its own computer to handle all salaries, personnel records and surveys. He had had indications that an independent investment society might be allowed to access the Treasury computer, whereas a credit union would create precedents. Hamish Beckett hoped that, if this became necessary, the word 'Investment' would not be used, members having become afraid of the word because of 'the mire that the PSIS had got into'. The good news was that the police had not bent to pressure to go with the PSIS.

Butterworth also warned against the problems of being tied up with the New Zealand Credit Union League, whose insurance company put limits on savings insured while the league itself aimed to absorb all members into itself. Walkinshaw, too, was not happy with the league taking 4 per cent of profits in fees.

Another problem Butterworth raised was the conflicting information about interest rates. A former Consumers Institute colleague assessed PSIS loans of 9 per cent proving to have a real interest rate of 16 per cent. Butterworth, strongly supported by Waugh, wanted a survey done. Butterworth would get his Consumer contact to do it, for $20!

Waugh attended the World Conference of Credit Unions in Australia, reporting that it was 'inspirational'. Meantime Moodie pressured the administration and the minister for access to the Treasury computer and by mid-July of 1979 Treasury had agreed that their earlier decision was unreasonable. A policy had to be developed with the SSC to ensure that no other credit unions could acquire the same access. Bad debts by now had been chased up. The board prepared to impose a penalty on 'unscrupulous members' who withheld repayments and then paid a lump sum, depriving the credit union of cash flow.

Butterworth stumped the country explaining to association and guild members the credit union philosophy that was developing here distinct from the Australian one. He and Moodie had abandoned the Australian approach of long term deposit facilities for first mortgages in favour of a more radical approach. This had come from Moodie's successful resolution of insurance negotiations to return some profit. This suggested members should consider cancelling personal insurance policies they did not need and divert this money into a long-term loan facility. Money coming direct from salary into a fund would avoid the inflation problems of insurance policies and contract savings schemes, whereby a $20,000 loan now would, in five years at 10 per cent inflation, hit $32,000. Butterworth and Moodie proposed that the fund be adjusted in line with movements in wage and price levels. The savings would be locked in for the period a member was in the police. The advantage was that, after five years, no member would have to look beyond the fund for long-term finance. As usual Moodie and Butterworth were a step ahead of everybody else.

Commissioner Walton's support was important to the success of the credit union. Here he hands to association staffer Wendy Davies his opening cheque for $500

NZ Police Association Newsletter

Page 36

POLICE AND FAMILIES CREDIT UNION

"OPERATION ONE MILLION"

Credit Union membership now stands at almost 1500—an increase of over 100% in the past five months. Forty-three members have already received loans totalling $72,750.

Most of the new members are making automatic payments to their sha... ...counts and this has built up the monthly cash flow to $15,000.

The interest rate on loans is 1% per month on a **reducing balan**... borrows $100.00 from the Credit Union and repays it over one year, p... of that money, that is it costs him 6.62% of the amount he borrowed... favourably with the actual rate of more than 15.5% charged at prese... 24% charged on Hire Purchase Agreements. On the other hand, inv... 4% on their funds, and this is expressed in the form of a dividend... profitability of the fund. If money is saved regularly and loaned pro... of **7% is possible, and this is on on-call money.** Whether... depends entirely upon the support given their Credit Union by me... of course, withdraw your savings at any time, but did you know th... Credit Union accumulates to:

At 4%			
5 years	1464.40	5 years	
10 years	3455.69	10 years	
20 years	8361.69	20 year	
30 years	15623.47	30 year	
40 years	26373.64	40 yea	

Imagine, by paying $10 per fortnight into the Credit Unior... that amount throughout their service, members of the Police can enjoy the ad... from an **available pool of low interest mortgage finance,** whilst at the same time accumulating for themselves a **retirement fund of the order of $30,000.** Additionally, mortgage repayment insurance is provided without charge, whilst savings of up to $2000 are doubled in the event of a member's death.

We aim to have 6000 members contributing to their shares account by the end of the year. If each of these saved only $10 per pay, our **cash flow would be $120,000 monthly; $1,440,000 yearly.**

HELP THE CREDIT UNION HELP YOU

BECOME A REGULAR C...

NO
CA...

FOR F...
The...
Poli...
P.O...

Moodie set a goal in 1979 of reaching $1,000,000 of credit union funds within a few years. One way was through hard-sell advertisements in the *Newsletter*. Another way was through the soft-sell cartoon

Alec Waugh (left) and Rob Moodie give each other credit for a union well done

At the end of 1979 Moodie was able to announce that they had met their goals for the first two years. The credit union had computerised automatic salary deductions, a self-supporting capital loans ratio, professional management and the confidence of members.

That confidence was to be sorely tested over the next few years by the succession of computer problems, a teething time for Treasury as much as the police. What stays in Waugh's mind is how the first three computer packages came close to disaster owing to poor advice by alleged computer experts and 'some fly-by-night salesmen'.

Moodie and Butterworth were keen to buy the latest and greatest computer; Pye's General Automation was the new byter on the block. Ian Bird of the administration had reservations, but Moodie told the 28 November 1979 board meeting it was 'a Rolls Royce among mini computers' compared with the noisy competitor not really understood by those who operated it. The Pye was also $2,000 below the Wang quote of $45,000. It was a costly mistake, but the company accepted Moodie's view that the machine did not achieve what was claimed for it. With mostly recompense money the $300,000 Wang was purchased.

Moodie was not, though, putting all his eggs in the computer basket. He brought in Wellington police with some get up and go, such as Jack Stevenson and Inspector Sherwood Young, to crank the credit union machine into action.

Young was easily persuaded at the mention of the credit union's aim to provide second mortgages of $5,000. He had his own house, but his antecedents had not been so fortunate. Grandfather Commissioner Young had lived most of his life in police houses and died leaving his widow an estate of £1,250. She had to vacate the police house. When Sherwood's father's cousin, Senior Sergeant Laurie Grimwood, died of cancer at the age of 53, his widow had to move out of the police house. They were typical examples. There were also the victims Young knew, those police who tried to save themselves money by breaking in a section at an age when they should have been taking it easy, and killed themselves in the process.

The main message Young heard from Moodie and Butterworth was that police must consider housing. The second mortgage facility might be, as McCombe had argued, the difference between buying or missing out on your own house. Young came on to the credit union board as treasurer in 1979. Assistant Treasurer Diann Stephen and, before her, Ann Rumble, handled the manual system for the first three years, when the operation stayed small.

Membership grew to 1800 by April 1980, with $300,000 share capital. The credit union was experiencing a slowdown in deposits and heavier withdrawals. Moodie told the board that the momentum so far achieved was in danger of being undercut by members' attacks. Compulsory contributions were the subject of complaints, with 40 Auckland members telling the department they did not want their subs to the welfare fund and credit union increased.

There were outside problems too. Butterworth was concerned at the legislation limiting loans to $5,000. Waugh called the Registrar of Friendly Societies 'a dictator clothed in democracy'. Moodie warned the directors that they might have to mount a campaign to protect their interests.

Contrarily, Butterworth accepted at the 16 April meeting that the union was for medium-term finance to $5,000, not for first mortgages up to $20,000. He was chastened by the bad experiences of the PSIS and the Post Office Investment Society trying to cope with large or 'hot' investments in a boom climate where money was whisked around to get the best return.

The following month the state computer broke down and it was expected to be some time before the SSC had the expertise to run it. This was a tricky time, with members threatening to cancel their automatic payments. By the end of the year Moodie reported the automatic system in place, boosting credit union capital to the half-million-dollar mark. The problem was that Treasury took 2.5 per cent as a servicing fee, something the PSIS and banks were not charged. Moodie fought against that as well as for computer compensation.

In March 1981 Moodie told the board it was time to have a permanent manager of the credit union, which now had assets of $700,000. He also reported his battle with Associate Finance Minister Hugh Templeton to get the 2.5 per cent back from Treasury; this money would help to pay for permanent management. There was bitterness expressed on the board about the government picking on a small organisation. Moodie, however, continued with his counter-attack and by mid-year had beaten Treasury down to half what it was charging.

Butterworth counselled against board intransigence when they had only 1707 members out of a potential 4900, so the board decided on an ultimately successful ploy. It would accept the government philosophy of user pays and the 1.25 per cent charge, but on the understanding that it would be reduced to a cost per member serviced, based on the current membership. As membership grew, the credit union's charges were reduced to 85 cents, and finally to 30 cents.

By mid-year the credit union had reached its million dollar mark. Moodie proposed as manager the staff member who had handled medical insurance but was underemployed since this was taken over by the underwriters. She had a successful track record marketing Turkish delight, but the board was not sure she should take over a million-dollar business. The decision was deferred.

The tool for rapid credit union development was a computer. This photograph shows the early computer days of the second half of 1980. On the left credit union chairman Alec Waugh observes assistant treasurer Mrs Diann Stephen receive a cheque from executive officer (personnel) Jack Harris. Behind them is the processor for the computer. At this stage only the credit union was on the computer, providing daily financial information and statements of share and loan accounts. Mrs Stephen was in at the beginnings of the modern credit union, working for the credit union and the association as an accounts clerk in 1978, helping assistant treasurer of the credit union Mrs Ann Rumble sort out several hundred membership records by hand. The following year Mrs Stephen took over as assistant treasurer. In 1988 she officially finished a decade with the credit union, by which time the computer was processing thousands of members. Now system administrator with the association, she keeps a motherly eye on the credit union, helping out when required

In August the Registrar of Friendly Societies was informed that the credit union was restructuring. To take account of the imbalance favouring borrowers in the traditional credit union monthly accounting system, the system was now to be six-monthly. The key to Philips' admission that their computer was not up to the job was that it could not implement this new savings and loan restructuring. Also, it had been incorrectly paying savers more than the stated interest and less than the 1 per cent per month on loan repayments.

In 1982 David Petterson became financial controller of the three service organisations. In December he told the board that the Wang was just about on stream, there were 6130 account holders, $1,640,000 invested, $1,590,000 on loan to 690 members. Moodie reported that, despite the rush of the credit union legislation through Parliament, most of their recommendations had been adopted. The credit union was poised to surge, with still much the same personnel—including Waugh as the chairman, Young as treasurer and vice-chairman, Monk, Walkinshaw, Basil Johnson, Gibson and Beckett, and Petterson, Butterworth and Moodie.

In March 1983 Moodie was effusive about the difference the Wang made, placing a lot of the credit with Petterson's handling of the software specifications. The credit union was centralised, computerised and structured into a competent financial organisation.

Young rates the health plan as the breakthrough for the credit union. Its viability depended on every member paying regularly into the credit union. Every police officer wanted to be in the health plan, hence the surge in membership. Many were using the credit union only to cover their welfare fund and insurance contributions. Young says the challenge of the early 1980s was to make those 1500 accounts more active. One way he managed this was to argue successfully for increasing subscriptions by $5 to build up the account, which would also mean more money could be lent.

Although the loan limit was $5,000, 87 per cent of the $2,000,000 assets was out on loan in 1982 to 1200 members. Over half was borrowed for family items, another 40 per cent for cars. The most significant loan, in Waugh's view, was the unsecured third mortgage finance at moderate interest rates, the difference between buying a house or missing out.

Over the next three years, under new manager Gary Fulton from 1985, the assets trebled to $6,500,000. Much of the growth was related to the input of Tom Robbie, as claims and promotions manager, and the extra cut from the handling of the superannuation mortgage lump sum. Robbie says the credit union might have felt that it was made use of by the welfare fund as an accounting function, but it was paid for its services. He points out how much the credit union benefited from his promotions around the country with Keith Morrow.

Robbie was prominent at credit union board meetings in the 1980s. On 6 June 1985 he told the board that, over the previous year, he and Morrow made 80 addresses around the country and at the Police College to recruits, members and retirees. The fortnightly payment from PIPS, the government computer, to the credit union had increased by $40,000 per pay or $1,000,000 per annum. The health plan brought the credit union an extra $50,000 a year.

At the August meeting Butterworth reported problems resulting from the administration being secretive about early retirement negotiations. The administration had, however, now expressed confidence in Robbie and guaranteed full and frank discussion with him.

Moodie left the board in October, Butterworth the following April. It was the end of the era when Moodie ran all three service organisations, and encouraged the presence of guild members on the welfare fund and credit union boards. When the association effectively took over the welfare fund four years later, the credit union retained its core board members Waugh, Young, Walkinshaw and Monk. Their career prospects may well have been held up by their unpaid dedication to transforming the credit union into a multimillion-dollar loan facility for members.

The late 1980s saw a move towards a stand-alone status for the credit union, in financial control free of the welfare fund and the association. New manager Gary Fulton set the scene in his 14-page submission of June 1986 to Associate Finance Minister David Caygill. The legislation was felt to be restrictive. All shares had to rank equally, and this stopped variable interest rates on incentive savings plans and fixed-term deposits. No interest or claim was available over $10,000. The result was that members used the credit union to accumulate funds to a reasonable level, then removed their money to where they could get a better return. The credit union could not counter this without offering an exorbitant lending rate as well as return, and this would defeat the organisation's purpose. Australian credit unions were so successful because they did not suffer such restrictive legislation. The submission asked for a $100,000 limit when a credit union reached assets of $10,000,000.

In 1986, too, Monk and Walkinshaw replaced Waugh and Young as president and vice-president, although both stayed on the board and policy did not change. A new ingredient, though, was Wray Smart delivering a computer lecture to the 28 April 1987 meeting. The data processing manager told them they needed a current computer, while the association and the welfare fund could cope with a much smaller one. Warning that the Wang was reaching the end of its useful life, he also told his audience that he was trying to make staff more computer confident, but there was considerable suspicion and diffidence. Effort had gone into getting it running, but its job of long-term planning had been lost sight of. 'The system,' he said, 'sort of drifted.'

Fulton called for a computer sub-committee. Monk warned of the difficulty of reaching a consensus on what should be done with the other two organisations' boards, a total of 30 people. Smart was not impressed with a sub-committee, given that the past was littered with people making decisions without knowing what the implications were, lacking the necessary skills to assess proposals. The credit union used the computer 60 per cent of the time, the association 25 per cent, the welfare fund 15 per cent. This needed to be rationalised. Despite this, the board decided to support the concept of a joint sub-committee.

The sub-committee talked and talked, and Smart was not happy. He needed to know computer requirements. He told the board on 24 October 1987 that lead time was critical. Fulton agreed, but thought the sub-committee useful and the computer still had two years in it.

By December it was agreed the Wang would go. Smart brought in the Altos system, first for the mortgage fund, then, by the following February, for the health plan. It was agreed by now to amalgamate with the government computer system. Bureaucratic sluggishness held matters up for several years. Then, in February 1989, Treasury wanted to increase the 30 cent fee; it was agreed to be set at 50 cents.

In 1989 the Touche Ross management consultant review of the three umbrella organisations was the final persuader for the credit union to go it alone. The report favoured the union manager being responsible to the president of the association, with the president reporting back to the union board. This did not suit the credit union. The report also appeared to overlook its responsibility to members outside the association—those in the guild, non-sworn police staff, and family and retired members.

The credit union now ranked fifth in New Zealand. Although Caygill had given the credit union more freedom, he had also proposed that it should be taxed. Tony Biss, audit partner of Spicer and Oppenheim, told the 25 September 1989 board meeting that their improved computer system and office procedures were overcoming high costs

The 1986 Australasian Federation of Police Credit Unions Conference was hosted in Wellington by the New Zealand Police and Families Credit Union because it was the New Zealand police centennial year.

Two significant developments occurred because of that conference—firstly the conference elected Les Day, the manager of the Queensland Police Credit Union, as spokesman in a discussion with Associate Minister of Finance, David Caygill, relating to the intransigence of the PIPS (Personnel Information and Payroll Service) over the continued charging of a percentage commission for each transfer of money from PIPS to the credit union. A flat transaction charge resulted from Day's submissions. This saved the shareholders of the credit union many thousands of dollars each year.

Secondly, a membership survey conducted by the Victorian Police Credit Association encouraged the New Zealand police credit union to engage a consultant, Peter Gurney of Christchurch, to conduct a survey of members' needs. A thousand questionnaires were mailed out to members selected at random, and over 800 replies were received. From this very high return rate it was possible to chart a course of action for the credit union which assisted in building its assets to $8.5 million by June 1991 of interest rates on loans and steep administration costs, but the credit union must think carefully about how to serve its members. It was not in the business of making a lot of money, but rather of using the combined resources of members to extend a helping hand to others. They were caught between raising interest rates to competitive levels and thereby reducing the standard of service and help to members. He believed members remained loyal not because of the rates offered, but because of how the money was used. It was a communication not an arithmetic problem.

Morrow brought up the question of his salary, now that the government had directed the administration not to pay it. He suggested a 60/20/20 split between the three service organisations. Although it would not affect him as he was resigning, it certainly affected the credit union. Discussion was vigorous. Robbie, another due to retire, argued that the association president put in a lot of promotional work for the credit union. Morrow said he did work for the union other than being on the board.

Walkinshaw seemed unimpressed. He said the credit union was trying to go down its own path and staff salaries would be paid in full by the union. They wanted a fulltime manager and a departure from the percentage situation in the national office. He thought, in the light of the credit union change, that it was strange to get a request from the President for 20 per cent. C.M. Maling made the telling point that over one-third of credit union members were not in the association. Fulton argued that the union was dependent on the policing environment and its successes rested on the guidelines of the president. Morrow said the president's promotion was a stamp of approval for the credit union and it could be guaranteed. The arguments for going alone were more convincing. Although a motion was passed that the board agree to pay a percentage, the amount was not determined.

At the 30 November 1989 meeting new association president Steve Hinds promised to promote the credit union under the umbrella concept. Brian Benn agreed they had voted to pay him, and suggested $1. Any further remuneration, suggested Walkinshaw, could be a matter for the association, while the credit union got on with paying its own staff. Young argued that there were dual roles in the health plan and welfare fund, but the board voted to control its own staff, and against paying anything towards the association president's salary.

Fulton resigned at the end of the year to take up a position as Deputy Chief Executive of the New Zealand Credit Union League in Hamilton, whose 156 unions, with 110,000 members, had assets of $120,000,000.

Hinds rationalised the cost structure. Harding became national secretary, John Turner moved from being financial controller to secretary of the welfare fund, Wray Smart was appointed manager of the credit union. Two jobs were wiped out of the top of the umbrella organisation, saving $130,000 a year. Hinds says this put them on a more equitable footing, but it did him no good in getting any more money out of the credit union for his own salary.

The credit union did agree to share the swanky new premises in Willbank House, Willis Street, Wellington. Young retired as a trustee at the 1990 agm, to return as the guild representative on the board. Smart announced that the credit union paid its own staff and did its own promotion around the country's police stations.

Monk expressed the view that there was insufficient dialogue between the association and the credit union on the new Police Plan. This could have been a remark about dialogue generally between the two organisations. The credit union was alongside but standing alone, and all the stronger for it. Smart, in his annual report, noted another milestone in credit union funds, in a year up another $1,100,000 to $8,400,000. The union had not quite reached the heights Waugh had envisaged, but Smart was keen to see it heading in that direction. Certainly the credit union had come a long way since its beginnings two decades before, when present chairman, Alan Monk, and a few police colleagues, seated around his Hataitai kitchen table, had started a self-help credit facility for the police.

Appendix I

Office Holders and Inaugural Proceedings

Deputation to Minister Proposing Association, 8 August 1936
Sergeant Tocher, Auckland and Whangarei
Sergeant T. Kelly, Hamilton
Detective A. Jenvey, New Plymouth
Constable H. Shields, Palmerston North
Constable G.A. McCurrach, Gisborne
Constable D. Bowick, Napier
Constable F.W. Edwards, Wanganui
Constable T. Smith, Wellington
Constable F.H. Healey, Nelson
Sergeant J. Isbister, Greymouth
Constable W. Calwell, Christchurch
Senior Sergeant D. Hewitt, Timaru
Chief Detective J.B. Young, Dunedin and Invercargill

Signatories to the Application for Incorporation
T.F. Smith
C.L. Spencer
L.B. Revell
J.B. Wakelin
F.H. Healey
J. Gracey
R.R. Tripney
W.R. Murray
J.M. Pointon
J. Henderson

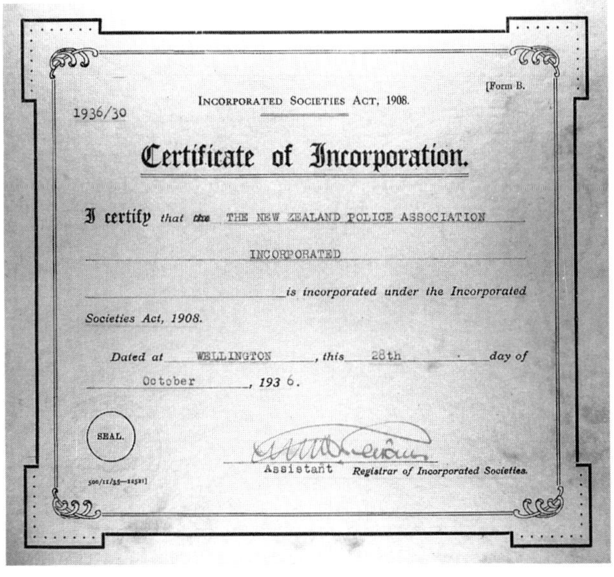
1936/30 INCORPORATED SOCIETIES ACT, 1908. [Form B.

Certificate of Incorporation.

I certify that the THE NEW ZEALAND POLICE ASSOCIATION INCORPORATED is incorporated under the Incorporated Societies Act, 1908.

Dated at WELLINGTON, this 28th day of October, 1936.

SEAL.

Assistant Registrar of Incorporated Societies.

E. Burnett
A. Johnston
P.A. Hardie
T. Brosnan
J.M. Ogilvie

Delegates to the First Conference, 8 December 1936
F.W. Edwards, Wanganui
D. Hewitt, Timaru
J. Isbister, Greymouth
A. Jenvey, New Plymouth
F.W. Johnsen, Dunedin
T. Kelly, Hamilton
A.B. Meiklejohn, Auckland
W.R. Murray, Wellington
C. Petersen, Nelson
H. Russell, Wellington
H. Shields, Palmerston North
F. Sinclair, Christchurch
G. Sivyer, Napier
T. Smith, Invercargill
T.F. Smith, Wellington
E. Wigmore, Gisborne

Original Management Committee
W.R. Murray, President
J.W. McHolm, Vice-President
W.S. Brown
A. Johnston
J.M. O'Connor
G.W. Kilgour
L.B.J. Revell
C.L. Spencer
T.F. Smith, Temporary General Secretary

Association Presidents

Murray, William Robert	1936
Young, John Bruce	1938
Johnston, Thomas Evan	1943
Pointon, John Morris	1944
Quin, Alphonsus Gerard	1947
Scott, Fergus Oliver	1950
Rodgers, Michael John	1954
Naylor, Cyril William	1956
Tait, Gideon	1959
Richardson, Harold Clifford	1960
Gibson, Bryan William	1962

1947 11th Annual

Front W A Calwell, Miss L Hunter (Association Secretary), W Madden, J M Pointon (President), P Fraser (M of Police), J Meltzer (General Secretary), J Robertson

Middle D G Campbell, J H S Hogg, F S Quinn, G H L Holt, C S Rouxel, E E Strawbridge

Back C G Cleverly, F G Day, L F Ward, M J Rodgers, J R Gedye, N Thompson

Former Association President Gideon Tait, also active in the guild

Past presidents of the association assemble at its 50th jubilee in 1986. Back row, left to right: Cyril Naylor, William Back and Alan Monk. Front, left to right: Dan Ingram, Bill Murray, Bryan Gibson and Rob Butler

New life members of the association at the October agm annual dinner 1985. Left to right: Ian Paterson, Bill Murray and Hamish Beckett

Life member Dave Paterson, living up to his status by still working for the association as its archivist and history project researcher

Back, William Alfred Peter	9163
Butler, Robert Laurie	1964
McCombe, Harold Eric	1969
Ingram, Daniel Nason	1971
Butler, Robert Laurie	1973
Monk, Alan John	1976
Morrow, Keith James	1981
Hinds, Stephen Philip	1989-

Association Secretaries

Smith, Thomas Frederick	1936
Campbell, Ian Drummond	1936
Meltzer, Jack	1940
Lee, David Clifford	1966
Thomas, Hamish Stewart	1969
Moodie, Robert Alexander	1976
Fulton, Gary Charles	1985
Harding, Graham Douglas	1989-

Industrial Advocate

Harding, Graham Douglas	1985-1989

Life Members

Stevens, Eric Albert
Tucker, Robert Sydney
Edwardson, Alfred Fairclough
Dynes, George
Craig, John Robert Duncan
Ingram, Daniel Nason
Murray, William Robert
Paterson, Ian Charles
Beckett, Hamish Oliphant Talbot
Butler, Robert Laurie
Moodie, Robert Alexander
Stevenson, Paul Stewart
Paterson, David Skinner
Eathorne, Maurice Christopher
Halpin, Ronald Stephen Francis
Nelson, Wallace Renfrew
Tozer, Trevor Owen
Morrow, Keith James
Olsen, Anthony Steven

The New Zealand Police Officers' Guild
Incorporation 1 June 1955, by Sub-Inspector Frederick Walter Edwards

Signatories to the Application for Incorporation
Superintendent J. Edwards, Wellington
Inspector W.S. Brown, Wellington
Inspector J.R. Corston, Wellington
Inspector D. McKenzie, Wellington
Inspector E.J.C. Hay, Wellington
Inspector G.S. Norris, Lower Hutt
Sub-Inspector M. Conway, Wellington
Sub-Inspector C.L. Spencer, Wellington
Sub-Inspector F.W. Edwards, Wellington
Superintendent J. Southworth, Auckland
Inspector R.T. Kearton, Auckland
Sub-Inspector P. Kearney, Auckland
Sub-Inspector H.E. Campin, Auckland
Sub-Inspector M.E. Parker, Auckland
Sub-Inspector F. Taylor, Auckland

Delegates to the First AGM, 28-29 July 1965
W.J. Robertson, Auckland
T. Jones, Hamilton
C. McKenzie, Christchurch
J.G. Williams, Dunedin
A.I. Knapp, Wellington District
G.A. Dallow, Wellington Headquarters

Presidents

Edwards, John	1955
Carran, William	1956
Norris, George Stephen	1957
Howes, Gordon Allen	1959
Craigie, William Smith	1963
Howes, Gordon Allen	1964
Knapp, Albert Ian	1965
McKenzie, Philip John	1968
Saunders, Joseph William	1969
Hollinshead, William Edward	1972
Baker, Arthur Walter	1973
McEwen, Stuart Blair	1977
Scott, Bruce Fergus	1979
Glynn, James Francis	1983
Wilson, Colin Walter	1985
Hartley, Brian Stanley John	1989-

Vice-Presidents

McEwen, Stuart Blair	1975
Rusbatch, Stephen Alexander	1977
Cummings, Maurice Daniel	1978
Dougall, Jean Aleen Mae	1979
Beatson, Trevor Alan	1983
Hartley, Brian Stanley John	1985-1989
Rowe, Bryan John	1985-1991
Hunter, Lindsay John	1989-
Coomber, John	1989-
Dallow, Ross Philip	1991-

Officers Guild Vice-President, Steve Rusbatch

Secretaries

Spencer, Carl Leslie	1955
Edwards, Frederick Walter	1955
Wootton, Burt Wesley	1956
Callaghan, George Edward	1957
Hansen, Hans Otto Lauritz	1958
Tanner, Charles Edward	1959
McGuire, William Alfred Thomas	1960
Trask, Earnst Royden	1965
Nancarrow, Jim	1967
Glynn, James Francis	1970
Joyce, Ronald Cecil	1971
Quill, John Michael	1972
Cooper, Leslie Earle	1973
Hartley, Brian Stanley John	1977
Waugh, Alec Kynaston	1985
Strong, Wayne Francis	1989-

Treasurers

Harman, John Reginald	1965
Young, Sherwood Ivan	1981

Executive Directors

Moodie, Robert Alexander	1989
Butterworth, Graham Victor	1991-

Life Members

Baker, Arthur Walter	1986
Harman, John Reginald	1986
Glynn, James Francis	1987
Cooper, Leslie Earle	1991

NEW ZEALAND POLICE OFFICERS' GUILD

Executive and Delegates to the Guild Conference Including for the First Time Members of the N.Z. Traffic Safety Service.

ANNUAL CONFERENCE : WELLINGTON 12-13 NOVEMBER 1991

Rear Row, Left to Right:
G. H. LAING (Delegate : Region 2), J. P. SCHOUTEN (Delegate : Region 5), P. L. ROBINSON (Delegate : Region 6), R. P. DALLOW (Vice President), G. J. GILPIN (Delegate : Region 4).

Middle Row, Left to Right:
L. J. TOOMAN (District Manager: Traffic Safety Service: Hamilton), R. G. DAVIES (District Manager: Traffic Safety Service: Lower Hutt), J. D. WHITE (Delegate : Police National H.Q.), R. H. PINKHAM (Delegate : Region 3), K. J. McMINN (Delegate: Region 1), L. J. DUNCAN (Delegate: R.N.Z. Police College).

Front Row, Left to Right:
G. V. BUTTERWORTH (Executive Director), W. F. STRONG (Secretary), L. J. HUNTER (Vice President), B. S. J. HARTLEY (President), J. COOMBER (Vice President), S. I. YOUNG (Treasurer).

NEW ZEALAND POLICE OFFICERS' GUILD

Incoming Guild Executive
For 1992

Annual Conference :
Wellington
12-13 November 1991

Rear Row (Left to Right) :
Inspector Wayne STRONG (Secretary), Superintendent Ross DALLOW (Vice President), Chief Inspector Sherwood YOUNG (Treasurer), Mr Graham BUTTERWORTH (Executive Director).

Front Row (Left to Right) :
Chief Inspector Lindsay HUNTER (Vice President), Superintendent Brian HARTLEY (President), Inspector John COOMBER (Vice President)

New Zealand Police Staff Benevolent and Welfare Fund Inaugural Meeting 4 October 1968 at Wellington. The following were elected Inaugural Board of Directors

Board of Directors
Butler, Robert Laurie
Kuzmich, John Stephan
Mills, Ian Lindsay
Toomey, Brian Anthony
Ingram, Daniel Nason
Lee, David Clifford
Quirke, John Francis

Subscribers to the Memorandum of Incorporation
Butler, Robert Laurie
Tibble, Kapapawaho Kururangi
Kuzmich, John Stephan
Mills, Ian Lindsay
Ingram, Daniel Nason
O'Shea, Bernard Thomas
Quirke, John Francis

Chairmen
Butler, Robert Laurie
McCombe, Harold Eric
Ingram, Daniel Nason
Holland, Kevin John
Monk, Alan John
Cummings, Maurice Daniel
Halpin, Ronald Stephen Francis
Mairs, Peter Ronald
Joblin, Pauline Beatrice
Glynn, James Francis
Morrow, Keith James
Hinds, Stephen Philip

Secretaries
Isaacs, Peter Thomas
Thomas, Hamish Stewart
Moodie, Robert Alexander
Fulton, Gary Charles
Turner, John Charles

Directors
McCombe, Harold Eric
Gilmour, Sidney George
Paterson, David Skinner
Thomas, Hamish Stewart
Glynn, James Francis
Holland, Kevin John
Bardwell, Paul Maclean
Stebbings, Margaret Eveline
Gill, Barry Thomas
Monk, Alan John
Maher, Leo James
Penrose, Thomas Mitchell
Matheson, Peter William
Boyd, David Stuart
Bos, Hendrikus Egbertus
Revington, Ross
Waugh, Alec Kynaston
Morley, Trevor Walter Alexander
Moodie, Robert Alexander
Cummings, Maurice Daniel
Ingram, Daniel Nason
Trendle, Neville Berkeley
Dynes, George
Halpin, Ronald Stephen Francis
McNeil, Wayne Todd
Mairs, Peter Ronald
Houston, Barry George William
Petterson, David Ross
Morrow, Keith James
Bull, Robert James Richardson
Valentine, Robert Attwell
Twentyman, George Edward
Robbie, Thomas James
Buist, William John
Gardiner, Ian Murray
Fulton, Gary Charles
Jacobson, Robert Owen
Monk, Alan John

MR. R. L. BUTLER

Walkinshaw, Brian Kenneth
Walton, Robert Josiah
Boyd, Wilfred Basil
Todd, Lindsay James
Asher, Diane Frances
Mayes, Trevor Raymond
Richardson, Ronald David
Hinds, Stephen Philip
Mangnall, Stuart Duncan
Joyce, Aporo Julian
Cooper, Leslie Earle

New Zealand Police and Families Credit Union
Credit Union proposed by association president H. E. McCombe at its 1967 agm. No formal record of transactions until ad hoc administration replaced by board of directors on 8 May 1978.

The 1978 Directors, Trustees and Supervisors

Directors
Waugh, Alec Kynaston (chairman)
Beckett, Hamish Oliphant Talbot
Brown, Robert David
Dynes, George
Gibson, Bryan William
Johnson, Basil Terence
McGuire, James William
Monk, Alan John
Stevenson, John Francis
Walkinshaw, Brian Kenneth
Manager—Moodie, Robert Alexander

Trustees
Brown, Robert David
Walkinshaw, Brian Kenneth
Waugh, Alec Kynaston

Supervisors
Hohaia, Charles William
Mullane, Brian Gregory
Webber, James Alfred Gerard

Chairmen

Waugh, Alec Kynaston	1978
Monk, Alan John	1986
Coster, Peter Valentine	1991

Vice-Chairmen

Young, Sherwood Ivan	1980
Walkinshaw, Brian Kenneth	1986
Coster, Peter Valentine	1988
Marshall, Robert	1991

Managers

Moodie, Robert Alexander	1978
Fulton, Gary Charles	1985
Smart, James Wray	1990

Directors

Monk, Alan John
Johnson, Basil Terence
Stevenson, John Francis
Gibson, Bryan William
Walkinshaw, Brian Kenneth
Waugh, Alec Kynaston
Young, Sherwood Ivan
Matthews, Barry Eldon
Benn, Brian Kingsley
Maling, Christopher Mulgrave
Marshall, Robert
Hall, Bowen Dudley
Hinds, Stephen Phiilip
Hamill, Marion Joan
Cox, Barry William
Williams, John Meirion
Coster, Peter Valentine
Mathews, John
Wilson, Colin Walter
Beckett, Hamish Oliphant Talbot
Eades, Barbara
Bull, Robert
Brown, Robert David
Bull, Roger
Dynes, George
McNeill, Wayne Todd
Morrow, Keith James

The 'terror' had to wait until the middle of another world war to arrive, and was well tamed by a cautious administration. The real face of women policing is one, as seen opposite here, that many a lost or upset child has good cause to thank

Appendix II

Policewomen in the Association and the Guild

The October 1940 *Police Journal* carried a two-page article by Marie Best, MA, of Wellington, headed 'I Want to Be a Policewoman'. She had been saying so frequently since October 1939. Women, she argued, were needed to handle cases affecting young women and girls—for taking evidence, inspecting suspected brothels, escorting female prisoners, staffing and supervising probation institutions, crime prevention activities such as identifying and helping young women at risk of shoplifting and prostitution, and other welfare work. She added that she felt quite capable of pacing a beat or running in drunks.

Nowadays such an applicant would be snapped up, but then society's controllers were still adjusting to women taking degrees, let alone publicly speaking their minds. A bastion of male employment such as the police was still gearing up to employing women, two years after this had been legislated for.

In the middle of 1938 Peter Fraser had responded to the lobbying of the National Council of Women and announced government approval of women police. Since 1895 women had been employed officially as matrons who searched, looked after and escorted female prisoners and mental patients. Now women were to be granted sworn police status.

As usual, Fraser's rhetorical intentions were a little ahead of their implementation. In April 1941 the *Police Journal* reported an urgent question to Fraser in the House from Mrs G.S. Stewart, the government MP for Wellington West, about when women would be sworn in. The increasing numbers of assaults on girls made the appointment of women police imperative. Fraser said the selection process was proceeding.

There were 150 applicants, aged 25 to 40, unmarried or widowed. Commissioner Denis Cummings chose 10, including three from Auckland, three from Wellington, one from Christchurch and one from Dunedin.

Senior Sergeant Daniel Beard trained the recruits at the Police Training Depot in Newtown, Wellington, in law, first aid, jujitsu, general police studies, drill and court practice. Edna Pearce was nominated No. 1 graduate of the three-month course. Women now represented 0.66 per cent of the total police strength of 1509.

In August 1942 the *Police Journal* reported that the three women MPs, Mrs M.M. Dreaver, Government Waitemata, Mrs Stewart and Mrs A.N. Grigg, National Mid-Canterbury, urging in the House that women police be put in uniform, since this would enhance their authority and usefulness. There should also be more women police. The Police Department disagreed, maintaining that women were more useful not in uniform. It took another decade to get women into a uniform of a heavy navy wool serge skirt and tunic and navy felt slouch hat. Whangarei's first policewoman, Myra Lane, found the outfit stifling.

Association involvement in the policewomen's cause was restricted to occasional articles and snippets in the *Journal*. In 1947 action was prompted by the numbers of policewomen dwindling as women resigned to marry or take other work, and were not replaced. Women police were on lower pay and there was great reluctance among senior policemen to employ them. The 1947 conference proposed raising their status from temporary constable to constable because 'no reason exists for the Women Police being treated in any other way than male members of the Force'. Many women had been employed for some years, but could not function efficiently if still declared temporary. It could also hamper police efficiency, if they gave evidence in court and were identified as only temporary, thus detracting from the value of their evidence.

In 1949 women were accepted into the detective branch and patrolled streets, hotels, waterfronts, parks, dance halls and racecourses, attended female prisoners and spoke to women's groups. In December 1952 eight were uniformed, required to work in pairs unless accompanied by a

The first women recruits at the police training school, Wellington South in 1941. Back row, left to right: Lynn Brockett, Nancy Aitchison, Vera McConachie, Tina Smith, Mary Berridge, Margaret Holden. Front row, left to right: Edna Pearce, Eileen O'Connor, their instructor Senior Sergeant Daniel Beard, Molly Speakman, Mary Callaghan. They were the privileged 10 chosen by the commissioner from 150 applicants

male officer. In the February 1953 *Journal* Meltzer printed a long letter from his New South Wales counterpart on equal pay for policewomen there, and other conditions that were better than those in New Zealand.

Commissioner Compton published the instruction that women who married could not stay in the force. The management committee had been prepared to contest the validity of this instruction with an Auckland member who had applied to the commissioner for permission to marry a male colleague, but she had resigned. The management committee was, however, committed to resisting the instruction.

At the October conference there was considerable discussion of an Auckland proposal that the 46-strong Women's Division have separate representation. Most delegates were unimpressed, suggesting that women seeking separate representation could lead to others doing the same, and in any case women's problems were not much different from men's. One delegate suggested that a woman could be voted on to the national council, and indeed there was the precedent of Miss May Beatrice Kelly of Invercargill serving on the management committee from 1945 to 1948. The conference voted against separate representation for women.

In 1958 came the first successful sitting of a sergeant's exam by a woman officer. Two years later the conference was told that a policewoman in Auckland had passed the senior sergeant's exam, but was wondering whether it was worth carrying on and taking the commissioned officer's exam. There was, Meltzer said, general dissatisfaction among women and the association had felt for some time that it was unjust to have a salary bar after three years. The commissioner dodged the issue by saying that he would await the outcome of government deliberations on equal pay.

The Police Amendment Act 1965 introduced equal pay and the notion of a Women's Division was abandoned, but the departmental quid pro quo was that policewomen should carry batons and perform the same duties as their

TROUSER SUITS FOR OUR GIRLS TOO?

This attractive trouser suit is currently being worn by

The *Police Journal* was a mild supporter rather than a proponent of women police

male counterparts. The association joined the public outcry, its 1966 conference sharing the general view that batons not be issued to women. Meltzer became emotional

Constable Roa Morrissey did receive permission to marry a policeman, but was punished for challenging an order to cater for policemen involved in the 1953 Royal Tour. The punishment was to transfer her away from her husband, causing public and association protest. *Minhinnick cartoon courtesy* New Zealand Herald

at the idea 'that a woman should be put in the position of risking physical violence'. Delegate Mooney told the assistant commissioner that the department was being 'rather more literal than practical' about the equal pay legislation. The association had, he said, consistently sought better conditions and pay for its women members, but had never asked for equal pay because they did not believe there was equality of work in the job, and nor was there between two men. Mooney might also have been accused of being too literal.

McCombe thought the least that could be done was to teach women police judo. The assistant commissioner demurred, saying the department wanted women to keep their femininity and not 'develop into a race of Amazons'. McCombe did not think judo likely to develop women 'unworthily'. Incoming national secretary Dave Lee thought women enjoyed protection at present by virtue of their sex, but the public might be less likely to intervene in an assault on a woman carrying a baton.

The matter was concluded with the promise of more representations to the department. The politicians, however, saw which way the wind was blowing and reviewed the decision to have policewomen carry batons.

That December Betty Bennett was appointed New Zealand's first woman inspector, and the *Journal* featured her prominently. In 1970 the *Newsletter* featured Mrs Margaret E. Stebbings as a member of the management committee. It was mentioned in passing that she was married to fellow police member Jim Stebbings, but their relationship was not by now considered an issue.

The biggest issue the association perceived involving policewomen was the wearing of trousers. Readers were invited to respond on the subject in a small paragraph tucked away at the bottom of a column in the March/April 1977 *Newsletter*. Seven of the eight pages of the following June/July *Newsletter* were devoted to the responses. No other issue ever attracted as many published letters.

At the end of these responses was another small paragraph saying that the comments of 'our girls' have been brought to the attention of the commissioner, who was having a number of trouser suits made up to be worn on a trial basis in the main centres. Moodie told the 28 July 1977 management committee meeting that he and Butterworth had made progress on women's uniforms only because of the tremendous response from the grass roots level.

At the 1 July 1977 management committee meeting Alec Waugh had raised an example of reverse sexism—a superior officer objecting to a male member wearing a gold earring stud. Waugh noted that female members were not permitted to wear earrings, bangles or beads.

Through 1978 there were hold-ups on women's uniforms from administration and from policewomen's objections. In August, for instance, Auckland women complained that the white top made them look like ice creams and that the red, white, blue and black colouring was 'bitsy'. The suggested blue top was to be investigated. The women's trousers cartoon that had been used in the July 1977 *Newsletter* was repeated in the July 1979 issue, and this time MP Marilyn Waring complained to the Human Rights Commission that it was 'degrading and sexist'. Ms Waring argued, from the 'limp waving, apathetic hand and arm' and the 'large bust and large bottom' provoking carnage, that by extension a woman asked to be raped because she wore a mini-skirt or no bra. The correspondence over this was printed in the September 1979 *Newsletter* along with the response: 'Marilyn, don't be bloody ridiculous.' It was a remark that could only fairly have been made by a man who publicly wore a dress and represented police men and women. From this year through to 1983 Jean Dougall was vice-president of the guild.

In October 1979 Moodie asked the commissioner to give women the option of joining the superannuation fund. This, he argued, particularly affected women constables married to members in the fund; they received nothing from the fund if they intended having children, unless they also intended to continue with their careers. Deputy Commissioner Thompson objected that the time was not right, but the management committee supported the secretary's proposal.

In 1982 policewomen and batons were again an issue,

JUVENILE DELINQUENT

this time the placing of the monadnock or long baton. Moodie's solution was that all officers wear the baton suspended from a belt ring. He also told Commissioner Walton of the management committee proposal that the administration employ a designer, who would work with a committee of women drawn from frontline officers to improve the uniform trousers, skirt and optional culottes. (These were a success with English policewomen.) Deputy Commissioner Thompson replied that the administration had worked through the clothing inspectors of the Ministry of Works and Development and, via a Hamilton firm and a Wellington tailor, slacks were now available. Moodie accepted the slacks, but pressed for the women's committee to fine-tune belts, location of and access to pockets, blouse cut and other matters. The department agreed.

Although the police were ahead of the private sector workforce with equal pay status, it had taken a 1973 memo from Commissioner Sharp to require equality of opportunity from their male colleagues. There were lingering macho male doubts about whether women could do the job.

Moodie had no doubts; he employed women readily, notably *Newsletter* editor Rebecca Macfie, whose final issue in April 1985 carried her thoughtful article proposing that the police exemption from the provisions of the Human Rights Commission Act be dropped. This exemption permitted more men than women to be recruited for the purposes of dealing with violence. She pointed out that the act provided the police with a handy excuse to bypass women. Statistics showed that women made up 5.2 per cent of the New Zealand Police, and only 2.6 per cent of women achieved rank—seven at the last count—compared with 26 per cent of men. Although conceding reasonably enlightened deployment of women, she argued that, in the new climate of community policing, women were ideally positioned to arbitrate, conciliate and act as 'an agent for peace in the community'.

In the next issue of the *Newsletter* former policewoman Jacqueline Rorani argued that, with frontline policing so stretched, women who had left the police to have families could be employed part-time, dealing with enquiries and freeing up male staff. In the United States they were called auxiliaries. There were still 'hard-nosed individuals within the Police service', while others thought women could not cope with night shifts and violence. She did not accept this. With more female offenders there should, she argued, be more policewomen. She did allow that the bad old days had gone when 'the meaningful thing a girl could do was pin her hair up off her collar and babysit a lost child'.

The policy of recruiting women aged 19 to 22 tends to guarantee that they will be lost to the service as they leave to have children. The increase in non-sworn staff has, however, seen a big increase in women in the service—700 non-sworn at the end of 1989 compared with 338 sworn women. Although 58 per cent of sworn women staff felt disadvantaged within the service compared with 26 per cent non-sworn, this could readily change. The non-sworn members, 69 per cent women and mostly clerical, represent a significant number of the 6128 staff. Their numbers will grow. The association has started accepting them as

June/July 1977, N.Z. POLICE ASSOCIATION NEWSLETTER

(b) A loop in the waistband at the rear of the skirt and trousers where you could attach the handcuff pouch.

W.R. STOCK
(Palmerston North)

Dear Sir,

1. TROUSERS

I feel that trousers would be a most practical uniform for night shift. At present with the skirts we are issued because of the width of them it is more than a little difficult at times to climb a fence, chase anyone etc with any ease. Trousers would also save on the amount of pantihose torn, ripped etc while engaged on normal police duties, regarding the aspect of warmth and comfort, trousers would be ideal as the weather during winter in most centres is far from comfortable.

2. JACKET

A jacket for the trouser suit would have to be of a practical length i.e. to thigh length, for both warmth and attractiveness. The jacket should also be fitting. The one jacket would be sufficient for both trousers and skirt.

3. SKIRT

The present skirt we have does not enable us to carry our notebook with the cover, consequently it gets torn and scruffy. Also we have no pocket in our uniform large enough to accommodate our handcuffs. It is totally impractical to carry our handbags on the beat. I suggest that the new uniforms have more pockets of a larger size in the skirt.

4. GREATCOATS

While we have an opportunity to comment on our new uniforms could the issue of a greatcoat be discussed especially as they are now making them in blue for the new uniforms for men. I realise that we are going to be issued with a new style overcoat for day wear this would be quite sufficient but for night wear they will not be thick enough.

(Lower Hutt) M.M. EDWARDS

70

Dear Sir,

1. TROUSERS

The issue of trousers for Policewomen is most definitely a good idea, both in respect of practicality and warmth. To undertake active police duties with the present uniform can be very difficult when occasions call for climbing fences, walls, etc. pursuit of persons, and even more normal duties such as taking complaints at building sites etc. Skirts do not allow the freedom that trousers can provide. They would prove indispensible during the winter months, particularly at night, as well as lessening the amount of stockings torn/ripped whilst engaged in normal police duties. They would therefore provide enormous warmth and comfort generally.

2. JACKET

A suitably designed jacket could be used for both trousers and skirt. The jacket must be quite long so as to be smart in appearance irrespective of the size of the wearer. It must also be suitably tailored and contain at least one pocket designed to accommodate a note book and cover. It is not always practical to use one's handbag and the present uniform's pocket is not big enough to take a cover for one's notebook.

3. SKIRT

The present skirts are far too narrow to be practical as well as very smart. A new skirt I feel should be slightly flared with either a belt to accommodate a handcuff pouch, or pockets big enough for this purpose. Depending on the length of the jacket, handcuffs carried at the belt or in the pocket should not detract from the general line of the uniform. At present no policewoman can work with ease unless their uniform skirt is worn fairly short.

4. GREATCOATS

Could the issue of greatcoats be considered for policewomen. Our present two coats are definitely not suitable for night wear during the winter months and whilst the proposed new coats will be suitable for the daylight hours, they would not be warm enough for night. Perhaps the Association could discuss that women could be issued with identical thick coats as the new issue for men.

C.F.T. REIDY

New Zealand
Police Association
newsletter

July 1979 ★ Vol. 11, No. 7 ★ Part series of "NZ Police Journal"

IN THIS ISSUE

Published by R.A. Mosdic, 11 Manners Street, Wellington, on behalf of the New Zealand Police Association (Inc.).
Printed by Bayley's Services Ltd, Wellington, and Registered at the Manners Street Post Office, Wellington, as a Registered Magazine.

Dear Sir,

The idea of trousers for Policewomen is a good one, however knowing the Department's ability to design uniforms, the idea would have to be thrashed out thoroughly before a style is decided upon.

The majority of uniform policewomen these days are working shift hours — late shifts, swing shifts, and night shifts. They are invariably on incident patrols and become involved in all sorts of strenuous activities, ranging from walking through scrub, looking for missing children to hopping over fences to cordon off a building. The present uniform is inadequate for these jobs. The skirts are not full enough to allow free movement and pantyhose are easily laddered or holed. The question of decency also arises!

As well as this, a night shift in the middle of winter can produce temperatures close to freezing point, and a covering of only nylon about the legs is not adequate. The coats supplied to women police are archaic and most use their nylon raincoats. A pair of trousers, then, would produce extra warmth.

I cannot stress enough, though, of the need for design to be by a competent **woman** with experience in uniform design — e.g. Air New Zealand: NAC or the N.Z. Wool Board. A commissioned Officer in H.Q. is not able to design uniforms, especially for women, and should not be given any say in the matter, apart from colour and badge requirements.

The other matter that comes to mind is the variation in shapes and sizes of the women members and I think that trouser-suit wear should be limited to shift duties. The present skirt and tunic should still be worn to Court, official functions, etc.

M.A. KELLY
(Wellington)

In 1977 policewomen's uniforms provoked the biggest letter-writing response the *Newsletter* had known. Two years later the *Newsletter* reprinted a cartoon that incurred the disapproval of feminist MP Marilyn Waring members. With national secretary Harding's trade union experience with women workers, there is every chance that, in the 1990s, women members of the association will start to shake up their lords and masters.

Note: Valerie Redshaw is writing the history of policewomen in New Zealand. She is a former policewoman who is now a non-sworn member.

Appendix III

Death in the Line of Duty

Sergeant Edward John Garvey, aged 30, lost his life in a snowstorm on 25 September 1863, when reporting on a new gold rush in the Kakanui Ranges north-east of Naseby. He was buried in the Dunedin Southern Cemetery, his gravestone noting that he had survived participation in the Charge of the Light Brigade and had been presented with France's highest award for bravery. He was believed to be the first New Zealand police officer to have died in this country doing his duty.

A century later the New Zealand Police Association initiated a rededication of his neglected Dunedin monument. Local association secretary Jack Craig, who helped to organise this, researched and recorded for the first time some of the police who died in the line of duty in New Zealand.

Police association members view the rededication of the memorial to the first policeman to die in New Zealand in the course of duty. *Otago Daily Times*

Former Constable Jack Craig, who did so much to record police who died in the execution of their duty, receives life membership of the association in 1977

THE NEW ZEALAND POLICE ASSOCIATION

(DUNEDIN BRANCH)

invites

to be present at the Southern Cemetery, DUNEDIN
at 2:30 p.m. on Tuesday, 8th October, 1963 on the
occasion of the centennial rededication of the
memorial to the late Sergeants

EDWARD JOHN GARVEY,

Chevalier de l'Ordre Imperial de la Legion d'Honneur,
who died in a snowstorm at Mount Ida Goldfield on the
25th September, 1863 in the execution of his duty;
Aged 30 years.

AND JAMES GRENNAN,

Chevalier de l'Ordre Imperial de la Legion d'Honneur,
who died at Dunedin on 19th January, 1866.
Aged 36 years.

Both these men were members of the Otago Mounted
Constabulary, were survivors of the memorable charge
at Balaclava, and held the badge of France's order
of Knighthood and Chivalry.

E. C. Adams,
President.

J. R. D. Craig,
Secretary
Phone 86-873.

Appendix IV

Stevenson's Cartoon Gallery

Former policeman John Stevenson's long-running cartoon series in the New Zealand Police Association *Newsletter* is a visual record of recent police industrial relations history.

HE OBVIOUSLY DOESN'T LIKE ME!
WONDER IF IT'S THE WAY I DRESS OR THE LENGTH OF MY HAIR OR EVEN PERHAPS WHAT I STAND FOR — MAYBE HE'S JUST RECEIVED SOME STEREOTYPED VIEW FROM THE MEDIA

OH NO MAN
IT'S THE FUZZ!

Department to save money by dishing out 2nd HAND UNIFORMS to W.D's - Where will it end?
SORRY— BUT all we've got left is one dog collar!
E.H. STEVENSON '80

INSPECTOR "FRILL-YO" APPROVES
OF YOUR NEW COLD WEATHER GEAR
"RENKO" BUT I THINK HE'S
TAKEN EXCEPTION TO THE
BASEBALL CAP AND PUMP ACTION !
OLICE
POLICE

J.H. STEVENSON
YOW!!!
KAWAKAWA
WHANGAREI
DISTRICT COMMANDER
NICE DISTRICT COMMANDER HELPS CONSTABLE TRANSFER

ALL RECOGNISED FRONT LINE STAFF TO BE TESTED FOR 'HEPATITIS B' . . .
PRETENDING YOU'RE A PROPERTY OFFICER WON'T SAVE YA MOOSE! ALL TEAM POLICING MEMBERS WILL BE TESTED - WHEN THEY'RE FOUND!!

POLICE
MEDICAL
INSURANCE SCHEME
For coverage
from DANDRUFF
To FOOTROT
POLICE

WHAT DID SANTA BRING YA?
TEN CAR CONVERSIONS— NINE WILFUL DAMAGES— EIGHT BRUTAL MURDERS— SEVEN WEIRD DOMESTICS SIX 'SAULTS ON COPPERS— FIVE BURG-LA-RIES!...
FOUR HIT & RUNS— THREE THEFT EX— TWO D.I.C'S AND A....
PART-RIDGE IN A PEAR TREE!
NO WAY!!
WE PASSED THAT ONE ONTO THE S.P.C.A!

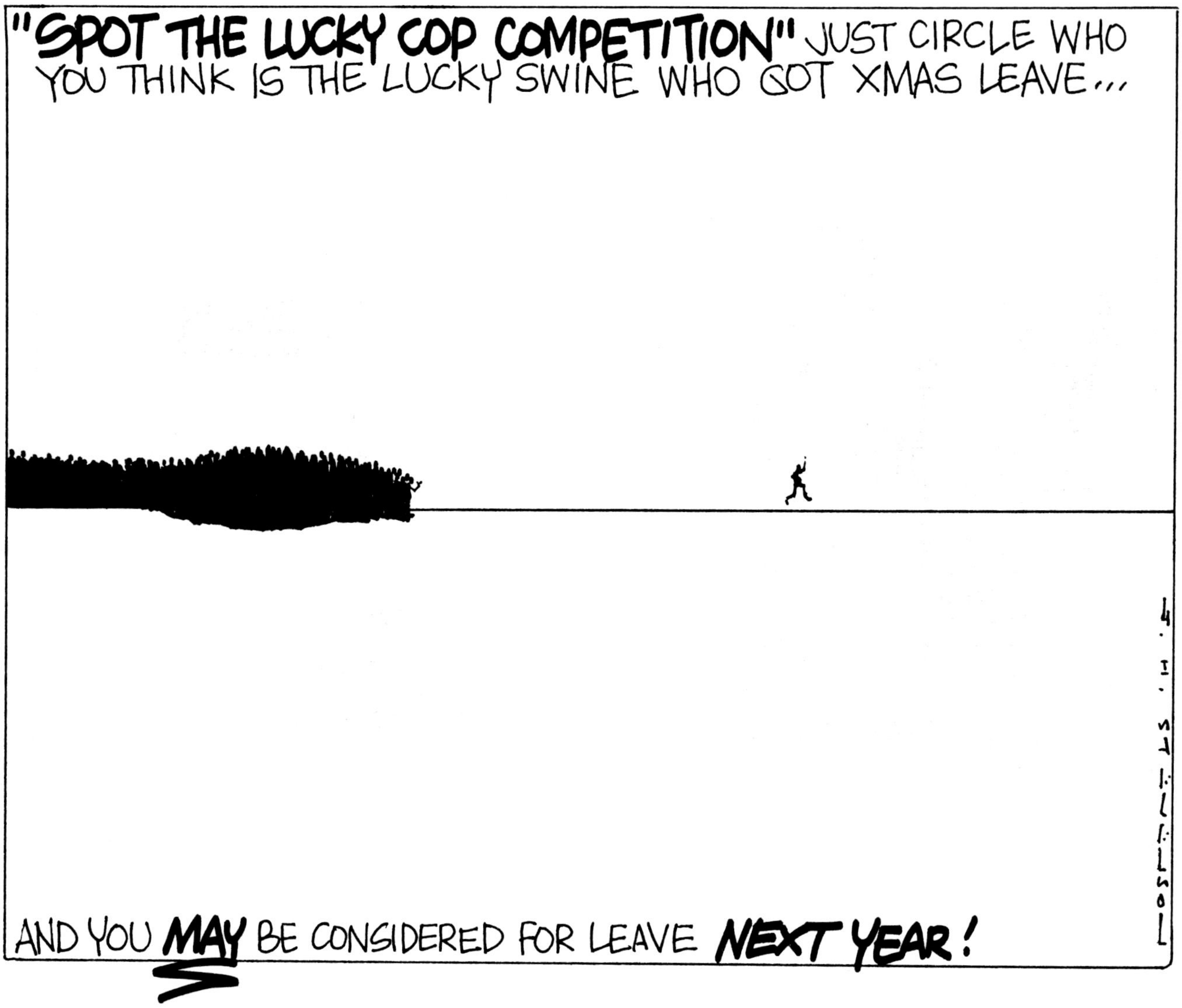
"SPOT THE LUCKY COP COMPETITION" JUST CIRCLE WHO YOU THINK IS THE LUCKY SWINE WHO GOT XMAS LEAVE...
AND YOU MAY BE CONSIDERED FOR LEAVE NEXT YEAR!

CALL IT "BREACH OF CONTRACT" OR THEFT - NO DIFFERENCE! HE'S COMING WITH US!!
POLICE GOVT. SUPER
P.M.s OFFICE
J.W. STEVENSON

BIG DAY HUH T.Y. JONES-
FINALLY SWAPPING YA
BUS PASS FOR SHIN PADS!
BUS STOP
INSTR.
GRADE 'A'
DRIVERS ONLY
GRADE B
GRADE C
GRADE D

POLICE ANNUAL BUDGET ONLY EQUAL TO TWENTY ONE DAYS OF SOCIAL WELFARE 'GOBBLING' !!?
SOCIAL WELFARE
BURP!
AW-GEE INSPECTOR MARSH –"THEY DO GET–EEEN!"
BELCH
BURP
J H STEVENSON

BACK OFF – OR I'LL.... I'LL
HIT US WITH YA PALMER PILLOW?
HA HA HA HEE
POOR MISUNDERSTOODS
PR24 REPLACED BY LIMPY WHIMPY 'PALMER PILLOW'
J H STEVENSON 88

NO
GO AWAY !!!!
POLICE CIVILIANS
POLICE ASSOCIATION

LAWRENCE
POLICE STATION
OPEN
YOU'RE IN LUCK SIR
— WE'RE OPEN TODAY!

LOOKS LIKE WE'LL HAVE T' PAY YA IN BEERS AGAIN, JACKO !
JUGS $7.00
SUPPORT OUR LOCAL COPPER

COMMISSIONER SAYS "MEMBERS WILL BE DEALT WITH HUMANELY"
HEEL !!!
GOOD BOY !
POLICE
LAST DINNER
J. H. STEVENSON

WHERE ARE ALL THE OFFICERS WITH 'GET UP AND GO'?
THEY GOT UP AND WENT!
QUIGLEY REVIEW STRATEGOS
PERSONNEL
UNIVERSITY OF VIC.
STEVENSON
© POLICE NEWS

We feel loved
BANKSEY LOVES US
LOVE
NATIONAL Banksey POLICE
WILL HE STILL RESPECT US IN THE MORNING?
J.H. STEVENSON

References and Acknowledgements

The principal sources are the association and guild holdings in the Manuscripts Section of the Alexander Turnbull Library and National Archives, and those records retained by the association and guild, including minutes books of the service organisations' executive and annual meetings, extensive box files and the complete set of the *Police Journal* and *Newsletter*. There are also the files and clippings books kept by Jack Meltzer and held by the association, and personal collections by A.F. Edwardson, J.J. Taylor, Brian Walkinshaw and Sherwood Young.

I am grateful to Geoff Terpstra for the oral histories he recorded for the association and to those who provided me with extensive interviews, namely Rob Moodie, Graham Butterworth, Tom Robbie, Sherwood Young, Alec Waugh, Graham Harding and Steve Hinds. I had the benefit of working alongside Dave Paterson on this project, and his invaluable research was particularly useful in culling material from Hansard and the *Police Bulletin*.

Richard Hill's police histories were invaluable in backgrounding the conditions that required a police association. In the lead-up to its formation, other valuable material came from the 1898 Royal Commission and the two that followed early this century; the memoirs of Constable Thom; Charles Belton's *Outside the Law in New Zealand*, Gisborne Publishing Company, 1939; S.R. Holford's manuscript 'The Evolution of the New Zealand Police Force 1840–1922'.

Valuable material came from the many local police histories, notably those of Auckland and Christchurch. Sherwood Young and police historian of the modern era Graeme Dunstall have been most valuable in conversation and in various published essays and chapters of Dunstall's work in progress. Sherwood Young and Dave Paterson have been supportive throughout this project, and I thank them and those others in the service organisations who have been so willing to help, including John Turner, Tui Hunter, Tania Winkels, Steve Hinds, Graham Harding, Lindsay Hunter, Alan Monk and Graham Butterworth.

Association president Steve Hinds (left) welcomes first official association secretary Ian Campbell and his wife to the opening of the new police service organisations' offices at 57 Willis Street, Wellington, on 16 July 1991

We are police, We are family—the police service organisations have their motto for the 1990s, and the poster image to go with it shows Naenae detective Jim Taare, his wife Linley and son Nathan. Linley's father H.E. 'Buzz' Smith was an Upper Hutt detective for 21 years

Index

Photo taken at the official opening of Te Awamutu Police Station 1942. Standing from left: Constable A. Findlater, Sergeant S. Clist, Constable L. Gordon, Constable H. Shaw. Sitting: Commissioner P. J. Cummings, Honourable P. C. Webb, Inspector G. B. Edwards.

New Zealand Police Association

TENTH ANNUAL CONFERENCE OF DELEGATES

Held at Wellington on October 3rd, 4th and 5th, 1945

Standing:—Left to Right Senior Sergeant W. J. Irwin (Invercargill), Constable F. Lemm (New Plymouth), Constable C. J. L. Matheson (Timaru), Detective Sergeant J. Thompson (Wellington), Constable R. A. Moore (Gisborne), Sergeant T. E. Johnston (Nelson), Sergeant J. Sutherland (Hamilton), Detective B. Constable (Greymouth), Constable J. R. Ryan (Napier), Sergeant J. Devlin (Dunedin), Constable H. McLean (Christchurch).

Sitting:—Sergeant F. W. Edwards (Auckland), Constable W. A. Calwell (Palmerston North), Miss P. McLeod (Asst. Secretary), Constable J. M. Pointon (President), Mr. J. Meltzer (General Secretary), Constable D. A. Almond (Wanganui), Constable M. J. Rodgers (Whangarei).

New Zealand Police Associaton

ELEVENTH ANNUAL CONFERENCE OF DELEGATES

Held at Wellington on October 1st, 2nd, 3rd, 1946

Left to Right:

Back Row:—K. W. MILLS, (NAPIER.) A. A. GUDSELL, (HAMILTON) J. ROBERTSON, (TIMARU) J. GIBSON. (INVERCARGILL)

Middle Row:—D. A. ALMOND, (WANGANUI) H. McLEAN, (CHRISTCHURCH) P. J. MAGEE, (NELSON) J. H. S. HOGG, (DUNEDIN) B. H. CONSTABLE, (GREYMOUTH) J. O'DONOGHUE, (NEW PLYMOUTH) M. J. RODGERS. (WHANGAREI)

Front Row:—J. R. GEDYE, (GISBORNE) F. W. EDWARDS, (AUCKLAND) Miss E. LEDGER, (ASST. SECRETARY) J. M. POINTON, (PRESIDENT) J. MELTZER, (GEN. SECRETARY) W. A. CALWELL, (PALMERSTON NTH.) J. THOMPSON. (WELLINGTON)

New Zealand Police Association

15th ANNUAL CONFERENCE OF DELEGATES

Held at Wellington on 4th, 5th and 6th October, 1950.

Left to Right:

Back Row:—CONSTABLE W. J. HILL, (Greymouth) CONSTABLE L. J. STEPHENSON, (Wanganui) SERGEANT D. M. CAMPBELL, (Gisborne) CONSTABLE J. W. THOMPSON, (Dunedin) DETECTIVE SERGEANT F. O. SCOTT. (Wellington)

Middle Row:—CONSTABLE T. R. M. WILLIAMS, (Timaru) CONSTABLE H. S. LINDSAY, (Whangarei) DETECTIVE SERGEANT C. D. TAYLOR, (Hamilton) SERGEANT E. WIGMORE, (Napier) DETECTIVE SERGEANT J. H. ALTY, (Palmerston North) SENIOR SERGEANT J. H. DENNEHY, (New Plymouth) CONSTABLE L. J. BRAZIER. (Invercargill)

Front Row:—SENIOR SERGEANT C. H. REARDON, (Christchurch) MRS. E. URQUHART, (Asst. Sec.) MR. J. MELTZER, (Gen. Sec.) MR. J. B. YOUNG, (Commissioner of Police) SERGEANT A. G. QUIN, **(President)** SERGEANT T. JOHNSTON, (Nelson) SENIOR SERGEANT F. W. EDWARDS. (Auckland)

17TH ANNUAL CONFERENCE 1952

18TH ANNUAL CONFERENCE 1953

27TH ANNUAL CONFERENCE 1962

28TH ANNUAL CONFERENCE 1963

NATIONAL COUNCIL AND OFFICERS - 39th ANNUAL CONFERENCE

FRONT ROW: (left to Right)- Messrs J. Dumble,H.S. Thomas (Exective Director),D.N. Ingram,(Life Member), R.L. Butler (President),A.J. Monk (Vice President), P.T. Isaacs (Treasurer),P.R. Hawarth

BACK ROW (Left to Right) Messrs B.R.McAvoy, I.C. Patterson, S.G. Morton, H.O. Beckett (Vive President),N. Smith, D.A.Duffy, T.J. Owen, I.A. Sutherland, A.C. Harding, M. Penn, G.W.Russell, L.F.Smith, E.J. Niven, FK. Parfitt

NATIONAL COUNCIL AND OFFICERS -42nd ANNUAL CONFERENCE

BACK ROW: M.A. Penn, A.E. Clarke, I.A. Sutherland, K.J.Morrow, R.J. O'Connell, J.R. Isaacson, J.L. Ongaro, A.K. Waugh, F.B. McWilliam, B. Nalder, J.K. Sawers. P.D. Wood, L.F. Smith, R.D. Richardson.

FRONT ROW: R.L. Butler (Immediate Past President) D.S. Boyd, A.J. Monk (President), Dr.R.A. Moodie (National Secretary), H.O.T. Beckett,, G.V. Butterworth (Research Officer)

The New Zealand Police Staff Benevolent and Welfare Fund

BOARD OF DIRECTORS, 1982–83

VALERIE STUDIO WELLINGTON

Back row: **G. V. BUTTERWORTH** (Asst. Secretary) **R. A. MOODIE** (National Secretary) **G. TWENTYMAN** **R. VALENTINE** **Ms P. JOBLIN** **J. TAYLOR**

Front row: **G. DYNES** **P. MAIRS** (Chairman) **Hon. M. B. COUCH** (Minister of Police) **Mrs T. HUNTER** (National Office)

Insets: **Mr A. MONK** **Mr R. HALPIN**

NEW ZEALAND POLICE STAFF BENEVOLENT AND WELFARE FUND
Board of Directors 1985-86

VALERIE STUDIO WELLINGTON

Back row: W. BUIST O. JACOBSON R. VALENTINE R. S. HALPIN R. J. R. BULL.
Front row: I. M. GARDINER J. GLYNN P. MAIRS Ms P. JOBLIN G. DYNES G. C. FULTON (National Secretary).
Absent: A. J. MONK (Chairman).

NEW ZEALAND POLICE ASSOCIATION (INC.)

MANAGEMENT COMMITTEE 1983/84

VALERIE STUDIO WELLINGTON

Back row (l. - r.): **W. BOYD** **A. MONK** **R. BULL** **I. REVELL.**
Front row (l. - r.): **R. MOODIE** (National Secretary) **R. HALPIN** (Vice-President) **K. MORROW** (President) **J. TAYLOR** (Vice-President) **D. DAVIDSON** (National Office).
Inset: **G. BUTTERWORTH.**

NEW ZEALAND POLICE ASSOCIATION INC

MANAGEMENT COMMITTEE 1986-87

Back Row: G C FULTON (National Secretary) W B BOYD I M REVELL A J MONK
Front Row: Mrs T HUNTER (National Office) J J TAYLOR (Vice President) K J MORROW (President) R D RICHARDSON (Vice President) Miss S M CLIFFORD (National Office)
Absent: P L SHAUGHNESSY G D HARDING (Industrial Advocate)

NEW ZEALAND POLICE ASSOCIATION

NATIONAL COUNCIL 1987 - 88

Back Row: M EASTWOOD (Hutt) C ROPER (Christchurch) B RAFFAN (Hamilton) L MATHIESON (Otago) G SMITH (Timaru) J MALCOLM (Whangarei) S HINDS (Kapiti-Mana) K McKAY (Auckland) R MANNING (Napier) I FRANKLYN (North Shore) R STEEDMAN (Dunedin) R HIBBS (Greymouth) I SUTHERLAND (Palmerston North) N JAMES (Nelson) L NADEN (Gisborne)

Front Row: D LAWFORD (Henderson) S MANGNALL (Otahuhu) M C PEDERSEN (Tauranga) K DEAN (Rotorua) J J TAYLOR (Vice President) K J MORROW (President) R D RICHARDSON (Vice President) Mrs TUI HUNTER (National Office) G HODGE (Wanganui) I GARDINER (New Plymouth) B SMART (Invercargill) A HUCKSTEP (Christchurch Rural)

Absent: K BURT (Wellington)

Mimo Photography, Wellington

HIS DAD'S A POLICEMAN!
ERIC HEATH